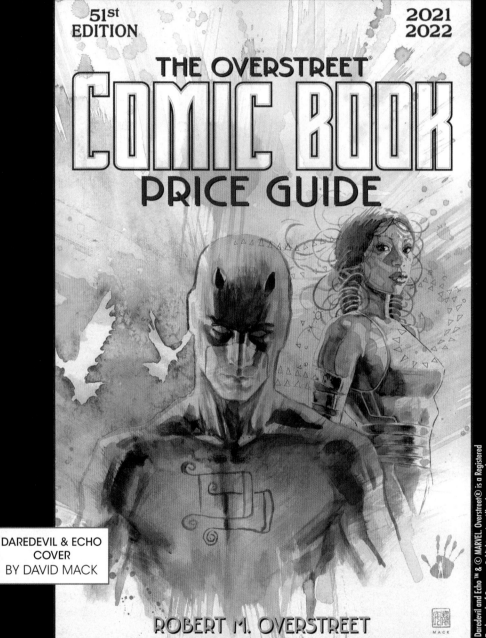

OVERSTREET @ 50

FIVE DECADES OF THE OVERSTREET COMIC BOOK PRICE GUIDE

By ROBERT M. OVERSTREET

DAVID T. ALEXANDER, THOMAS ANDRAE, E.B. BOATNER,
STEVE BOROCK, GARY M. CARTER, STEVE GEPPI, STEVEN HOUSTON,
MARK HUESMAN, JOE JUSKO, PAUL LEVITZ, MATT NELSON,
CHARLES S. NOVINSKIE, GEORGE OLSHEVSKY, BUDDY SAUNDERS,
AMANDA SHERIFF, BEAU SMITH, JOHN K. SNYDER, JR., BILL SPICER,
DAVID STONE, HARRY B. THOMAS, MAGGIE THOMPSON, AND J.C. VAUGHN
CONTRIBUTING WRITERS

MARK HUESMAN
LAYOUT & DESIGN

OVERSTREET HALL OF FAME ENTRIES WRITTEN BY
J.C. VAUGHN WITH MATT BALLESTEROS, ARNOLD T. BLUMBERG,
BRAELYNN BOWERSOX, SCOTT BRADEN, LEONARD (JOHN) CLARK,
STEVE GEPPI, MARK HUESMAN, MICHAEL KRONENBERG,
TOM MASON, DEAN MULLANEY, ROBERT M. OVERSTREET,
S.C. RINGGENBERG, AMANDA SHERIFF, JIM SHOOTER,
BILLY TUCCI, MARK WHEATLEY, AND CARRIE WOOD

MARK HUESMAN + AMANDA SHERIFF + J.C. VAUGHN
EDITORS

SPECIAL THANKS TO
SCOTT BRADEN, LANDON CHESNEY, COMICLINK, KEN FINNERTY,
STEPHEN FISHLER, JOSH GEPPI, DAWN GUZZO, GARY GUZZO, HAKE'S AUCTIONS,
JAMES HALPERIN, MARK L. HAYNES, HERITAGE AUCTIONS,
WILLIAM HUGHES VINTAGE COLLECTIBLES, NICK KATRADIS, JIM MCLAUGHLIN,
MYCOMICSHOP.COM, JOSH NATHANSON, ROSS RICHIE, JOSEPH RYBANDT,
MORT TODD, LINDSAY WALLACE, ALEX WINTER, AND VINCENT ZURZOLO

GEMSTONE PUBLISHING

GEMSTONE PUBLISHING • HUNT VALLEY, MARYLAND
WWW.GEMSTONEPUB.COM

FROM THE PUBLISHER

Although I've written a number of these "I never expected to" type columns and interviews this year, it's safe to say that I never expected to be writing a Publisher's Note in a companion book celebrating the 50th anniversary of *The Overstreet Comic Book Price Guide*. In fact, I wasn't all that sure there would be a second *Guide*, let alone a golden anniversary edition.

When I completed the first edition of the *Guide* in 1970 and it went on sale, I continued my research and took copious notes for corrections and updates, but it wasn't with any great assurance that the field would actually need a second edition. So, consider how surprised I must be to be writing this in 2020!

Five decades is an amazing time to spend working on one of your passions, yet here we are, celebrating fifty years of *The Overstreet Comic Book Price Guide*! Incredible! I consider myself very fortunate to be able to have done all the things I've done, met the people I've met, and seen the things I've seen.

I hope you'll enjoy all of the articles and our cover gallery, too. We've had some amazing artists featured on the *Guide* over the years and it's very exciting to see them collected in one place, along with some covers that never were (in the form of unused concept sketches).

As I write this, it's a tumultuous time in the world, but I'm still confident that there are better days ahead. We've had our facsimile edition of the first *Guide* turn into a surprise hit, *The Overstreet Comic Book Price Guide* #50 is selling briskly, and this book about to go to press. We've seen four different comic book issues sell for $1 million or more, and I suspect that there will be more in the not-too-distant future. We aim to make sure that the *Guide* will be with you for those times.

Thanks for joining in our celebration!

Robert M. Overstreet
Publisher

GEMSTONE PUBLISHING

STEVE GEPPI
PRESIDENT AND
CHIEF EXECUTIVE OFFICER

J.C. VAUGHN
VICE-PRESIDENT
OF PUBLISHING

ROBERT M. OVERSTREET
PUBLISHER

MARK HUESMAN
CREATIVE DIRECTOR

AMANDA SHERIFF
ASSOCIATE EDITOR

BRAELYNN BOWERSOX
STAFF WRITER

YOLANDA RAMIREZ
SENIOR RESEARCH ANALYST

MIKE WILBUR
DIRECTOR OF OPERATIONS

TOM GAREY
KATHY WEAVER
BRETT CANBY,
ANGELA PHILLIPS-MILLS
ACCOUNTING SERVICES

WWW.GEMSTONEPUB.COM

TABLE OF CONTENTS

INTRODUCTION

Sometimes the best introductions come from letting others do the introducing. While we think Bob Overstreet's accomplishments with *The Overstreet Comic Book Price Guide* over 50 years speak for themselves, we have to admit that these gentlemen do a rather fine job of introducing the subject matter on their own.

James Halperin, Co-Chairman of the Board, Heritage Auctions: "50 years ago, long before ubiquitous computers and the Internet, indexing and estimating values at multiple condition levels for every U.S. comic book known was a Herculean task that few mere mortals could hope to accomplish. Bob Overstreet's brilliant work set the trajectory for comic books to become one of the most liquid, valuable and popular collectibles in the world."

Vincent Zurzolo, COO, Metropolis Collectibles: "I will never forget the first *Overstreet Comic Book Price Guide* I ever held in my hands. It was issue #11 with that great L.B. Cole cover. I got goosebumps up and down my arms and still do to this day every time the new *Guide* comes out! An invaluable resource that I have been proud to be a contributor to since 1993. Thanks, Bob, for letting a young upstart dealer become an advisor. It is a title I hold with pride and a sense of responsibility to the comic collecting community. Here's to 50 more years! Make that 150!"

Stephen Fishler, CEO, Metropolis Collectibles: "Met Bob at a show in Chicago for the first time around 1983. Up to that point, all I knew was his name and the incredible impact he had on the comic book market during the previous decade. Felt very fortunate to know the man as well. Clearly, his passion for comic books was the driving force behind *The Overstreet Comic Book Price Guide*. That much became obvious to me."

Jim McLaughlin, President, The Hero Initiative: "I think one thing that gets overlooked among all the pricing data is what an exhaustive reference tool the *Guide* is. I mean, if you want to know the sixth appearance of the Legion of Super-Heroes or that Jim Starlin drew the splash page for *Son of Satan* #1... yeah, there it is. It says, 'Price Guide' on the cover, but it's an encyclopedia as well."

Ross Richie, Founder, BOOM! Studios: "*The Overstreet Comic Book Price Guide* is the gold standard of the hobby. Inside its pages, I've combed through comic book history and learned of treasure troves of stories, creators, and publishers I never knew existed. It's opened worlds of wonderment to everyone. For 50 years it's been a support to our incredible world of creativity, and I will be forever grateful it exists."

Nick Katradis, Collector: "The *Guide* is the holy book of comic collecting. Every collector of comics, new or seasoned, keeps it on hand. Whether they need publishing information for a particular issue or to determine the price of any comic ever published, the *Guide* is the prime source of information. It is hands down the most comprehensive and informative publication about comics ever created."

Josh Nathanson, President, ComicLink: "Without the impact *The Overstreet Comic Book Price Guide* made on me when I was a 9-year-old kid – alerted to the fact that I could read and enjoy comic books *and* have them be worth more than I paid in the future – I'd not have gotten into comic collecting. If I'd not gotten into comic collecting, there would be no ComicLink.com! So, the *Guide* is a significant part of this origin story, for sure. I first met Bob in my early to mid-20s, and so appreciated how generously encouraging he was to me as the new kid on the block. At the time I viewed him as a legendary, almost mythological figure, and I was shocked that not only was he nice to me, but he even knew what ComicLink was! A true steward of the hobby, the impact Bob made with the *Guide* in terms of dissemination of valuation and information will be there for as long as there is a comic book hobby. Thanks Bob, and Happy 50!"

We hope you'll enjoy this book, a loving tour through five decades of the *Guide*!

OVERSTREET @ 50

by Paul Levitz

Former President & Publisher, DC Comics

...the price guide became a well-worn tool in my search...

Photo credit: Seth Kushner

It's hard for a data-rich generation to understand the game-changing phenomenon that the first edition of the *Price Guide* was in 1970. Check the app on your phone for the first appearance of the character starring in the next big budget comics movie, then a few fast motions of your fingertips, and you can choose between bidding on it in an auction or buying it outright from dealers across the world. But back in the day, not only were there no big budget comic book movies (or even small budget comic book movies), most fans didn't even have a way of figuring out what a true first appearance was.

When that first edition came out, fandom was just entering the era of accumulating information on comics. No one had bothered to keep track of what comics were published, much less who the mostly anonymous creative people were who produced them or how many copies were sold. But as the '70s began, fandom had reached a passion for accumulating all this data. Databases hadn't been created on a scale that ordinary people could use, so these scattered facts were being compiled in fragile, mimeographed fanzines or simply in loose-leaf notebooks full of carefully gathered information. A few individual fans, indexers, started to trade information, but it was scarce as gold.

There were previous attempts at assembling a price guide for comics, but they were thin, light on detail, and showed no ambition to be comprehensive. The first edition of *Overstreet* defied all these norms. Envisioning a range of possible readers, it explained "how to start collecting" and our secret jargon, terms like "x-over" which have since, er, crossed over into the mainstream. It didn't get all the facts right, and even though only a fraction of the comics that would be published over the next 50 years existed, it missed quite a few. But it accumulated more information in one place than any comic fan had ever had access to before, and for the active collector, it became the invaluable roadmap to defining and building their collection.

As one of those early fans, the *Price Guide* became a well-worn tool in my search for the scattered first appearances of the Legion of Super-Heroes, and when I gained access to the DC Comics library a year or so later, I quickly did my part to fill in gaps in the information. It's too long ago for me to remember the handful of corrections I was able to offer Bob on that first edition, but it earned me a listing as an 'advisor' in the next. Best part about that was being able to tease Steve Geppi decades later that I'd been an Overstreet advisor before he was...of course, he got to buy the *Guide* and take it to the next level as its publisher.

My well-worn copy still sits on my reference shelf near the desk, next to the current volume. It's mostly a reference to how much simpler life was: *Adventure Comics* #247 with the first appearance of the Legion isn't even called out as anything special, just listed at $2 in mint like the surrounding issues. Now two generations later, that's less than the cover price of the newest *Legion* #1, and that issue of *Adventure* in Mint lists at the price of a pretty decent new car. Collecting's become a bit less of a treasure hunt and more of an organized hobby thanks to Bob Overstreet, but what I'll always thank him for is the valuable trove of information he unlocked.

OVERSTREET @ 50

by Maggie Thompson
Former Editor, Comics Buyer's Guide

And here we are, half a century later, still benefiting...

Much of the research for Bob Overstreet's first *Overstreet Comic Book Price Guide* came via his painstaking research of dealers' advertised price lists. I also saw his contributor Jerry Bails at a 1960s Detroit Triple Fan Fair going through dealers' boxes in search of such basic data as title and issue number in addition to each issue's price sticker. In both cases, even after a decade of comics fan communications, detailed information concerning such data was still largely unknown.

In his first publication of the *Guide* in 1970, Bob told readers that prices in the early days of comics collecting had been unstable. "However, the market seems to have stabilized over the past two years, making it now possible to have a realistic, dependable Price Guide."

In the early days of the *Guide*, Maggie Thompson and her husband Don provided a welcome wealth of data.

But here's what was so important about what he did: Bob clearly didn't consider the job finished, though it already represented countless hours of meticulous notetaking. While it must have been a relief to have his information finally released in a saddle-stitched volume of 244 internal pages, he didn't stop working.

Bob wrote in that first publication, "Please notify me of any omissions, corrections, or deletions of data in this volume so that I may include it in the 2nd Edition." Two years later, he released a "completely revised" squarebound tome of 338 internal pages. In the first edition, he had written, "Comic books with little or no value have been left out of this edition, but will be included in future volumes if and when their value increases." By the second volume, a concerted search for *all* available information had become the goal, and contributions had come in from such other sources as Don Thompson and me.

Because that was among the challenges of the incredible project: After a decade of enthusiastic collecting by countless comics aficionados, each collector continued to focus on personal interests, rather than on the art form as a whole. As a result of the interests of many of those pioneering fans, there was a huge focus on costumed heroes, with the 1970 volume even reporting, "Superman gave rise to a 'Golden Era' in the history of comics, technically referred to as 'The First Heroic Age of Comic Books.' For a full decade, the fellows in the long underwear ruled supreme." That "technical" reference was, indeed, the term coined and then adopted by fans and collectors whose personal focus lay in such costumed characters.

The basics of supply and demand pricing in that first volume reflected the nostalgia for stories of costumed characters. Many of the initial published high prices (*Action Comics* #1 at $300, *Marvel Mystery* #1 at $250, and the first issue of *Whiz Comics* at $235) were largely associated with action and adventure. Although costs of such issues as *Walt Disney's Comics & Stories* #1 were hefty ($115), they tended to be less than half the prices of key costumed characters. Nevertheless, as information grew, the "technical" term morphed to "Golden Age," because there were important non-heroic comics in that era, too. The point has turned out to be that, just because something is super-rare doesn't mean it's super-valuable. But that doesn't mean we don't care about the details of all forms of comics.

And here we are, half a century later, still benefiting from Bob's determination to make the project the best and most encompassing it could possibly be – for fans, for buyers, for sellers, and for historians. He not only had the idea, he also had the integrity, the meticulous organization, and the ongoing commitment that has brought us all a vital resource.

As part of the "Overstreet at 45" panel at the 2015 Comic-Con: San Diego, Maggie was joined by J.C. Vaughn, Matt Nelson, Steve Borock, Mark Waid and Mark Huesman.

OVERSTREET @ 50

by Buddy Saunders
Lone Star Comics / MyComicShop

The Overstreet Comic Book Price Guide has been a part of my life for all of its 50 years.

When Bob Overstreet brought his new baby, *The Comic Book Price Guide*, into the world, I was 23 years old. Now *The Guide* has turned 50 and I'm 72. I like to think both of us have held up pretty well over those 50 years, which have seen many changes in comic book collecting and in the comic book industry as well.

With issue No. 17 (Disney cover) *The Guide* became "official," assuming the longer title, *The Official Overstreet Comic Book Price Guide*. Then with #40 it dropped the "Official," to be as it is to this day, *The Overstreet Comic Book Price Guide*.

Over the years other guides have come and gone, but "official" or not, *The Overstreet Comic Book Price Guide* stands unchallenged as <u>the</u> guide we go to every time.

I began selling comics in 1960, just months after I began reading and collecting them. I would buy new comics at the Big World Drug for 12¢, then sell them at 25¢ to 35¢ through ads in early issues of *G.B. Love's Rocket's Blast Comic Collector*. Back then I shipped orders book rate at 4¢ a pound.

Among the comics I sold at 25¢ was a fresh-off-the-newsstand *Fantastic Four* #1.

My early ads mirrored others of the time, "All comics listed are VG to NM unless otherwise indicated," and my teenage pricing amounted to my best guess.

Overstreet changed all that. *Overstreet* gave comic fans and retailers two things, the first being a reliable baseline for pricing by grade, and the second a commonly agreed upon codification of standards, beginning with the letter grade system consisting of NM, VF, FN, VG, GD, FR, PR, and followed by the more exacting ten point system.

Fans and comic dealers simply refer to the comic world's "blue book" of comics as *The Overstreet*, a pricing tool along with articles and insights on market trends. "Let's check the price in *Overstreet*," is heard wherever comic fans gather. And that's exactly what I did over the years – check *Overstreet*. My original first printing white cover edition isn't mint. Far from it. It served me well the two years that

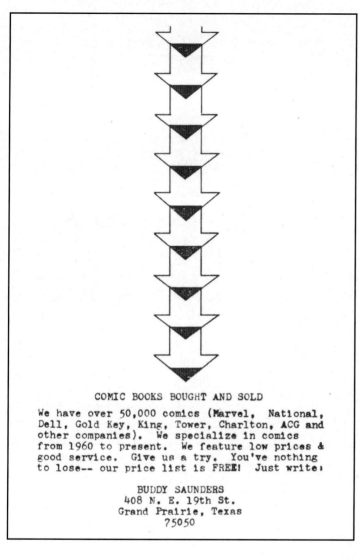

COMIC BOOKS BOUGHT AND SOLD

We have over 50,000 comics (Marvel, National, Dell, Gold Key, King, Tower, Charlton, ACG and other companies). We specialize in comics from 1960 to present. We feature low prices & good service. Give us a try. You've nothing to lose-- our price list is FREE! Just write:

BUDDY SAUNDERS
408 N. E. 19th St.
Grand Prairie, Texas
75050

up, it remains that for most comics *Overstreet* represents a reliable benchmark.

Comics that were back then unbagged and unboarded or in make-shift bags from dry cleaners or grocery stores are today bagged and boarded using materials specifically produced for comic preservation. The brown wax-coated chicken box has been replaced by comic boxes better suited for comic handling and storage. The new age of national comic book chains predicted by Mel Thompson never happened. But the internet did, altering the comic book collecting and selling landscape as never before! The direct market arrived and flourished, peppering the nation with comic book stores. The air freight war came and went as did the distributors who

passed between its publication and the release of #2 in 1972. The cover is half off but still attached, a gray smudge showing on the page edges where my ink-stained thumb visited countless times. As I grew as a comic collector and retailer, the *Overstreet* and I became fast friends, its issue numbers advancing even as my own years advanced.

Not that the *Overstreet* prices are set in stone. "Guide" is as important a word in the title as any other. But while prices may fluctuate, sometimes rising or falling too quickly for *Overstreet* to keep

started the war. Comic creators came and went. Publishers, too.

But through it all, and pointing the way to tomorrow as it always has, *The Overstreet Comic Book Price Guide* has remained an invaluable gift to all those with an appreciation of the world of comic books. For that, I thank Robert Overstreet and those, especially Steve Geppi, who have brought us unfailingly each new edition of *Overstreet*.

"Excelsior" and "Up, up, and away'" to the *Overstreet* at 50 and beyond!

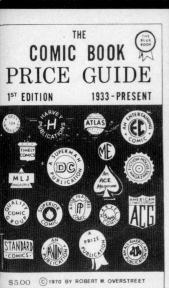

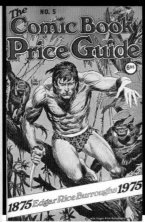

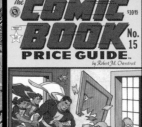

THE COMIC BOOK PRICE GUIDE
1ST EDITION 1933–PRESENT

$5.00 ©1970 BY ROBERT M. OVERSTREET

ACTION COMICS
June, 1938 – Present
National Periodical Publications

Issue #	Good	Fine	Mint
1-Origin Superman, Intro. Zatara.	200.00	250.00	300.00
2	50.00	60.00	70.00
3	40.00	50.00	65.00

CAPTAIN AMERICA
Mar., 1941 – #78, Sept., 1954.
#74 & 75 titled Captain America's
Weird Tales.
Marvel Comics Group

Issue #	Good	Fine	Mint
1-Origin Captain America & Bucky By Simon & Kirby; Hurricane begins.	90.00	125.00	150.00
2	40.00	50.00	60.00

Detective (Continued)

Issue #	Good	Fine	Mint
27-First app. of The Batman.	175.00	225.00	275.00
28	50.00	60.00	75.00
29,31-Batman covers.	40.00	50.00	60.00
30,32	35.00	45.00	55.00
33-Origin The Batman; Batman cover.	45.00	60.00	75.00

MARVEL MYSTERY (Marvel Tales #93 on)
Nov., 1939 – June, 1949 (Content
Change)
Marvel Comics Group

Issue #	Good	Fine	Mint
1-Origin Human Torch, Sub-Mariner, Kazar the Great; Intro. The Angel, The Masked Raider.	165.00	200.00	250.00

The Semi-Secret Origins of the Overstreet Comic Book Price Guide

By J.C. Vaughn

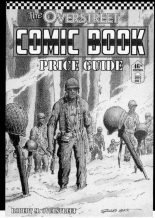
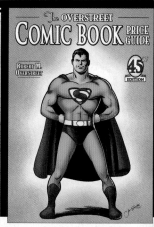

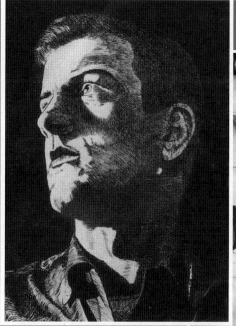

When Robert M. Overstreet first produced
The Overstreet Comic Book Price Guide, *it was in
many regards the logical culmination of collecting
habits and skills he had honed since childhood.
It was also the start of an entirely new career.*

With his calm, studious approach – frequently punctuated by moments of excited smiles at some new discovery – Overstreet first released his Guide to fandom and the marketplace in 1970. Not only did its success warrant a second printing, it also meant he had to update the prices and produce a second edition, something he hadn't contemplated when he started.

Still very active with the Guide today – he continues to handle all the pricing himself – Overstreet talked with J.C. Vaughn, Gemstone Publishing's Vice-President of Publishing, with whom he's worked for about 25 years (Vaughn previously freelanced for Overstreet Publications prior to its acquisition by Steve Geppi's Gemstone).

Sometimes the seeds of something big are planted very early. That was the case with Bob Overstreet. Known to literally hundreds of thousands of readers as the author of The Overstreet Comic Book Price Guide, he not only started with comics early in life, he started with them early each day.

"I read comic books in the late '40s. One of my favorite comics was Fox And The Crow. I would have Kix cereal in the morning and I would read my Fox & the Crow comics eating Kix," he said.. "My older brother Jerry had more comic books than I did. And we always had comic books around the house. I even ordered the Atomic Bomb ring advertised on the Kix box back in 1947."

You mentioned Fox And The Crow. Were funny animals your favorite?
With my brother's comics I remember Captain Marvel, Daredevil (the '40s Daredevil, that is). It was a mixed bag of superhero and funny animal, but I mainly remember reading the Fox And The Crow comics. I really enjoyed those at that time, but my favorite superhero was the Gleason Daredevil. At 11 years old in 1949, I was Daredevil! I had hand-walked power lines across the street, could jump my own height, and poll-vaulted across ditches.

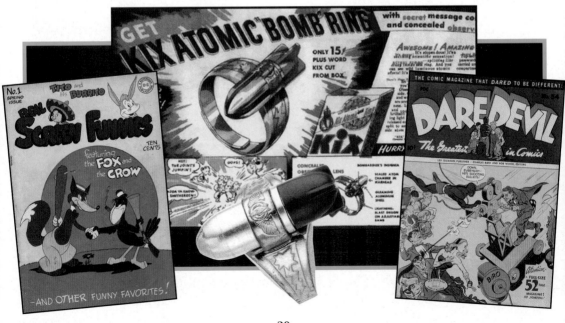

What was your family background? Did your dad have a furniture business?

Dad was in the furniture business. He owned his own store. He worked in the coalmines back in the 1930s in West Virginia. That's where I was born. Then he went to work for Sterchi's, which was a big furniture chain rooted out of Knoxville, Tennessee. They transferred him to Cleveland, Tennessee in 1944.

And that's when you moved there?

Yes. And then he opened his own store after he'd been there a while. Before he opened the store, though, he left Sterchi's and went to work for the newspaper. He became publisher of the Cleveland newspaper between 1948 and 1952. In '52 he opened his own furniture store. He kept that for 10 years and then he sold it. He didn't do well with it. I don't know if he ever showed a profit. Then he sold it and went back to West Virginia in the early '60s.

How old were you when you hit the ECs?

I was 13.

How did you discover them?

I met Landon Chesney when I was in the eighth grade. L.C. was very intelligent, and he collected ECs. He collected them seriously. He loved the art, and he was a great artist himself. I was always interested in art, so

when I met him he introduced me to EC Comics. He was an early member of the EC Fan-Addict Club. His number was 47. And he also introduced me to the idea of collecting comic

books. I never thought about collecting them before that. He was a really interesting person. He collected comics, and was interested in magic. He did a lot of artwork. He was interested in theater. He could imitate almost anybody. In high school he was in theater. He enjoyed that. I would take him to high school parties with me and he'd be the entertainment for the party because he could imitate Jimmy Stewart, or Jerry Lewis or Peter Fontaine or just about anybody famous. He was really good at it. He was a natural.

Did you guys meet other collectors at that point?

We were the two comic book collectors in the town. We had friends that had comic books, but we were the only ones who were serious about it. We were always seeking EC comics to complete our sets, and so we discovered a few EC comics from our friends, but not many.

Once you started getting really diligent about tracking down all the ECs, how did you start meeting other collectors?

Back in the early '50s I also collected coins. I always bought the *Red Book* when it came out each year. Back in those days, you could still go through change and find a lot of rare coins in it. It wasn't a big investment other than time. So I went to the bank and they would give me the parking meter money, and I would go through it looking for rare coins. And then I would count the coins and roll them for the bank.

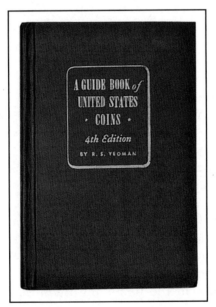

So you traded your services for the chance to cherry pick coins from the bank?

Right. I found a lot of rare coins. I put together complete sets of almost all the rare 20th century coins. I would even find Indian Head Pennies or Barber coins going back to the 1800s [*Editor's note: Barber coins were named after their designer, created as dimes, quarters and half dollars by the Mint from 1892 to 1915*]. Buffalo Nickels were very common and Jefferson Nickels were very easy to get, even the rare Jefferson 1950 "D" Nickel. I found at least a roll or two of them. I sold them to coin dealers for $2.50 a piece and I was paying 5¢ each. I was really into coins. We would have a *Red Book* party when the *Red Book* came out each year there in Cleveland. There was a coin dealer, and we would all get together when the *Red Books* arrived. We really looked forward to that.

This background was pretty important, I think. At the same time, I was really into EC Comics and trying to locate the back issues, other collectors, dealers, or anyone that had a source for those comics. Pretty early on we met two other collectors in Tennessee. One was Billy Hoover, who lived in Manchester, Tennessee, and he had a comic book mail order business. He sent out price lists of comic books and he collected EC, Disney, westerns. I still have postcards from Billy that date 1955 and other collectors that date 1954.

Was he one of the earliest dealers?

He was an early one. He collected all the westerns, some superheroes... he loved the Disneys, he loved Barks, and he loved the ECs. His name was listed in *EC Bulletin #4*, September 1954, which was my first bulletin after joining the EC Fan-Addict club.

So, we wrote to him, and he wasn't that far away from us, so we started corresponding with him. He was also an artist and loved drawing comics. We met him through the mail and then drove over and actually met him in person. He was the first person I bought back issue ECs from. He would type his lists up on tissue paper, on toilet paper, on paper bags, whatever paper he had available. It was weird. I still remember ordering a stack of ECs from him and waiting on that package.

Were these ones you hadn't seen or just upgrading the copies you already had?
I had never seen them.

You must have been really excited then.
I would have dreams about what might be on the covers. We had never seen these early ECs.

Did they live up to your expectations?
Oh, yeah, they were fantastic. They were all early ones. He packaged them in a shoebox and put it in the mail. When the box arrived it didn't survive very well in the postal system. The comics were loose inside the box. There were gaping holes in the box. Probably the comics were damaged, but back in those days you were just happy to have a copy if it was complete, even if today it would be considered VG or whatever.

How long before you started wanting really good copies?
From the beginning I always wanted mint copies and mint was a grade we used back then, but mint copies were next to impossible to find. In Tennessee, old comic books were very

hard to find. We went to Nashville, Chattanooga, Atlanta, and it seemed like nobody had old comic books. There were very few collectors we knew of in the South. We also met Harry Thomas, another collector, from Sweetwater, Tennessee. He collected superhero comics. We collected the ECs almost exclusively. So Harry introduced us to the superheroes and to the fact that a lot of people around the country collected them. We had a lot of arguments about which were the best. [laughs] We would always argue that ECs were aimed at an older audience and they were better than the superheroes, which were aimed at a younger audience. I remember when we first met Harry he had a few Golden Age comics. And we had never seen any Golden Age comics - there were no used bookstores with them for sale, no one we traded with had them, you just didn't see them in Tennessee. So he brought down a little stack of Golden Age comics. I bought from him an *All Star* and a *Green Lantern* #18, the Christmas cover, and he kind of introduced me to the other types of comics outside of EC. I was desperately trying to put an EC collection together, but funds were limited and that's all I could afford.

In the mid-1960s while working for Hiwassee Land Company, the forestry division to Bowater Southern Paper Corp., an ad auctioning Golden Age comic books appeared in one of the fanzines. It was placed by an antique dealer in Spring City, Tennessee, which is where our company had a branch office. In the next couple of weeks, I was there with a Bowater accountant on a business trip. I couldn't remember the name of the antique dealer, but soon got their address. It was unbelievable! The dealer took us down to the basement where there was a chest of drawers packed full of comic books and a full size bed with stacks of comic books. The auction did well with many of the books sold. One of the famous early fans, Jerry Bails had bid on the *All Star #3*, among others. I asked the dealer if she had any of the EC comics? She pulled out the top drawer and said "You mean like these?" There was *Weird Science #12/1* and several other early ECs. I was literally blown away. I asked the accountant with me if he had some money? He said "Yes, I've got you covered." (Thinking you should be able to buy comics for a few cents each). I asked her, how much? She said "I want $1.00 each." The dealer told me that one of the bidders didn't come through which was a nice stack of early Golden Age books, such as *Batman #9*, *Captain Marvel #2*, *Green Hornet #1*, *Superman #6*, and others. We didn't have enough money to pay for them then, so I had to come back that night with the money.

At what point did you figure out what you thought you wanted to do for a career?

At that time, I was very interested in astronomy. I was grinding telescope lenses, making telescopes. I had friends in the community, older friends, and one guy owned a machine shop. He was very interested in science and geology. He had has own laboratory in his home. I'd go over and visit him every week. He made me a telescope mount and made my rack and pinion gear at his machine shop. I bought the kit for the mirror and ground my own mirror. It took me two years to grind

Blue Chip Stock

Bob's funny books have increased greatly in value since some boy—perhaps 25 years ago—paid a dime apiece for them. The copy of the Green Hornet in Bob's right hand is the first issue and is now worth about $50. After 20 years in obscurity, Bat Man—now riding the crest of his television wave—has returned to popularity. The Bat Man No. 9, Bob is holding, is worth $17 and rising.

Newspaper clipping from 1966.

24

that mirror. I was learning about how to do that. That was another hobby of mine. I thought that when I grew up I wanted to be an astronomer. I never thought of anything else. I was always out late at night with the telescope. Later, I got a camera and learned how to take pictures through the telescope. Some of these pictures were actually published in an astronomy magazine back in the '60s. I didn't know the pictures had been published. A local person called me and asked me if I was the Bob Overstreet that took the pictures he had seen in this book he bought. That was the first I had heard of it, so I ran to the bookstore, found the book, and there were my pictures.

How did they get the photos?
After I built my own, I bought a good quality telescope. I sent the pictures to the telescope company. They had them published to promote their telescopes.

What were you doing for a job at that point?
Working for my dad at the furniture store. I was the credit manager and the bookkeeper.

So you did that until he sold the business?
Yes. Then I was put out on the street. [laughs] I moved around from one job to another. My training was bookkeep-ing. I got a selling job, which I hated. I was never a salesman. Then I got a bookkeeping job and then a credit job. Then finally I got a really good job at Bowater Paper Company, one of the largest employers in our area and one of the biggest paper plants in the country. They were close by, and they ran an ad for a statistician. I applied and got it. I launched the price guide while I was there.

So you were gaining knowledge of printing at that point. Did that help with the price guide?
Well, while my dad was publisher of the newspaper they also did job printing. I guess I had ink in my blood. He was really strong in advertising and he convinced me that I needed to sell ads for my first price guide, so that's what I did.

And your book was the first price guide to carry advertising in it?
Certainly in this hobby, but I had never seen another one with ads in it even in other fields.

Before you started actually putting the *Guide* together, was there one exact moment when you knew you had to do it, or was there a series of events that lead you to consider it?
I think it was several years of slowly discovering other collectors in the area and then around the country. We discovered science fiction fandom in the early '50s.

And they were much more organized than comics were at that point?

They were organized, and they were putting out newsletters. There was one guy in Dalton, Georgia, 30 miles away, who was in science fiction fandom. The guy who was the president of that group was in Birmingham, Alabama. And Chesney went down to see him, and his name was Alfred McCoy Andrews. From science fiction fandom we got names of people who had comic books. So we joined that group so we could locate other collectors, who shared our interest. When Chesney and I were in high school we spent a lot of our time writing and drawing comic books.

You did an extensive article in *CBPG* #30 about that.

Right. So we drew some stories and published some of them. Among them was this one story that I republished in that article. At the end of that story we wrote in Alfred McCoy Andrews' name on a newspaper as a tribute to him. But we also met another collector down in Georgia, down below Atlanta, and he collected horror. He had almost every horror comic. And we went down and met him. He had ECs and everything else, and he also had some superhero comics. I remember trading him a duplicate EC I had for a *Superman* #2. And we thought, "Who knows? This may be worth something someday." I was a little reluctant to give up an EC for a superhero comic, but I picked that book up and thought it was kind of neat. We went down to see this guy a couple of times. He had walls of paperbacks. He had all the comic books on bookshelves, stood up on end, and he had gone through and taped the spines on all of his comics with Scotch tape.

Ouch.

So his whole collection was ruined. So we met a lot of people and found new sources. This went on all through the '50s and '60s.

As you had this network of people, is there one point where you think there's just got to be a price guide...?

All through the '60s I was hoping that someone would put out a price guide on comic books because one was needed.

Did you recognize that because of your experience in coins?

Yes. I wanted to see a *Red Book* in comics. I didn't know if it would ever happen. I didn't know if comics would ever become a legitimate collectible field like coins. I was hoping it would. I was hoping that someone would someday put out a guide on comics. I just didn't know it was going to be me.

What brought you to the point of deciding it was going to be you?

The comic market was really taking off in the '60s. Prices were escalating rapidly. Almost any 10¢ comic was worth money. You had the *Rocket's Blast - Comic Collector* (RBCC) coming out and going to all the comic people, and I subscribed to that. I had all the *RBCC*s and I also had all the price lists from the early dealers like Claude Held and Howard Rogofsky. I could see the market was growing. Like I said, prices were escalating. There were a lot of details that were basically unknown and there was still a lot to be discovered about comics, and there was no single source of information to go to in those days.

I was buying everything off the stands in the '60s beginning with *Amazing Spider-Man* #1, so I had all this stuff. I had a great inventory of Silver Age books. I bought duplicates, so I set up Sonny Johnson to be a dealer. I gave him an inventory to get him started. He ran an ad and the comics sold just like that. I couldn't believe how fast they went. Then I decided I better stop selling the books. They were still going up in value. He sold my two copies of *Spider-Man* #1, so I didn't get them back.

I also had a relic collection because I hunted arrowheads all through the '50s. The relic market was flat during the '60s while the comic market was taking off. So I sold most of my relics to raise money to buy comics. In the mid '60s I actually started working on an arrowhead price guide. I was going to draw each arrowhead. Instead of using photography, I was going to illustrate each point because that's how all the books down in that market were done. Many of them still are today, in fact. I started doing the research on the types, doing the drawings and so on. I was actually getting into the book. But the comic market was getting so hot...

Then there was a big collection that turned up in 1967. Sonny found this big collection of Golden Age comics in Pennsylvania. He was paying $2.50 a piece for them. The guy who had them was sending him a list every week, and he was picking out the best ones. He didn't buy them all. He bought the #1s and the more valuable ones for $2.50. So he had a box of comics coming in every week. This was all stuff none of us had ever seen. And this was all the *Action* [*Comics*], *More Fun* [*Comics*], *Superman*, *Adventure* [*Comics*], *Detective* [*Comics*], *All Star*

[*Comics*], *All-American* [*Comics*], *Daredevils*, reprint comics from the '30s and '40s. One weekend he got *Superman #1*, *All Star Comics #3* and *Detective Comics #27*, all at the same time. I was sitting there with not a lot of money, so I was selling everything I could to buy these books. At that time I had a stack of EC annuals. There was a guy in Florida who put out an EC fanzine. He stopped through Cleveland back in the '50s and he gave me a stack of EC annuals. So I sold and traded some of the annuals for those comics. Sonny became a national dealer almost overnight because of that Golden Age collection. He sold to other dealers and collectors all over the country.

In of all this, you realized that there's not only a need for a guide, it was going to take someone to get it started?
I began putting together the page format of what the book would look like, and what would go in the book. I was showing it to Harry, L.C., Sonny, and Bob Jennings in Nashville, who put out the fanzine *Comic World*. I was trying to get somebody interested in putting out a price guide because we needed one. I kept working on it. I kept typing up information, putting it in price guide form and showing it around to people. Nobody wanted to do a price guide. It was too much work. They kept on kicking it back to me. "Why don't you do it?" they said. "We'll help you." [laughs] So finally I ended up doing it.

Aside from the guys you just mentioned, did anyone else have any input into how it looked or what

went into it?
Jerry Bails, of course, was another one that I kept sending information to. He was the one I wanted to do it.

Were they all supportive of what you showed them?
Yes.

As long as you were the one doing the work?
Right. [laughs] Bails said he would help me. He had other interests. He was more interested in continuing his research. He didn't want to do a price guide.

Once you began, did they still help?
They all faded out once the work started. I was typing up complete pages and sending them to Jerry. He would lay onionskin paper over my pages and make notations as to what he thought the prices would be. That got to be too much work and he only did a few pages, then he quit. But I had his good wishes to go ahead and do it myself. [laughs]

Over the years since the first guide, you've developed an extensive network of advisors, but what did you base the original prices on?
I went through every piece of information that I had accumulated up to that time, which was quite a few years' worth of material. I had a lot of price lists, all the back issues of *RBCC*, Bill Thailing's catalogs, fanzines and every other bit of information I had. One price list I got from the beginning was from Bob's Book Barn. They sold everything. That's where I got a lot of initial information as to what existed because they would list titles, issue numbers and very important dates,

28

which a lot of people didn't list. That was good information. I began setting up an index card file for every title I could find. I would put the information on them.

Did you start seeing the first indications of the regionalism in the market then?
No, that was something that we didn't really see until the market became more national. That wasn't even something we thought about in the early stages.

Who were some of the others you had lists from?
There were a lot of people who advertised in *RBCC*. I had a lot of individual price lists of collectors. I still have a lot of correspondence from when I was seeking back issue ECs. I corresponded with a lot of collectors. I actually wrote to everybody listed on the EC Bulletins, every one of those people. I found one guy who still had his set of ECs out of all those names. I began buying his back issue ECs. He said he paid through the nose for them, so they were going to be expensive. He was going to have to have a dollar a piece for them. I bought all the rare ones and the early ones, then I got him down to 50¢ on the next batch. Then I tried to get him down to a quarter, and that's when I lost him.

What was the print run on the original *Guide*?
The print run on the first book was 1,000, and on the second edition it was 800.

How did you come up with the retail price of the book?
I just felt that $5 was a fair price. I sold a lot of copies at a pre-publication price, which was less. I vaguely remember $3.50.

How did you gauge your success?
RBCC was going to about 2,000 people at the time, so I thought my audience was 2,000 people. If I could sell 2,000 copies I would have hit a home run. I did sell about 1,800 copies.

How was it printed?
It was a very small printer who was doing the book. He would run off the pages and then bring them over to my house, and then I had to fold them, collate them, and staple them. I had to do that myself. All he did was the actual printing.

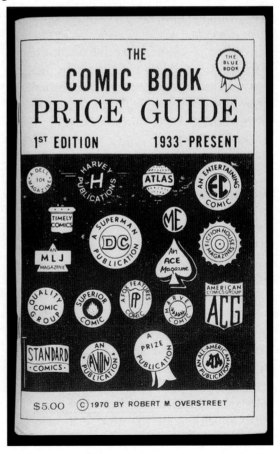

THE
COMIC BOOK
PRICE GUIDE
1ST EDITION   1933–PRESENT

$5.00 ©1970 BY ROBERT M. OVERSTREET

glaring ones. I retyped those pages on the reprint. I was getting feedback immediately when I was shipping books out.

What were the reactions to the book from collectors and dealers?
That's the first time anyone had put comic book retail values in a book and published it. There was a lot of criticism about the prices being too high, and there was a lot about them being too low. But everybody bought the book. That was the main result; the book was accepted. I remember Phil Seuling, who was throwing the New York conventions, didn't support the price guide until I had put out four editions. Then he was interested in buying it. He started distributing it after that. It took several years before some of the other powerful people in the market began accepting it.

When you put out a price guide, most people don't respond directly to you at all. They'll talk about the book to

Why did the second printing have a blue cover?
I went to a blue cover because the printing was so bad. The black ink was washed out on a lot of the copies. I thought if I put a color in the background that would minimize the washed out black. That's why I went to blue.

How did the book sell initially?
It came out in the fall. It took me through 1971 to sell out the first two printings, then I started coming out in spring with the second edition and the *Guide* has been there ever since.

Did you make corrections between the first and second printings of the first Guide?
Yes. I can't remember what they were specifically, but there were mistakes in the first edition and we corrected the most

Bruce Hamilton with Carl Barks
in 1982

someone else, and that other person might call you and tell you about it if you're lucky. Bruce Hamilton was one person who got involved after the first guide. He came to see me right after it came out. He drove to Tennessee. It really got him. He became one of my early advisors, and he stayed with me to his death in 2005. He was very important in the early development of the price guide. He helped a lot in pricing theory, among other things.

Who were your earliest advertisers?
Howard Rogofsky, Robert Bell, Bruce Hamilton, F.L. Buza, Jerry Bails, Richard Burgess, Clint's Bookstore, Buddy Saunders. Passaic Book Center, Grand Book, Inc., Sonny Johnson, to name a few.

Once the *Guide* started getting established, did you or any of the early naysayers start advertising or begin supporting it?
It took a few years of exposure, attending some of the early conventions to meet many collectors and dealers. Phil Seuling, who put on the New York convention, resisted support at first, but by the fourth edition came on board and presented me with an Ed April award at the 1974 convention for publishing the price guide.

What made you decide to start having original art on the cover of the *Guide*?
After running comic book covers on #2 and #3, it was a natural transition to have original covers for future guides done by the master comic book artists. My first professional cover was done by Don Newton, a friend of Bruce Hamilton's, who recommended him to me. His cover of the Justice Society of America was a beautiful piece of art

which itself inspired top artists like Joe Kubert (Tarzan), Will Eisner (The Spirit) and Carl Barks to do the next covers in line. After that, it was easy to solicit covers.

There's a great story – one Ed Catto documented in a ComicMix column – about The Spirit cover by Will Eisner on *CBPG* #6. What can you tell us about it?
In the fall of 1975 DC Comics recommended that I contact Crown Publishers in New York about bookstore distribution for the *Guide*. I called them and they preordered 10,000 copies of my next book, which was *The Overstreet Comic Book Price Guide* #6. I contacted Will Eisner to do a 1776 theme since it was our country's 200th anniversary in 1976. He finished the art right away and upon receiving it, I sent Crown a copy of my new cover.

They called me on Christmas Eve 1975 and told me that Eisner could not have his name on the cover because his illustrated cookbook series had sold awfully. I had to call Eisner on Christmas Eve to ask him if it would be okay to drop his name off the cover art.

This was very hard for me and something I did not want to do. I got him on the phone and surprisingly he agreed for me to delete his name from the cover art. However, I just couldn't do it. I left his name on the cover, much to Crown's chagrin.

Incidentally, it ended up selling very well. This was so important because this was my very first book for bookstore distribution worldwide.

What are your personal favorite *Guide* covers?

How can you not like all the early covers? I loved them all!

You're probably sick of me saying it at this point, but with Kubert, Eisner and Barks, followed by Bill Ward, Wally Wood, and Alex Schomburg, you really threw down the gauntlet to those of us who have had to pick covers for the *Guide*. Which recent ones do you think are our best for keeping up your grand tradition?
I think all the recent covers are excellent and am very happy with the way you have kept the standard high with them.

When you look back on it, did you ever still expect to be doing it today?
When I did the first book, I didn't think I'd have to do another one. [laughs] The first book was a lot of work. I didn't know... I hadn't

Bob Overstreet holding early *Price Guide* cover art in 1979. This photo was run in the *Chattanooga News Free Press*.

thought that much about the future. I hadn't thought about having to do this book every year. But as the decades roll by, the book has actually become my life. My love for comics from the start has prevailed now for more than 68 years and will continue as far as I can see.

Were you hoping that a professional publisher would come along, take over, and do it like the *Red Book*?
Oh, yeah. There was a point after a few years that I sent copies to major publishers and tried to get them to take it. They all turned me down and said the market didn't need a book like that. Because the first one was such a success, though, there had to be a second. And the second one was twice as successful as the first one, and that meant there had to be a third one. The circulation of the *Guide* was increasing every year. I really had the proverbial tiger by the tail. I was stuck with it, making enough money to keep it going. I couldn't drop it. The most amusing thing to me when I put out the first *Guide* was that every day when I went to the mailbox there was a check. I couldn't believe that it was so easy. You just run an ad... and all these people send money in. That's what made it great because it eventually gave me the freedom to do this full time.

One of the biggest changes in the market since I've been working with you clearly has to be the arrival of third-party, independent grading and certification. What do you think first CGC and now CBCS have brought to the market?
I've always thought that the comic market needed professional grading to survive into the future. The coin market went through this transition successfully, so why not comics.? Value is based on an acceptable certified grade which opened up our market to many auction houses or anyone that had a certified comic for sale and has propelled our market to the top along with coins, art, antique cars, antiques, etc.

The *Guide* is now five decades old. What other significant market changes would you note from that time?
Certification has made our market acceptable to all levels of society and has to be as important an event as the publication of the *Guide* itself. With certification, now anyone can acquire books with confidence that the grade will be accurate and that the book is as advertised.

For *The Overstreet Comic Book Price Guide* #40, you were a guest of Comic-Con International: San Diego. As I recall, that was the first time you ever let a convention pay your way. Why was that?
Through all the early years, attending

conventions was important for me in research pricing with dealers and collectors where I controlled my time. When you attend a convention at their expense, your time is controlled by them and you are obligated to at least do some of the things they have lined up.

After you made your appearance at that show, it was clear that from our sales and the level of participation from some of the Overstreet Advisors and retailers that people were very happy to see you were still so involved with the *Guide*. What sort of reactions did you experience?
I enjoyed very much seeing everyone and meeting some of the new advisors.

The Hero Initiative hosted a private luncheon at that show for five winners who bid on lunch with you as a fundraiser. What was that like?
It was thoroughly enjoyable and interesting to meet fans in this way. You don't realize how you have touched the lives of people over the years, which this luncheon brings out.

For the rest of us on the staff, it was very similar when you and Carol

were at San Diego for the *Guide's* 45th anniversary. You were greeted like a rock star, like a long-lost friend. How did it seem to you?
I was immensely flattered and beginning to realize how long the *Guide* has been around, when now the grandkids of collectors/dealers I knew back in the 1960s are collecting and buying the *Guide* now.

The early editions of the *Guide* have commanded premium prices for years now, but what do you think of the prices we've seen for #1 the past couple of years?
I guess it is a natural progression of a growing market as values continue to escalate. The *Guide* has become a collectible itself and the prices it is bringing at auction are beyond belief.

When did you notice that some folks were collecting the *Guide* itself?
Early on as the *Guide* proved to be a dependable series that would come out every year, collectors were encouraged to put a set together.

You mentioned earlier that after you finished the first *Guide* that you didn't even know you'd have to do a

second one. What do you think your younger self would have said if you told him that you'd still be working on the *Guide*?
It would strongly reinforce why I put out the first edition and the importance of a price guide on comic books to begin with. And surviving 50 years would have been totally unbelievable!

Looking back over the last five decades, do you have any favorite moments with the *Guide*?
I enjoyed the early years at San Diego Con when a group of dealers and I would go to a local restaurant down the street and have pizza. You would walk through a grocery store to get to the restaurant in the back. There, many deals were negotiated and consummated.

On another trip to Phoenix, Arizona to visit Bruce Hamilton, my plane arrived late when Bruce was there to pick me up. While leaving the airport he turned on the radio. Phoenix has several radio stations and before the *Guide*, Bruce worked at a radio station. We were shocked that they were talking about *The Overstreet Comic Book Price Guide*. Now what are the chances of that, at that precise time and date that Overstreet would even be in Phoenix, Arizona. Bruce couldn't have set this up to amuse me because my plane was late, so it wouldn't have worked. When we arrived at his home, we called the radio station and went out over the air. They were shocked to find out that I was listening and was in Phoenix and their audience really got an unplanned treat.

In 1974, Phil Seuling invited me to be in a discussion panel at the New York Comic Convention which would be my first real exposure to a collectors' audience. I arrived at the room where this would take place and sat down in the back of the room. No one knew who I was and soon Phil entered the room and began making some convention announcements while waiting on the guests to arrive. I noticed they were setting up TV cameras to televise the event. Soon it was time for me to go to the front of the room and I quickly realized that the panel was only Phil and myself. The television was being broadcast into Canada. Phil introduced me to the audience and the questions began. They were firing questions at me about the *Guide*, how the pricing was done, etc. and Phil was great in backing me up and helping me answer the questions. When it was all over, many were asking for my autograph. It went well. Also at that time I received the Ed April award plaque honoring the *Guide*.

While there, Phil told me a story about him and a partner going to see a guy close to New York who had a comic collection for sale. Between them, they only had a few dollars to spend. While going through the collection, they were shocked when before their eyes was a copy of *Superman* #1. They tried to hide their anxiety and couldn't believe they had found such a treasure. They just barely had enough money to buy the books including the *Superman* #1. They couldn't believe that they actually bought a *Superman* #1 and were leaving with it. They worried that the guy would change his mind and take it back. They made it out to their car ready to leave when the guy shouted to get their attention. They thought, on no! He has changed his mind about selling the *Superman* #1. But he said, "Would you be interested in buying another copy of *Superman* #1"? He had two copies of *Superman* #1. Unbelievable!

In 1976 I was honored by a visit from Carl Barks and his wife Gare. He drove all the way from California to Tennessee to meet me. He was impressed with the price guide and wanted to see how it was put together and published. He spent the night and we had a charming visit. While there he photographed my Barks painting "Nobody's Spending Fool." He accepted my request to create a *Guide* cover for #7. I wanted a Disney cover, but Disney would not allow me to run a cover until *CBPG* #17 due to their licensing restrictions. Later I remembered that Barks did do a Porky Pig cover for Warner Bros. back in 1944, *Four Color Comics* #48. Carl agreed to paint me a Porky Pig cover, so Warner Bros. was contacted to acquire permission which they gave with no problem.

In the Fall of 1980, after *CBPG* #10, was released I took Cooksey Shugart, a long-time friend of mine, to New York to negotiate the distribution of his book *The Complete Guide to American Pocket Watches*, which I was about to publish. The comic guide was being distributed to bookstores by Crown Publishers and we took the galleys of Cooksey's book to sell Crown on picking it up for distribution. We had a great meeting with Bruce Harris, who wanted the book and placed an order for 10,000 copies for bookstore distribution when it came out in 1981. While in New York, we had some time to kill, so I told Cooksey that there was a comic book store in Manhattan that owed me money. I wanted to walk through the city and try to find the store. We did find it, and I walked in with Cooksey and told the manager who we were and that we were there

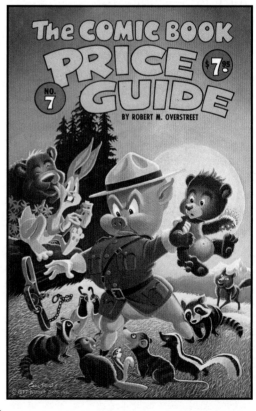

to collect the money that was owed. The store had several Golden Age comics displayed on the wall and in cases. I told the manager that I would take comics to pay the debt. He then called the owner on his phone and told me the owner would be there shortly. Next door was a bar, so Cooksey and I went into the bar and thought we could kill time and have a cocktail. We ended up having several cocktails waiting on the manager to show up. He finally came into the bar and offered me some cash and the comics that I picked out to settle the debt. At that time, I remembered that I had an appointment with Associated Press back at our hotel room about the *Guide*. With my head spinning from the cocktails, we flagged a cab and rushed back to the hotel. I was going to be late for the appointment, but as we arrived at the hotel, we saw an Associated Press guy leaving the hotel. We stopped him in time and proceeded to my room for the interview which went well. The article came out all across the country and this was *CBPG* #10 with the Schomburg cover. Orders began streaming in and I had to go back to press.

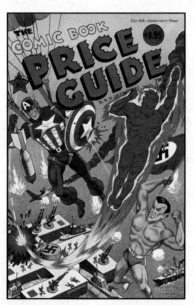

On one of several trips to California there was one special day when Bruce Hamilton and I had breakfast with Carl Barks, and then drove to Los Angeles to visit Dave Smith at the Disney archives. While we were there, Disney allowed us to see a special showing of a recent Disney movie and gave us a tour of a western town on set that was used in some of the '50s westerns. We finished the day having dinner with Floyd Gottfredson, the premier Mickey Mouse artist, followed by a visit to his studio. So, in one day, we had the unbelievable chance to visit the premiere Donald Duck artist and the premier Mickey Mouse artist.

All through the 1980s, Chuck Rozanski would take a briefcase full of Mile High comics to Baltimore to sell to John Snyder, who in turn would sell them to Steve Geppi, me, and others. I remember one trip when Steve Geppi drove down to Tennessee to show me the Mile High run of *Captain America* that he just acquired. Snyder also made several trips to Tennessee to sell me books. At that time, I owned a beautiful maroon and black 1931 Chevrolet coop (all original) and on his visits John became fascinated with the car. Then there was a visit with John and Steve. Steve brought down an *Action Comics* #1 that he had just acquired. I wanted the *Action* #1 and John wanted the car, so a trade was worked out where John got the *Action* #1 to trade to me for the 1931 car. Then John and Steve had to find a way to pull the car back to Baltimore.

On one of my many visits to Baltimore to see Steve, I arrived on the day that he had just bought the famous Pennsylvania pedigree collection. I was visiting Snyder in Virginia and we drove up to Baltimore to visit Steve. Steve's house had boxes of this collection on the floor everywhere. These books were all very high grade and I just had to go through the collection and buy some of these beautiful books. We kept Steve up until 3 AM pricing the dozens of books that I wanted to buy. On another visit to see Steve, he had just received the Mile High run of *Planet Comics* that he had bought from a collector in Houston, Texas. I couldn't resist and left with the *Planets*.

On one of my New York comic con trips, Don Phelps had made arrangements to have a visit with John Stanley, the Little Lulu artist, who lived in a small town on the Hudson river north of New York City. We arrived in the afternoon and had a wonderful visit with John and family. When John drew Little Lulu he would write the stories and draw them in pencil. He would write in cursive the dialogue in the word balloons. He would send the finished stories (in pencil) into the Dell New York office where someone else would ink the finished art. I asked John if he would consider creating a cover for the price guide. He accepted and after my visit, he sent me several cover idea roughs. However, for some reason, he changed his mind and never did the finished cover. He did do some Lulu cover recreations for Phelps, however, after our visit. John didn't attend comic conventions and pretty well stayed away from his fans and was very difficult to reach. Our visit went past midnight, when we left to drive back to New York.

In 1989 I was contacted by Russ Cochran who informed me that Bill Gaines was ready to open his vault of

EC's and put them up for sale along with all the EC art which he had kept. They wanted me to participate in the event. For a lifelong EC collector, this was an unbelievable opportunity for me. I flew to New York City and we arrived at Gaines' penthouse in Manhattan on Friday, August 11, 1989 and worked opening and bagging the EC's through Sunday, August 13. Entering his apartment, I couldn't help but notice the real shrunken head on top of his bookcase. This reminded me of the cover to *Haunt of Fear* #8, and then I knew I was at home. From the beginning of the New Trend EC's, Gaines tried to keep 12 copies of each. The 12 copies of each issue were wrapped in brown paper and placed in a box. He kept his entire EC file copies in six large boxes in the closet of his apartment. We wore white cotton film editor's gloves and opened each package one at a time. We discovered that there were between 6-12 copies of each and only one copy of *Vault of Horror* #12. Gaines wanted to

keep four of the sets for his family and sell the rest. On Friday, August 11, we processed *Vault*, [*Tales from the*] *Crypt*, *Haunt* [*of Fear*], *Crime* [*SuspenStories*] and *Shock* [*SuspenStories*]. On Saturday, August 12, we did *Weird Science*, [*Weird*] *Fantasy*, *Incredible Science Fiction*, *Weird Science Fantasy*, all the New Direction titles, *MAD* and *Panic*. On Sunday we were joined by Sylvia Cochran and Angie Mayer and did *Two-Fisted* [*Tales*], *Frontline* [*Combat*], 3-D's and all *Picture Stories*. The actual sets of books were put together Sunday afternoon which finished the project. I wound up this trip by taking Jerry Robinson out to dinner Monday night at the Gotham Bar & Grill to discuss him doing a Batman cover while Cochran and company went to a Broadway play.

When I worked at Gemstone in Timonium, MD from the mid 1990s to 2006, Steve Geppi would have many dinner meetings with other comic people and me. Steve had put together a poem based on "The Night Before Christmas" that he would recite to everyone from memory. Steve was always a talented entertainer and he would have a smug look on his face and a penetrating stare to everyone sitting at the table and in animated style blurt out, "It 'twas the night before Overstreet and all through the con, not a comic was sold from dusk until dawn!" and so on. Everyone always enjoyed his poem and I kept pushing Steve to write it down, so that I would have a copy. He finally emailed me with a copy in June, 2011. His poem only had a few verses and I was able to add more verses and put it in a finished form which we put our *Scoop* email newsletter at that time and shared with the comic book world.

A shorter version of this article appeared in Gemstone's Scoop email newsletter with the release of The Overstreet Comic Book Price Guide *#33. It was expanded, updated and revised by Overstreet and Vaughn in December 2016 for* Back Issue *magazine, and expanded again in October/ November 2019 for this publication.*

Overstreet's childhood friend Landon Chesney had a profound influence on the early editions of the *Guide*. Shown here are some of his thumbnail sketches for cover designs. Included is a Tarzan sketch for the 5th edition (although Joe Kubert did his own design). Chesney submitted an Invaders cover for the 30th edition, but Overstreet "settled" for Al Feldstein and Al Williamson instead.

This cover by the late Don Newton, originally commissioned but never used for the *Guide*, became a variant cover for the first printing of *The Overstreet Guide To Collecting Comics* (2012), giving Newton the first art cover edition on two different Overstreet books.

40

THE CLOAK

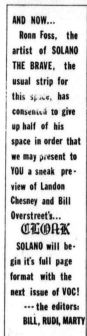

AND NOW...

Ronn Foss, the artist of SOLANO THE BRAVE, the usual strip for this space, has consented to give up half of his space in order that we may present to YOU a sneak preview of Landon Chesney and Bill Overstreet's...

CLOAK

SOLANO will begin it's full page format with the next issue of VOC!

--- the editors: BILL, RUDI, MARTY

Overstreet worked on the first installment of "The Cloak" with Landon Chesney. The strip ran in the early issues of *Voice of Comicdom*, fandom's first newspaper, which began publishing in the mid-1960s.

IN MEMORY OF JOHN VERZYL

The John Verzyl Overstreet Advisor Award is named in honor of our friend, comic book dealer, and longtime contributor John Verzyl, who passed away far too young. The award is presented annually to an Advisor or Advisors whose knowledge, contributions, ethics and reputation are held in the highest esteem by his or her peers. John's many insights and observations informed our work for many years and *The Overstreet Comic Book Price Guide* would not be all that it is without his tireless efforts. He is and always will be missed.

– RMO

THE PRICE-KEEPER

This homage to EC's Crypt-Keeper and Vault-Keeper host characters was illustrated by Bob Overstreet's lifelong friend, Landon Chesney, for *CBPG #6* in 1976.

"I wanted Chesney to do a new Price-Keeper strip every year,
but he only did this one," Overstreet said.
We expect The Price-Keeper to make a return some day.

OVERSTREET @ 50

by David T. Alexander

DTA Collectibles

50 YEARS WITH BOB

In late 1967 I found out about the *Rocket's Blast Comicollector* and organized comic book collecting. That was a revelation that altered the course of my life. Moving from North Georgia to California took most of my attention for the next few months. When I finally landed I took a subscription to *RBCC* and decided to sell some of my childhood collection. Dealers catalogs and *RBCC* ads helped me determine values. As you can imagine prices were all over the map. Quickly I realized that issues with origins, special artist or writer appearances were more popular and more valuable. Obtaining checklists and indexes from other collectors became very important to me. The more information you had increased your chances of success in the hobby. With the thousands of issues published to this point and the thousands of creators involved, it would be fantastic if someone compiled all the information in one place.

At the first San Diego Comic Con in 1970 I can recall conversations with collectors and dealers about the need for a centralized information source. Many of the early fanzines

were key sources for historic info about comics and their creators but they were published on a very random basis and lacked any type of quality control. Enthusiastic fans were generally behind these and they were often in the 12-19 age range. Some of these had character, artist or writer checklists but it was still difficult to amass info to direct your collecting efforts.

Bob Overstreet was a name I had never heard of until I saw his ad in a late 1970 edition of *RBCC* offering the first edition of *The Comic*

Rocket's Blast Comicollector #76 had an ad for the 1st Guide.

Book Price Guide for sale. His original ad looked more professional than most that appeared in *RBCC* and it conveyed that a lot of time and effort had been put into this publication. His original price was $5 and I could not get my dough in the mail fast enough. I was in contact with a number of local Los Angeles fans and there was an ongoing buzz about this new publication.

I do not recall if he had the book available when the ad appeared or if he was printing based on preorders but it really didn't take too long to arrive. The day the *Guide* hit my mail box was quite a thrill and for several days my time was absorbed devouring the information it provided. In retrospect I can say that if I had devoted myself to my college studies in the same way I was absorbed with Bob's first book I would not be writing this today but would have followed some other more scholarly endeavor. I will admit that comics have had some narcotic effect on me since that late summer day in 1948 when my father showed me Johnny Thunder and his horse in the water on the cover of *All-American Comics* #101 and the *Guide* just reinforced it.

One of the great things about the *Guide* is that it gave relevance to all eras of comic books. In the earliest days of comic fandom many long time collectors paid high esteem to the 1930s and early 1940s super hero and newspaper reprint comics but looked down on issues from the late 1940s and 1950s. Bob included everything. His early promotions highlighted the inclusion of "western, romance, funny animal, war, horror, science fiction, and crime comics", and "issues from the second heroic age of the 1960s". As history shows many of these books are quite valuable.

The first *Guide* was a robust effort at over 240 pages in a saddle stitched digest format that lost centerfold pages with repeated use. With a short print run of under two thousand copies the original edition was passed around from collector to collector at cons and comic shops and most remaining copies show repeated use. They have become quite valuable today.

Unfortunately for me I was not aware of the first *Guide* far enough in advance to put an ad in it. I did get an ad in the second edition and have had ads in every subsequent edition for my mail order operation or for my various comic book store chains. Almost every major dealer and many collectors have placed ads in the *Guide* during the last 50 years. Looking back at the ad pages for the last five decades is like seeing a "Who's Who" of comic book collecting. The ad sections alone tell us a lot about the history of collecting.

Pricing information has been the major thrust of the *Guide* from the beginning. An amazing asset is that the pricing info comes from long time dealers and collectors who contribute to each annual edition. Originally Bob developed the pricing scales from dealer's catalogs and first hand info he received from personal contacts. He always opened the door for knowledgeable hobbyists to submit pricing info for any area of the field in which they had first hand knowledge. Grading definitions and standards were important concepts in the early *Guide*s and have been refined over the years with the input of many collectors. During its existence the *Guide* has grown from 200 pages to over 1000 pages. That is a lot of information for Bob to process every year. Thousands of comic books have been created and added to the *Guide* in the last 50 years. The *Guide* has made the comic book market stronger and helped provide respect when compared to other popular collectibles such as stamps, coins, cards and related items. It has been a useful and recognized tool used in court proceedings, estate settlements, insurance settlements, etc.

In the mid 1970s there were some unstable years where dealers were not adding inventory and collections were not easy to buy. I

DAVID T. ALEXANDER........

                    P. O. BOX 2921.....

                         HOLLYWOOD, CALIF., 90028

    RARE COMIC BOOKS AND PULP MAGAZINES FOR SALE !!!!

****

                        NOW AVAILABLE:

GOLDEN AGE: SUPERMAN, BATMAN, CAPTAIN AMERICA, FLASH,
            SHADOW, CAPTAIN MARVEL, GREEN HORNET,
            DAREDEVIL, BLACK TERROR, CATMAN, ETC.

MARVEL COMICS: ALL ISSUES FROM 1960 TO DATE.

MONSTER MAGAZINES: FAMOUS MONSTERS, EERIE, CREEPY,
             SCREEN THRILLS, SPACEMEN, ETC.

E. C. COMICS: MAD, WEIRD SCIENCE, WEIRD FANTASY,
              TWO-FISTED TALES, AND ALL THE REST!!!!!!!!

PULP MAGAZINES:DOC SAVAGE, SPICY MYSTERY, KA-ZAR,
            DOCTOR DEATH, WINGS, ASTOUNDING STORIES,
            DANGER TRAIL, SKY FIGHTERS, SHADOW,
            JUNGLE STORIES, TERROR TALES, ETC.

******MORE*****MORE*****MORE*****MORE*****MORE*****MORE***

    SEND FIFTY CENTS(50¢) FOR LATEST PRICE LIST

SPECIAL***** FIFTY (50) OLD (50's & 60's) COVERLESS
            COMICS.......ONLY $3.29 ORDER NOW !!!!

SUPER SPECIAL***** 100 PROTECTIVE PLASTIC BAGS....
            GREAT FOR COMICS AND PULPS... $2.50 !!!!!!

  "I BUY COMICS AND PULPS. WRITE ME IF YOU WISH TO SELL"

The earliest David T. Alexander
price guide ad, in the 2nd edition.

46

believe that the *Guide* was a stabilizing influence in this era and added confidence to the market. As prices began to rise I think there were many dealers who could not have made progress without the help of the *Guide*.

Later editions of the *Guide* have featured charts and graphs to evaluate rising prices for the most valuable comics among different categories: Golden Age, Silver Age, Pre-Code Horror, Western, War, Romance, etc. Research such as this has helped comics to be viable investments. There have been many years where comics have performed much better than the Stock Markets.

Imagine that a comic book considered as a child's plaything in the past can now command a King's Ransom. How does this happen? Does the buyer think he might ever re-sell it? Does the seller know how to price it? Will it ever happen again? Do similar items exist? *The Comic Book Price Guide* has helped answer these questions.

Comics have provided a massive amount of pleasure for me and I have been selling them full time for over 50 years. I have very few regrets but one of them is that in the late 1960s during my final three years in college in North Georgia I lived about 75 miles from Bob but had no idea what he was working on and no way to contact him. Fortunately things have changed.

We have to say thanks to Bob Overstreet for his dedication, perseverance, study, research and determination that led to the creation of *The Comic Book Price Guide*. Bob has tried to capture all the data about comics and determine current values. Providing pricing and grading updates annually for 50 years is a monumental effort. In addition to that, cataloging beginning and ending dates for titles and publishers, artist and writer appearances, origins, first appearances and key issue information is a tremendous service to fans and collectors. Great job Bob, keep it going for another 50 years.

OVERSTREET @ 50

by Joe Jusko
Cover Artist

I could not have considered it a greater honor...

From the Savage Sword of Conan *to* Vampirella *and from* Heavy Metal *to the 1992 Marvel Masterpieces trading cards, Joe Jusko has painted most of the great comic characters and plenty of the newer or lesser-known ones, too. The lighting, tone, character physiques and dynamic action of his paintings has earned him a distinct reputation, one that we were eager to employ on the cover of* The Overstreet Comic Book Price Guide.

Once we knew he was interested in doing a Guide *cover, we just had to find the right subject. For CBPG #42, we narrowed it down to John Buscema's awesome cover for* The Avengers #58, *and the result was magic. Jusko not only captured the real feeling of the original, he added more power to it.*

Jusko returned for a second Overstreet cover, this one his powerful depiction of

Thanos for the Hero Initiative exclusive edition of The Overstreet Comic Book Price Guide #48. *Presently working on the creation of new covers for all of Edgar Rice Burroughs classic novels, we asked him to talk about the* Guide *and specifically his cover for #42.*

Ever since I was a kid working in a New York City comic shop, I've known that you had to be seen as one of the most respected artists in the industry to make the cover of *The Overstreet Comic Book Price Guide*. Each new edition proved it: Kubert, Eisner, Barks, Wood, etc., all the way through to the greats of today.

When I was chosen for a cover a few years back, I could not have considered it a greater honor to join the pantheon of supreme talent that came before me. The *Guide* cover has always seemed like a reward more than just another job, sort of an acknowledgment that you've hit a certain level of respect in the industry. I am so totally flattered to have been asked, and to be asked a second time is truly humbling.

INSIDE THE COVER

A lot of things contribute to *Avengers* #58's "classic" status. Aside from the incredible composition, it's from the year of Marvel's big expansion, 1968, when they truly became the industry powerhouse. It's drawn by one of comics' greatest artists, "Big" John Buscema, whose art became the "house style" at Marvel for a generation and, most importantly, it's the climactic issue to a story arc revealing the origin of one of Marvel's most popular characters, The Vision.

While many artists diverge to a great extent from the source material when doing an homage, I like to keep as much of the original cover's identity as possible. I think keeping the proportions, composition and especially the color true to the original helps evoke a sense of nostalgia in the minds of the fans. It's easier with artists whose work is realistically rendered, like Buscema or John Romita Sr., than it is with Jack Kirby, whose anatomy was very stylized and requires a lot more thought when translating his drawing to a more realistic interpretation.

Buscema was the artist who most influenced my career path and from whose work I learned to draw as a kid. Since I was so familiar with his work I was always the "go to" guy at Marvel when it came to painting over him. Always an honor but always an intimidating assignment, as well. John's figure work was beyond reproach. He was able to convey mass, weight and movement in a way that made the most fantastical characters seem real. With a subtle (but not simple to draw) twist of a hip or turn of a head he could project such natural mood and attitude. His figures didn't sit on a chair, they sat in a chair. While he was a true fan favorite during Marvel's Silver Age, and certainly fondly remembered by fans from that era, I think he has become more of an artist's artist in recent years, held up on a pedestal for his pure draftsmanship.

For *The Avengers* issues from that era, everything was still pretty new, Marvel Comics as we know it only being six to seven years old. Some of the most popular characters today were being introduced on an almost monthly basis, and the art

Steve Geppi with Joe Jusko and his Tarzan painting at the 2012 San Diego Comic-Con.

and stories were a revelation from everything else done before or even at that time from other companies. On *The Avengers*, Roy Thomas and John Buscema were as perfect a writer/artist team as there will ever be and seemed to feed off each other to create really exciting, memorable comics. John's interpretations of Roy's plots and Roy's dialogue, obviously written expressly to the postures and attitudes of John's figures jelled into perfect storytelling.

Different sensibilities certainly come into play when doing recreations and reinterpretations. The spontaneity of creating my own work is replaced with a more technical approach because I now have to determine the best way to interpret someone else's work in a totally different medium. Many times, the compositions are not something I would have chosen for a painting or the anatomy needs to be tweaked to make the painted figure work, while keeping the original artist's spirit intact. I did a recreation of *Avengers* #4 by Jack Kirby several years ago and enjoyed the challenge of translating the King's unique figure work to a more realistic vision, while still keeping the quirkiness of his poses evident.

I think simply rendering the line drawings into a painted medium brings a lot of my stylistic identity to the finished product. Hard for it not to, even though my main objective is to retain as much of the original artist's soul as I can.

In September 2018, Joe Jusko began creating new cover art and frontispieces for all 80 of Edgar Rice Burroughs' novels, kicking off the first unified Burroughs library by one artist.

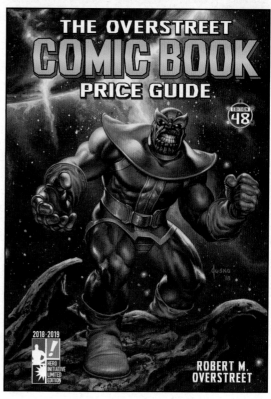

GUIDE COLLECTING:
Important Details
& Variations
by David Stone

Like the comic books captured in its pages, The Overstreet Comic Book Price Guide *has itself become a collectible. Throughout its run, the* Guide *has experienced different cover formats, multiple printings, cover art and design variations, and specialty editions.*

In a series of articles originally published in Heritage Auctions' Comic & Animation News, collector David Stone offered a deep, highly detailed, authoritative exploration of the history of the Guide. His work, which we have excerpted here, provides context on these printing factors and availability in the collecting market.

Our thanks to Stone and Heritage Auctions for this look at the Guide's *first edition and noteworthy variations in the soft cover and hardcover formats.*

The Overstreet Comic Book Price Guide #1

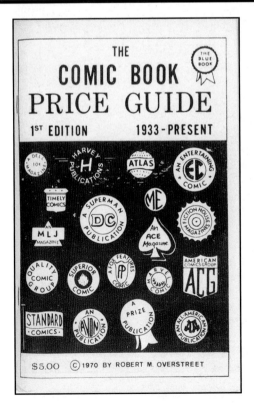

Bob Overstreet published the first edition of *The Overstreet Comic Book Price Guide* in November 1970. Overstreet reports that he believed the *Guide* would be a one-shot deal and did not anticipate turning out yearly updated editions until later. Curiously, however, the first edition was numbered, so the possibility of future editions must have been in the back of his mind, at least on a subliminal level. Sales were brisk, so a second printing, with a few corrections and a blue cover, was accomplished in 1971.

In his introduction to *The Overstreet Comic Book Price Guide* #1, Bob Overstreet notes it would have been impractical to produce a price guide for comic books at an earlier time, as the market in the 1960s was very volatile, with constantly changing prices and only a rudimentary grading system. While comic book fandom largely grew out of the long-established science fiction fandom, the grading system was largely borrowed from coin collecting. The grade Very Fine was not listed in *The Overstreet Comic Book Price Guide* #1 (it was added in 1977), and prices were given for copies in Good, Fine, and Mint condition. The most expensive comic book listed in *The Overstreet Comic Book Price Guide* #1 was *Action Comics* #1 at $300 in Mint, closely followed by *Detective Comics* #27 at $275.

The content of the two printings was very similar, but some minor corrections were made, and the placement of some advertisements was altered. An errata slip was issued for the first printing and found tipped in some copies.

```
     *    NOTICE OF CORRECTION    *

Insert following name and address for the "Auction
Block" ad on page 230: Thomas Altshuler, 14501
LaBelle, Oak Park, Mich. 48237
```

The ad for the *Auction Block* was omitted in the blue cover second printing and Jerry Bails' ad for the *Collector's Guide: The First Heroic Age* was printed in its place (Bails' ad appeared on the final page of the first printing). Canadian dealer Ken Mitchell's

ad was also moved from the final page of the first printing to the top of page 240 in the second printing, to replace the ad for the Able-Man Book Shop, leaving the final page of the second printing blank. Apparently, Thomas Altshuler cancelled his advertising in the second printing, as he was a principal of both the *Auction Block* and the Able-Man Book Shop in Hamtramck, Michigan. The *Auction Block* was a fanzine that ran for four issues in 1970. It had ceased publication by the time the second printing of *The Overstreet Comic Book Price Guide* #1 was published, so no advertising was needed. Advertising for the Able-Man Book Shop was resumed in *The Overstreet Comic Book Price Guide* #2.

Bob Overstreet advertised in most of the popular fan publications of the time, including the ad for the white cover first printing in the *Rocket's Blast and Comicollector* #76, the ad for the blue cover second printing in the October-November 1971 edition of *Comic Zine*, and the ad for the second printing, with a plug for the upcoming second edition, in the *Rocket's Blast and Comicollector* #85.

Bob's ad in *Rocket's Blast Comicollector* #72 for the first printing and his ad for the blue cover second printing in *Comic Zine*'s October-November 1971 edition.

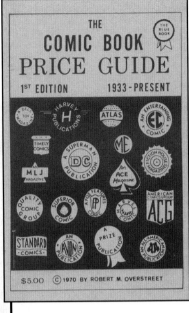

Bob's ad in *Rocket's Blast Comicollector* #85 for the blue-covered second printing.

The first printing (white cover, November 1970) had a print run of 1,000 copies, while the second printing (blue cover) had a print run of 800 copies. More copies of the blue cover edition are seen today, perhaps because the white cover first printing was more heavily used by dealers and collectors at the time of issue, while the blue cover second printing was more likely to be preserved by collectors. Alternatively, some sources indicate the second printing had a higher than reported print run, perhaps as high as 1,200 examples, but that figure is undocumented. Both editions were easily disbound, as the 242-page book was just stapled to-gether in a saddle-stitched fashion (Bob Overstreet and his family collated the books and stapled them together themselves). Exactly how many copies of each printing have survived is unknown. Since CGC only recently began to certify *The Overstreet Comic Book Price Guide* #1, no meaningful Census data is available. Old time collectors believe as many as 200 copies of the white cover first printing may be extant in collectible condition, but NM copies are very rare. Certainly many copies have changed hands over the years in both public and private transactions, but records of these sales are seldom available.

Editor's Note: Through his research, Stone found 47 known copies of *The Overstreet Comic Book Price Guide* #1 (white cover). Most of those copies were noted during their sales and additionally, a number of known copies have been noted as extant without actual sales data. While Stone's complete list was reported in Heritage's Comic & Animation News, here is a sample of those copies:

NM. One of Bob Overstreet's personal signed copies was offered in ComicConnect's June 9, 2016 auction and realized $1,300.

NM CGC 9.2. A copy offered on eBay on September 2, 2018, for a reserve of $1,500, was later sold by Heritage in November 2018 for $9,000. A number of tiny white specks appear in the black box with comic icons on the front cover.

VF/NM. One of Bob Overstreet's signed copies sold by Hake's Auctions in July 2013 for $2,277. It has light age toning on the covers and the top of outside pages.

VF+. A copy sold by Heritage in December 2002 realized $529. It has a few black ink marks above the "C" in "Comic" on the front cover.

VF+. ComicConnect sold a copy on December 8, 2017 for $2,655. It has some browning on the covers and a diagonal ink mark near the top of the front cover.

VF CGC 8.0. A copy offered on eBay by Sparkle City Comics sold for $2,575 on January 7, 2018.

VF. A copy originally purchased from a comic shop was sold on eBay in May 2018 for $1,495. The tip of the top left corner of the rear cover is torn.

VF. Heritage sold a copy in May 2009 for $657.25. It has a faint crease on the lower right front cover and discoloration along edges.

VF CGC Restored 8.0. A copy that was offered on eBay circa August 2016 was later graded CGC Restored 8.0 with a small amount of color touch and glue on the cover. It was then offered on eBay by My Comic Shop for $1,270 and was sold on January 7, 2018. It has a stamp of Richard Hamlin Mosso/Commercial Artist/17 Summer Street/Auburn Mass. 01501 on the title page.

FN/VF. Heritage sold a copy in May 2016 for $1,553.50. It has a light mark near "Over" on the back cover.

FN+. A copy from the Phillip M. Levine Collection was sold by Heritage in February 2016 for $597.50. It has ink initials low on the front cover.

Fine. Hake's sold a copy in January 2007 for $632.50. It has light handling wear and dust soiling on the covers and slight pulling at the staples.

VG/FN. Heritage offered a copy along with one of the blue cover second printings in August 2014, which realized $1,075.50. The spine is frayed at staples and there's discoloration at the "st" in 1st.

GD. A copy with several cover creases, tape on staples, and two detached center folios sold with a copy of *The Argosy Comic Book Price Guide* on the CGC Forum in April 2010. *Argosy* brought $500 and the *Guide* brought $375.

GD. A first and second edition were sold by Hake's in June 2006 for $443.52. There is tape at top and bottom of the spine and along the entire bottom of the front cover.

Bob Overstreet began publishing regular issue hardbound volumes with his second edition in 1972. The hardbound editions have always been much scarcer and more valuable than their softbound counterparts, especially the early issues. Collector demand for the hardbound volumes was hard to judge in the early years, resulting in a recurring cycle of over and under ordering on the print runs throughout the first decade. Number 3 had a small print run of 75 copies, and it was difficult to fill all the orders, so Overstreet increased the print run dramatically to 1,000 copies for hardbound #4. This proved too optimistic, and many copies went unsold, so he cut back on the print run for #5. The print runs continued to oscillate through the first 10 volumes, as Overstreet finetuned his operation to calculate the optimum number of copies to produce. Accordingly, #3 and #5 are rare, while #4 and #6 are relatively common in today's market. The same holds true, to a lesser extent, for #7 and #9 (scarce) and #8 and #10 (common), but the advent of eBay and Amazon have made all these books more available in recent years.

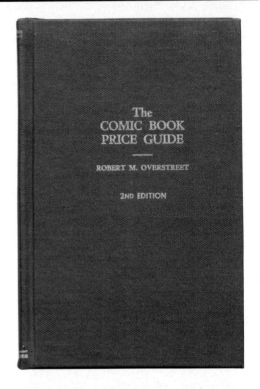

At first hardcover #2 and #3 had simple blue cloth covers with gilt lettering on the front and spine. The hardbound *Overstreet Comic Book Price Guide* #2 had two print runs that featured slightly different cover designs, with varied arrangements of the gilt text.

Pictorial front covers began with *The Overstreet Comic Book Price Guide* #4 and the books usually featured paid advertising on the back cover (for some reason, the back cover of hardbound #5 was blank). The rapid success of the *Guide* soon made it possible to commission some of the foremost artists in the comic book field to produce the art for the covers, like Carl Barks for *The Overstreet Comic Book Price Guide* #7.

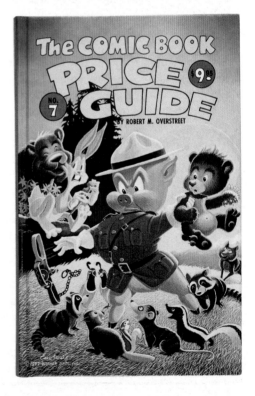

Alex Schomburg's original artwork for
the cover of the 10th edition. It sold for
$38,837.50 in a Heritage auction in 2007.

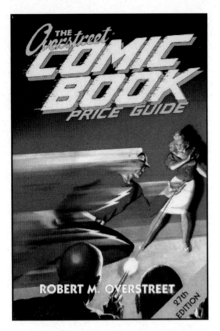

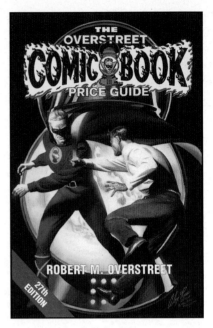

Regular editions featured only one cover design for both hard and softcover for #2-26. Beginning with #27, two cover variants were produced each year, both available in hard or softcover format.

This practice continued up to #44, but #45 offered four cover variants featuring Captain America, Superman, Captain Action, and X-O Manowar, all available in both formats. This was done to celebrate the 45th edition of *The Overstreet Comic Book Price Guide* and made possible by the cooperation of four different comic book publishers. For some reason, the Captain Action and X-O Manowar cover versions are seen with less frequency in public offerings.

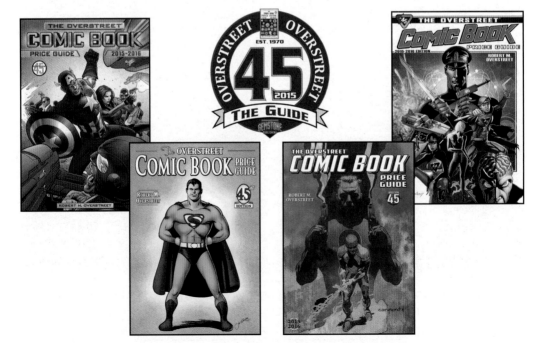

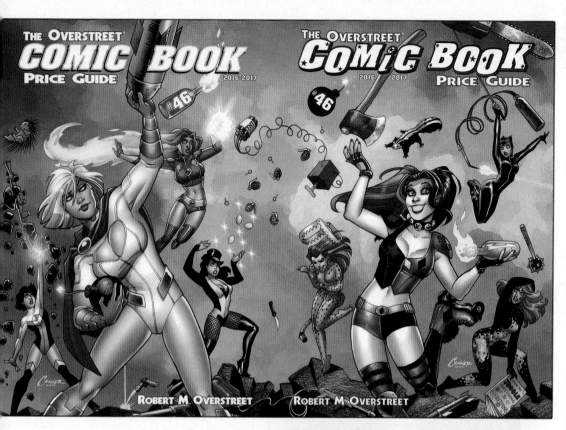

With #46, Overstreet produced a joint cover concept for its regular issue *Guides*, where the two independent cover designs, both produced by artist Amanda Conner, could be combined side-to-side to produce a larger picture. Also with #46, a third cover option was started, sometimes referred to as the "Hall of Fame" edition. The first of those was a Silver Age Sgt. Rock tribute by Russ Heath, folowed by Walt Simonson and Michael Kaluta.

There have been a few extra giveaway gimmicks included with the *Guide* over the years. For instance, the two-sided ONE/OWL grading card was issued with #22 (both hard and softcover), but the cards were easily lost and few copies on the secondary market include one today.

Quality control has always been pretty good for the hardbound editions, but a few errors have slipped by over the years. At least one copy of hardbound #16 is known with the contents bound in upside down with respect to the covers. As of 2020, including the first and second printing versions of hardbound *Overstreet Comic Book Price Guide* #2, there are 78 different cover variants in the regular issue hardbound series.

The *Overstreet Comic Book Price Guide* has been issued in many formats over the years, but the direct market softcover editions are the version most collectors are familiar with. The history of the softcover editions follows the same course as the hardbound editions in most respects, but there are a few exceptions. Unlike the hardbound version, the softcovers have been issued with square-bound pictorial covers since the second edition, in 1972 (pictorial covers started with #4 on the hardbound editions). For #2-26, a single cover design was offered every year. The cover design for the direct market softcover editions usually followed that of the hardbound version, but on #18 the softcover has a black background and the hardbound has a white background.

For #27 through the present, two cover designs were offered every year except for #45, which had four cover variants, featuring Golden Age Superman, Captain America, Captain Action, and X-O Manowar. The Captain Action and X-O Manowar versions are more difficult to locate than the other two cover designs. For #46 through #49, there has been a third regular cover, sometimes referred to as the Overstreet "Hall of Fame" cover. It started with Russ Heath's Sgt Rock and continued with offerings from Walt Simonson, Howard Chaykin and Michael Kaluta. The 50th edition had 3 regular covers, but with Overstreet Hall of Famer Todd McFarlane supplying the Spawn/Spider-Man main cover, the HOF designation wasn't used.

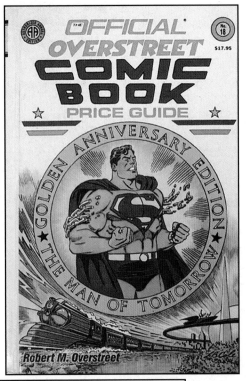

L.B. Cole's B&W artwork was photocopied then hand colored to create these two versions: the softcover with the black background and the hardcover with the white background.

Like its hardbound counterpart, softcover *The Overstreet Comic Book Price Guide #22* was issued with the combination OWL/ONE grading card, but the cards were easily lost, and they are seldom included with the books in public offerings today. Fortunately, the cards were also issued in foil packets with the 1992 *Overstreet Comic Book Grading Guide* and can still be purchased individually on the Gemstone website.

Also like the hardbound volumes, #46 featured a dual cover by artist Amanda Conner. The two cover variants produce a larger single picture when placed side-to-side.

None of the regular issue softcover editions are really rare in the absolute sense, but some of the early issues are condition rarities in high grade. Of particular note are the early printings of the softcover The *Overstreet Comic Book Price Guide* #2. Bob Overstreet printed a total of 3,800 copies of his softcover *The Overstreet Comic Book Price Guide* #2, more than twice the print run of the first edition. According to his advertisement in the *Rocket's Blast and Comicollector* #95 (see image to right) it required three different print runs to satisfy collector demand for the issue.

In his article "A Price Guide for Price Guides, 1992" which

appeared in *Comic Book Marketplace* #16, Gary Carter noted there were two cover variants for the issue, although the basic design was exactly the same. The second edition was a tremendous success with collectors and the books were heavily used, with most examples suffering wear and attrition along the way. Back issue demand for #2 developed at an early date. Fortunately, Overstreet had some unused interiors leftover from the early print runs (he and his family glued the covers on the softcover #2 volumes themselves). He simply ordered more covers for those interiors and issued the new copies. For some reason, possibly related to the paper stock the printer had on hand, the covers for the

later printing did not quite match the color of the earlier printings. The first printings had a dark magenta-red color, while the later issue had a lighter orange-red color. The dark colored issues were used for the interior softcovers on the hardbound *Overstreet Comic Book Price Guide* #2, so we know they were produced first. They can be found in public offerings with a little patience today, but they are almost never seen in better than Very Good condition. The lighter colored covers are seen with equal frequency, and they can sometimes be found in high grade.

Quality control was usually good for the softcovers, but some #2s have slightly wrinkled covers, possibly due to the amateur binding efforts of Bob Overstreet and his family. At least one copy of softcover *Overstreet Comic Book Price Guide* #3 is known with the final page out of order. One copy of the softcover *Overstreet Comic Book Price Guide* #3 has the interior of the Canadian #3 edition, with no ad copy, bound in the regular softcover with the contents upside down.

Many back issues, including a few single digit issue numbers, are still available in Mint condition on the Gemstone Publishing website.

SOURCES

The Overstreet Comic Book Price Guide #1

1. Andresen, Eric, "Looking Back 22 Years to Price Guide #1," *Comic Book Marketplace* Vol. 1 #16 (1992), pp. 46-50.

2. CGC Message Boards thread on hardcover *Overstreet Comic Book Price Guide* #2 https://www.cgccomics.com/boards/topic/437370-2nd-edition-overstreet-price-guide-hardcover/?tab=comments#comment-10324157.

3. Carter, Gary, "A Price Guide for Price Guides," *Comic Book Marketplace* Vol. 1 #2 (1991), pp. 65-67.

4. Carter, Gary, "A Price Guide for Price Guides 1992," *Comic Book Marketplace* Vol. 1 #16 (August 1992), pp. 53-55.

5. Carter, Gary and Mallette, Jack, "A Price Guide for Price Guides 1995," *Comic Book Marketplace* Vol. 2 #25 (July 1995), pp. 64-67.

6. Heritage Auctions online archives.

7. Mallette, Jack, conversations in July 2017.

Regular Issue Hardbound Volumes

1. Carter, Gary, "A Price Guide for Price Guides 1992," *Comic Book Marketplace* Vol. 1 #16 (August 1992), pp. 53-55.

2. Carter, Gary and Mallette, Jack, "A Price Guide for Price Guides 1995," *Comic Book Marketplace* Vol. 2 #25 (July 1995), pp. 64-67.

3. Wilbur, Mike, Director of Operations at Gemstone Publishing, emails on various topics.

Direct Market Softcover Editions

1. Carter, Gary, "A Price Guide for Price Guides 1992," *Comic Book Marketplace* Vol. 1 #16 (August 1992), pp. 53-55.

2. Mallette, Jack, conversations in July 2017 and November 2018.

3. Olshevsky, George, "Conversation with Bob Overstreet," *The Collector's Dream* Vol. 1 #4 (1978), pp 12-22, 26.

4. Overstreet, Robert, advertisement in the *Rocket's Blast and Comicollector* #95.

5. Wilbur, Mike, Director of Operations at Gemstone Publishing, emails on various topic.

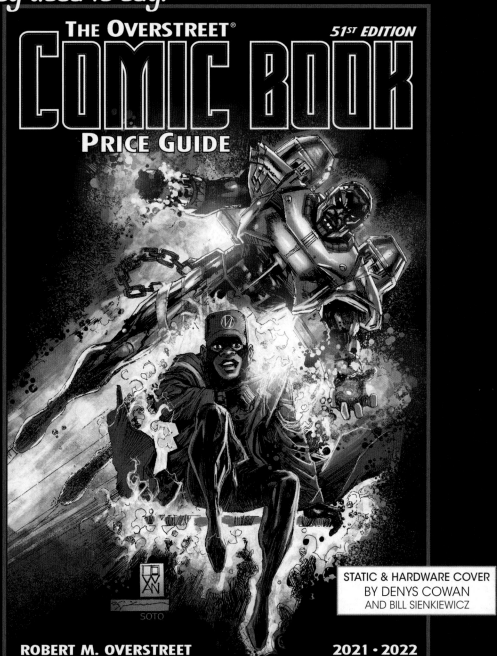

OVERSTREET @ 50

by Steve Geppi

President & CEO,
Gemstone Publishing

*Its existence confirmed
what I had suspected ...*

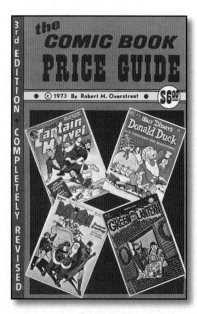

Stephen A. Geppi, Sr., the Chairman and CEO of Geppi Family Enterprises, purchased The Overstreet Comic Book Price Guide *from Bob Overstreet's Overstreet Publications in 1994, but that was hardly his first experience with comics. At the age of nine, his first job was bundling comics and magazines for a local used magazine dealer and he opted to receive part of his compensation in comics. After starting a family and working as a postal carrier, he rediscovered comics as a young adult. By 1974, he opened his first Geppi's Comics World store. In 1982, he started Diamond Comic Distributors.*

In 1973, when I was still a mailman, walking my route and asking people along the way if they had comics, before I ever opened my first Geppi's Comic World store, I discovered an ad for *The Overstreet Comic Book Price Guide*, which was then its third edition. Its existence confirmed

what I had suspected: that comics had real value beyond cover price and in addition to sentiment.

It might have been in a fanzine or *The Buyer's Guide To Comic Fandom* (*TBG*, later *CBG*), I'm not sure, and in truth the location of that doesn't matter. But its content mattered a lot.

Before Overstreet, everyone in the hobby would hear about *Superman* #1 selling for $100 or a handful of other comics selling for what seemed like incredible prices, but when I got the *Guide* is was like a revelation. There I was, sitting with this book, taking it in, surrounded by comics, some of which I already had duplicates of...

I was now armed and ready to go sell comics!

Fairly early on, I made contact with Bob Overstreet and began to be listed as an advisor in *CBPG* #6, the one with the Spirit cover by Will Eisner. I can't even tell you what an honor I thought it was just to talk to Bob Overstreet. He was like the king, and still is in my book.

He was so kind to me, so encouraging, and he embraced my input. He felt that I had a good perspective. I believe that he thought I was honest (just as we all have seen about him through all these years), and that was a big factor for him. Although he had only been producing the *Guide* a few years at that point, he had already sensed that a lot people would try to inflate prices.

At that time Bob also became a great customer. Over the years I sold him many wonderful comics (when I bought the *Guide*, I also purchased his collection, so I got many of those comics back), so our relationship developed further.

Eventually he started holding Overstreet Advisor meetings in Gatlinburg, Tennessee. Bob would rent a huge chalet that had 11 bedrooms or some such craziness, and everyone in attendance would spend the whole weekend talking comics. The only time we left was one night we would go out to dinner at a restaurant called The Burning Bush. The rest of the time, it was all comics.

I've been asked a few times over the years when I first thought "Wouldn't it be neat to own the *Guide*?" It was definitely early on, but in truth I think I was plotting to buy his collection before I was actually thinking about buying the *Guide*. Somewhere along the line, though, I made the assumption that they were a package deal; I thought there was no way that Bob was going to sell his collection and keep the *Guide*.

Bob Overstreet and Steve Geppi at 2015's San Diego Comic-Con.

It was early on. I just remember that every time I talked to Bob, I felt like I was talking to the number one guy in comics. I think a very good argument can be made that *The Overstreet Comic Book Price Guide* is the most significant publication ever produced for the comic book industry.

When I purchased the *Guide* in 1994 and Bob came to work for me at Gemstone Publishing, I knew that there would be people – even some good friends and longtime customers of mine – who thought I was going to be setting the prices. That was never going to be the case, but I understood that it would take time to prove that to some.

And I believe that time has done just that. My deal with Bob was based on honor. I knew that he took his responsibilities as a sacred trust. He was the guy who was rightly considered the authority on pricing. It just wouldn't make any sense for

The 25th edition, the first produced by Steve Geppi's Gemstone Publishing.

me to ever put him in a position where I would call him up and suggest what a price should be.

Steve Geppi and John Verzyl celebrate at the opening for Geppi's Entertainment Museum.

The growth and stature of *The Overstreet Comic Book Price Guide* has in its foundation Bob Overstreet's credibility. He secured his status by making every Advisor feel the way I did: information and opinions are always welcome, the contributor's ideas are always heard and considered, and that in the end Bob will go with the evidence at hand in the most judicious way possible.

The best part about this is that it's not an act. This is who Bob Overstreet has been and who he is. In fact, he has played it so straight, that he never even let a comic book convention pay his way until the

Batman legend Jerry Robinson with John Snyder and Steve Geppi.

San Diego Comic-Con brought him as a special guest to honor him for the *Guide's* 40th anniversary in 2010.

He inspires that in the people around him as well. Owning *The Overstreet Comic Book Price Guide* is a sacred trust. In at least some sense, it belongs to the whole industry, and I'm just happy to be its custodian.

Steve Geppi is the Chairman of Geppi Family Enterprises, which in addition to Gemstone Publishing includes Diamond Comic Distributors, Alliance Game Distributors, Diamond International Galleries, Hake's Auctions, and Baltimore Magazine, among other companies.

Paul Levitz, J.C. Vaughn, Steve Geppi, and Jim Shooter at Steve's 70th birthday party.

OVERSTREET @ 50

by John K. Snyder, Jr.

Former President,
Diamond International Galleries

He was the right person with the right idea at the right time...

I met Bob Overstreet for the first time not long after *The Overstreet Comic Book Price Guide* #4 was released in 1974 (I had seen #3, but #4 was the first one I purchased). It was the first edition to feature original cover art (Don Newton illustrated the Justice Society of America), kicking off another facet of what made the *Guide* an annual tradition.

As I began to devour the information contained in that edition, it was immediately apparent that an incredible amount of thought, organization, and preparation had gone into it. I didn't know then – but I would soon learn – that this methodical approach very accurately reflected the man who put it all together.

When I met Bob, we really hit it off. Not only was he immensely likeable, but he clearly was the mind behind this incredible blessing to our hobby. He was the right person with the right idea at the right time, and I don't think that's a mistake. He had all the right attributes.

He was very astute, well educated, and research-oriented, and he really enjoyed investigating the history of the comics. He had a tremendous memory and just the right disposition.

By the time the *Guide* launched in 1970, Bob was a highly experienced coin collector. From the way coin collectors were organized, the ideas of a price guide, grades, and various editions was already in place. He understood that it wasn't much of a leap to apply similar logic to comic book collecting. If anything, comic books had a built-in advantage because they were sequentially numbered.

Bob took his skills, his knowledge of comics, and his understanding of collecting and combined them with another attribute, probably the single biggest thing that made him the man for the job: He was an incredible listener.

Our field isn't that different from others because it has many different voices with an equal number of conflicting opinions. What makes it different is that Bob Overstreet had and has maintained an

John Snyder with Martin Luther King III at the opening of Geppi's Entertainment Museum in 2006.

true for the development of the grading standards. Bob had many opinions, but he was dedicated to finding a consensus among dealers and collectors about how to honestly and succinctly describe the condition of the comics. Without the steps he took in *The Overstreet Comic Book Price Guide*, the first edition of *The Overstreet Comic Book Grading Guide* in 1992, the grading system that eventually followed and the present level of liquidity in the market would not have come to pass.

unwavering tendency to be open-minded. His only dogmatic leaning is toward doing the best job possible to get things right. While in the end he might not side with one view or the other, he will always give the views due consideration and will likewise reevaluate his decisions in the light of new information.

This has been true through the collection of data for the listings, and it has also been

Everyone who collects comics seriously owes a major "Thank-you!" to Bob for his dedication, insight, and integrity.

John K. Snyder, Jr. was the President of Diamond International Galleries and Geppi's Entertainment Museum, and a longtime Overstreet Advisor. A former Acting Under Secretary of Commerce, he resides in his native Indiana.

Disney comic creator Don Rosa and John Snyder proudly displaying the first Gemstone-published issue of *Uncle Scrooge* (#319) in 2003.

MILLION DOLLAR COMICS

It seems incredible that a 10¢ or 12¢ investment could turn into a million dollar payday. Such is the magic of comics...

Action Comics #1 CGC 9.0
$3,207,852
by Darren Adams on eBay
on August 24, 2014

Action Comics #1 CGC 9.0
$2,161,000
by ComicConnect
in December 2011

Action Comics #1 CGC 8.5

$2,052,000

by ComicConnect in June 2018

This copy previously sold for

$1,500,000

by ComicConnect in 2010

Marvel Comics #1 CGC 9.4
Windy City Pedigree

$1,260,000

by Heritage Auctions
on November 24, 2019

Amazing Fantasy #15
CGC 9.6
$1,100,000
by ComicConnect in 2011

Detective Comics #27
CGC 8.0
$1,075,500
by Heritage on February 25, 2010

Action Comics #1
CGC 8.0
$1,000,000
by ComicConnect in 2010

THE TOP 10 FROM OVERSTREET #50

As we celebrate our first five decades, these 10 comics sit atop the rankings in *The Overstreet Comic Book Price Guide #50*. Many of them are perennial powerhouses; all of them are highly collectible. All prices are for NM- (9.2) condition.

1970 PRICE
$300

Action Comics #1
First appearance of Superman
$4,600,000

1970 PRICE
$275

Detective Comics #27
First appearance of Batman
$3,000,000

1970 PRICE
$250

Superman #1
Superman's origin
$1,700,000

1970 PRICE
$50

All-American Comics #16
First appearance of Green Lantern
$880,000

Batman #1

Debut of the Joker and Catwoman

$860,000

Marvel Comics #1

First Sub-Mariner and Human Torch

$750,000

Action Comics #7

Second Superman cover

$550,000

Captain America Comics #1

First appearance of Captain America

$550,000

Amazing Fantasy #15

First appearance of Spider-Man

$425,000

Pep Comics #22

First appearance of Archie

$385,000

THE TOP 10
SINCE 1970

Many new comics have been published since the *Guide* debuted, and likewise many of them have connected with collectors. Here are the Top 10 Comics published since 1970 as ranked in *The Overstreet Comic Book Price Guide #50*. All prices are for NM- (9.2) condition.

Star Wars #1 (35¢-c)
Starts adaptation of first movie

$12,000

Teenage Mutant Ninja Turtles #1
1st app. & origin of the Turtles

$8,000

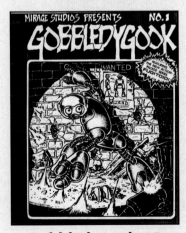

Gobbledygook #1
T.M.N. Turtles appear on back-c ad

$6,600

Incredible Hulk #181
First full Wolverine story

$5,500

Iron Fist #14 (35¢-c)
First appearance of Sabretooth
$4,400

House of Secrets #92
First appearance of Swamp Thing
$3,350

Cerebus the Aardvark #1
Debut of Cerebus
$3,200

Albedo #2
First appearance of Usagi Yojimbo
$3,200

Scooby Doo #1
First comic book appearance
$3,000

Marvel Spotlight #5
First appearance of Ghost Rider
$2,800

OVERSTREET @ 50

by Beau Smith   Comic Book Writer

ONCE UPON A TIME IN COMIC BOOKS

WE ALL HAVE GUIDEPOSTS IN OUR LIVES. THEY ARE THERE FOR DIFFERENT
REASONS, SOME OF THE HEART, SOME OF THE MIND, AND OTHERS,
WELL – IN MY CASE – TO GET ME BACK INTO COMIC BOOKS.

As far back as four years old, I can remember being drawn to comic books, nowadays I'm drawn into them – literally – by artists. Yes, I put myself into comic books that I write, not so much from ego, but because I love the medium of comic books so much, I want to not just be in them, I want to be them.

There's something about words and pictures that makes so much sense to me and has for a lifetime. Some people see life as a film in their head, I've always seen it in the form of a comic book, pages, panels, and word balloons. I wasn't just a comic book reader, I was a comic book collector as well. When I was younger, comic books were much less expensive than they are today, they were also harder to find. There were no comic book stores, no internet, and the only way you could find back issues was to trade comics with your buddies on the porch in what always seemed to be summertime. You could also buy back issues from Howard Rogofsky and Robert Bell, two gentlemen that placed ads in the pages of Marvel Comics in the 1960s. I remember wanting to complete (at the time) my *Daredevil* collection, and the only way that I was going to do that was by buying #7, #8 and #10 from one of these gentlemen via the mail. I remember saving up my money and finally coming up with $9 to buy these three issues. (Howard Rogofsky was selling them for $3 each.) That was a lot of money for me in the '60s, but I had to have those treasured issues. I sent the cash in the mail and in a short couple of weeks, I had my issues. They were actually in better shape than the comic books that I bought new off the rack. One of the best purchases I ever made.

Every year my family went to Wrightsville Beach in North Carolina for summer vacation. I loved those trips, the surf, the sand, and scouting out the local grocery stores, news-stands, and drug stores for new comic books somewhere other than my own hometown. I loved reading my comic books under the raised porch of our beach house. It was there one summer (1972-1973) that I met a kid staying in the place next to us. He saw me reading my comics and he confessed to being a comic book reader as well. He ran back to his place, grabbed the comic books he had brought, and we looked over each other's traveling collections. We decided to trade a few, and it was then that I discovered *The Overstreet Comic Book Price Guide.*

Robert Bell not only placed ads in Marvel comics, he also had the back cover ad on the first edition of the *Guide.*

79

He not only had some comics to trade, but he suggested we trade by value. He had this wonderful book called *The Overstreet Comic Book Price Guide*. I had never seen or heard of it before. He was nice enough to give me some background on it. He was from a much bigger city than I was, so he had access to stuff like this in bookstores. I was mesmerized by this book. It had values of almost every comic book I had or had heard of, and many that I never heard of. I truly felt this was the holy grail of comic books. For the rest of the week he was kind enough to let me write down the prices of comic books I knew I had at home. I never worked that hard in school. I left at the end of the week with a notebook filled with information and prices. That truly was a week at the beach I will never forget.

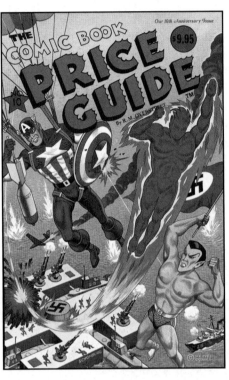

Needless to say, when I got home, I bugged our local newsstand to find me a copy of *The Overstreet Comic Book Price Guide*. They had no luck, or just didn't care because I wasn't able to find a copy until much later, 1980, when I discovered *The Overstreet Comic Book Price Guide* #10 with an amazing Alex Schomburg Invaders cover. I wore the pages of that book out.

But, I'm getting ahead of myself. Let me make a confession here, it wasn't long after my return from that summer vacation that I stopped buying and reading comic books for almost ten years. It was a time when other teenage activities engulfed my life, sports, girls, cars, and stuff you don't need to hear about. Oh, I would purchase a comic book now and then, but nothing like that of my youth.

It wasn't until 1980, when I was out of college, married, working and what you'd call settled down, that I found my way back to the love of my youth, comic books. In 1980 we actually had a real comic book store open up. There were not only comic books, but fanzines and magazines about comic books. It was wonderful. I bought a few comics and before you knew it, I was hooked again.

The only thing was, I had a lot of catching up to do. So much had changed since my time in the Silver Age of comics. While looking through one of the fanzines, I saw an ad from a comic book shop in North Carolina (of all places) called Heroes Aren't Hard To Find. It was run by one Shelton Drum. They were selling the latest edition of *The Overstreet Comic Book Price Guide*, and when you bought a copy you also got 100 free comic book bags to go with it. That was good enough for me! From there on out, that was where I bought my copy of *The Overstreet Comic Book Price Guide.*

Guide #10 was a dream for me. It was a thick "textbook" of comic book history that I spent so much time absorbing and studying. Everything in it was of interest to me. I filled up notebooks of book lists, checklists, comics to buy, duplicates to trade, values, notes on particular issues and so much more. There was so much for me to learn and to be honest, I had most of it right there in my hands thanks to Robert "Bob" Overstreet. In my opinion, he, Steve Geppi, J.C. Vaughn, and his great group of advisors and experts, were my academy of comic book professors. They helped fill in every gap I had missed in the last ten years. They also help send me out on a hunt that continues to today in 2020. I have to say I have not missed an issue of the *Guide* since #10, the *Guide* has become a part of my life, it's become a friend and a member of my family.

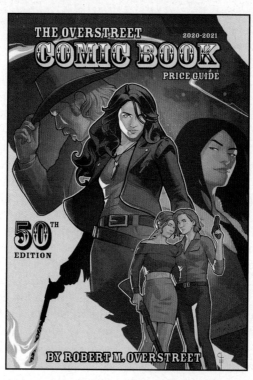

I also can count Bob Overstreet as a friend, something back as a teenager I could only dream of. Through my 33 years of being a comic book writer and marketing executive, I have been so lucky to have spent personal time with Bob and his wife Carol on many an occasion, and to be frank, during those times, in my head there is teenage Beau screaming, "You're talking with Robert Overstreet!"

My career writing comics as well as having a TV series based on one of my characters, Wynonna Earp, truly became legit for me when not only are all the comics I have written listed in *The Overstreet Comic Book Price Guide*, but my character Wynonna Earp graces the cover of the special *Overstreet Comic Book Price Guide* #50. To me, that is the honor among all honors. It is one of the pinnacles of my career and my creative life along with having lunches with Stan Lee, becoming personal friends with Don Heck, and having a character I created being on the cover of the most respected and authoritative publications on the subject of comic books – *The Overstreet Comic Book Price Guide.*

The *Guide* that returned me back to my first love – comic books. Robert Overstreet is the ultimate matchmaker.

Thank you, Bob.

OVERSTREET @ 50

by Matt Nelson
Primary Grader, CGC

*I wrote a letter to Bob when I was 15;
by that point I was all in...*

It's hard to believe I'm writing this in celebration of the 50th edition of *The Overstreet Comic Book Price Guide*. I bought my first *Overstreet* in 1988 when I was only 14, and though that was over 35 years ago, I wasn't even born when the first edition was released.

How Bob's *Guide* changed the hobby has been discussed many times over the years. How it opened people's eyes to the value of comics, slowing, and eventually halting their ongoing destruction. How it began to accumulate what would become the definitive source of historical information that was otherwise lost to the ephemeral wastebasket of time. How it ultimately stabilized a burgeoning market, leading comic books to become one of the most sought-after collectibles in history.

But the *Guide* is so important to me for personal reasons too. It put me on my path to a lifetime career, although I didn't know that at the time. All I remember is quickly falling in love with comic books, then realizing how vast that world

was, stretching decades back in time, which felt overwhelming. Once I came across my first *Overstreet*, I held in my hands something that crystallized all of that. I try to imagine how frustrating it must have been for someone like me in the '60s, feeling the same rush of excitement but having nowhere to turn for information.

I immediately felt a personal connection with the *Guide*, initially because it had Bob's name on it, but as I connected with other collectors and dealers and devoured any literature I could get my hands on, it soon became clear that it was more than just a last name on a book; Bob *was* the *Guide*. He seemed to be omnipresent, an invisible force guiding the cosmos as everyone waited with bated breath to see what changed in each year's new edition.

I wrote a letter to Bob when I was 15; by that point I was all in, spending every free moment I had on comic books. He quickly returned the letter with his handwritten answers in the margin. I still have it. I remember how excited I was to have connected with Bob, and it seemed to galvanize my focus even more. We wouldn't meet in person until the Overstreet Advisor conference held in Timonium, Maryland in 1994, shortly after Steve Geppi bought Bob's *Guide* and his collection. Being invited and meeting Bob and all the others was absolutely one of the great highlights of my career.

As with so many great achievements, Bob's creation of the *Guide* was a combination of passion, vision, ambition, intellect, timing, and luck. Even though the concept of a collectible price guide was not new, how he executed and evolved it was unique, and showed that his *Guide* wasn't just another passing fad. In fact, there was quite a bit of resistance to it initially, which seemed to take the better part of the '70s to subside. By the time I picked my first one up, the *Guide* had been nicknamed "The Bible," which given my near reli-gious devotion to comics I find to be quite an appropriate moniker.

Having had the privilege to spend more time with Bob over the years, what I think is most striking is the contrast between his personality and his legacy. If you've ever met Bob, you know that he very soft spoken, friendly, and unpretentious. And from this man came what I consider the single most important published work in our field, loudly overflowing with so much knowledge and information it resembles to me the archetypical musician who says little, but speaks volumes through his instrument.

Bob, I profoundly thank you for what you did for all of us. I wouldn't be here without you.

A veteran comics historian and Overstreet Advisor, Matt Nelson is the Primary Grader for CGC, an independent, third-party grading service for comic books.

Matt Nelson enjoys a convention moment with Gary Carter and Bob Overstreet in 2015.

OVERSTREET @ 50

by Steven Houston
Torpedo Comics

"Wow! Robert M. Overstreet reads my work!"

I first became aware of the name Robert "Bob" Overstreet in 1985, after purchasing a copy of *The Overstreet Comic Book Price Guide* #15. At the time I was 18 years old and had the grand number of two years of comic collecting under by belt.

I devoured that *Guide* from page to page, from advertisements to articles and yes, the price listings. I was in awe of this publication, and I remember thinking to myself "What type of God could have all this comic knowledge?" while also lamenting that I, a newbie comic collector from a small town in England, would never get the chance to meet the legend himself, Robert Overstreet.

Who would have guessed that some 30 years later, that dream would come true! While prepping my booth at Comic-Con on July 7, 2015, J.C. Vaughn, Vice-President of Publishing for Gemstone Publishing, informed me that Bob was going to be at the show the next day,

meeting with various dealers, and he wanted to meet me. I was like a giddy school kid, my heart racing. I remember trying to keep my composure in front of J.C. My fellow workers at Torpedo Comics overheard the conversation and asked me to stay calm – Ha! As if that were possible. My mind exploded with a million possible conversations that I could have with Bob, what would be important enough to bring up to Bob? Would I make a fool of myself?

I often wonder about comic collecting pre-*Overstreet*. Shortly after discovering the *Guide* myself, I learned that it was first published in 1970. I was immediately struck with one thought: What did collectors do when putting a want-list together before the *Guide*? The next thought that hit me was this: Who on earth would have the gall to try and put together a guide regarding this unknown and obviously massive medium?

I was obviously very fortunate, when I came into collecting, I could put together a want list, either by title or even publisher. I can only imagine collectors and dealers arguing over a title like *Crime and Justice*

(published by Charlton in the 1950s), debating whether someone once saw an issue 26, or did it end with issue 25?

The impact of the *Guide* cannot be overlooked. We are talking about an immense project that brought order to a wild and chaotic hobby with no guidelines – just rumor, or the word of a dealer. I can't imagine a comic collecting world being as big as it is today, without *The Overstreet Comic Book Price Guide*.

The next night, July 8, during the so-called "Preview Night," I was working away at the booth when suddenly out of nowhere, Bob and his wonderful wife, Carol, were there standing in front of me. I shook Bob's hand and held myself together. I had a billion things to ask, but I kept myself in check and began the conversation with my introduction to his work in the *Guide* of 1985.

We talked for a good 45 minutes, as I brought up name after name, all who had referenced Bob over the years. I fell silent as Bob explained about pivotal moments in the *Guide's* history, sneaking a look at

Carol's proud face, while she also revealed some great accounts of the *Guide's* creation. I had some photos taken, and after Bob and Carol left to continue their dealer meet-and-greets, I was spent, utterly exhausted. I had just met my (reference) publishing idol, what more to life was there? I must admit July 8, 2015 is to date the greatest day of my comic collecting (dealer) life. As an advisor to the *Guide* I hope to keep contributing as much as I can, always with this thought in mind: Wow! Robert M. Overstreet reads my work!

Stephen Houston at his Torpedo Comics store in Las Vegas with Gemstone's Creative Director Mark Huesman.

OVERSTREET @ 50

by Steve Borock
President & Primary Grader, CBCS

Here's to another 50 years of the Guide!

Christmas morning! Wait! Even better! Our day is the day the new edition of *The Overstreet Comic Book Price Guide* comes out! Yay!

That's exactly how I felt as a kid and, believe it or not, still do to this very day! I get to look up prices, scour some amazing market reports, read cool articles and look at all the new advertisements.

Bob Overstreet did not just create our hobby's Bible, he created a real community for all of us. Yes, it started out as a simple price guide (though the work that went into it was not so simple), but now it has become the one book so many of us use every day. By forming the Overstreet Advisors group, Bob gave us new friends, and along with them, their different perspectives on our hobby and the marketplace.

There are no words that can totally encompass how much joy Bob has given us for so many years with his passion and hard work, but I have to say again, I feel like a kid every year the *Guide* comes out.

I'll tell anyone about how much I love the *Guide*, I want to share an extra bit of appreciation for Gemstone's support of our hobby's greatest charity: The Hero Initiative. Hero gives back to those in need who created or worked on the wonderful characters we all enjoy with food, medical, housing and other help that is needed. While this year is the *Guide's* Golden Anniversary, it also marks the 11th year that there has been a Hero Initiative limited edition of *The Overstreet Comic Book Price Guide*. What's more, Steve Geppi, Bob Overstreet, and the team at Gemstone don't take a cent for this ver-

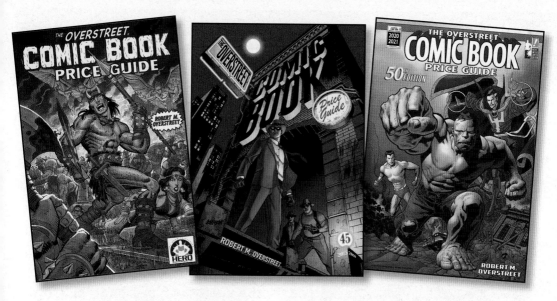

sion so that Hero, a 501(c)(3) charity, can get everything they can out of it.

In just about every market report I write for the *Guide*, I offer the same advice: "Buy what you like and can afford." It's really that simple, which is why it's been my war cry for so many years. And strangely enough for a price guide guy, Bob would tell you the same thing. It's fantastic when your comics go up in value, but if you already love them, it's not such a concern.

As is evident in the *Guide* each and every year, Bob has been sharing his passion for comics with us for five incredible decades. Just enjoy collecting and reading comic books, enjoy the amazing friendships we make in this wonderful hobby. Look around and enjoy all the cool stuff this hobby has to offer from original comic art and comic books, to the movies and TV shows based on the characters we all love so much, to comic memorabilia, going to the conventions and so on. It will all seem worth it in the end.

I would not be where I am in our great hobby today if it was not for Bob and *The Overstreet Comic Book Price Guide.* For that, and all the friends I have made through the *Guide* and all the many, many hours of fun leafing through the *Guide*, I have to say:

Congratulations, Bob! Here's to another 50 years of the *Guide*! Thanks for your friendship, the knowledge you have shared with me, and for all the great things you have done for our hobby! You are a rock star in my book!

A longtime Overstreet Advisor, Steve Borock is the President and Primary Grader of CBCS, an independent, third-party grading service for comic books.

Steve Borock and J.C. Vaughn at Geppi's Entertainment Museum.

OVERSTREET @ 50

**1st Edition
1st printing - 1970**

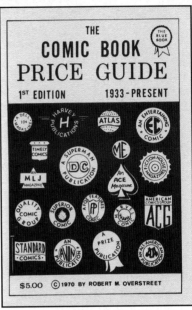

**1st Edition
2nd printing - 1971**

**2nd Edition - 1972
Patriotic flag covers**

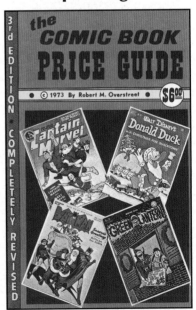

**3rd Edition - 1973
Christmas covers**

4th Edition - 1974
Cover by Don Newton
1st art cover for the Guide

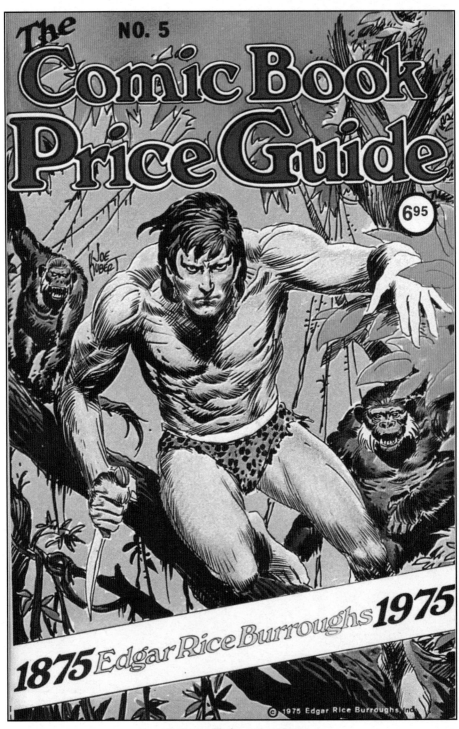

5th Edition - 1975
Cover by Joe Kubert
Voted Most Popular Cover (2010)

6th Edition - 1976
Cover by Will Eisner
1st bookstore distribution edition

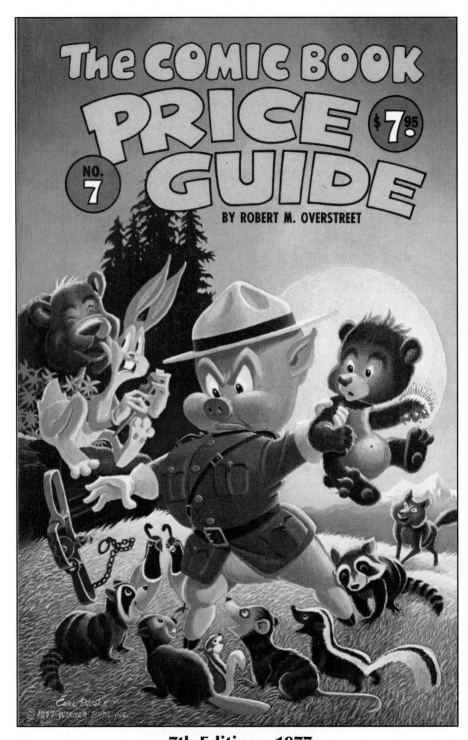

7th Edition - 1977
Cover by Carl Barks
Legendary Disney artist painting Porky Pig and Bugs Bunny

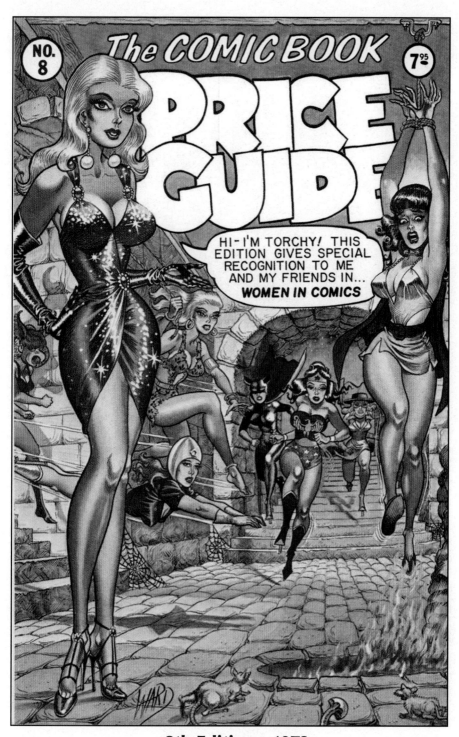

8th Edition - 1978
Cover by Bill Ward
Spotlight on women in comics

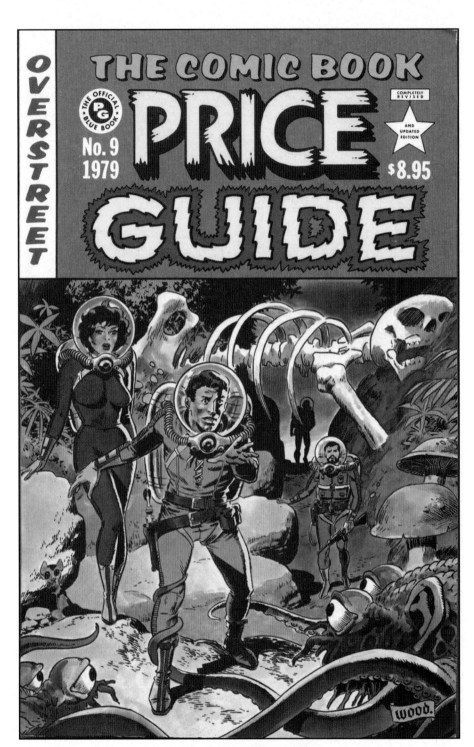

9th Edition - 1979
Cover by Wally Wood
EC science fiction tribute

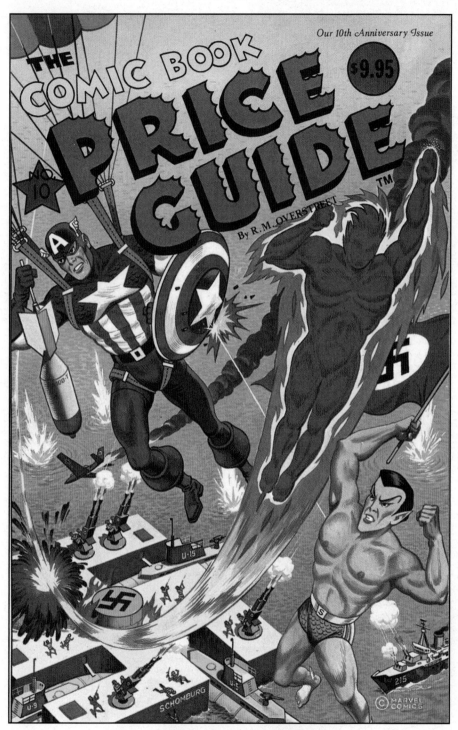

10th Edition - 1980
Cover by Alex Schomburg
Timely World War II characters

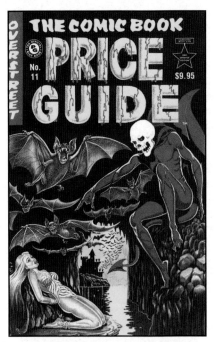

11th Edition - 1981
Cover by L.B. Cole
Pre-Code horror style

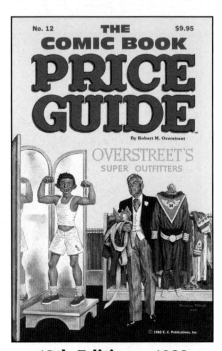

12th Edition - 1982
Cover by Norman Mingo
Bob Overstreet appears on cover

13th Edition - 1983
Cover by Don Newton
First repeat cover artist

14th Edition - 1984
Cover by Bill Woggon
Katy Keene #1 recreation

15th Edition - 1985
Cover by C.C. Beck
Includes article on Mister Mind by C.C. Beck

16th Edition - 1986
Cover by John Romita, Sr.
25th anniversary article by Stan Lee

17th Edition - 1987
Cover by Ron Dias
Snow White's 50th anniversary

18th Edition - 1988
Cover by L.B. Cole
Hardcover has white background

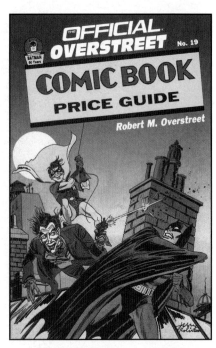

19th Edition - 1989
Cover by Jerry Robinson
Co-creator of Robin and The Joker

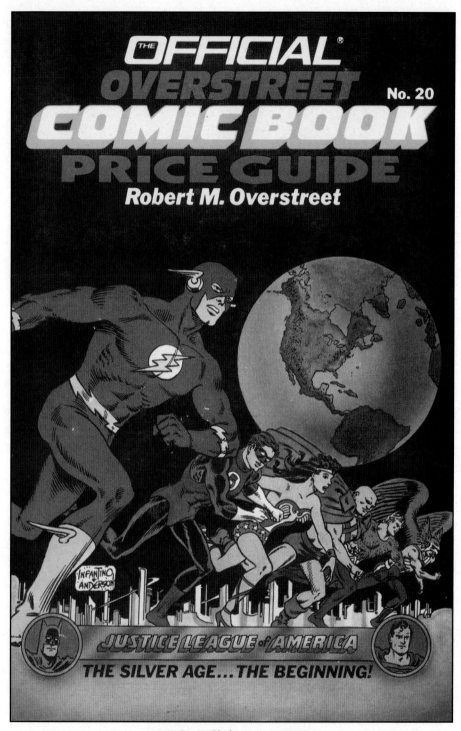

THE OFFICIAL OVERSTREET COMIC BOOK PRICE GUIDE No. 20

Robert M. Overstreet

JUSTICE LEAGUE of AMERICA
THE SILVER AGE...THE BEGINNING!

20th Edition - 1990
Cover by Carmine Infantino & Murphy Anderson
30th anniversary of the Justice League

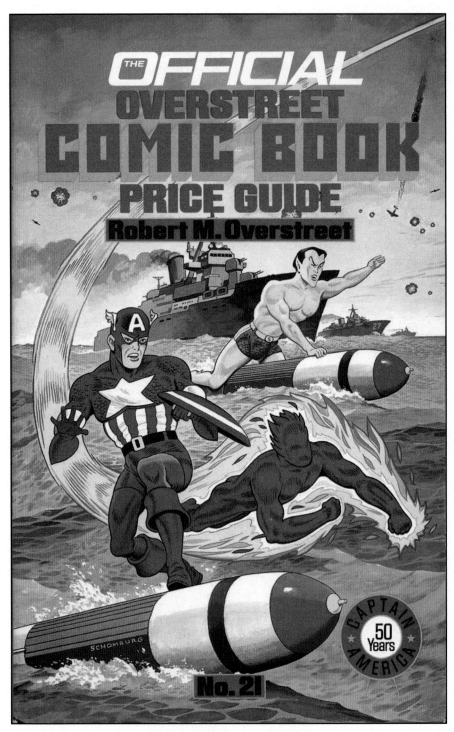

21st Edition - 1991
Cover by Alex Schomburg
Captain America's 50th anniversary

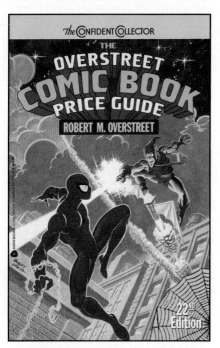

22nd Edition - 1992
Cover by Mark Bagley
and John Romita, Sr.

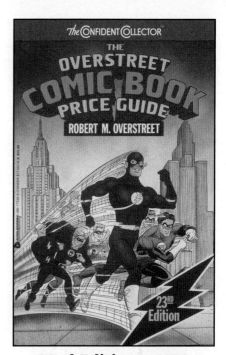

23rd Edition - 1993
Cover by Carmine Infantino
Flash/Green Lantern team-ups

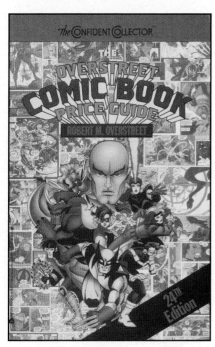

24th Edition - 1994
Cover by Mike Parobeck
X-Men in animated style

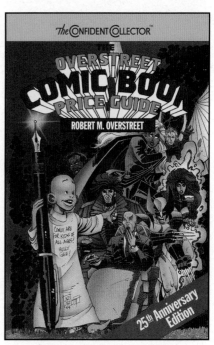

25th Edition - 1995
Cover by John Romita, Jr.
1st Gemstone Publishing edition

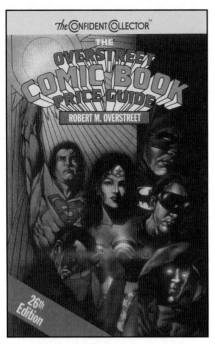

26th Edition - 1996
Cover by Tony Harris
Harris' Starman appears

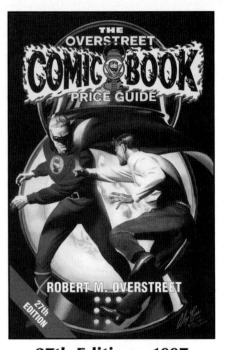

27th Edition - 1997
Cover by Alex Ross
First edition with multiple covers

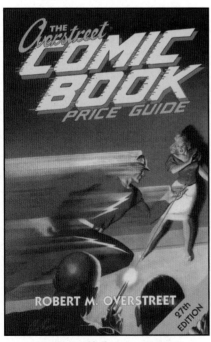

27th Edition - 1997
Cover by Alex Ross
First edition with multiple covers

28th Edition - 1998
Cover by Murphy Anderson
Justice League and Adam Strange

28th Edition - 1998
Cover by Murphy Anderson
Quality & Fox heroes

29th Edition - 1999
Cover by Alex Ross
Homage to *Avengers* #4

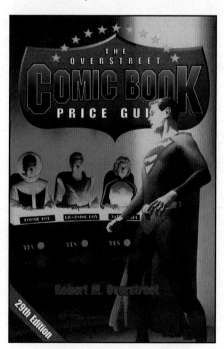

29th Edition - 1999
Cover by Alex Ross
Homage to *Adventure Comics* #247

30th Edition - 2000
Cover by Al Williamson
Celebrates EC's science fiction

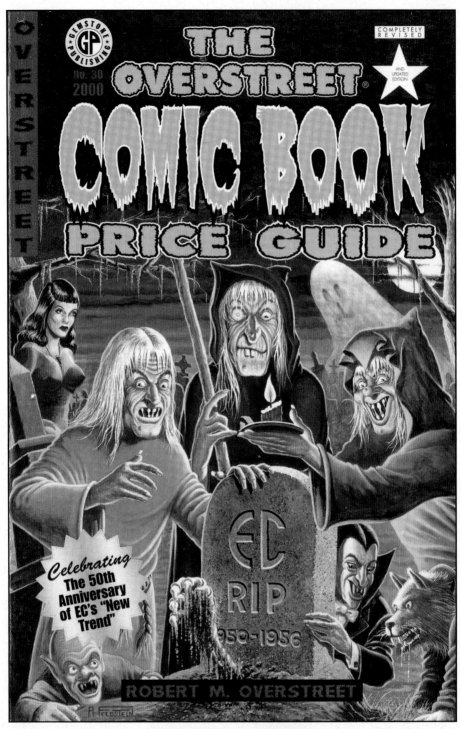

30th Edition - 2000
Cover by Al Feldstein
The Vault-Keeper, the Old Witch, and the Crypt-Keeper

31st Edition - 2001
Cover by John K. Snyder III
Direct market edition of the *Fantastic Four* #1 homage

31st Edition - 2001
Cover by John K. Snyder III
Book market edition

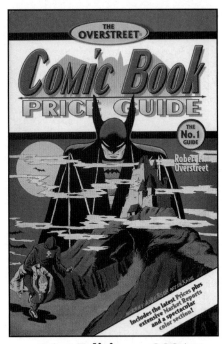

31st Edition - 2001
Cover by Murphy Anderson
Recreation of *Detective Comics* #31

32nd Edition - 2002
Cover by Murphy Anderson
Very Fine price added in listings

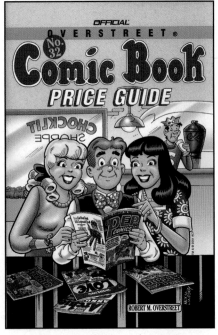

32nd Edition - 2002
Cover by Rex Lindsey
60th anniversary of Veronica

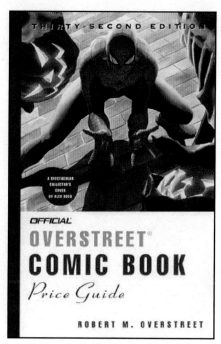

32nd Edition - 2002
Cover by Alex Ross
Spidey/Goblin rematch from *Guide* #22

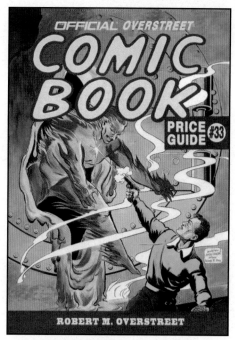

33rd Edition - 2003
Cover by Murphy Anderson
Guide page size increases

33rd Edition - 2003
Cover by John K. Snyder III
Six prices now shown in listings

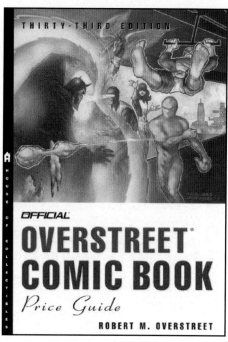

33rd Edition - 2003
Cover by John K. Snyder III
VG & VF/NM prices added

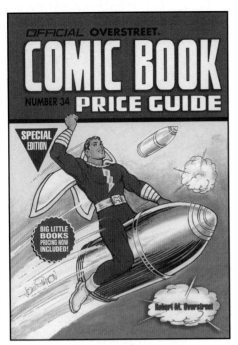

34th Edition - 2004
Cover by Joe Simon
Top listed price changes from NM to NM-

34th Edition - 2004
Cover by Daan Jippes
Donald Duck's 70th anniversary

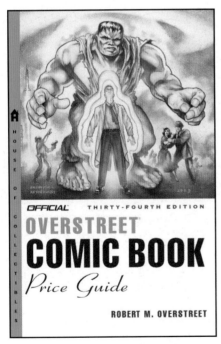

34th Edition - 2004
Cover by John K. Snyder III
Homage to *Incredible Hulk* #1

35th Edition - 2005
Cover by John Stanley
Little Lulu and Tubby

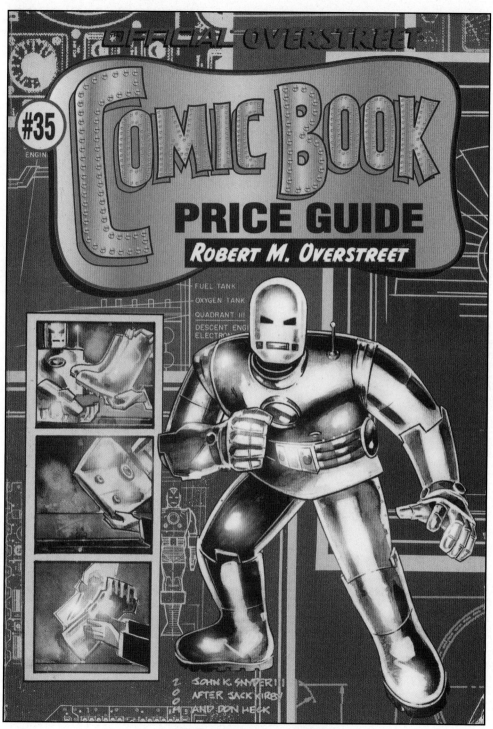

35th Edition - 2005
Cover by John K. Snyder III
Homage to *Tales of Suspense* #39

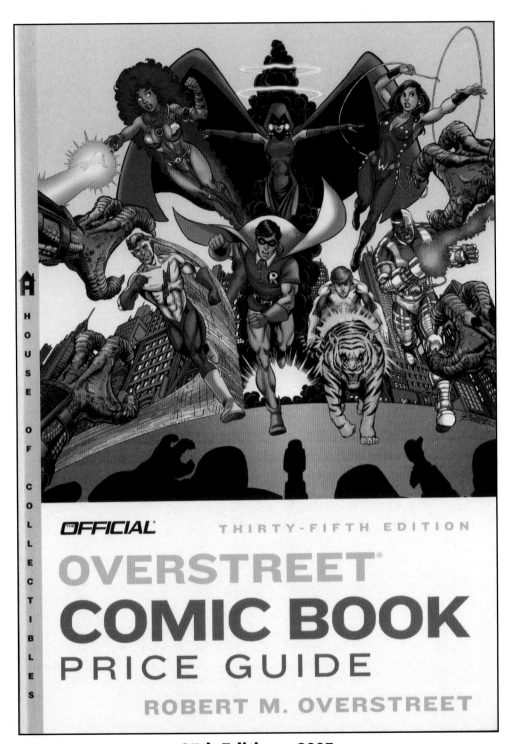

THE OFFICIAL
THIRTY-FIFTH EDITION
OVERSTREET
COMIC BOOK
PRICE GUIDE
ROBERT M. OVERSTREET

HOUSE OF COLLECTIBLES

35th Edition - 2005
Cover by George Pérez
25th anniversary of *New Teen Titans* #1

36th Edition - 2006
Cover by John K. Snyder III
Homage to *Journey Into Mystery* #83

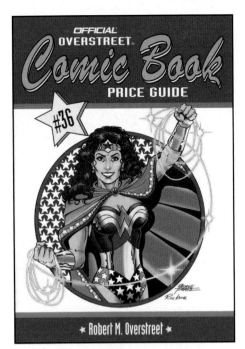

36th Edition - 2006
Cover by George Pérez
Main creator for WW's 1987 reboot

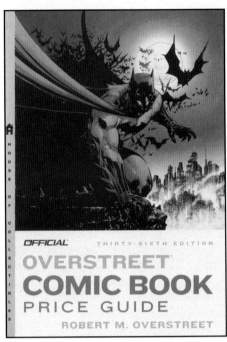

36th Edition - 2006
Cover by Jim Lee
Printed art was pixelated

37th Edition - 2007
Cover by Billy Tucci
Tucci's first *Guide* cover

37th Edition - 2007
Cover by John K. Snyder III
Daredevil #1 homage, red costume

37th Edition - 2007
Cover by Mark Sparacio
Wolverine, Luke Cage, Spider-Woman as Avengers

38th Edition - 2008
Cover by Mark Sparacio
Marvel villain spotlight

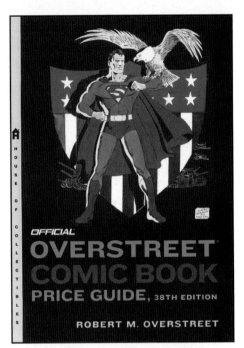

38th Edition - 2008
Cover by Murphy Anderson
Recreation of *Superman* #14

38th Edition - 2008
Cover by Doug Wheatley
The *Guide*'s 1st Star Wars cover

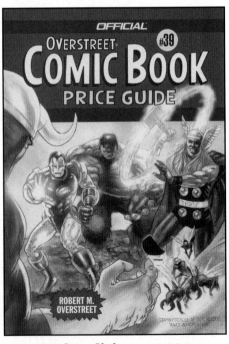

39th Edition - 2009
Cover by John K. Snyder III
Homage to *Avengers* #1

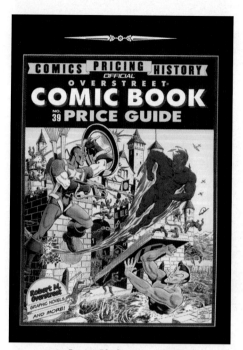

39th Edition - 2009
Cover by Murphy Anderson
Recreation of *All-Select Comics* #1

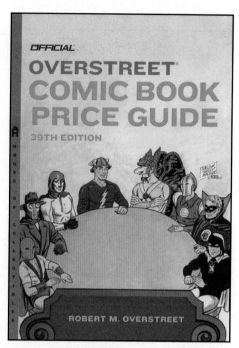

39th Edition - 2009
Cover by Sheldon Moldoff
Recreation of *All Star Comics* #3

• A number of artists from Alex Schomburg and L.B. Cole to John Romita, Jr. and Billy Tucci have illustrated more than one *Guide* cover, but only a handful have had multiple covers in the same year: Alex Ross (#27 and #29), Murphy Anderson (#28), John K. Snyder III (#33), and Amanda Conner (#46).

• Murphy Anderson and John K. Snyder III each clock in with eight covers on their résumés.

• The cover of #12 is the only one to feature Bob Overstreet himself, as illustrated by *MAD* artist Norman Mingo. Thirty-eight years later, the Gemstone staff had an homage/Easter Egg based on this cover in the "About This Book" section of *CBPG* #50.

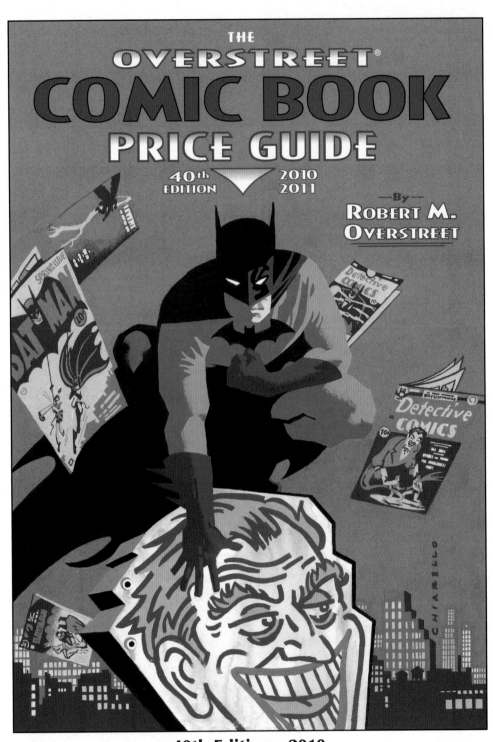

40th Edition - 2010

Cover by Mark Chiarello

The *Guide*'s release moved to July starting with this edition

40th Edition - 2010
Cover by Darwyn Cooke
1st time *Action* #1 & *Detective* #27 prices topped $1 million

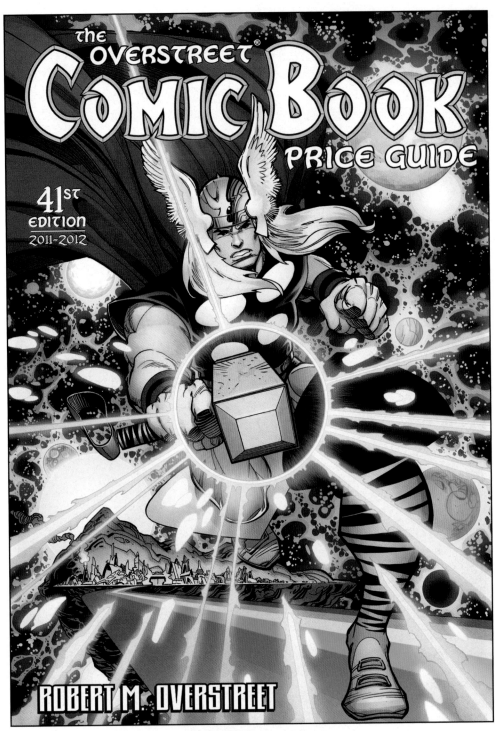

41st Edition - 2011
Cover by Walt Simonson
Defining Thor artist's first *Guide* cover

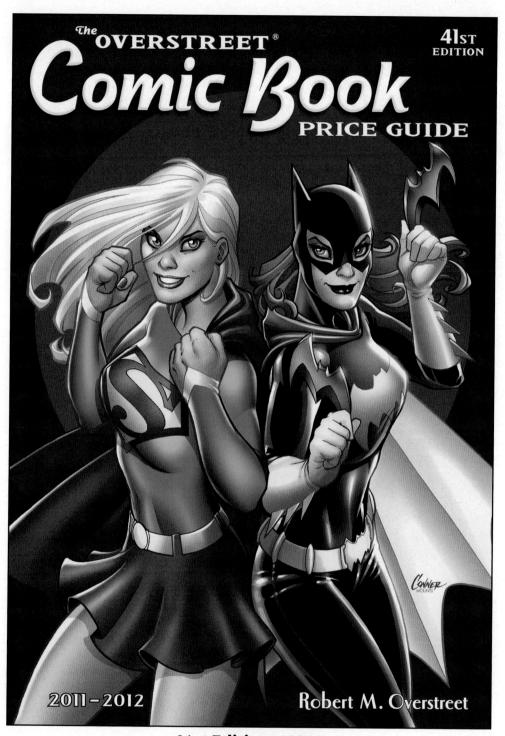

41st Edition - 2011
Cover by Amanda Conner
1st *Guide* cover drawn by a woman

42nd Edition - 2012
Cover by Adam Hughes
Copies of *Guide* #1 are peeking out of Catwoman's bag

42nd Edition - 2012
Cover by Joe Jusko
Avengers #58 recreation

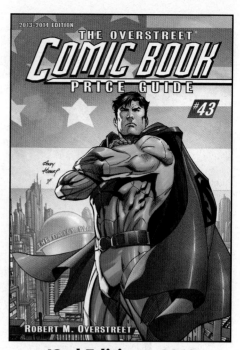

43rd Edition - 2013
Cover by Andy Kubert
Superman from DC's New 52

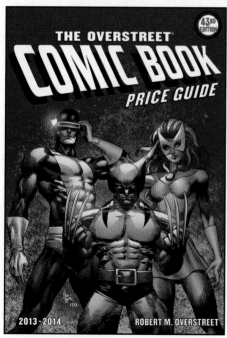

43rd Edition - 2013
Cover by Mike Deodato Jr.
Multiple eras of X-Men

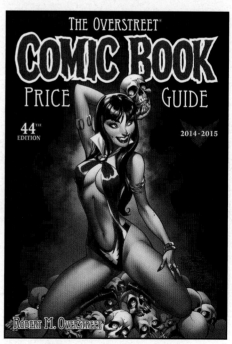

44th Edition - 2014
Cover by J. Scott Campbell
Later *Vampirella* #3 (2019) cover

44th Edition - 2014
Cover by J.G. Jones
Homage to artist J.C. Leyendecker

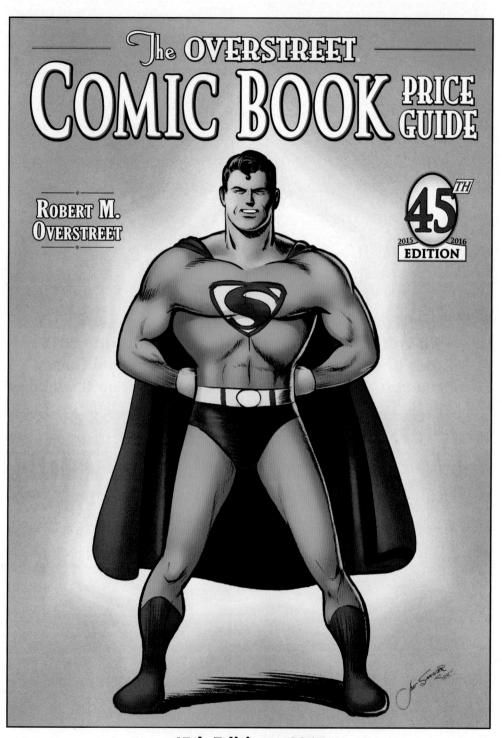

45th Edition - 2015
Cover by Joe Shuster
Custom Shuster sketch for Yankees great Lefty Gomez

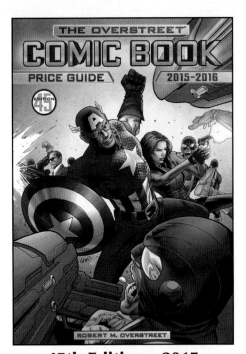

45th Edition - 2015
Cover by Greg Land

Agents of S.H.I.E.L.D. TV characters appear

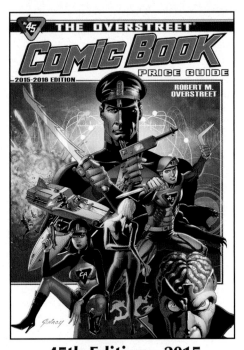

45th Edition - 2015
Cover by Paul Gulacy

1st Captain Action *Guide* cover

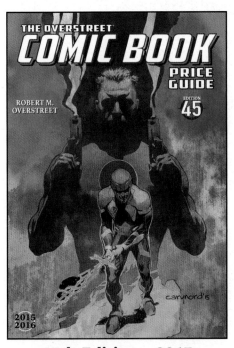

45th Edition - 2015
Cover by Cary Nord

1st Valiant on regular edition

46th Edition - 2016
Cover by Russ Heath

1st Hall of Fame edition • Sgt. Rock

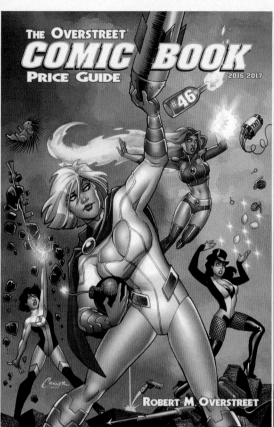 

46th Edition - 2016
Covers by Amanda Conner

Even before her incredibly popular tenure on *Harley Quinn*, Amanda Conner's stints on *Power Girl* and in *Wednesday Comics* had elevated her to superstar status. Her cover for *The Overstreet Comic Book Price Guide* #41 had proven popular with new fans and established collectors alike, so she was a logical choice when the decision was made to have the two covers of *The Overstreet Comic Book Price Guide* #46 link up to form one larger image.

"We had the idea of doing covers that joined up a few years early. That never really came together, but it proved to be worth the wait. The results by Amanda Conner, colorist Paul Mounts, and our own Mark Huesman on production were amazing," said Gemstone's J.C. Vaughn, "Mark's contributions were subtle, but critical."

Because there are slightly different specs for the hardcover and soft cover editions, Conner had to draw a bit more on the right edge of the Power Girl cover and on the left edge (spine side) of the Harley Quinn cover. Huesman's job was to make both the hardcover and soft cover editions line up seamlessly despite the differences.

The difference that's easiest to notice is that the spiral cord between the plunger (on the Harley Quinn cover) and the dynamite (on the Power Girl cover) is longer on the hardcovers.

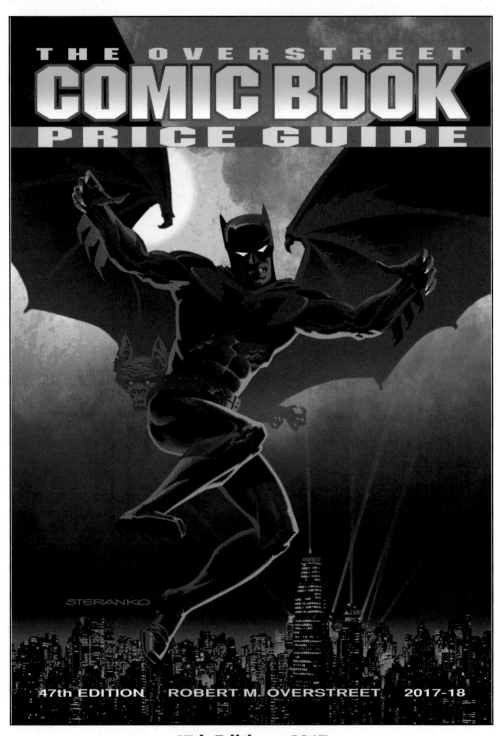

47th Edition - 2017
Cover by Jim Steranko
Steranko designed the cover logo as well

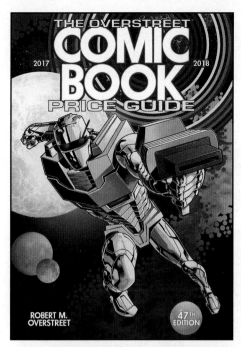

47th Edition - 2017
Cover by Gabriel Rodríguez
Rom: Spaceknight appears

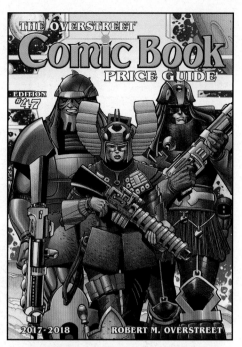

47th Edition - 2017
Cover by Walt Simonson
Hall of Fame • Star Slammers

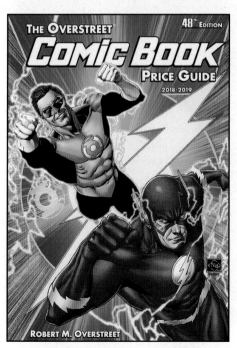

48th Edition - 2018
Cover by Ethan Van Sciver
Artist on Rebirth series for both

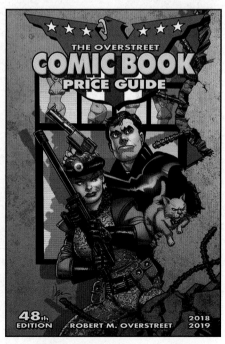

48th Edition - 2018
Cover by Howard Chaykin
Hall of Fame • American Flagg

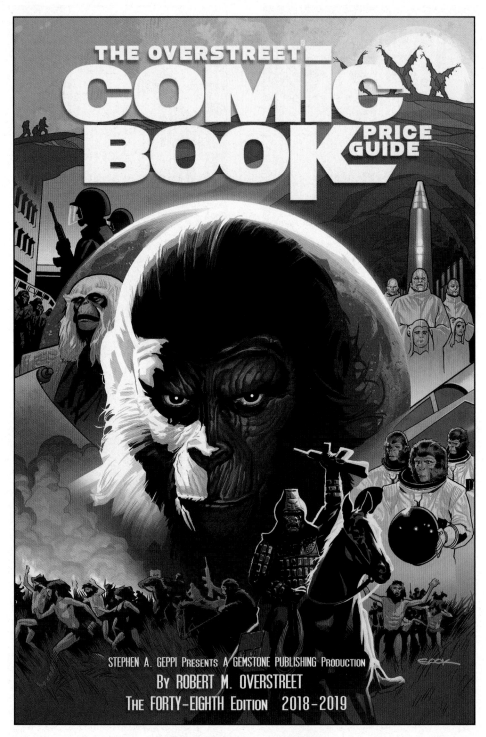

48th Edition - 2018
Cover by Ryan Sook
Only cover with Steve Geppi's name

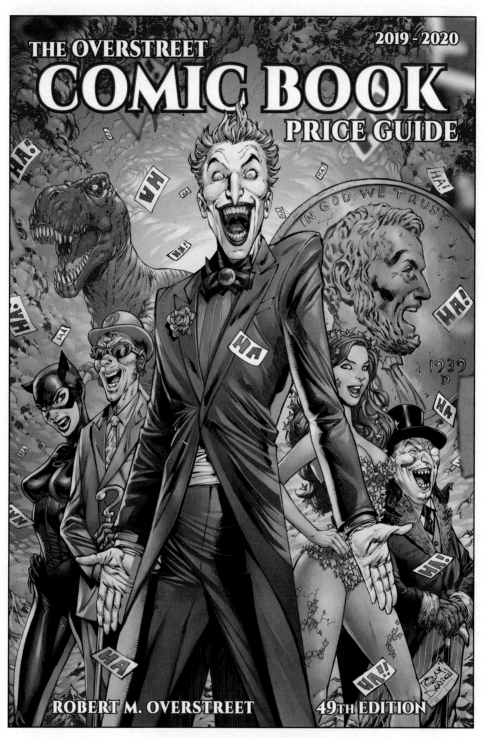

49th Edition - 2019
Cover by Tony Daniel
Released same year as *Joker* movie

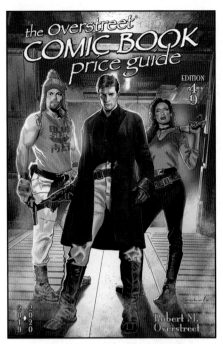

49th Edition - 2019
Cover by Diego Galindo
Firefly/Serenity characters

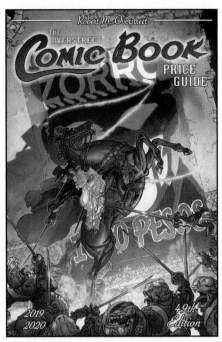

49th Edition - 2019
Cover by Michael Kaluta
Hall of Fame • Zorro

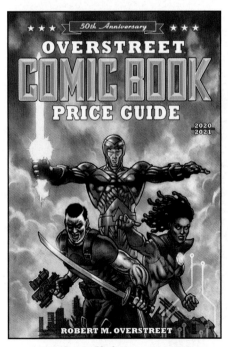

50th Edition - 2020
Cover by John K. Snyder III
Snyder's 1st Valiant cover

50th Edition - 2020
Cover by Chris Evenhuis
Beau Smith's Wynonna Earp

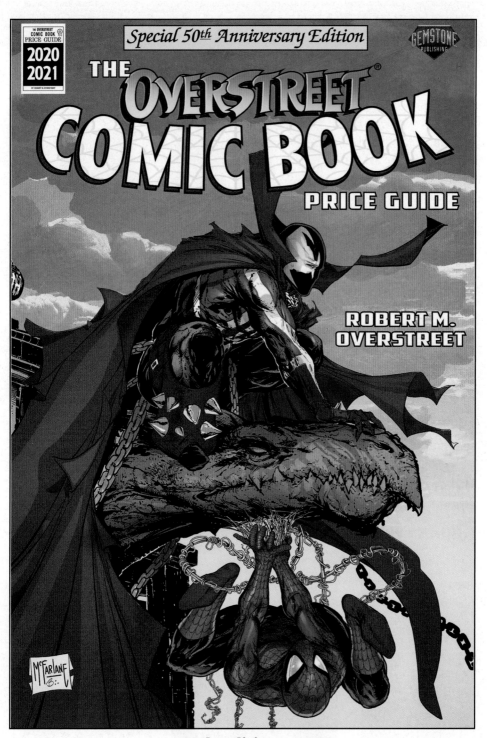

50th Edition - 2020
Cover by Todd McFarlane
McFarlane's 1st published team-up of these characters

The BIG, BIG Edition

When our oversized limited edition, *The Big, Big Overstreet Comic Book Price Guide*, was introduced, we initially used our bookstore cover art to make sure that comic book shops had access to those great cover images (#31-37). Since this version returned with #42, all have featured original art.

31st Edition - 2001

32nd Edition - 2002

33rd Edition - 2003

34th Edition - 2004

35th Edition - 2005

36th Edition - 2006

37th Edition - 2007

38th Edition - 2008

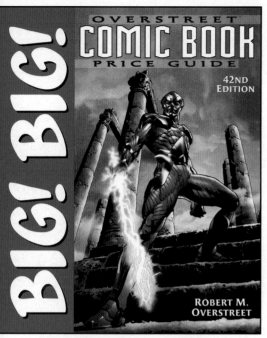

42nd Edition - 2012
Cover by Lewis LaRosa
1st Valiant character cover

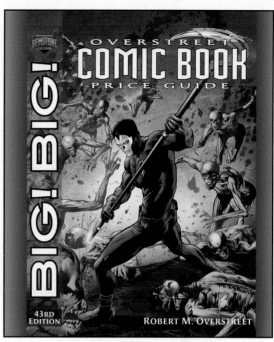

43rd Edition - 2013
Cover by Will Conrad
Valiant's Shadowman

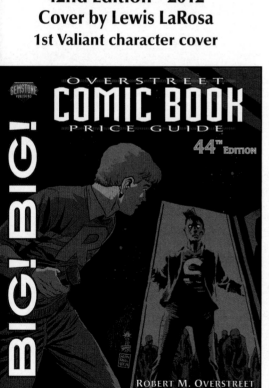

44th Edition - 2014
Cover by Francesco Francavilla
Based on *Afterlife With Archie*

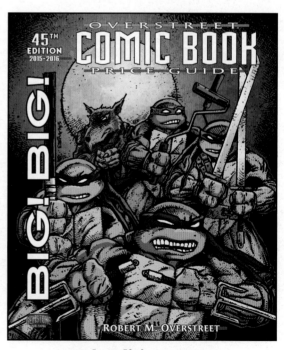

45th Edition - 2015
Cover by Kevin Eastman
1st Teenage Mutant Ninja Turtles cover

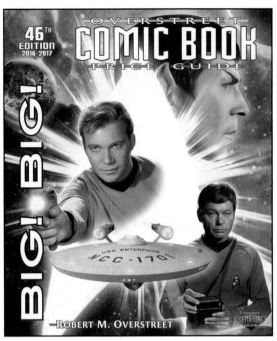

46th Edition - 2016
Cover by Joe Corroney
1st Star Trek cover

47th Edition - 2017
Cover by Billy Tucci
Last spiral bound edition

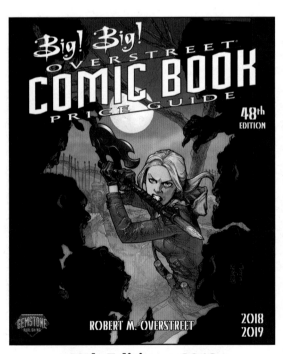

48th Edition - 2018
Cover by Georges Jeanty
Buffy the Vampire Slayer

49th Edition - 2019
Cover by Billy Tucci
25th anniversary of Shi

134

50th Edition - 2020
Cover design by Mark Huesman
Homage to the cover design of the 1st edition

THE HERO INITIATIVE EDITION

By Charles S. Novinskie

The Overstreet Comic Book Price Guide and Hero Initiative have teamed up to raise funds to help comic creators in need by publishing a special limited hardcover edition of the *Guide* for each of the past 11 years.

"I first mentioned the idea to Hero's Jim McLauchlin about five years before we were able to do it. Then, as we were working on *CBPG #40*, I ended up in charge of the day-to-day operations at Gemstone and found the opportunity to greenlight the project. Jim liked the idea from the beginning, so from that point the goal was to find some willing partners," said J.C. Vaughn, Vice-President of Publishing for Gemstone Publishing.

"J.C. called me up and asked if I thought it was a good idea, and if it would sell. I responded in the affirmative to both! It was Conan's 40th anniversary year in comics along with Overstreet's 40th, so that seemed a natural connection, and we were off," McLauchlin said.

That edition began a series that has run each year since. The edition is limited to 500 hardcover copies, all of which are sold by Hero or their affiliates.

"Gemstone doesn't sell any of those copies, though just about every year the covers are so good that we wish we did. We have had some truly amazing covers by some of the top folks in the business," Vaughn said.

"The *Guide*, for many artists, is a bucket-list type achievement, and we always want to pick the best artists in the business. With the Hero Initiative edition, there are additional factors. If we can pick someone who is an active supporter of Hero, or someone who's been helped by Hero, that's a big plus," he said.

"They sell, and typically very fast. Each one has been a limited edition of 500 at $35 a pop, and they've all sold out. So that's money in the coffers. We sell most direct ourselves but have wholesaled a number to retailers such as Graham Crackers Comics, A-1 Comics, and Heroes Aren't Hard to Find," said McLauchlin. "It's a great collector item. *Overstreet* is really an every-year evergreen, and I'm happy that people have enjoyed these and pick them up. I know I'm supposed to say all of the covers are my favorites, but honestly that first one, the *Conan The Barbarian #1* recreation by John Romita, Jr., Klaus Janson, and Dean White is an all-time fave," said McLauchlin.

"Because of Hero's 501(c)(3) status, neither Gemstone nor our printer takes any fee for this edition. That's one of the real joys to us. We've been able to make it so that whatever Hero gets from the project, it all goes to that great cause. The Hero Initiative is about one of the best, least controversial causes I know. They do great work, and for those of us who collect the *Guide*, you just want to help them," Vaughn said.

A longtime industry figure and Overstreet Advisor, Charles S. Novinskie serves as disbursement secretary for the Hero Initiative.

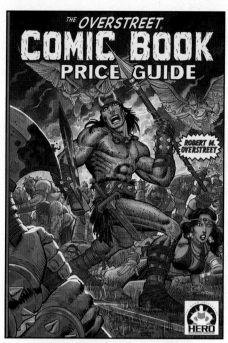

40th Edition - 2010
Cover by John Romita, Jr.
and Klaus Janson

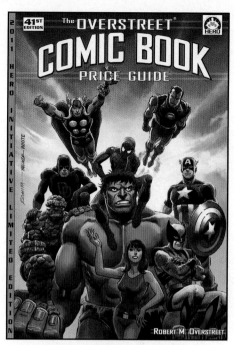

41st Edition - 2011
Cover by John Romita, Sr.
and Tom Palmer

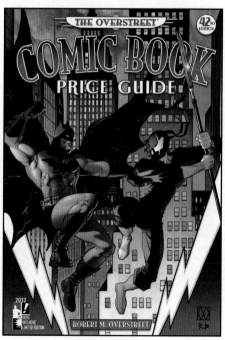

42nd Edition - 2012
Cover by Matt Wagner
1st Grendel cover app.

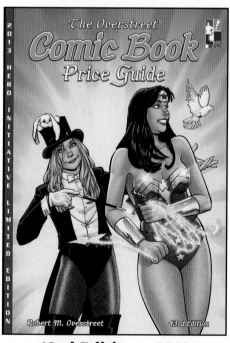

43rd Edition - 2013
Cover by Terry Moore
Strangers in Paradise cosplay

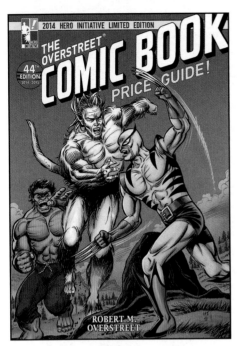

44th Edition - 2014
Cover by Herb Trimpe
and Tom Palmer

45th Edition - 2015
Cover by Dave Johnson
1st Spirit cover since *Guide* #6

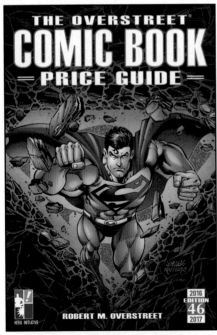

46th Edition - 2016
Cover by Dan Jurgens
and Norm Rapmund

Bob Overstreet with 45th edition
cover artist Dave Johnson at the
Hero Initiative booth at the
2015 San Diego Comic-Con.

47th Edition - 2017
Cover by Rob Liefeld
Co-creator of Deadpool

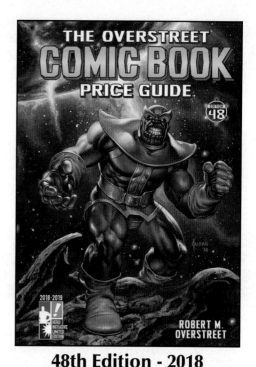

48th Edition - 2018
Cover by Joe Jusko
Released just after *Avengers: Infinity War*

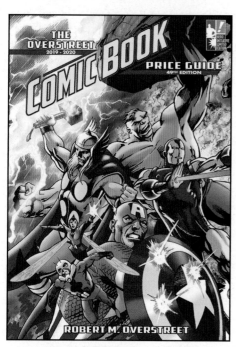

49th Edition - 2019
Cover by Alan Davis
Released just after *Avengers: Endgame*

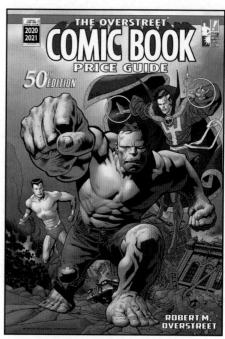

50th Edition - 2020
Cover by Kevin Nowlan
Homage to *Marvel Feature #1*

OVERSTREET @ 50

by Mark Huesman

Creative Director, Gemstone Publishing

> *I've had one of the best possible opportunities to learn more...*

Gemstone Publishing Creative Director Mark Huesman has been familiar with The Overstreet Comic Book Price Guide *for most of his life. He discovered the book as a preteen and has spent the past 23 years working on the* Guide *in a multitude of capacities, becoming integral to the development and production of each new volume.*

After the milestone 50th edition of the Guide *was finished, Huesman reflected on his history with the publication, starting with that childhood introduction, to the layers of responsibilities he now holds in bringing the book to readers.*

Overstreet: What was your first experience with *The Overstreet Comic Book Price Guide?*

Mark Huesman (MH): I started collecting comics when I was 5, focusing on Batman because of the Adam West series, and eventually I found the *Guide* at the mall bookstore. I was probably 11 or 12 then (circa 1978), and I leafed through, first checking my *Green Lantern/Green Arrow* issues with the Neal Adams art because those were my most expensive comics (and they probably still are).

Overstreet: Your acquaintance with Steve Geppi way predates your time at Gemstone Publishing, though, doesn't it? What's the story there?

MH: I probably met Steve earlier than anyone else in his various companies. I was 9 years old in August 1975, and my brother Paul and I were riding with our next-door neighbor and fellow comic collector John Compton and his mom on an errand and I spotted the sign outside Steve's first store, the basement below the TV repair shop on Edmonson Avenue in Baltimore. We stopped in and I saw a much larger comic selection than my local 7-11 could ever have. I bought a *DC Special #17* with the Mike Grell Green Lantern cover and planned to bring my allowance for future visits. "An allowance that helped build an Empire." It's almost operatic...

Turns out Steve lived in my neighborhood at the time and my parents arranged for hand-drawn gift certificates for my brother and me for that next Christmas. I was also at the store on my 10th birthday and continued with 5-6 visits a year.

Overstreet: How long have you worked at Gemstone and what positions have you held?

MH: I started in June 1997 as the Pricing Coordinator, gathering data from advisors, updating the *Guide* listings with the new comics, typing in all the price changes, and placing those three comic covers on the top of each pricing page. I'd also update content on other Gemstone books, like the Hake's Guides and Arrowhead books. I dabbled in some of the production aspects of the books my first few years, so when the managing editor left, I added his responsibilities, mostly with editing and readying the computer files for the printer. In 2009, the previous Creative Director left, so I had those responsibilities added to all the previous ones, plus dealing with some advertising tasks. I've never had an underling to take over some of my original tasks, so while I'm doing the design work, I still add the new comics data, still type new prices and still put those 2,000-plus covers at the page tops of each edition.

Overstreet: What does your position as Creative Director entail?
MH: I'm the custodian of the computer files that get updated and refreshed for each new edition. The look of the book is in my hands, from the cover logos and art placement, article design, Hall of Fame, market reports, Top 100/Top 10 lists, section headers, ad placement, and various tweaks. I also connect with the 150-plus advisors to get their market reports (on which I do the initial formatting and editing) and pricing data. I also create the promotional print ads appearing in *Previews*. Not everything that goes in the *Guide* fits perfectly, so I made the adjustments, so it looks seamless. At deadline time, I prepare the files for the printer and give every page the final proofing before the printing. Then I start the next one.

Overstreet: Start to finish how long does it take to put the *Guide* together?
MH: The easy answer is a full year minus a weekend. Usually the files for one *Guide* are finished and approved on a Friday, then the new files for the next one are started the next Monday. In the case of #50 with the 6-week delay due to the pandemic, I started on #51 as soon as new comics were released in May while finishing up #50 in mid-July.

Overstreet: When you're working on the *Guide*, which tasks do you enjoy most?
MH: The most satisfying is working on the covers, since those are the first things to be finalized, and a good cover can energize me for the work on the inside of the book. A close second is the arrival at the very last keystroke on the very last price change, on usually a Zorro title. I start with a Pete Townsend windmill arm gesture, maybe 4 rotations, then hit that key, and bask at the end of a process that has usually stretched out for 5-6 weeks.

Overstreet: What do you find most challenging about designing the book?
MH: There's a juggling act with the page map with late additions and subtractions, so I need to be ready to expand or contract a layout by a page or two at the last minute. I also try not to overuse any particular fonts, although I do use lots of Optima Bold.

Overstreet: How much creative freedom do you have when you are laying out the articles?
MH: If I can, I try to collaborate with the authors to see what they feel is essential to include art-wise, and then I send them the first draft and second and third if necessary. I'd hate for them to see their work for the first time in the finished book before they can add their input.

Overstreet: For the *Guide* covers, you've designed the Overstreet logo to match the style of the cover art for almost every version beginning with #40. Tell me about that process.
MH: The first step is looking at cover logos on the comics that are best known for the cover subject. In the case of Thor, Conan, Deadpool and Spawn, they each

have a cover logo in a specific font that I use to create the words "Comic Book" as the main part of the *Guide*'s title logo. Even if I don't have all the letters I need in the original logo, I can extrapolate from what I'm given. I used to do the same thing at a previous job in sportswear lettering where a customer might want the team name "Beer Sox" in the style of the Red Sox logo. I did some of that with a pen and ruler, but now the computer makes it quick and painless.

If there's no existing logo to mimic, then I scroll through my array of a hundred or so fonts until something clicks. It helps to let my mind wander and imagine that it's the day the finished books arrive and I'm peeking over my future self's shoulder to see what's in the box and what I ended up designing, then I poach that design from myself, like Bill and Ted going to the future to steal their historic song from their future selves. "How is it stealing, if we steal it from ourselves?"

Overstreet: What's your favorite cover so far?
MH: Catwoman by Adam Hughes on #42 is my favorite for many reasons. I wanted him to do a *Guide* cover, so I just walked up to him at his San Diego Comic-Con booth and asked and he said yes. That was almost too easy. DC's New 52 had just started and someone else was given the cover duties for the new Catwoman title, so I thought he'd welcome the opportunity to show DC what they were missing. I gave him a basic idea and told him to do whatever he wanted. The first glance I got months later took my breath away. I reacted like the father in *The Christmas Story* movie seeing the leg lamp award for the first time. Then I had to design the cover logo worthy of the artwork, and luckily, I remembered the Harrington font I used to design my cousin's wedding program. The letters were seductively curvy, some with little cat claw ends. When I saw Adam Hughes the following year at San Diego, his giant ceiling banner featured that

Overstreet artwork and he complimented me on my logo design. That was my favorite collaboration so far.

Overstreet: The *Guide*'s 50th anniversary has faced challenges due to the COVID-19 pandemic. How did it affect your work on the book?
MH: I worked from home starting in mid-March, but distractions were minimal. Due to the delay, I was able to finish the *Big, Big Overstreet* #50 first since there was no advertising to consider, and I also prepared the PDF version for Heritage Auctions early as well. It was also an opportunity for two additional proofing run throughs. It was an unusual feeling having many of the post-*Guide* projects already finished once I completed the main guide.

Overstreet: For the *Big, Big Overstreet* #50, you created an homage to *Overstreet* #1 with a cover featuring only publisher logos, so now you're a *Guide* cover artist. What's it like to be in such lofty company?
MH: I assumed fellow *Guide* cover artist Billy Tucci would have taught me the secret handshake by now. Seriously, it's a nice honor, but it would feel more legitimate if, like previous cover artists, I put pencil and ink on a blank sheet of paper and drew some superheroes. I did lots of comic-style drawing during my early collecting days (age 8-12) but I gravitated to other hobbies when I reached my teen years.

Overstreet: You have become an integral part of handing out the *Guide* to dealers each year at Comic-Con International: San Diego. What is that experience like for you?
MH: The preparation starts a week or two earlier, compiling lists of who will be there and where the booths are located. Lists and maps are printed. Then we worry about the books arriving at the convention center on time.

Finally, around 4 PM on Preview Night, "It's showtime!" as Beetlejuice would say. We usually start with Terry O'Neill and bring a book and a smile and a hearty handshake to 30-40 advisors over the next three hours. Like Santa's elves, we give each excited advisor a present they've been waiting a year to receive, and their joyous reactions are heartwarming.

Overstreet: What are the biggest changes that have happened to the *Guide* since you've been working on it?

MH: The day to day production of the *Guide* hasn't changed drastically since my start in 1997, but the method of getting the files to the printer has changed so much for the better in the last 10 years. I still remember the dread of deadline time in the early 2000s when the layout files and linked picture files and fonts needed to be burned onto many CDs, then matched with up-to-date printouts of all 1,200-plus pages, and boxed with customs forms for shipment to Canada and the UPS guy would be there for pick-up in 20 minutes and if the CD currently burning had a disk error, then you had to start again, and then a typo was found, and now it's 10 minutes to pick-up. There was me and two other people accessing the same layout files, and our fonts didn't always match so text would overflow the text boxes, or a picture wasn't cropped properly because we had different versions of the same image.

Now it's just me making single page PDFs to quickly upload to the printer's website. We get a 2 to 3-day breather for final edits, and I can easily substitute revised pages until I give them the go ahead to "Print it." The work still needs to be ready at deadline time, but the last-minute hazards and aggravations have been removed.

Overstreet: Outside of the main *Guide* what are some of your favorite Overstreet books that you worked on?

MH: Last year we did *The Overstreet Price*

Guide to Batman, and I felt like I really brought my A-game to the production. Whatever image was needed for the layout, I was able to find a perfect fit thanks to my lifetime's extensive Bat-memory. That's the one book where I think to myself, "That looks much better than I remember during the production time."

Overstreet: How has working on the *Guide* affected your perspective on comics and collecting?

MH: In my 23 years working on the *Guide*, I've had one of the best possible opportunities to learn more about the rich history of the comics, the characters and the creators. I enjoy mentioning on Facebook my recent collaborations with notable artists like Todd McFarlane, Amanda Conner, Kevin Eastman, Terry Moore, and, yes, even Rob Liefeld. This job also made possible my opportunity to sit in a 1966 Batmobile, with the door opened for me by the original designer George Barris.

My comic collecting is mostly confined to the current releases. My back-issue purchases are dollar-bin Archies when I visit a comic shop. My main collecting focus is on game-worn sports apparel with 1970s baseball jerseys as my passion. Regardless of my own collecting tendencies, I recognize what an invaluable resource the *Guide* has been and I put forth my best effort every year to maintain those impeccable Overstreet standards.

JOSEPH RYBANDT

First as a research editor, then in other positions, Joseph Rybandt worked on The Overstreet Comic Book Price Guide *and related publications during his tenure at Gemstone Publishing. Rybandt, who is now the Executive Editor at Dynamite Entertainment, reflected on his time at Gemstone, shared his experiences working on the* Guide *and* FAN, *how working in retail influenced his perspective, and his favorite contributions to the publication.*

Overstreet: Let's start with your job at Gemstone: What did you do?

Joseph Rybandt (JR): I was hired as a research editor, but became Price Guide editor and then a contributing editor as the magazine expanded. When I started, the magazine had not yet started, but the *Guide* was in active production, so everyone was working on that. I think Bob [Overstreet] wrangled everything back when it came to the *Guide*, whereas the monthly magazine took the full staff. Not that the *Guide* wasn't work, but clearly, Bob knew how to do it.

Overstreet: Did you read the *Guide* before you worked at Gemstone?

JR: Read and used. I worked in comics as a retailer in the Midwest before moving to the East Coast. So, I knew about, and used the *Guide*, on a regular basis… We always used Overstreet for pricing, even when the market had embraced speculator pricing mags like *Wizard* in the '90s.

Overstreet: What did you like about working on the *Guide*?

JR: The entirety of the experience at Gemstone is one thing to me, after all these years. So, I don't know that I can segment the *Guide* from the magazine, but being part of the history of it all, as well as working with Bob (and Carol) and the roots of organized fandom was really very special. The offices were amazing, we were right down the hall from the Gemstone Gallery and there was just an air of comics culture in every aspect. But it was a business, and that marriage was an important building block in my own professional development. Learning the mechanics of publishing was also something that stuck with me, even though those mechanics have changed a good deal. Some of the basics still remain (there will always be a deadline).

Overstreet: Putting the *Guide* together is a huge undertaking. What was your impression of being a part of that process?
JR: It wasn't just the *Guide*, but it was any of the "big" books because they were that: *big* books. Just a massive amount of coordination and attention to detail. It still ran smooth though, from what I recall (I never spent the night in the office, though I'm sure there were those that did).

Overstreet: What was the difference in how things were being priced for the *Guide* vs *Overstreet's FAN*?
JR: *FAN* was more focused on the newer books with a sampling of "classic" pricing from the *Guide*, though the two did work in tandem. Pricing the flavor of the week was tricky, but I relied on a retail network that was well established and that was key. Having come from retail myself, I knew how the stores and consumers thought and reacted (most of the time), so it was a lot of common sense stuff... The movement on the bigger books was a much more involved affair. Lots of cooks in the kitchen because there had to be as that market at the time was *big* business and has only grown *bigger*.

Overstreet: What are your favorite contributions to the *Guide* and *FAN*?
JR: I don't know that I had any articles in the *Guide*, though there may have been some things from *FAN* that made it

in, but my writing contributions to *FAN* involved interviewing creators like Alan Moore, Grant Morrison. Neil Gaiman, James Robinson, and so many more that would go on to define the current and future generations of storytellers. And that list of creators – along with populists like Jeph Loeb at the time, were where my head was at in terms of the medium. We really tried hard to push people towards the good stuff. What we thought was the good stuff... and in competition to *Wizard*, I think we succeeded, though they certainly were a larger footprint on pop culture of the time.

Overstreet: Has your perspective on the comic collecting hobby been influenced by working on the *Guide*?
JR: Yes, but not in any way that I put to use. More an understanding and appreciation of those that make up collecting, rather than honing collecting myself. I'm a bad collector in the sense that I drop in and out. I also rarely ever used collecting as a way of making money, though there was some speculation when I was working retail. I just bought what I liked and understood it had a value at that moment, that might stay, deflate or inflate given any number of factors.

Overstreet: How did your time at Gemstone affect you in terms of the subsequent chapters in your career (if it did)?
JR: Without Gemstone I wouldn't be here now, that's for sure. I've told Steve as much and also told him that it was the professional air that ran throughout Diamond that stayed with me as well. It was all a real business and it was my first "real" business work. But, when the magazine folded, it was people I knew in the industry that recommended me to my next employer and that kept me in the space and it's been a trip and fall up the ladder of various pop culture enterprises ever since.

MARK L. HAYNES

In his positions at Gemstone Publishing and Diamond Comic Distributors, Mark Haynes contributed to The Overstreet Comic Book Price Guide *and* FAN *through technological advancements and design. Looking back on his time at Gemstone, Haynes talked about the link between visual art and business appeal, what he liked about working on* FAN *and the* Guide, *working for Diamond Comic Distributors to design company websites and create online tools, doing layouts and designs for Gemstone later as a freelancer, and the career hats he's worn since working with Gemstone and Diamond.*

Overstreet: How did you get your start at Gemstone Publishing?
Mark Haynes (MH): In the mid-1990s, I was working for a company called Towson Computer. They were a Mac dealer at the time (this was before the days of getting a Mac at Best Buy or the Apple Store) and I was one of their installation and support technicians. Although I had graduated with a degree in marketing and advertising and was looking for a job as a graphic designer, I worked at Towson Computer because it allowed me to get a sense of all of the graphic design shops running around town (including a pre-Steve Geppi *Baltimore Magazine*) and see which one would be a good fit. Also, I figured I'd have an edge over other candidates if I could fix the equipment I'd be using.

I landed at Gemstone after the order came in for an office's worth of Mac equipment and since my boss at Towson knew I was

into comics I got the gig to install the equipment. It was going to take several days so I staged the equipment in the conference room at Gemstone and, since she was my contact, struck up a conversation with Carol Overstreet. She'd just relocated to Baltimore along with Bob and some of his other staff from Tennessee to Maryland and was in the process of setting up the office. Ultimately, our conversation that took place over me elbow-deep in the computers became an interview and she made me an offer.

Overstreet: What was your position?
MH: I was the Assistant Art Director.

Overstreet: What did you enjoy about being a designer for Overstreet's *FAN*?
MH: The most enjoyable thing is the friends that I've made – for life it seems. Really, no matter what I do or say to try and dissuade them, they insist on keeping in touch. Ha!

Seriously, though, it's hard to pick out any single thing. Top of mind is that it was where I first started getting a sense of the business aspects that drive and support creative projects and how the two are intertwined. Even as a creative person designing page layouts, covers, and other graphics in that setting, you always had to keep in mind that you were solving a business question. I still find that fascinating in my current endeavors.

Overstreet: Are there issues of *FAN* or the *Guide* that stand out as your favorites?
MH: *Overstreet's FAN* #1 with the Superman vs. Alien cover. Although I thought it was strange that a 225-page full color magazine only had seven paid ads in it, it is the issue where I met one of my very best friends in the world, J.C. Vaughn, who was a freelancer at the time. I knew we'd be friends since we were both in our 20s at the time, but we liked what are now known as "dad jokes." For example, one of his favorites is, "Two nuns walk into a bar. You think the second one would've ducked." Anyway, I knew we'd become best friends when we realized that making people groan when they hear them was even more enjoyable than the joke itself. Ha!

Beyond that, I was very proud of the indie comic creator coverage *Fan* was able to provide. In the pre-internet, pre-social media days of the 1990s, there are creators today that got surfaced in our pages that they honestly wouldn't have gotten from our competition without a big outlay of ad dollars. I don't want to say that some creators today who can look back on a 20-plus year career owe that to anything other than their amazing talents – but in some cases *FAN* was the first place they got wide coverage.

Overstreet: As a part of Gemstone, what were your thoughts on *The Overstreet Comic Book Price Guide*?
MH: Not only is it a valuable reference, it's essential for home defense since it's so huge. Ha!

From a production standpoint, I always remember how we'd shift work around to accommodate it in the schedule and in some cases ended up working around the clock to get everything done (which I didn't mind since that meant the company would pick up dinner). Tony Overstreet, Art Director and my boss at the time, shouldered most of the load while I and the rest of the production team, including the amazing Jeff Dillon, switched back and forth between "the book," as we called it, and the magazine.

From a collecting standpoint, it was cool to get to know some of the Overstreet advisors as well as look at the *Guide* as one of the definitive historical records of our hobby. The biggest bonus, of course, was being able to walk down the hall to Diamond International Galleries and see the actual comics – first appearances of characters, the first work from people who would become giants of the medium – being documented in *The Overstreet Comic Book Price Guide*. Of course, some of them you could only see through glass, but it was still cool.

Overstreet: After Gemstone, you took a position with Diamond Comic Distributors. What did you do there?
MH: I joined the Information Technology team at Diamond. I remember clearly the job being described to me by Bill Larduskey, head of the department, as being "50% Mac support and 50% building a website." I also remember clearly this being around 1996 and responding "That sounds great. What the hell is a website?"

From that humble beginning, as they say, I helped Diamond and its sister companies build up their online presence and grew the "Web team" to include programmers, designers, and content creators. By far, though, our biggest priority was supporting the retailers who make our hobby possible. As such, we worked very closely alongside the customer service team to come up with new – at the time – online tools that would make their jobs easier.

Beyond that, supporting Diamond's marketing and communications team with new tools to promote our hobby to the end customer was also very high on our list. Diamond is unique as distribution companies go as it is one of the few that takes on the responsibility of helping drive customers to their local comic shop. To support that, I was part of the team that developed the original online version of the Comic Shop Locator Service. Now, in the age of Google Maps and "Siri, tell me where the nearest comic shop is," it doesn't seem like that big of a deal but in the early 2000s, it was pretty cool.

One of the last things I had the opportunity to participate in was bringing Hake's Auctions to the world of modern, online auctions, while still preserving their unique approach to auction closing, with timers on specific items. The majority of the work was done by one of the best programmers I've ever had the pleasure to work with, Sam Kirchmeier, and I'm happy to see it's still supporting Hake's to this day.

Overstreet: What did you do after Diamond and before your present job?
MH: After Diamond, I moved to Los Angeles to pursue screenwriting and worked for writer-producer-director Marc Scott Zicree (known for his book *The Twilight Zone Companion* as well as TV shows like *Sliders, Star Trek: The Next Generation, Star Trek: Deep Space Nine*, and many, many more).

From there, I worked for a non-profit, overseeing an information technology transformation project and then, through 2018, I worked for the home office of Zurich Insurance, Ltd, managing the global rollout of a new intranet to its – at the time – 60,000-plus employees around the world. That was a great job and gave me a renewed appreciation for international business and how it drives just about everything.

Overstreet: Even after you left, you contributed layouts and designs for Gemstone's *Guide to Collecting* line and *Comic Book Marketplace Yearbook*. How did that compare to earlier projects?
MH: Well, as a freelancer, I could do most of the work in my pajamas, which was very cool and very different than being on staff at Gemstone where we still had to wear ties when I was there. The main difference, though, would have to be having more control over the consistency of the book's appearance. Unlike *FAN*, which had widely varying layouts throughout, with varying success, these later book projects, I felt, should showcase what they were talking about rather than the flashiness of any presentation I could come up with. They often featured retrospectives of great artists and creators of the hobby, so I thought why not let their work speak for itself? As a result, I lean toward huge images or zooming in on cool details that support the accompanying text. The reader, of course, is the final judge, but I like the layouts I was able to contribute.

Overstreet: How have your experiences at Gemstone affected your career since then?
MH: As mentioned above, the realization that any creative endeavor in a commercial space is inextricably linked to the business side of the same venture. That's not to say the art should be governed by business considerations, but it, and the artist creating it, should be informed by them.

Additionally, it taught me to question everything, not in a challenging way but in a way that the person being asked, who was usually higher on the organizational chart than me, knew I was asking because I wanted to support what they were trying to do. Over time, this evolved into a standard approach on any project that most people know as reverse engineering. Basically, tell me what you'd like to achieve or where you'd like to be at the end of this – whatever 'this' is – and let's figure out how to get there. If the other party is cool with that, it usually ends up being more fulfilling for both of us.

Overstreet: What are you doing now?

MH: I've recently secured funding and have opened a production company here in Los Angeles to develop film, television, podcasts, and other entertainment products. We've already got one pilot nearly ready to go with Roddenberry Entertainment (yes, *that* Roddenberry) and a second one with interest from a new film production studio coming online in the next month that has first-look arrangements with the major streamers like Amazon, Netflix, and Hulu. Plus, we have several fiction podcasts and other ideas in the works, as well.

LINDSAY (DUNN) WALLACE

Lindsay Dunn (now Lindsay Wallace) joined the Gemstone Publishing staff as an editor for The Overstreet Comic Book Price Guide *and the e-newsletter,* Scoop. *In that capacity, she did copious amounts of research each week. Wallace shared what she liked about working on the* Guide *and how it influenced her perspective on comics and collecting.*

Overstreet: What did you do for the *Guide*?
Lindsay (Dunn) Wallace (LW): I helped research comic book history – I fact-checked by studying the past, as well as assisted with editing and writing articles. I also remember a lot of roundtable brainstorming.

Overstreet: Why did you want to work for Gemstone Publishing?
LW: Gemstone was hiring at a time when not many companies were. It was 2007 and right smack in the middle of the recession. Once I met with J.C. Vaughn and he and I began to discuss our love for writing and antique collecting, I knew

I would love nothing more than to dive further down the comic collecting rabbit hole. It was all so interesting!

Overstreet: What did you like about working on the *Guide*?

LW: I loved researching and learning. I thought I knew a bit about comics...but I quickly found I had no idea. I loved that my job was to become completely immersed in the pop culture phenomenon of comics. I greatly enjoyed reading everything I could about them. How they started, what they meant to kids – especially during the Golden era of comic books. I loved visiting Geppi's Entertainment Museum and feeling absolutely awestruck by its collection. It was truly the most enjoyable job I have ever had the pleasure of investing my time in.

Overstreet: What did you find most challenging?

LW: I suppose just getting the book to the printer on time was a bit of a challenge. I remember working on the book late one night the evening before we had to ship it to the printer. I remember running it into the post office for delivery moments before they closed. We were sweating we wouldn't make it on time! It was very close, but we got there and had it overnighted. I felt very superhero myself that day.

SCOTT BRADEN

Scott Braden was a comics enthusiast before working at Gemstone Publishing and maintains that perspective now as an Overstreet Advisor. While working at Gemstone, Braden studied pricing trends and comic history, which he presented in the Guide *and in* Overstreet's FAN. *Remembering his time at Gemstone, Braden talked about the* Guide's *significance, his experience working with Robert Overstreet, and his appreciation for comics.*

Overstreet: What was your position at Gemstone and what did it entail?

Scott Braden (SB): I was the company's research editor. My job had me do everything from researching comic book information to collecting pricing info from retailers to writing articles for both the *Guide* and our monthly magazine, *Overstreet's FAN.* I also traveled and assisted Bob when he would venture out and photograph arrowheads for his bestselling *Arrowhead Guide.*

Overstreet: Did you read the *Guide* before you worked at Gemstone?

Overstreet: How did you feel about coming into a mostly male-dominated industry? Did it impact your job?

LW: I worked with a group of great guys. I never once felt out of place. I think the group of amazing women who were hired and worked in our little office building were all treated with the utmost professionalism.

Overstreet: How did working on the *Guide* shape or change your perspective on comics?

LW: My career has not followed an editorial path after Gemstone, but I still absolutely use the knowledge I acquired during my time there. I have a vast knowledge of comics and collectibles and they always come in handy in my current profession because it allows me to connect on a personal level with a very wide audience. Everyone loves comics. It's been a great ice breaker on so many occasions. I am always asked about my career history and having the pleasure to humble brag that I was an editor for *The Overstreet Comic Book Price Guide* always makes me vastly more interesting person to talk to...and it's always fun discovering another comic geek in the room to nerd out with. There's always at least one.

SB: Absolutely. The *Guide* is required reading for every true comic book fan. Period.

Overstreet: What was your experience working with Bob?

SB: Bob was both a mentor and a father figure to me. When we traveled together, we would talk comics, as well as about comic book movers and shakers he met in the early days – like Stan Lee and Jack Kirby and C.C. Beck and William M. Gaines – and retailers from all over the country. He is a font of information and working with him was a true education. In fact, let's face it, Bob has forgotten more about comics and collectibles than I will ever know. He's that knowledgeable.

Overstreet: What appealed to you about working on the *Guide*?

SB: Steve Geppi created a wonderful environment where we could learn about and truly love comics and premium collectibles. I mean, let's face it – our job was to talk about, promote, and read comics. You can't beat that!

Overstreet: How did your interest in comics history shape your approach to working on the *Guide*?

SB: Although I understood the importance of the pricing information for the *Guide*, I was always driven towards the comic book info itself. The *Guide* offers collectors from all different backgrounds the most complete history of the four-color medium in existence. Not only did I know that going into my job, I truly appreciated that fact after working for Gemstone.

Overstreet: What do you consider your best contributions to it?

SB: While working at Gemstone, I considered myself the "enthusiastic" one. Every day, there was a palpable sense of wonder in what we were doing – and I had no problem sharing that with the team.

Overstreet: Did it change your perspective on the comic collecting hobby?

SB: Working for Gemstone only expanded my love for the art form. And things I learned as Gemstone's research editor have only colored what I do as an Overstreet advisor today.

THE OVERSTREET
HALL OF FAME

The Overstreet Hall of Fame was conceived in 2006
to single out individuals who have made great contributions
to the comic book arts.

This includes writers, artists, editors, publishers and others
who have plied their craft in insightful and meaningful ways.

While such evaluations are inherently subjective, they also
serve to aid in reflecting upon those who shaped the
experience of reading comic books over the years.

NEAL ADAMS

Neal Adams is one of the greatest artists our medium has ever known. He is also the single most influential artist in the history of comic book publishing. An amazing number of artists, including many whose styles are nothing like Neal's, many you'd never guess, started out trying to emulate Neal. He has personally trained a small army of artists. Not only a master of the visual, Neal writes as well, and also does, it seems, whatever else he wishes to with ease and grace. His brilliance extends beyond the printed page. He works with light, motion and sound. He creates three-dimensionally. Any medium is his medium. And, everything he does, he does with rare excellence. He brings insight to any endeavor. Most importantly, he truly creates. New ideas. Original thoughts. Genesis! Beyond that, he has always been a force in the industry -- a righter of wrongs, a bringer of change, a leader. Neal is a genius and a giant who has lifted up us all.

– Jim Shooter

**ALL-NEW COLLECTORS'
EDITION C-56**
1978. © DC

MURPHY ANDERSON

Born July 9, 1926 in Asheville, North Carolina, Murphy Anderson began his life-long career in comic books in 1944 working at Fiction House, where he pencilled and inked for several years. Beginning in the Golden Age, he worked steadily for a number of companies in the industry, including Ziff-Davis, and DC Comics (where he would become a mainstay with work spanning five decades).

He worked also on newspaper strips, notably including taking over the reins of the *Buck Rogers* strip from creator Dick Calkins, and he also produced the military's *P.S. Magazine* (following Will Eisner and preceding Joe Kubert, both also Overstreet Hall of Fame members).

Anderson helped to propel the Silver Age of DC Comics with work on such characters as Adam Strange, The Atom, Flash, Green Lantern, Hawkman, and many others, including his inks over artists Curt Swan and Carmine Infantino.

Widely regarded as a gentleman of the old school, Murphy Anderson was a member of the first class inducted into The Overstreet Hall of Fame in 2006.

BRAVE AND THE BOLD #61
August-September 1965. © DC

JIM APARO

Jim Aparo was considered to be "the definitive Batman artist" by a generation of comic readers, but he also left his mark on numerous other characters. In a career spanning 1966 to early 2000s, he created memorable portrayals of Aquaman, The Spectre, The Phantom Stranger, Green Arrow, The Outsiders and the guest stars of *The Brave and the Bold*.

His comics career started in 1966 at Charlton Comics working on "Miss Bikini Luv" in *Go-Go Comics*. Brought to DC Comics by editor Dick Giordano, Aparo began work on *Aquaman* and *The Phantom Stranger* before landing the regular assignment on *The Brave and the Bold* starting with #100 and lasting until the title's end with #200. During that time, he also contributed art for the Spectre in *Adventure Comics* and short mystery stories. His Batman work in the late 1980s included the story that killed off the second Robin, Jason Todd. He continued to work until his retirement in the early 2000s.

– Mark Huesman

BRAVE AND THE BOLD #111
February-March 1974. © DC

SERGIO ARAGONÉS

Who knew that all those gutters could be so funny? Sergio Aragonés never let panel borders get in the way of telling quick and delightful comic stories, and his margin cartoons ("marginals") in the pages of *MAD Magazine* not only raised doodling to a high art but packed the periodical with laughs in every conceivable corner. Thanks to the marginals and his "A Mad Look At..." features, Aragonés – often called "The World's Fastest Cartoonist" – has been a beloved fixture of the magazine since 1963. In 1982 he also introduced us to Groo, a lovable and seriously inept barbarian that has an insatiable love of cheese dip and an unerring knack for getting into, or causing, trouble. In all of his work, Aragonés' melodic, hyper-detailed style is instantly recognizable (as is his trademark moustache), and his joy in sharing humor with the world is evident in every line.

– Dr. Arnold T. Blumberg

SERGIO ARAGONÉS
GROO THE WANDERER #60
December 1989.
© Sergio Aragonés

MATT BAKER

One of America's first major African American cartoonists, Matt Baker (1921-1959) is best known for his "good girl" comics and his romance comic work. He is considered by many to be a master in drawing the female form. He clearly adored women and enjoyed drawing them and all their beauty.

Not just a pin-up artist, his attention to detail and his ability to use the background details to help set a scene was something very few of his peers were doing at the time. Educated at Cooper Union in New York City, he got his start with Iger Studios in the mid-1940s, providing art for St. John, Fox, Fiction House, Quality and Atlas. His work included the genres of Westerns, Romance, and Jungle Adventure, but he is mostly remembered for his work on the *Phantom Lady* series. So provocative for the day, one of his *Phantom Lady* covers was used in Fredrick Wertham's book on the ill effects of comic books on America's youth, *Seduction of the Innocent*.

– Amanda Sheriff

PHANTOM LADY #17
April 1948. © FOX

CARL BARKS

Originally known to fans only as "The Good Duck Artist," in 1935, Carl Barks went to work for the Disney Studios and storyboarded cartoons such as *Donald's Nephews* and *Donald's Cousin Gus*. In 1942, Western Publishing asked him to work on the comic story "Donald Duck Finds Pirate Gold," and then to rewrite and draw a 10-page Donald story for *Walt Disney's Comics and Stories #31*. Soon, he became a regular contributor, lasting 25 years in the position, until his retirement in 1967. After retiring, though, Barks kept active. In 1971 he obtained permission from Disney to produce and sell oil paintings based on the Duck characters. In 1976 Disney withdrew permission, but in 1982 Another Rainbow Publishing, which had just secured a license from Disney to produce lithographs of Barks' paintings, commissioned him to paint two new oils per year. In 1995, Barks finally retired for real. He died on August 25, 2000, just shy of 100 years old.

FOUR COLOR COMICS #386
First Uncle Scrooge issue.
March 1952. © DIS

C.C. BECK

Cartoonist and comic book artist Charles Clarence "C.C." Beck is celebrated for his work on Captain Marvel at Fawcett and DC. His style captured the youthful essence of comics with slightly exaggerated cartoony flair. He joined Fawcett Publications in 1933 as a staff artist, creating pulp magazines. Then he was tapped to draw Captain Marvel, Spy Smasher, and Ibis the Invincible in *Whiz Comics* and other titles. Beck defined the look of Captain Marvel, so his role expanded to overseeing the art of the character in various comics and he opened his own New York City comics studio in 1941. The studio provided art for the Marvel Family titles with Beck acting as chief artist, but when Fawcett folded their comics line, he left the industry. Beck returned to comics in the mid-1960s with a three-issue run of his creation, *Fatman the Human Flying Saucer*. In 1973, he was the initial artist on *Shazam!*, the Captain Marvel revival, but left after creative differences. In his later years he painted cover recreations of Golden Age comics and served as the editor for *Fawcett Collectors of America* in the early '80s.

– *Amanda Sheriff*

SHAZAM! #3
June 1973. © DC

JOHN BUSCEMA

Inspired by the work of Hal Foster, Alex Raymond, and Burne Hogarth, John Buscema began his career at Marvel Comics in 1948, when it was still Timely Comics. He stayed on staff there for a year and a half, afterward freelancing for a number of companies. After leaving the comics field to go into advertising in 1958, Buscema returned to comics — and Marvel in particular — in 1966, when his old boss Stan Lee brought him back to the "House of Ideas." His Silver Age output could be seen within the pages of *Avengers, Conan the Barbarian, Fantastic Four, Nick Fury: Agent of S.H.I.E.L.D.*, and *Silver Surfer*, among others. He also co-wrote *How to Draw Comics the Marvel Way* with Stan Lee. His final published comics work was DC Comics' *Just Imagine Stan Lee with John Buscema Creating Superman*. His is a talent that is greatly missed, but lives on in myriad four-color tales.

– *Scott Braden*

AVENGERS #58
November 1968. © MAR

SAL BUSCEMA

With a track record that included virtually all of their top tier characters throughout the 1970s and '80s, Sal Buscema was a staple of the Marvel Comics bullpen. A skilled pencil and ink artist, Sal was known initially for his collaborations with his brother, John, but soon found his own artistic voice. Among his extensive credits are runs on *The Avengers, Fantastic Four, Thor, Daredevil, New Mutants, Ms. Marvel, Howard the Duck, Master of Kung Fu*, and the three major Spider-Man series – *Amazing Spider-Man, Spectacular Spider-Man*, and *Web of Spider-Man*. He also penciled definitive moments of *Captain America* and *The Defenders*, as well as a 10-year run on *The Incredible Hulk*. While he worked solely for Marvel for nearly 30 years, Buscema later provided work on such DC titles as *Birds of Prey: Manhunt, Shadow of the Bat, Detective Comics, DC: Retroactive –The Flash, Superman Beyond*, IDW's *Rom, G.I. Joe Annual* and *Dungeons and Dragons: Forgotten Realms*, and for others.

– *Braelynn Bowersox*

AVENGERS #71
December 1969. © MAR

HOWARD CHAYKIN

INDUCTED IN 2018

From his first published work in DC Comics' mystery, war and romance titles, Howard Chaykin hit the ground running and has never let up. Almost out of the gate he was creating his own characters, from Ironwolf to Dominic Fortune to Cody Starbuck. But he's also worked on a *Who's Who* of Marvel and DC characters: Batman, Wolverine, Punisher, Nick Fury, Challengers of the Unknown, Blade, Black Canary, Hawkgirl, Rawhide Kid and a revamp of The Shadow that set a high bar for modernizing a dusty pulp character. He's also worked for a variety of publishers, Atlas-Seaboard, Vortex, Bravura, Image, Vertigo, Wildstorm, BOOM! and others. He even spent some time in the Star Wars universe, adapting the original movie. He took side trips to places like *Heavy Metal*, original graphic novels like the acclaimed *Time²*, and television work on shows like *The Flash*, *Viper* and *Mutant X*, but he always returned to comics. Howard's influence is widely felt across modern comics, and techniques he pioneered in his own ground-breaking *American Flagg!* (many in conjunction with letterer Ken Bruzenak) and other titles have been copied and adapted by others in the medium in the years since.

– *Tom Mason*

AMERICAN FLAGG! #1
October 1983. © First Comics &
Howard Chaykin

MARK CHIARELLO

INDUCTED IN 2013

From illustrating the 1993 National Cartoonists Society Award for Best Comic Book for *Batman/Houdini: The Devil's Workshop* to editing *Wednesday Comics*, *Solo*, *Batman: Black & White* and *Before Watchmen*, to co-writing *The DC Comics Guide to Coloring and Lettering Comics* and *Heroes of the Negro Leagues*, and to his *Star Wars* work, Mark Chiarello's creativity, innovative sense of design, and bold execution has helped establish him among the highest regarded artists in and out of the comic book business. A prolific designer, as an editor he has frequently demonstrated an impressive ability to match other artists with the right projects. Among his diverse comic book work readers can find his cover art on *Wolverine*, *The Many Armors of Iron Man*, *Animal Man*, *Ray Bradbury Comics*, *Vigilante: City Lights*, *Prairie Justice*, *Terminal City* and *Terminal City: Aerial Graffiti*. He also illustrated the cover to *The Overstreet Comic Book Price Guide #40*.

WEDNESDAY COMICS HC
2010. © DC

CHRIS CLAREMONT

INDUCTED IN 2009

Chris Claremont has written many wonderful things. He's passionate about everything he writes. Especially notable, of course, is his work on the X-Men. Chris gets a good deal of credit for the success of the X-Men, but not nearly as much as he deserves. Not only did he do an outstanding job as writer, he built the team that built the team. He recruited artists when needed. He made sure the lettering and coloring were consistent and top drawer. He spent time, effort and money out of his own pocket to insure the quality of the book. He sweated the details. He fought like a Wolverine to defend the integrity of his vision, his work, his words.

If there's a Hall of Fame for Caring, Trying and Outworking Everyone, he should be there, too.

Babe Ruth didn't create the Yankees and Chris Claremont didn't create the X-Men, but each of them built the house.

– *Jim Shooter*

X-MEN #100
August 1976. © MAR

DAVE COCKRUM

INDUCTED IN 2007

Dave Cockrum began his career in comics as an assistant to artist Murphy Anderson (another Overstreet Hall of Fame member), who was at the time responsible for various DC titles starring Superman and Superboy. This included *Superboy*, which featured back-up stories of The Legion of Super-Heroes, which Cockrum took over and redefined with his style and sequential storytelling.

Marvel's *Giant-Size X-Men* #1 hit the stands with the debut of the new team of X-Men, including Cockrum's co-creations, Storm, Nightcrawler and Colossus. Since then, it has become one of the most sought after comics of the Bronze Age. Working initially with writer Len Wein and then Chris Claremont, he helped relaunch the regular title, *Uncanny X-Men*, with issue #94. He continued on the series through issue #107, working with writer Chris Claremont, and then returned for another run (#145-163). After his second stint with the X-Men, Cockrum produced *Marvel Graphic Novel #9: The Futurians*. It became a short-lived series for Lodestone and was published as a collection by Eternity.

Cockrum passed away in 2006.

X-MEN #94
August 1975. © MAR

DARWYN COOKE

INDUCTED IN 2016

Known for his clean line work, superb composition, and strong storytelling, Darwyn Cooke's first published comic book artwork appeared in *New Talent Showcase* #19, but he ended up working in magazines, product design, and animation (*Batman: The Animated Series*, *Superman: The Animated Series*, and *Men in Black: The Series*) before landing in comics again with *Batman: Ego*. Cooke teamed with writer Ed Brubaker to revamp Catwoman in 2000 in *Detective Comics* #759–762 and spinning off *Catwoman* in 2001. He wrote and drew *Selina's Big Score*, a prequel graphic novel, in 2002, then went on to *DC: The New Frontier* (2004), *Solo* #5 (June 2005, which won an Eisner Award for "Best Single Issue"), *Batman/The Spirit* (2006), The Spirit (2006), *Superman Confidential*, *Richard Stark's Parker: The Hunter* (July 2009), *The Outfit* (October 2010), *The Score* (July 2012), and *Slayground* (December 2013). He wrote and illustrated *Before Watchmen: Minutemen* and co-wrote *Before Watchmen: Silk Spectre* (2012–2013). His animated short for Batman Beyond was released in April 2014 to celebrate Batman's 75th anniversary.

DC: THE NEW FRONTIER
VOLUME ONE
TPB. 2004. © DC

PALMER COX

INDUCTED IN 2009

Palmer Cox (April 28, 1840 – July 24, 1924) was a Canadian-born cartoonist whose best known work revolutionized the world of comic characters and comic character merchandise. As the creator of The Brownies, Cox can be credited with the first successful recurring characters, the first internationally successful characters, and with developing a principled road map for producing character-themed merchandise for children. Appearing in serialized form in *St. Nicholas* magazine, the fairy- or pixie-like characters had special powers, appeared only to the virtuous, and were collected for the first time in *The Brownies, Their Book* (1887). The Kodak Brownie camera featured the characters on its box, and items ranging from sheet music to candle holders were offered, creating a road map followed regionally by The Yellow Kid and internationally by Mickey Mouse and Superman.

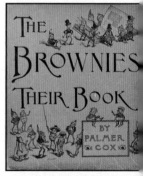

THE BROWNIES THEIR BOOK
Hardcover book. 1887.
© The Century Co.

JACK DAVIS

The general public might recognize his style from his covers for *TV Guide* and *Time* or his movie poster and promotional work for such films as *It's a Mad, Mad, Mad, Mad World*, *Viva Max!* and *Kelly's Heroes*, but comic book fans have long known the distinctive art of Jack Davis in a variety of genres. At EC Comics, his horror stories included appearances in *Tales from the Crypt*, *The Haunt of Fear*, *The Vault of Horror*, *Crime SuspenStories*, and *Shock SuspenStories* and later the "Picto-Fiction" series *Terror Illustrated*. His action-adventure work appeared in *Frontline Combat*, *Two-Fisted Tales* and *Piracy*, and his material was also seen in *Incredible Science-Fiction*. As much as he won fans for all of his work (including Westerns for Atlas such as *Rawhide Kid*), though, it was in humor where he defined himself. His work appeared in almost all the early issues of *MAD* (and many later ones, too), all 12 issues of *Panic*, as well as *Trump*, *Humbug*, *Help!* and even *Cracked*.

TWO-FISTED TALES #30
November-December 1952.
© WMG

DAN DECARLO

Born on December 12, 1919, Dan DeCarlo established the visual house style of Archie comics for the modern age. DeCarlo created Sabrina the Teenage Witch, Cheryl Blossom, and Josie and the Pussycats (he named Josie after his wife) for the company in addition to his work on the various other Archie titles.

He broke into the four-color medium working for Timely Comics in 1947, drawing such classic titles as *Millie the Model*. He also freelanced for *The Saturday Evening Post*, *Argosy*, and the Humorama line of pin-up cartoon digests. He won the National Cartoonists Society Award for Best Comic Book in 2000 for *Betty & Veronica*.

The prolific artist has also been cited to be a strong artistic influence on *Love & Rockets* creators Jaime and Gilbert Hernandez, among others, and his work can be seen in a new line of "best of" hardcovers from Archie and IDW Publishing.

– *Scott Braden*

ARCHIE: THE BEST OF DAN DECARLO VOL. 1
May 2010. © AP

MIKE DEODATO, JR.

Watching his father draw and write comic books in his spare time inspired the young Mike Deodato's interest. Growing up in Brazil, he has said that Portuguese-language Uncle Scrooge comics were likely his first exposure to American comics, and that Superman and Spider-Man were his first American super-heroes. His father also introduced him to the work of such masters as Will Eisner, Hal Foster, Alex Raymond and Burne Hogarth, and while his style is an action-filled blend of photo-realistic and more illustrative elements, those influences can be detected. After a strong roster of Brazilian comics in the 1980s, 1990 brought his first American assignment, *Santa Claws*. It led to *Beauty and the Beast* for Innovation Publishing, and then *Lost in Space*, *Quantum Leap* and *Mac Bolan: The Executioner*. They were followed by work on titles such as *Megalith*, *Miracleman: Triumphant*, and *Turok*. After attention-getting stints on *Wonder Woman* and *Thor*, he illustrated *Incredible Hulk*, *Batman*, *Amazing Spider-Man*, *Dark Avengers*, *New Avengers*, *Secret Avengers*, *Thunderbolts*, and other titles.

NEW AVENGERS (2ND SERIES) #20
March 2012. © MAR

STEVE DITKO

No artist other than Jack Kirby had as much influence on the formative years of the Marvel Comics universe as Steve Ditko. Although he was not as prolific as Kirby, the style, substance and mood of his artwork defined Spider-Man, Doctor Strange and numerous other characters for the publisher. His work debuted in *Black Magic* Vol. 4 #3 and *Captain 3-D* #1 at about the same time in 1953. He worked for Marvel predecessor Atlas on horror, monster and science fiction stories. *Tales of Suspense*, *Journey Into Mystery*, *Amazing Adventures*, and *Tales to Astonish*, all featured his work at Marvel, but it was *Amazing Fantasy* #15 and his subsequent 38-issue run on *Amazing Spider-Man* and his Doctor Strange stories in *Strange Tales* that made him a fan favorite. At Charlton, he worked on Captain Atom, Blue Beetle, The Question, and other characters, and at DC he created Shade The Changing Man, among other works.

AMAZING SPIDER-MAN ANNUAL #2
1965. © MAR

KEVIN EASTMAN

Kevin Eastman co-created a pop culture giant in the *Teenage Mutant Ninja Turtles*. In 1984, he and Peter Laird self-published their first issue of *TMNT* through their newly-formed Mirage Studios. Despite a print run of only 3,000 for the first printing of #1, the Turtles' popularity flourished. Soon *TMNT* became ubiquitous when the pair licensed them for products, a long-running animated TV show, feature films, video games, movies, and an Archie comic series in addition to their own publication. Eastman founded the short-lived Tundra Publishing, which notably published the first appearance of Mike Allred's *Madman* among other projects. He purchased sci-fi/fantasy magazine *Heavy Metal* in 1992, continuing the publication's long history of serializing European comics in the U.S. market. He sold the magazine in 2014. Laird eventually bought Eastman's share of *TMNT* and then later sold the property to Viacom in 2009. Eastman returned to *Teenage Mutant Ninja Turtles* as a frequent writer and cover artist at IDW Publishing.

– Amanda Sheriff

TEENAGE MUTANT NINJA TURTLES #1
1984.
© Mirage Studios

WILL EISNER

Considered by many to be the father of the American graphic novel, Will Eisner was a writer, artist, master storyteller, and businessman. In a career that spanned eight decades, he created The Spirit, John Law, Lady Luck, Uncle Sam, Blackhawk and numerous other characters.

He co-founded the Eisner – Iger Studios, then created *The Spirit* sections which were issued weekly in newspapers across America, and developed and packaged *P.S. Magazine* for the U.S. Army.

His book *A Contract With God* is widely regarded as the first American graphic novel (it wasn't, but it was an early and significant work in the format), and he continued to produce numerous other important works well into his 80s with the quality for which he was known. His innovative panel design and artistic choices seemed always to be in service to the story, rather than simply demonstrating his impressive skills. At one Harvey Awards ceremony at the Pittsburgh Comicon, he received honors for works produced 60 years apart (*The Spirit* and *Last Day in Vietnam*).

Eisner passed away in 2005 following heart surgery, but he left an almost immeasurable legacy.

THE SPIRIT NEWSPAPER SECTION
August 25, 1940.
© Will Eisner Studios

GEORGE EVANS

INDUCTED IN 2014

George Evans was a superb realistic illustrator in comic books and comic strips with a fascination for aviation art. He began in comics in the mid-1940s. Working first at Fiction House on *Planet Comics,* and *Wings Comics*, and aviation pulp illustrations, he next worked at Fawcett. After that, he moved to EC, and then did work for *Classics Illustrated*. He did the Space Conquerors! strip in *Boys' Life* for several years in the '50s. During the early '60s, Evans contributed to Dell/ Western/Gold Key, drawing *Tales of Terror, The Twilight Zone*, and *Frogmen*. He also ghosted pencils on the *Terry and the Pirates* comic strip from 1960 to 1973.

During the '60s Evans contributed stories to *Creepy* and *Blazing Combat*, and illustrated a children's book, *The Story of Flight*. In the '70s, he contributed to *National Lampoon*, and drew war and horror and *Blackhawk* for DC, did work for Marvel, and periodically ghosted *Secret Agent Corrigan* before taking over the art and writing in 1980. He also contributed to Dark Horse, Pacific, and Eclipse. Evans did *Corrigan* until retiring in 1996.

– S.C. Ringgenberg

ACES HIGH #4
September-October 1955.
© WMG

BILL EVERETT

INDUCTED IN 2009

As the creator of Namor, the Sub-Mariner, Bill Everett (1917-1973) was responsible for one of Timely Comics' three main characters (the other two were Captain America and The Human Torch). Namor was likely the first very successful anti-hero in the comic book world, since he was near-ly constantly at war with the surface-dwelling humans. *Motion Picture Funnies Weekly* #1 featured the character's first appearance, which was then expanded for *Marvel Comics* #1. He wrote and drew the character in a number of different titles for the publisher both before and after his service in World War II. During the 1950s, he illustrated Marvel Boy, Venus and the first appearance of Simon Garth, The Zombie, among other work. Timely had become Atlas and then Marvel Comics when he illustrated the first issue of *Daredevil*. His last lengthy work in comics was a 1972-1973 run on his original character, Sub-Mariner.

DAREDEVIL #1
Everett & Kirby cover. April 1964.
© MAR

AL FELDSTEIN

INDUCTED IN 2008

As an editor with EC Comics, Al Feldstein created, wrote, illustrated and edited titles in one of the most influential comic book lines in history. With a body of work ranging from horror (*Tales from the Crypt*) to sci-ence-fiction to crime and suspense, his contributions have been reprinted numbers of times over the years. They also stood up to the harshest critic: time. In 1955, he became editor of *MAD*, which had started as part of EC's comic book line-up and survived the demise of its sister publications by graduating to magazine format. Under his editorship, the magazine's circulation steadily increased from 375,000 to almost 3 million. Using his own pen name, he christened Alfred E. Neuman, *MAD*'s trademark charac-ter, and made short work of many social conventions. In 1984, Feldstein retired from *MAD* to devote his time to painting, something he continued in his Montana home until his passing in 2014.

WEIRD SCIENCE #13 (#2)
July-August 1950. © WMG

LOU FINE

INDUCTED IN 2014

Despite the brevity of his comics career, Lou Fine is remembered as one of comics' best draftsmen. He began in comics in 1938 at the Iger & Eisner shop; his first published work was "Wilton of the West" in *Jumbo Comics* #4. He also supplied covers and stories for Fox, including "The Blue Beetle" and "The Flame," a series he co-created. At the same time, he established himself as an artistic superstar on "Dollman," "The Black Condor," "The Ray," and "Uncle Sam" for Quality Comics. However, by 1944, Fine had left comics to concentrate on newspaper and advertising strips. He ghosted the inking on Eisner's *Spirit* from 1942 until 1945. After this, Fine drew the syndicated strips *Taylor Woe* (1949) and *Adam Ames* (1959-1962). From 1965 until 1967, he drew the hard-boiled detective *Peter Scratch*. His sole '60s comic book work was the two-page, "The Man From Aeons" for *Wham-O Giant Comics* in 1967. His final strip was "Space Conquerors," which appeared monthly in *Boys' Life* until his death in 1971.

– *S.C. Ringgenberg*

NATIONAL COMICS #3
September 1940. © QUA

BILL FINGER

INDUCTED IN 2013

Arguably the non-credited co-creator of Batman with Bob Kane and Green Lantern with Martin Nodell, the prolific Bill Finger also created the Golden Age hero Wildcat with Irwin Hasen. Kane said of Finger that he was a contributing force on Batman right from the beginning. Finger's talent wasn't just found in comics. He also wrote for Hollywood with films and television shows like *The Green Slime, Hawaiian Eye* and *77 Sunset Strip*. Finger also wrote a two-part episode for the live action *Batman* series from the 1960s. It was called "The Clock King's Crazy Crimes / The Clock King Gets Crowned." Finger, who passed away in 1974, was posthumously inducted into the Jack Kirby Hall of Fame and the Will Eisner Award Hall of Fame. In 1985, DC Comics also named Finger as one of the honorees in the company's 50th anniversary publication *Fifty Who Made DC Great*. And, to further honor him, Comic-Con International established the Bill Finger Award for Excellence in Comic Book Writing.

– *Scott Braden*

DETECTIVE COMICS #38
April 1940. © DC

GARDNER FOX

INDUCTED IN 2014

The astonishingly imaginative and prolific Gardner Francis Cooper Fox was one of the Renaissance men of Comics. He wrote comic book scripts for several decades for a range of publishers including Timely, Avon, E.C., Marvel, and Warren, but was most closely associated with DC Comics. His career at DC lasted almost 30 years, and encompassed the creation of Zatanna, Hawkman and Hawkgirl, the Atom, The Justice Society of America, Johnny Thunder, the Flash, the Sandman, the Shining Knight, and Adam Strange. He also made significant contributions to the very earliest Batman stories, including creating Batman's parents, Thomas and Martha Wayne, the Bat-Gyro, the Batarang, and Batman's first use of his utility belt. At the same time he was the head writer for Max Gaines' All-American Comics line, he was also a productive writer of pulp fiction, especially horror and science fiction (though the versatile Fox also wrote adventure stories, westerns, sports stories, and romances). In the '60s, Fox returned to Batman, creating the new Batgirl (Barbara Gordon), and reinventing the Justice League, the Atom, and Hawkman. His story "Flash of Two Worlds" in *Flash* #123 introduced the concept of Earth I and Earth II, thereby establishing the DC Comics multiverse, a concept that's been used ever since. With 1,500 DC scripts to his credit, he was DC's second-most prolific scripter (after Robert Kanigher).

– *S.C. Ringgenberg*

BRAVE AND THE BOLD #28
February-March 1960. © DC

FRANK FRAZETTA

INDUCTED IN **2009**

Frank Frazetta started illustrating comic books and comic strips with a wide variety of themes before becoming the almost universally lauded master fantasy illustrator he became. He worked in the western, mystery, humor, and other genres including stories for EC Comics, National's Shining Knight, Avon and other publishers (his collaborations with EC's great Al Williamson and the talented Roy Krenkel are particularly noteworthy). His work on *Buck Rogers, Famous Funnies, Li'l Abner, Flash Gordon* and *Johnny Comet* still shine, but when he turned his hand to a series of Conan book covers he found a depth and a serious connection to a legion of fans. From the 1960s to the 1990s, he illustrated more than a dozen movie posters. His own characters, such as the Death Dealer, have taken on lives of their own on posters, album covers, and in comic books. He is truly a legend whose true impact on the artists who follow him is yet to be fully felt.

– *Robert M. Overstreet*

WEIRD FANTASY #21
September-October 1953.
© WMG

NEIL GAIMAN

INDUCTED IN **2009**

Even though they thought they had something special, when DC Comics released *Sandman* #1 in 1989, it would have been impossible for them to know what they had on their hands since it really hadn't happened before. By the time the series ended with *Sandman* #75 (March 1996), it had given birth to DC's Vertigo imprint (*Sandman* #47), introduced or re-introduced the comic book world to a number of exceptional artists, and established Neil Gaiman as one of the medium's most distinct voices. Lyrical, moody, sensitive, and painterly, his ability to take readers to the world in which his characters lived captured and kept readers from beyond the normal fan base. With spin-offs such as *Death: The High Cost of Living*, he rounded out that world and soon began carving out others, in comics, novels, and other media.

Popular world wide, his *Sandman* has never been out of print since it debuted, finding success in multiple formats.

SANDMAN #1
January 1989. © DC

M.C. GAINES

INDUCTED IN **2010**

Pioneer, publisher, promoter and advocate Maxwell Charles Gaines is known for creating the idea in 1933 of repackaging the Sunday newspaper comic strip into the format we recognize as modern comic books and distributing them to the newsstand. Comic strips had been collected into books since the 1800s, but he felt by folding a full tabloid page of eight or sixteen pages down twice to produce a 32-page or a 64-page comic magazine that it could be sold for 10¢, even during the Great Depression.

He tried first with *Funnies On Parade*, then with *Famous Funnies, A Carnival of Comics,* both done as promotional comics. *Famous Funnies*, Series 1, was the following step. The next issue, also #1, dated July, 1934 was distributed as the first newsstand comic magazine. The series lasted In 1938 Gaines (with Jack Liebowitz) started All-American Publications, which was a separate company co-marketed with DC Comics. In 1944, DC bought out Gaines, who then started a new line, Educational Comics (EC). He died in a boating accident in 1947.

– *Robert M. Overstreet*

ALL STAR COMICS #3
Winter 1940. © DC

WILLIAM M. GAINES

Best known on the national stage as the founder and publisher of *MAD* magazine, Bill Gaines suddenly found himself in charge of a floundering comic book company after the accidental death of his father, industry pioneer M.C. Gaines. Over the course of the next few years and in the course of trying to capture the latest trends, the younger Gaines published westerns, romances, and thrillers. Along the way, though, he began assembling an unparalleled roster of contributors, starting with writer-editor-artists Al Feldstein and Harvey Kurtzman and including Al Williamson, Jack Davis, Graham Ingles, Johnny Craig, Reed Crandall, George Evans, Wally Wood, John Severin and many others. With titles like *Tales From The Crypt*, *Weird Science*, *Two-Fisted Tales*, and *Shock SuspenStories*, in just a few years Gaines and company created titles that still influence other creators today. *MAD*, of course, became a cultural icon and did its own brand of influencing.

CRIME PATROL #15
Debut of the Crypt Keeper.
December 1949-January 1950.
© WMG

JOSÉ LUIS GARCÍA-LÓPEZ

José Luis García-López has an extensive résumé as a penciller, with significant additional credits as an inker, colorist, and cover artist. He is an artist with the skills to match writers' grandest story ideas and the ability to draw characters in dramatic, albeit realistic, poses that propel the action. His long relationship with DC Comics began in 1975, inking the pencils of Dick Dillin and Curt Swan on *Action Comics* and *Superman*, respectively. Later in '75, García-López and Gerry Conway created the *Hercules Unbound* series, he worked with Michael Fleisher to launch the *Jonah Hex* ongoing series in '77, and teamed with Martin Pasko to kickoff *DC Comics Presents* in '78. García-López is celebrated for his illustrations in several DC style guides that are used for merchandise licenses around the world. Since defining the look of DC characters in that initial 1982 guide, he contributed to additional style guides for the next 30 years. García-López's work has appeared in most DC mainstays from *Action Comics* to *World's Finest Comics* in a career that spans 50 years.

– Amanda Sheriff

ACTION COMICS #484
June 1978. © DC

JEAN GIRAUD (MOEBIUS)

The term "visionary" is bandied about almost as much as the word "classic," but even in an era in which the meaning of the expression has been diluted through overuse, Jean Giraud was an edge-pushing pioneer, an artistic leader, and a true visionary. The French writer-artist passed away on Saturday, March 10, 2012 at the age of 73 after a long battle with cancer. Many American fans got to know his work through reprint collections published in the U.S. and through his collaboration with Stan Lee on *The Silver Surfer*, a two-part mini-series published in 1988-89. His range of topics was vast, and his impact equaled their scope. "The life of a storyteller like Jean Giraud cannot be evaluated simply by his prolific output or the elegance of his art or even by his commitment to his craft. Instead, in an earthly sense, we can only gauge his time among us by the impact he and his work had on others. In that sense, his effect is probably the definition of immeasurable," said Melissa Bowersox, Executive Vice-President of Geppi's Entertainment Museum.

SILVER SURFER: PARABLE
February 1998. Reprint of
graphic novel. © MAR

MARTIN GOODMAN

In 1931 Martin Goodman joined with future MLJ Magazines (Archie) co-founders Louis Silberkleit and Maurice Coyne to start pulp magazine publisher Columbia Publications. In 1932 he started his own business. His first publication was *Western Supernovel Magazine*, which premiered in May 1933, and he began building a variety of publishing companies from there. Under his umbrella came *Mystery Tales*, *Real Sports*, *Star Detective*, *Marvel Science Stories*, *Ka-Zar* and others.

In 1939, he contracted with Lloyd Jacquet's Funnies, Inc. to provide the content for what became *Marvel Comics* #1, which featured the Human Torch and the Sub-Mariner. With that comic as a hit, he hired his own staff, starting with writer-artist-editor Joe Simon. Timely Comics was born. A few years later, he hired his nephew by marriage, Stan Lee, as editor.

Eventually Timely Comics became Atlas Comics, and Atlas Comics became Marvel Comics. After selling Marvel in the late 1960s, he started a new Atlas line in 1974. While it didn't last at the time, it has recently been revived by his grandson, Jason Goodman.

MARVEL COMICS #1
November 1939. © MAR

ARCHIE GOODWIN

Ask the average fan to name the greatest creators in the history of comics and the name Archie Goodwin will not leap to the minds of many, because so much of Archie's brilliant work was behind the scenes or flew under the mainstream radar. But ask the creators with whom he worked! Ask other all-time great writers, artists, editors and creators! Gather the elders, the best of the best and ask them! His name will be among the first mentioned. Archie Goodwin was an amazing writer with outstanding story sense, penetrating insight, a gift for dialogue, an effortless knack for character, a flair for drama and utter mastery of the art of delivering the payoff. His sheer creativity ranks with the best ever. He was an all-time great editor and teacher. He made everyone he worked with better. On top of that, Archie Goodwin was a fine, wonderful, noble and honorable soul, loved and respected by everyone because he deserved it. This industry may never see his like again. How sad. He is desperately missed.

– Jim Shooter

EPIC ILLUSTRATED #1
Spring 1980. © MAR

MIKE GRELL

After inking Dave Cockrum's pencils on *Superboy* (with the Legion of Super-Heroes) #202, Mike Grell got the assignment to pencil the series beginning with #203. On the title, he developed many elements of his now-familiar style. His run on the series was followed by the marriage of Saturn Girl and Lightning Lad in the treasury-sized special *All-New Collectors' Edition* #C-55. His own creation, The Warlord, debuted in *1st Issue Special* #8 and then landed his own series beginning with *The Warlord* #1, the start of a 35-issue run as writer-artist. Grell then launched two creator-owned series, *Starslayer* (at Pacific Comics) and *Jon Sable Freelance* (at First Comics). He enjoyed another long run as writer-artist, 43 issues, on *Sable*. Following that, he undertook writing and illustrating the three-issue mini-series *Green Arrow: The Longbow Hunters*, which in turn spawned an ongoing *Green Arrow* series, which Grell wrote for 80 issues (periodically providing covers). Grell has continued to work on many characters, including revivals of *The Warlord* and *Jon Sable Freelance*.

ALL-NEW COLLECTOR'S EDITION C-55
1978. © DC

PAUL GULACY

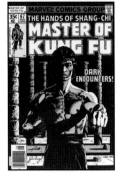

In the mid-1970s, after the exodus of Jim Steranko, Neal Adams, and others, there was a veritable creative void in mainstream comics. Bursting upon the scene to fill that gap was Paul Gulacy and his work on *Shang-Chi: Master of Kung Fu*. Gulacy broke Marvel's "House Style" mold. Influenced by Steranko, Gulacy's art was slick, detailed, and eye-catching. But it was his magnificent storytelling ability that left its indelible mark. Heavily impacted by movies, editor Archie Goodwin described Gulacy's work as "film on paper." Movie director Quentin Tarantino said, "My favorite comic when it came out was *Master of Kung Fu*."

After *Master of Kung Fu*, Gulacy teamed with writer Don McGregor to produce the graphic novel, *Sabre*. He would go on to work on such pop culture icons as James Bond, Batman, Terminator, Star Wars, G.I. Joe, along with a host of independent titles. He has always found ways to push the medium's creative limits.

– Michael Kronenberg

MASTER OF KUNG FU #67
August 1978. © MAR

LARRY HAMA

Writer-artist-editor Larry Hama began his long association with the comic book incarnation of G.I. Joe almost immediately following then Marvel Comics editor-in-chief Jim Shooter's meeting with Hasbro. "It was Larry's book all the way," Shooter said. And in the minds of many fans, that's how it has remained. During the title's 155-issue run at Marvel, subsequent appearance at Devil's Due Publishing, and revival at IDW Publishing, Hama's portrayal of the characters defined many of them permanently for their fans. He has, however, been far from all G.I. Joe. He broke into comics as an assistant for Wally Wood, served as editor for Marvel's Conan line and *The 'Nam*, created Bucky O'Hare, wrote such titles as *Kitty Pryde, Agent of SHIELD*, *Punisher: War Zone* and *Weapon X*, among others. He has also written video games, consulted for G.I Joe in feature films, and even appeared as an actor on *M*A*S*H*, but it's his work on G.I. Joe – including the acclaimed "Silent Interlude" in *G.I. Joe #21*, which he wrote and penciled – that continues to demand attention.

G.I. JOE, A REAL AMERICAN HERO #1
June 1982. © Hasbro

BRUCE HAMILTON

A towering figure in the history of American comic books, Bruce Hamilton was publisher of Gladstone Publishing, a comics historian, and an early fan activist. Known around the world for the licensed line of Disney comics he lovingly published, Hamilton was a central figure in detailing the history of the medium. Possessed of an imposing stature, a radio announcer's voice, and a fiery drive, Hamilton helped get the comics industry organized, first as a dealer in Golden Age comics, then in other collectibles such as original art, movie posters, and cartoon cels. He was among the first to suggest that classic material be repackaged into deluxe formats. He began a 20-year relationship with The Walt Disney Company in 1980 when he and Russ Cochran acquired a license to produce *The Fine Art of Walt Disney's Donald Duck*, a collection of Carl Barks' Disney-based oil paintings. He passed away June 18, 2005.

WALT DISNEY'S UNCLE SCROOGE #210
October 1986. © DIS

RUSS HEATH

INDUCTED IN 2016

Wait, stop! Read this!

If you are perusing this book, then you must have some interest in comics. Great! So let's discuss Russ Heath. Those of you who know and revere him, fantastic! Skim through this homage and get to the artwork. You know it, you love it… you are in awe of it! Those of you who are not familiar with Heath and his legacy, stop what you are doing and read this carefully: Russ Heath is a living legend and a master of the comic medium! He has influenced what you consider great, before great was even drawn. He developed art that inspired everything from young minds to cultural luminaries. He is one of the most remarkable artists of the comic art form. Now, let your eyes drink in his talent. Please, do yourself a favor, seek out his work and see his genius the way it was supposed to be enjoyed, in comic book form.

– *Matt Ballesteros*

**ALL-AMERICAN
MEN OF WAR #94**
November-December 1962. © DC

CARMINE INFANTINO

INDUCTED IN 2009

As a youngster, Carmine Infantino struggled to break into comics around the demands of his school schedule, making a number of sales and working on a variety of titles for different publishers including Hillman Periodicals, Fawcett, Holyoke, and DC Comics. He also worked for Joe Simon and Jack Kirby's Prize Comics during his early days. When editor Julius Schwartz paired him with writer Robert Kanigher on a revival of the Golden Age superhero The Flash in *Showcase #4*, though, lightning struck more than just the main character. Showing his illustration and design talents on characters ranging from the science fiction adventurer Adam Strange to serious superhero Batman to somewhat silly hero Elongated Man, Infantino became DC's Art Director, Editorial Director and eventually Publisher, supervising among other things the first Marvel - DC crossover, *Superman vs. The Amazing Spider-Man*. Following his staff tenure, he returned to work as a freelancer, illustrating *Star Wars*, *Nova*, and *Spider-Woman* for Marvel and various others for DC.

**AMAZING WORLD OF
DC COMICS #8**
September-October 1975. © DC

MICHAEL WM. KALUTA

INDUCTED IN 2019

Widely acknowledged as a master of the art form, Michael Wm. Kaluta began his rise to prominence illustrating Len Wein's adaptation of Edgar Rice Burroughs's *Venus* novels for DC Comics after breaking in with work on early fanzines. Soon after that he produced what is considered by many to be his signature work when he teamed with writer Dennis O'Neil for a run on *The Shadow*. His design sense reflects the influence of pulp-era illustrations, but his art is also highly detailed. His elaborate illustrations established him as a premiere cover artist, whose work has been seen on *Madame Xanadu, House of Mystery, House of Secrets, Conan The King, Spectre, Aquaman, Detective Comics,* and *Zorro*, among others. He was featured in *Epic Illustrated*. With writer Elaine Lee, he also produced a number of *Starstruck* tales for a variety of publishers. The Shazam, Inkpot, and Spectrum Award Grand Master has also visualized film properties and characters for animation and computer games.

– *Braelynn Bowersox*

THE SHADOW #1
October - November 1973.
© DC

JACK KAMEN

After his initial work for EC Comics, which came at the end of their "Pre-Trend" era on the final two issues of *Modern Love*, Jack Kamen quickly made himself a vital component of the company's "New Trend" efforts. He illustrated the very first "Old Witch" story (written by Al Feldstein) in *Haunt of Fear* #2 (#16/2) and frequently contributed to *Crime SuspenStories* and *Shock SuspenStories*. His classic "Squeeze Play" cover for *Shock SuspenStories* #13 (May 1954) was for Frank Frazetta's only solo story at EC, and he also provided covers for final three issues of *Crime SuspenStories*. Outside of his EC work, Kamen was known as one of the top "good girl" artists for his popular covers on Fox's *Zoot* and *Rulah* and Four Star's *Brenda Starr*, and he turned this to his advantage when his sexy "Kamen Girls" worked well for the *Crime* and *Shock* series. In addition, his art was seen in the George Romero – Stephen King film *Creepshow*, and on the cover of the *Creepshow* graphic novel.

– *Robert M. Overstreet*

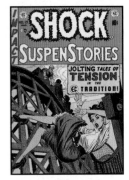

SHOCK SUSPENSTORIES #13
February-March 1954. © WMG

BOB KANE

Known near and far as the creator of DC Comics' Batman, Bob Kane joined the Max Fleischer Studio as a trainee animator in 1934, then subsequently worked for Jerry Iger and then the Eisner & Iger Studio. Following the surprising success of Superman in 1938, he and writer Bill Finger developed Batman in 1939. The character first appeared in *Detective Comics* #27. Although still credited in each issue as the creator of Batman, Kane's comic book career wound down in the 1960s, though he parlayed his Batman status into a bit of celebrity. Before that, among the Dark Knight's Rogues Gallery, Kane created Two-Face, Catwoman (first seen as "the Cat"), and the Scarecrow, among others. In his post-comics career, he painted and showed his works in galleries, created Courageous Cat and Cool McCool, and served as a consultant to the movies *Batman* (1989), *Batman Returns* (1992) and *Batman Forever* (1995). His familiar signature was even seen on a piece of art in the 1980 film.

– *Scott Braden*

DETECTIVE COMICS #27
May 1939. © DC

JACK KIRBY

A creative dynamo given human form, for many Jack Kirby defined with his work the very idea of what comic books should be. In his art and stories, the obvious brash doses of daring design and explosive action were infused with something more unexpected in the eras in which he worked: an equally bold excitement for the cerebral, philosophical and spiritual. Whether working with partners such as Joe Simon (with whom he co-created Captain America, the Fighting American, Boys Ranch, and many would say the romance comics genre) and Stan Lee

(co-creating the Fantastic Four, Thor, and the Silver Surfer, among others), or on his own (DC's "Fourth World" titles such *The New Gods*, *Mister Miracle*, *The Forever People*, or his creator-owned *Captain Victory* and *Silver Star*), Kirby worked as much in metaphor as he did in pencil. The number of creators and fans he influenced will never be known.

AVENGERS #4
March 1964. © MAR

ANDY KUBERT

INDUCTED IN 2013

In a vibrant and distinguished career, Adam Kubert has touched many characters, including work on the high profile *Before Watchmen: Nite Owl* mini-series in 2012, as well as stints ranging from *Batman vs. Predator* and *Adam Strange* to *X-Men* and *Wolverine: Origin*. Among many other assignments, illustrated Marvel's *1602* and DC's two-part "Whatever Happened to the Caped Crusader?" both written by Neil Gaiman. His work has appeared in *Uncanny X-Men, Batman, Flashpoint, Ghost Rider, Incredible Hulk, Ka-Zar, Captain America, Thor, Ultimate X-Men, Ultimate Iron Man,* and *Action Comics*, among others. The son of legendary writer-artist-instructor and fellow Overstreet Hall of Fame member Joe Kubert, he is a graduate of the not-coincidentally-named Kubert School, where he serves as a Vice-President, passing on his education to upcoming artists.

– *Scott Braden & J.C. Vaughn*

DETECTIVE COMICS #853
April 2009. © DC

JOE KUBERT

INDUCTED IN 2009

I don't know any other words that will as quickly put a fellow artist into that zone that exists between pure fandom and the cold sweats as the mention of writer, artist, editor, and educator Joe Kubert. In an industry predisposed to overuse words like 'legend,' Mr. Kubert truly is one. He started working in the business at age 11 in 1938 and for the rest of his career looked for ways to push himself and the medium for all its worth. While he is no doubt best known for his work on Sgt. Rock, he also poured his efforts into DC's other iconic war titles such as *G.I. Combat, Our Army at War* (and characters like Enemy Ace and the Haunted Tank), his art also graced titles like *Hawkman* and *Tarzan*, all of which would be enough for any artist. Not him. He founded the Joe Kubert School of Cartoon and Graphic Art in 1976, wrote and illustrated *Tor, Abraham Stone, Fax from Sarajevo,* and *Yossel: April 19, 1943*. To put it bluntly, he is my biggest influence and my comic book hero!

– *Billy Tucci*

OUR ARMY AT WAR #112
November 1961. © DC

HARVEY KURTZMAN

INDUCTED IN 2008

Harvey Kurtzman was a cartoonist, writer, editor, artist and master storyteller. Best known as the founding editor of *MAD* in its original comic book form at EC Comics, Kurtzman was also the driving force behind EC's *Two-Fisted Tales* and *Frontline Combat*. He also created *Hey Look!, Trump, Help!,* and *Humbug*. Throughout his career, he worked with artists such as Will Elder, Jack Davis, Wally Wood, John Severin, and Russ Heath, among others, but his method of scripting and providing page layouts had the impact of making a Harvey Kurtzman story come out looking like a Harvey Kurtzman story no matter who illustrated it.

His war comics are generally considered among the best the genre has ever experienced even though they clearly portray the high cost of war on individuals rather than more typical war stories. The long-running comic book industry Harvey Awards are named in his honor.

MAD #4
April-May 1953. © WMG

JIM LEE
INDUCTED IN 2006

Over the past twenty years, Jim Lee has created many of the classic comic book images with his sense of style and attention to composition garnering plenty of fans. A native of Seoul, South Korea, he started his comics career in 1989 drawing *Uncanny X-Men* before helping to launch the record-breaking *X-Men* with co-writer Chris Claremont.

In 1992, Lee joined fellow comic creators in the founding of Image Comics, creating and co-creating new characters under his WildStorm Productions imprint including *WildC.A.T.s* and *Gen13*.

In 1998, Lee sold WildStorm to DC Comics. While he continued to work with the company he founded, he also began working on DC's iconic characters as well. He illustrated the 12-issue story arc "Hush" in the pages of *Batman* with writer Jeph Loeb, followed by a run on *Superman*. Much of his time has been spent closely developing the look of the characters and settings in DC's new online game with Sony.

In 2010, Lee was appointed co-publisher of DC Comics with Dan DiDio, succeeding Paul Levitz.

BATMAN #608
December 2002. © DC

STAN LEE
INDUCTED IN 2008

"Captain America Foils the Traitor's Revenge," a text piece in *Captain America Comics* #3 (May 1941) might not have been the most auspicious debut in the history of the comics, but it is nonetheless an important event. It marked the first published comic book work of young Stanley Martin Lieber, better known as Stan Lee, the writer, editor, creator, co-creator, publisher and pitchman who developed and relentlessly promoted the identity of Marvel Comics. After two decades in which Lee was forced to do comics as others wanted them done, he finally he tried them his way. The Fantastic Four, Spider-Man, Thor, The Avengers, The X-Men, The Incredible Hulk and others were the result. Eventually moving to the west coast to spearhead the company's Hollywood ambitions, this entertainment icon has lived to see many of his favorite creations hit the silver screen as Hollywood special effects finally caught up to his imagination of 40 years ago.

FANTASTIC FOUR #51
June 1966. © MAR

PAUL LEVITZ
INDUCTED IN 2009

He started out as a fan, established a broad base of historical and contemporary knowledge about the field, developed as a writer, and eventually became the leader of one of the two biggest comic book companies. After writing and co-publishing the long-lived fanzine *The Comic Reader*, Paul Levitz could have called it a day and still been lauded for his contributions to the four color world. Good thing for us, though, he didn't stop there. As a writer, he's known for writing the Earth II adventures of the Justice Society of America in the revived *All Star Comics* in the 1970s, a period in which he co-created The Huntress. In the 1980s, he wrote a lengthy run on Legion of Super-Heroes, and he recently returned to scripting for a run of *JSA*. He's probably best known, though, as the President and Publisher of DC Comics, where he has worked tirelessly to promote their characters as well as the history and future of the medium.
– *Stephen A. Geppi*

DC SPECIAL #29
August-September 1977. © DC

ROB LIEFELD

From his earliest days as a professional, Rob Liefeld has channeled a raw kinetic energy and given it form in his comic book artwork, much to the pleasure of a cadre of loyal fans. His first published work was a five-issue *Hawk and Dove* mini-series for DC Comics in 1988. It led to more work at DC, and then *Amazing Spider-Man Annual #23* for Marvel. He began his stint as pencil artist on *New Mutants* with #86. After introducing the bombastic Deadpool and the anti-hero Cable, he transformed the title into the blockbuster *X-Force #1*. He departed Marvel, co-founded Image Comics (which was launched with his *Youngblood #1*), and introduced a full slate of characters. Since then, he departed Image, founded new publishing ventures, and returned to Image. During that time he has also enjoyed stints at both Marvel and DC, including working on *Cable and Deadpool, Onslaught Reborn, The Savage Hawkman, Grifter,* and *Hawk and Dove*, as well as work for other publishers.

NEW MUTANTS #98
February 1991. © MAR

RUSS MANNING

Whether one knows his work from his long run on the *Tarzan* newspaper strip, a too-brief stint on the *Star Wars* newspaper strip, or creating the comic book series *Magnus Robot Fighter*, the illustrations of Russ Manning (1929-1981) pack clean, crisp line work and solid storytelling into every panel. With a design sense dictated by the stories (His *Star Wars* or *Magnus* are substantially different than his *Tarzan*), he became influential with comic artists, even though his work was never published by Marvel or DC.

In recent years, Dark Horse has reprinted many of his Tarzan stories in collected editions, sharing them with new generations of fans. Each year The Russ Manning Most Promising Newcomer Award is an award presented at Comic-Con International: San Diego to a comic book artist whose first professional work appeared within the previous two years. In 1982 the first recipient was the late Dave Stevens, who had worked as an assistant of Manning's.

MAGNUS, ROBOT FIGHTER #5
February 1964.
© Random House

WINSOR McCAY

It's a daunting task to bring the world of dreams to vivid, waking life, but Winsor McCay (1867-1934) managed to do that for newspaper readers every week through his landmark artistic achievements, the ground-breaking strips *Dreams of a Rarebit Fiend* and *Little Nemo in Slumberland*. Chronicling the night-time adventures of a little boy as he navigated a wonderland of imagination from 1905-1927, McCay's *Nemo* was a powerful exploration of childlike discovery and lush, expressive art. As an animator, McCay was a pioneer that introduced the world to Gertie the Dinosaur in 1914 and employed vaudevillian techniques to blend live-action and animation long before Roger Rabbit was born. His work in comic strips and cartoons inspired the likes of Walt Disney, Bill Watterson, Maurice Sendak and many more. It is absolutely fair to say that without McCay, the world of comic characters as we know it would simply not exist.

– *Dr. Arnold T. Blumberg*

**LITTLE NEMO IN SLUMBERLAND
SO MANY SPLENDID SUNDAYS!**
2005. © Sunday Press

TODD McFARLANE

INDUCTED IN 2009

Writer, artist, toy designer, businessman. All of these titles and others apply to Todd McFarlane, the former Spider-Man writer-artist who capitalized on incredible sales in 1992 and co-founded Image Comics. Following a back-up story in *Coyote*, which was then published by Marvel's Epic imprint, McFarlane began quickly making a name for himself. After illustrating Batman: Year Two and *Infinity, Inc.* at DC Comics and *Incredible Hulk* at Marvel, he landed the art duties on *Amazing Spider-Man*. After 28 issues on that series, he launched a new one, simply *Spider-Man*, which he wrote and illustrated. He parlayed the overwhelming sales for that series into the launch of Image Comics, where he wrote and illustrated his own series, *Spawn*, and created many others. McFarlane has built his McFarlane Toys into a serious force in the toy business, and continues to work in various areas in entertainment in addition to comics.

SPAWN #1
May 1992. © TMP

DON McGREGOR

INDUCTED IN 2015

The first word that comes to mind when one thinks of Don McGregor's writing is "humanity." Throw in "honesty" and "integrity," and a passion for the romantic and sometimes tragic nature of heroism, and you have a quintessentially poignant Don McGregor script. He started his comics career writing for Warren's *Creepy*, *Eerie*, and *Vampirella* before joining Marvel in the early 1970s. His stories featuring Killraven, the Black Panther, and Luke Cage remain examples of the best that comics can achieve. Often at odds with the editorial restraints of the era, he became a pioneer in creators' rights, and with artist Paul Gulacy created *Sabre*, the first graphic novel specifically published for the then-new comic book specialty store market in 1978. He followed with *Detectives, Inc.*, drawn by Marshall Rogers and, later, by Gene Colan, and *Ragamuffins* with Colan, all at Eclipse Comics. At DC, Don again teamed with Colan on *Nathaniel Dusk*. He also created the popular Lady Rawhide as a spin-off from the *Zorro* series he wrote for Topps in the 1990s, and then scripted Zorro's newspaper strip adventures, with artist Tom Yeates. Much of his work remains in print.

– *Dean Mullaney*

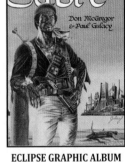

ECLIPSE GRAPHIC ALBUM SERIES #1
October 1978. © McGregor & Gulacy

MIKE MIGNOLA

INDUCTED IN 2010

Having worked for both Marvel and DC on titles like *Daredevil*, *Incredible Hulk*, Batman: A Death in the Family and *Gotham by Gaslight* (which launched DC's "Elseworlds" line), artist Mike Mignola blended his love of Lovecraft-like horror and pulp/B-movie monster mashes, tinkering at his table like a latter-day Frankenstein until the bulky, huge-handed, nearly hornless, bright red paranormal crusader known as Hellboy leapt from the pages of Dark Horse Comics in 1994. Broadening his accomplishments to include scripting many of Hellboy's tales, Mignola's distinctive artistic style mixed Jack Kirby-like intensity with a darker layer of expressionistic shadow and shape. Mignola has also brought his artistic eye to Hollywood with conceptual work on Coppola's *Bram Stoker's Dracula* and the *Lord of the Rings* prequels, *The Hobbit* series. He also had the rare opportunity to help usher his own creation onto the silver screen via Guillermo del Toro's two *Hellboy* feature films.

– *Dr. Arnold T. Blumberg*

HELLBOY: SEED OF DESTRUCTION #1
March 1994.
© Mike Mignola

FRANK MILLER

INDUCTED IN **2010**

After illustrating a few stories for Gold Key's *The Twilight Zone* and DC's *Weird War Tales* and *Unknown Soldier,* and following a story in Marvel's *John Carter: Warlord of Mars* #18, Frank Miller landed a two-part fill-in job on *Peter Parker, The Spectacular Spider-Man* #27–28, which guest-starred Daredevil, a character who he would define and which in return would define his early success. Miller took over as regular artist on *Daredevil* #158. By the time Elektra was featured on the cover of *Daredevil* #168, he was writing it as well. With inker Klaus Janson, he turned it into one of Marvel's most popular titles.

He also illustrated the first *Wolverine* mini-series, unleashed *Ronin,* and then turned his attention to Bruce Wayne's future with *Batman: The Dark Knight Returns,* which became a perennial best seller in its collected edition. Subsequently he wrote another run on *Daredevil* and Batman: Year One, both with artist David Mazzuccheli, before turning to creator-owned projects such as *Sin City* and *300.* He continues to create in both film and comics.

BATMAN THE DARK KNIGHT RETURNS #1
March 1986. © DC

TERRY MOORE

INDUCTED IN **2014**

Writer-artist Terry Moore's self-published *Strangers in Paradise* began as a three-issue mini-series at Antarctic Press, and then blossomed into two subsequent volumes from his own Abstract Studio imprint, the last of which ran 90 issues. The work earned him a very devoted fan following, which enabled the title to run more than 16 years. It spawned multiple reprints in soft cover, hardcover, and manga format editions, including a 20th anniversary omnibus in 2013. After the series concluded, Moore immediately launched *Echo,* an action-adventure science fiction series, which ran for 30 issues, and then *Rachel Rising,* a horror series. Like *Strangers in Paradise, Echo* and *Rachel Rising* feature strong female characters and realistic human interaction. Moore's success in self-publishing also lead to high-profile assignments in mainstream comics, including five issues of *Spider-Man Loves Mary Jane* and a nine-issue stint on *Runaways* for Marvel, and a variety of work for DC, Dark Horse, Bongo Comics, and Image Comics.

– J.C. Vaughn & S.C. Ringgenberg

STRANGERS IN PARADISE V2 #10
February 1996.
© Terry Moore

DEAN MULLANEY

INDUCTED IN **2011**

In 2007, Dean Mullaney created IDW Publishing's archival imprint The Library of American Comics, which he edits and designs. Almost immediately his efforts began to usher in a new Golden Age of classic comic strip reprint collections, significant in both the material itself and the manner in which it is presented. In its first four years, LoAC has been nominated for nine Eisner awards and other accolades, and it has been called "the gold standard for archival comic strip reprints."

Under his guidance, Milton Caniff's *Terry and the Pirates,* Alex Raymond's *Rip Kirby,* Chester Gould's *Dick Tracy,* Harold Gray's *Little Orphan Annie,* Archie Goodwin and Al Williamson's *Secret Agent Corrigan,* Chic Young's *Blondie* and other strips have been showcased for seasoned fans and new readers alike.

In 1978, he launched Eclipse Comics when he published Don McGregor's *Sabre,* the first graphic novel created for the comics specialty market. Eclipse championed creator ownership and the first line of Japanese manga in English translation, and had the first digitally-colored comic book.

ECLIPSE MAGAZINE #6
July 1982. © ECL

MARTIN NODELL

INDUCTED IN 2007

Martin Nodell was one of the shining lights of the Golden Age of comics. Best known as the creator of the Golden Age superhero the Green Lantern, Nodell took the character to All-American Publications, and his Green Lantern made its debut in the July 1940 issue of *All-American Comics* #16. The character proved popular and received its own title in the Fall of 1941. Nodell went on to illustrate for other publishers including Timely Comics, including cover art for *Captain America Comics* #74 and *Marvel Tales* #93.

In 1965, Nodell accepted an art director position at Leo Burnett Agency where he was a member of the design team that created the Pillsbury Doughboy which would go on to be another iconic character.

Starting in 1980, Nodell began attending various comic book conventions along with his wife, Caroline to meet the many fans and collectors who the Green Lantern and its creator had touched.

GREEN LANTERN #3
Spring 1942. © DC

DENNY O'NEIL

INDUCTED IN 2018

Comic book writer-editor Dennis "Denny" O'Neil carved out for himself a special place as a distinctive voice who also had an eye for developing others' best work. As a writer, while he has worked on many different titles, O'Neil is best-known for his collaborations with Neal Adams on *Green Lantern*/Green Arrow and DC's *Batman* titles (where they created Ra's al Ghul, revitalized the Joker and brought back Two-Face), with Michael Kaluta on *The Shadow*, and with Denys Cowan on *The Question* (on which O'Neil had a 36-issue run). He is also credited with much of the storyline for *Transformers* and naming Optimus Prime. He wrote *Iron Man* for four years and kicked off DC's *Batman: Legends of the Dark Knight* with its first arc. His work as an editor for both Marvel and DC spans many different series. Among his top credits are supervising Frank Miller and Klaus Janson's *Daredevil* at Marvel and serving as group editor of the Batman family of comics at DC.

BATMAN #232
June 1971. © DC

KATSUHIRO OTOMO

INDUCTED IN 2018

A manga writer and artist in addition to being a screenwriter and director in film, Katsuhiro Otomo is easily best-known for his legendary work on *Akira*. In the world of manga, Otomo's career began by doing a number of short stories for *Action* magazine in the late 1970s, before he started on his first long-form work, *Fireball*. He followed up with *Domu* in 1980, and that in turn was followed up with *Akira*, which began serialization in 1983. It was around this time that he began working in anime, first as a character designer before moving on to directing. The 1988 animated feature film *Akira* was directed by Otomo, though the manga was actually still ongoing at the time; *Akira* is considered one of the most influential anime films of all time. While Otomo has continued to work in animation on films such as *Steamboy* and *Metropolis*, his comics work has also continued with series including *The Legend of Mother Sarah* and *Hipira: The Little Vampire*. He also contributed to the *Batman: Black & White* limited series with the story "The Third Mask.".

– *Carrie Wood*

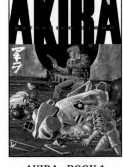

AKIRA - BOOK 1
English collection by
Kodansha Comics. 2009.
© MASH • ROOM Co. Ltd.

R.F. OUTCAULT

R.F. Outcault (1863-1925) was a comic strip writer, artist, and painter known for creating The Yellow Kid and Buster Brown. This pioneer worked as a technical illustrator for Thomas Edison before being hired by Joseph Pulitzer at the *New York World*. Outcault launched *Hogan's Alley*, a single panel illustration which featured The Yellow Kid, in 1895. It portrayed the struggles in city slums at the time and was successfully licensed on everything from children's toys and sheet music to liquor and cigarettes. Buster Brown first appeared as a color strip in the Sunday edition of the rival *New York Herald* on May 4, 1902. Buster was a pint-size prankster, constantly bedeviling those around him, then resolving to behave better in the future. His ever-present companion was Tige, a Boston terrier with an evil toothy grin. The strip ran until 1920 and was reprinted in collected editions. Buster Brown was licensed to more than 50 manufacturers of everything from bread to soap to harmonicas; the best known product was Buster Brown shoes.

THE YELLOW KID IN McFADDEN'S FLATS
1897. G.W. Dillingham Co.

ROBERT M. OVERSTREET

It started humbly with exposure to his older brother's Golden Age copies of *Captain Marvel, Daredevil* and the funny animal title *Fox And The Crow*, but when Bob Overstreet discovered EC Comics, look out! He began travelling to put together a full set of the EC titles, always searching for better copies and any bit of data he could find on them. A veteran coin collector, he quickly realized that what comics needed was a price guide. In 1970, after a lot more research, he published the first edition of *The Overstreet Comic Book Price Guide*. While some early fans thought the prices were way too high, time has proven him – and the *Guide* – right pretty frequently.

– Stephen A. Geppi

OVERSTREET C.B.P.G. #1
1970. © Gemstone

GEORGE PÉREZ

George Pérez is arguably one of the greatest comic book artists to ever hold a pencil. He began his career working on a serialized action-adventure strip called Sons of the Tiger in Marvel's *Deadly Hands of Kung Fu*. From there, Pérez moved on to work on Marvel premier superhero team, *The Avengers* (beginning with issue #141) and soon took over artistic duties on Marvel's First Family, *The Fantastic Four*.

After tackling two of Marvel's flagship books, Pérez jumped ship and moved over to work on *Justice League of America* at DC Comics. Soon after, he teamed up with writer Marv Wolfman to streamline the DC Universe in the epic maxi-series, *Crisis on Infinite Earths* (1985).

Pérez, at one time or another during his illustrious career has drawn every major character from both the Marvel and DC Universe, many of whom were featured in *JLA/Avengers* (2003), a crossover that was 20 years in the making.

CRISIS ON INFINITE EARTHS #7
October 1985. © DC

MAC RABOY

INDUCTED IN 2006

Emanuel "Mac" Raboy began his comic book career in 1940 working for the Harry A Chesler studio, which was known for completing work for a variety of comic publishers. He also notably used his artistic talents at Fawcett Publications on many of the company's classic titles including *Captain Marvel, Jr.*, *Captain Midnight*, and *Master Comics*.

His art carries a classic feel that can be easily identified by his use of composition and perspective. Mac later left Fawcett in 1944 and used his abilities on the comic book *Green Lama*. From 1948 until his death in 1967 Mac Raboy worked as the illustrator on the *Flash Gordon* comic strip for King Features Syndicate.

MASTER COMICS #30
September 1942. © FAW

MIKE RICHARDSON

INDUCTED IN 2010

When Mike Richardson launched Dark Horse Comics in 1986 with *Dark Horse Presents* #1, very few could have predicted the events of the next 24 years. Even when *Concrete* #1 started garnering critical acclaim (the series would eventually win 26 Eisner Awards during its run), no one really knew what an independent powerhouse Richardson was building in Milwaukie, Oregon. They soon would.

Whether acting as the creator of projects like *The Mask*, *The Secret*, *Living with the Dead*, and *Cut*, co-authoring non-fiction books such as *Comics Between the Panels* and *Blast Off!*, developing comic book-inspired films, or championing the work of other creators, he said he founded the company with the goal of establishing an ideal atmosphere for creative professionals.

Over time, creators such as Frank Miller, Geoff Darrow, Dave Gibbons, Stan Sakai, Sergio Aragonés, Arthur Adams, Harlan Ellison, Matt Wagner, Mike Allred, Mike Mignola, Mike Baron, Steve Rude, Jim Shooter, and Dave Stevens, and licensed properties such as *Aliens*, *Predator*, *Conan*, and most notably *Star Wars* have made their home at Richardson's company with dazzling results.

– *Stephen A. Geppi*

DARK HORSE PRESENTS #51
June 1991. © DH

JERRY ROBINSON

INDUCTED IN 2010

Jerry Robinson was a Columbia University student when he met and began working for Batman creator Bob Kane in 1939. He started out working on backgrounds and lettering, teamed with Kane and writer Bill Finger. He quickly became the main inker for the character. When Kane and Finger discussed adding a sidekick for Batman while preparing for *Detective Comics* #38, Robinson suggested Robin, drawing inspiration from N.C. Wyeth's illustration of Robin Hood. In time for *Batman* #1, he (along with Finger) is unofficially credited with creating the Joker as well.

After working for Kane, then on staff at DC and illustrating comic books for others, Robinson had a highly successful career in newspaper comic strips and editorial cartooning. He served as President of the National Cartoonists Society and the Association of American Editorial Cartoonists, founded the Cartoonists & Writers Syndicate. He, along with Neal Adams and others, championed the cause of Superman creators Jerry Siegel and Joe Shuster receiving royalties for their creation.

He passed away on December 7, 2011 at the age of 89.

BATMAN #12
August-September 1942. © DC

MARSHALL ROGERS INDUCTED IN 2008

Marshall Rogers visually defined Batman for a generation of fans. Teamed with writer Steve Englehart and inker Terry Austin, Rogers delivered the lead stories in a highly praised run on *Detective Comics* in the 1970s which introduced mob boss Rupert Thorne, Bruce Wayne's love interest Silver St. Cloud, and the Joker Fish. He simultaneously drew a memorable run of *Mister Miracle*. Rogers also worked with Englehart on *Coyote* in serialized form in the pages of *Eclipse Magazine, Madame Xanadu, Scorpio Rose, Silver Surfer* and later, again with Austin inking, on the mini-series *Batman: Dark Detective*. Rogers also illustrated a run on *Doctor Strange* and teamed with writer Don McGregor on the original *Detectives, Inc.* graphic novel. His work also appeared in *G.I. Joe, Howard The Duck, Green Lantern: Evil's Might, Batman: Legends of the Dark Knight*, and his own creation, Cap'n Quick and a Foozle. He passed away unexpectedly at the age of 57.

DETECTIVE COMICS #475
February 1978. © DC

JOHN ROMITA, SR. INDUCTED IN 2008

Even if they have never seen a comic book, anyone who saw the visual imagery in the first two Spider-Man feature films has seen the work of John Romita, Sr. (credited simply as John Romita for a good portion of his career). Imagery based on his strong, distinctive, character-rich comic book work permeated just about every important scene in those movies. He worked in the industry for years before he took over the art duties on *Amazing Spider-Man* from Steve Ditko, but his dynamic style and fluid linework put his stamp on Spidey almost immediately, forever associating him with the character. His influence on successive generations of Marvel Comics artists was foreseen by Stan Lee, who hired him as Art Director for the company. Although he is officially retired, his work still pops up from time to time, always to smiles from his fans and fellow professionals.

AMAZING SPIDER-MAN #100
September 1971. © MAR

JOHN ROMITA, JR. INDUCTED IN 2008

After making his American comics debut in the pages of *Amazing Spider-Man Annual* #11, John Romita, Jr. quickly established himself as a popular artist with a healthy run on *Iron Man*. He then launched into his first run on *Amazing Spider-Man*, the series that had made his father a fan favorite. He followed this with stints on *Uncanny X-Men, Daredevil, Daredevil: Man Without Fear, Star Brand, Punisher War Zone, Cable, The Mighty Thor*, a second run on *Iron Man,* *Wolverine*, a second run on *Amazing Spider-Man, The Black Panther, The Sentry, The Eternals*, and the "World War Hulk" event. He illustrated the Punisher-Batman crossover and his creator-owned *The Gray Area*, which was released by Image Comics. He has worked with John, Sr. on a number of special occasions, always to the delight of the comic-buying public, but has clearly worked to develop his own style, sometimes sharing only a commitment to great storytelling with his father.

AMAZING SPIDER-MAN #508
July 2004. © MAR

DON ROSA

Born in Louisville, Kentucky in 1951, Don Rosa developed a love of Carl Barks' Uncle Scrooge tales from early childhood. That led Rosa to the creation of his own Barks-inspired comics and characters, notably "The Pertwillaby Papers" for his college newspaper. After graduation, Rosa divided his time between self-created comics, comics fanzine work, and his family's tile company. In the mid-1980s Rosa began writing and drawing his first Duck stories. "The Son of the Sun" (*Uncle Scrooge* #219) marked the start of many years' active work with Scrooge and Donald: first for Gladstone, then for Sanoma and Egmont in Europe.

Perhaps Rosa's most celebrated achievement is his 12-part epic, "The Life and Times of Scrooge McDuck," which has been repeatedly anthologized around the world and is regarded as one of Disney comics' great milestones.

With numerous beloved, highly intricate Scrooge McDuck adventures to his name and an international fan following, Don Rosa ranks among today's most significant Disney comics creators.

– J.C. Vaughn & Leonard (John) Clark

THE LIFE AND TIMES OF SCROOGE MCDUCK
Trade paperback. 2005. © DIS

KURT SCHAFFENBERGER

The Marvel and Superman Families seldom looked better when handled by the skilled hand of Kurt Schaffenberger. Tackling the Big Red Cheese in the Golden Age for Fawcett Comics and the Bronze Age for DC Comics, the talented artist was also recruited by Otto Binder in 1957 to work on the Superman family of titles. He continued to work at DC for the next three decades, where he was the lead artist on *Superman's Girl Friend, Lois Lane* for the entirety of its first decade. It's been said that Schaffenberger's rendition of Lane became the "definitive" version of the character, and the artist was often asked by DC editor Mort Weisinger to redraw other artists' depictions of her in other DC titles in which she appeared. He retired from comics in the 1980s soon after penciling the second chapter of Alan Moore's pre-Crisis Superman tale, "Whatever Happened to the Man of Tomorrow?" Schaffenberger passed away on January 24, 2002.

– Scott Braden

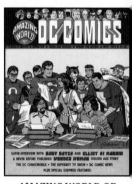

AMAZING WORLD OF DC COMICS #2
September 1974. © DC

ALEX SCHOMBURG

Alex Schomburg (Alejandro Schomburg y Rosa) was born May 10, 1905 in Aguadilla, Puerto Rico, and moved to New York City in the 1920s, where he began working as a commercial artist for the National Screen Service. In the 1930s he freelanced for Better Publications producing line art for their line of pulps, but he is remembered best for his brilliant and unique comic book covers that he produced for Timely Comics which included Captain America, Human Torch, Sub-Mariner and their other heroes, many of them in World War II images. He also produced covers for Nedor Comics like *Exciting Comics, The Black Terror, Fighting Yank, Best Comics, Thrilling Comics, Startling Comics, Wonder Comics*, and others. In addition to traditional line work, he developed a completely different style with an airbrush and signed those works "Xela" ("Alex" backwards). He left comics for magazines in the 1950s, but produced covers for *The Overstreet Comic Book Price Guide* #10 and #21, and accepted fan commissions at shows later in life. Schomburg passed away on April 7, 1998.

– Robert M. Overstreet

ALL SELECT COMICS #1
Fall 1943. © MAR

JULIUS SCHWARTZ

It's difficult to measure the impact Julius "Julie" Schwartz had on the comic book world. In fact, as we observed at the time of his passing, we would probably need to invent a new unit of measurement just to begin to cover it. He was Ray Bradbury's first agent and an important voice in science fiction before he ever joined All-American Comics in 1944. Working with writers such as John Broome and artists like Gil Kane, Murphy Anderson, Carmine Infantino, and Joe Kubert, he began the underpinnings of what would become the resurgence of superhero comics in the 1950s and '60s.

After re-introducing and revamping characters such as Flash and Green Lantern, he helped develop DC's "multi-verse" by having the then-current incarnations of characters meet their predecessors, kicking off one of the best-loved eras in the company's history. He was continually a force for reinvention of characters and served as a goodwill ambassador after his retirement.

AMAZING WORLD OF DC COMICS #3
November 1974. © DC

JOHN SEVERIN

Rarely has an individual been known for two so distinctly different genres of work in the field of comic art, but John Severin is known equally for illustrating action-adventure tales and humorous stories. From his days as one of the original artists on EC's *MAD* (often with Will Elder providing the inking) to a lengthy run at *Cracked*, Severin became one of the prime send-up artists working in the business. Due to the wider circulation of *MAD* and *Cracked* compared to many comic books, it's safe to think that many know him for that work rather than the action-adventure genre, but comic book fans have had a deep appreciation for his westerns, war stories, horror, and other pieces in *Two-Fisted Tales*, *Blazing Combat*, *Creepy*, *King Kull*, *The 'Nam*, *Sgt. Fury*, and *Conan*, setting standards whether providing pencil art, inking, or supplying both. Most recently he had illustrated *Desperadoes: Quiet of the Grave* and *Bat Lash*.

He passed away on February 12, 2012.

TWO-FISTED TALES #37
April 1954. © WMG

MARIE SEVERIN

Beginning with coloring *A Moon, a Girl...Romance* #9 (October 1949), Marie Severin became a highly regarded contributor to EC Comics. There she labored on the company's whole line, including the horror, action-adventure, science fiction and humor titles ranging from *Crime SuspenStories* to *MAD*, often working closely with her brother, artist John Severin, and writer-artist-editor Harvey Kurtzman. While noted as a colorist, she became highly capable in most artistic roles, including penciling, inking and lettering. When EC closed down, she worked at pre-Marvel Atlas before the industry took a downturn and she left. She reentered the business shortly before Atlas became Marvel and was there for the Silver Age growth. While continuing to color and deal with production issues, she illustrated *Captain America*, *Captain Marvel*, *Daredevil*, *Strange Tales* (taking over *Doctor Strange* from Steve Ditko), *Sub-Mariner*, *Tales to Astonish*, and *X-Men*. Her EC background (and perhaps her work with Kurtzman) influenced her wonderful stint on Marvel's self-parody series *Not Brand Ecch!*

CRAZY #1
February 1973. © MAR

JIM SHOOTER

INDUCTED IN 2007

It's perhaps fitting that a career punctuated by sensational successes and seemingly crushing defeats began with a spectacular misperception. Jim Shooter began writing comics when he was 13 years old. The editors, thinking he was older, called to accept the stories and ended up having to negotiate with his mother. Over the next four decades, he put a distinctive stamp on the Legion of Super-Heroes in *Adventure Comics*, helped propel *The Avengers* to the top of the Marvel Comics universe, and his stint as Editor-in-Chief at Marvel launched such notable runs as Frank Miller's *Daredevil* and Walter Simonson's *Thor*. He wrote *Marvel Super-Heroes Secret Wars*, which is still a best-seller. He helped develop and launch Marvel's recently resuscitated New Universe, then founded Valiant, Defiant, and Broadway Comics. In 2009, Dark Horse Comics hired Shooter to relaunch Gold Key's *Magnus, Robot Fighter, Doctor Solar, Man of the Atom, Turok, Son of Stone, Mighty Samson*, and *Doctor Spektor*, among others.

MARVEL SUPER-HEROES SECRET WARS #1
May 1984. © MAR

JOE SHUSTER

INDUCTED IN 2010

By the time his greatest creation had become a worldwide sensation in the late '30s and early '40s, he was already beginning to lose his eyesight, but artist Joe Shuster (1914-1992) had vision to spare when working with partner and writer Jerry Siegel to craft the quintessential hero – Superman. Based on a mutual love of science fiction and pulp adventure shared by the Cleveland teens, the Man of Steel debuted in 1938 in *Action Comics* #1 (DC) with Shuster's hand shaping the dynamic look that would remain more or less intact for the next 70 years. Although marginalized by the industry in later years, Shuster eventually earned permanent credit for his role in Superman's creation thanks to a crusade spearheaded by the likes of industry star Neal Adams. Today every Superman comic and production still proclaims: "Superman created by Jerry Siegel and Joe Shuster." For a man that saw the future clearly even through fading sight, there is no better epitaph.

– Dr. Arnold T. Blumberg

SUPERMAN #1
Summer 1939. © DC

JERRY SIEGEL

INDUCTED IN 2010

He was a Jewish kid from Cleveland with big dreams and a knack for writing high-flying adventure. Together with his friend, artist Joe Shuster, Jerry Siegel (1914-1996) created a character that would become the definitive comic book superhero for the next 70 years. Superman was a worldwide multimedia hit within a few years of his debut in *Action Comics* #1 in 1938, and although Siegel also created the creepy crusader known as the Spectre, it was the Man of Tomorrow that would cement Siegel's name in the annals of pop culture. Sadly, much of Siegel's later life was consumed more with legal battles than flights of fantasy as he (and later his family) fought to wrest control of his super-successful creations from DC. The ongoing courtroom saga has often obscured Siegel's accomplishments as one of the architects of the Golden Age and our modern mythology.

– Dr. Arnold T. Blumberg

ACTION COMICS #1
June 1938. © DC

BILL SIENKIEWICZ

INDUCTED IN 2012

Boleslav Felix Robert "Bill" Sienkiewicz is best known for his dynamic style of comic book and graphic novel illustration beginning with Marvel's Moon Knight in the pages *The Hulk* #13, later graduating with the character from the magazine to his own comic book series. Sienkiewicz grew up in rural New Jersey, taught himself anatomy to better his sketches, and worked construction to put himself through the Newark School of Fine and Industrial Arts. Starting his career on Marvel Comics' at the age of 19, he illustrated *Moon Knight* for several years, including its jump being available exclusively in the Direct Market only. Initially his work showed the strong influence of Neal Adams, but as he moved from assignment to assignment, it grew more expressionistic. It continued to evolve in the pages of *New Mutants, Daredevil: Love and War* (Marvel Graphic Novel #24), and *Elektra: Assassin*, as well as his acclaimed graphic novel Stray Toasters. He also has created advertising material, book art, CD covers, and film designs, among other projects.

– Scott Braden & J.C. Vaughn

ELEKTRA: ASSASSIN HC
1987. © MAR

MARC SILVESTRI

INDUCTED IN 2018

Marc Silvestri has been a pioneer in the comics industry for dozens of years, having been part of the original artist collective to establish Image Comics in 1992. His career started in the '80s, working for both DC and First Comics before moving to Marvel, where he worked on *Uncanny X-Men* and *Wolverine*. After founding Image, Silvestri established the Top Cow imprint, where he's worked on a number of different titles, including *Cyberforce, Codename: Stryke Force, Witchblade, Hunter-Killer,* and *The Darkness*, among many others. *Witchblade* was actually adapted into an anime series in 2006, which Silvestri executive produced; *The Darkness* has seen two video game adaptations, in 2007 and 2012. Silvestri continues to run Top Cow as its CEO, though he has also contributed to various *X-Men* titles for Marvel within the last few years as well.

– Carrie Wood

CYBERFORCE Volume 2 #1
November 1993. © TCOW

DAVE SIM

INDUCTED IN 2014

Dave Sim, the creator of Cerebus the Aardvark, is revered as one of the pioneers of the self-publishing and creators' rights movements. Although he has subsequently published interesting projects such as the online comic book biography of Canadian actress Siu Ta (entitled Sui Ta, So Far) and *Judenhass*, which Sim described as a "personal reflection on the Holocaust," and *Glamourpuss*, a comic book parody of fashion magazines, he is best known for his 300-issue, self-published comic, which he began in 1977. Initially a parody of Conan the Barbarian and Howard the Duck, *Cerebus* morphed into a vehicle for social satire that became increasingly sophisticated visually and explored weighty topics like politics, religion, metaphysics, and gender roles. The 300 issues of *Cerebus* (constituting 6,000 pages) have been collected into 16 volumes. In 2009, Sim's web series, *Cerebus TV*, premiered, with new episodes appearing weekly. To date, more than 100 episodes have been produced.

– S.C. Ringgenberg

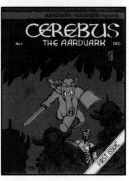

CEREBUS THE AARDVARK #1
December 1977 - January 1978.
© Dave Sim

JOE SIMON

Though best known as the co-creator of Captain America or as half of the Simon and Kirby team (with Jack Kirby), Joe Simon's prolific career as a writer, artist, editor and publisher has few parallels in comic book history. After freelancing for *True Story* and magazines, Simon reportedly came to the attention of Lloyd Jacquet, whose company, Funnies, Inc., packaged comic book material for publishers. A short while later, he met Kirby. They began working together on the second issue of *Blue Bolt* and became one of the most influential teams in the medium's history. They worked together until 1955, when comic sales nose-dived and Simon sought work outside the field. During that time, they produced *The Fighting American*, westerns such as *Boys Ranch*, and many others. They are credited with creating the romance comics genre with *Young Romance Comics*. Among the projects he later took on, he spent a decade working with *Sick*, a *MAD*-inspired humor magazine.

Joe Simon passed away on December 14, 2011 at the age of 98.

CAPTAIN AMERICA COMICS #1
March 1941. © MAR

LOUISE SIMONSON

Louise Simonson's comic book career began at Warren Publishing in 1974 as assistant editor on titles like *Creepy* and *Eerie*. This would lead to an an expansive body of work as an editor and later a writer for Marvel and DC, with additional entries at Dark Horse Comics, IDW, Image, and Valiant. In 1980, she joined Marvel, where she edited *Uncanny X-Men* for nearly four years during its most iconic period. Then credited as Louise Jones, she also edited *The New Mutants* as well. In 1983, she switched to writing. She created and wrote the first 40 issues of *Power Pack*. She took on writing duties for *X-Factor*, where she introduced Apocalypse, transformed Angel into Archangel, and suggested that the "Mutant Massacre" story become an *X-Men* line-wide crossover. Through the late '80s, she wrote *New Mutants* and co-created Cable. In 1991, she launched *Superman: The Man of Steel*, which she wrote until 1999. Simonson was among the architects of best-selling "The Death of Superman" storyline. She co-created and wrote the first 31 issues of *Steel*.

– Amanda Sheriff

SUPERMAN: THE MAN OF STEEL #1
July 1991. © DC

WALT SIMONSON

While attending the Rhode Island School of Design, writer-artist Walt Simonson created *Star Slammers*, a different version of which years later would become *Marvel Graphic Novel #6* and later a *Star Slammers* series from Malibu's Bravura imprint. Between those two periods he established himself as a creative force, chiefly with the award-winning Manhunter back-up feature in *Detective Comics*, on which he collaborated with writer Archie Goodwin. Following work on DC's *Metal Men* and *Hercules Unbound* and *Heavy Metal*'s *Alien* adaptation (again with Goodwin), he made his way to Marvel. Beginning with *Thor #337*, Simonson wrote and illustrated a definitive run on the title, eventually ending with *Thor #382*. Over the years, his other Marvel work included *Battlestar Galactica*, *Star Wars*, *Fantastic Four*, *The Avengers*, *X-Factor* (with wife Louise Simonson) and others. At DC, among other work, provided covers for *Jack Kirby's Fourth World*, wrote and illustrated 25 issues of *Orion*, illustrated *Elric: The Making of a Sorcerer*, and wrote the Catwoman and The Demon strip in *Wednesday Comics*.

OVERSTREET C.B.P.G. #42
2011. © MAR

JEFF SMITH

INDUCTED IN 2014

Jeff Smith, creator of the brashly funny and adventurous, all-ages *Bone*, is one of the most successful and honored of all self-published cartoonists, with 10 Eisner Awards, 11 Harvey Awards, one Inkpot Award, and two National Cartoonists Society Comic Book Awards, an astonishing legacy by any standards. While the 55 issues of *Bone* constitute the majority of his oeuvre, Smith has not rested on his many laurels. Since concluding the *Bone* saga in 2004, Smith's published works have included *Shazam!: The Monster Society of Evil* Prestige miniseries for DC, a retelling of the Golden Age Captain Marvel's epic struggle against the eponymous collection of villains, *RASL*, a science fiction series about a dimension-hopping art thief, the webcomic *Tüki: Save the Humans* (about the first humans to venture out of Africa), and the graphic novel, *Little Mouse Gets Ready*, a book intended for beginning readers. In 2007, Smith was named as the designer for Fantagraphics' complete collection of Walt Kelly's *Pogo* comic strips, which is only fitting, since *Pogo* was one of Smith's biggest influences as a cartoonist and writer.

– S.C. Ringgenberg

BONE #1
July 1991. © Jeff Smith

DICK SPRANG

INDUCTED IN 2020

Dick Sprang produced stylish, bold designs, iconic covers, and smooth pacing through innovative page layouts and panel structure. The penciler-inker's most notable work was largely centered on Batman and his titles during the Golden Age and Silver Ages. Following newspaper and magazine assignments early in his career, Sprang began illustrating Western, detective, and adventure magazines in the 1930s. After submitting art samples to DC Comics, he was assigned to *Batman*. His first published work for them came in *Batman* #19 (Oct.-Nov. 1943). For 20 years, he was a dominant force with the character. His portrayal of the Caped Crusader gave Batman such notable qualities as his expressive face, square chin, and large chest. With his crafting of these details, Sprang contributed significantly to Batman's early success. He had noted runs on *Batman*, *Detective Comics*, and *World's Finest Comics*, as well as in the Batman comic strip. He co-created villains like the Riddler, Killer Moth, and Kite Man, and redesigned the Batmobile.

– Amanda Sheriff

DETECTIVE COMICS #118
December 1946.
© DC

JIM STERANKO

INDUCTED IN 2010

His covers for Marvel's *Captain America*, *Incredible Hulk*, and *Nick Fury, Agent of S.H.I.E.L.D.* are some of the most iconic and innovative pieces of pop art from the 1960s. Jim Steranko (1938-) was, perhaps auspiciously, born the year the Golden Age began, but he is far more than just one of the most influential artists of the Marvel Age. His *Chandler: Red Tide* helped to define the very meaning of the term "graphic novel," his conceptual artwork for *Raiders of the Lost Ark* breathed life into Indiana Jones – the man whose name was synonymous with adventure – and his two-volume *The Steranko History of Comics* offered a unique insight into the development of the medium during the Golden Age. Today the award-winning Steranko stands as one of comicdom's living legends with awards and honors that serve as testament to his indelible contributions.

– Dr. Arnold T. Blumberg

NICK FURY, AGENT OF S.H.I.E.L.D. #1
June 1968. © MAR

DAVE STEVENS

Dave Stevens, whose first comic work was inking Russ Manning's pencils for the *Tarzan* daily, made a splash in the comic book world with the introduction of The Rocketeer as a back-up feature in *Starslayer* #2 from Pacific Comics. The character jumped from there to *Pacific Presents* to his own comics from a number of publishers, and eventually onto the silver screen. His story and art were steeped in the styles and history of the 1930s, and they drew praise for their historical accuracy as well as their breathtaking imagery.

For a relative small comic book output, Stevens was widely considered "an artist's artist." He received the first Russ Manning Award in 1982, and played a key role in reviving interest in Bettie Page. While he illustrated numerous other covers (including *Alien Worlds*, *Bettie Page Comics*, and *Jonny Quest*, among others), Dave Stevens remains best known for high-flying pilot Cliff Secord, The Rocketeer.

He passed away in 2008.

THE ROCKETEER:
THE OFFICIAL
MOVIE ADAPTATION
1991. © DIS

CURT SWAN

Douglas Curtis Swan, the artist most associated with Superman during the Silver Age of comics, produced hundreds of covers and stories from the 1950s through the 1980s. Following World War II and a stint on *Boy Commandos*, he began to pencil pages, leaving the inking to others, including famed inker Murphy Anderson (the pair's collaborative artwork came to be called "Swanderson" by fans). His first job pencilling the iconic character was for *Superman* #51. Swan felt, however, that his breakthrough came when he was assigned the art duties on *Superman's Pal, Jimmy Olsen*, in 1954.

Over the years, Swan was a remarkably consistent and prolific artist, often illustrating two or more titles per month. The artist illustrated the first chapter of the 1986 "last Silver Age" Superman story, "Whatever Happened to the Man of Tomorrow?" written by Alan Moore. Swan's last published story was five pages published posthumously in the 1996 special *Superman: The Wedding Album*.

– Scott Braden

SUPERMAN #423
September 1986. © DC

RUMIKO TAKAHASHI

Given her remarkable and lengthy career in manga, it's hard to say what Rumiko Takahashi is "best-known" for at this point. After spending time in a manga school founded by *Lone Wolf and Cub* author Kazuo Koike, Takahashi began publishing her own work, with her professional career taking off by the end of the '70s. Her first serialized work was the sci-fi rom-com *Urusei Yatsura*, which ran from 1978 to 1987. She followed that up with *Maison Ikkoku* and *Ranma ½* in the '80s and into the '90s, and saw massive international mainstream success with *Inuyasha*. Her most recent long-running work is *Rin-Ne*, which ran from 2009 to 2017, though she has also published dozens of short stories over her 40 years in manga. She has won the Shogakukan Manga Award twice: in 1980 for *Urusei Yatsura* and in 2001 for *Inuyasha*.

– Carrie Wood

INUYASHA Volume 1
1996. © Viz Media

OSAMU TEZUKA

After the conclusion of World War II, Osamu Tezuka created his first manga, *Diary of Ma-Chan*, at just 17 years old. This time period in Japan featured a huge boom in manga – similar to the rapid expansion of comic books in America – and Tezuka's work contributed greatly to it. Tezuka's complete portfolio contains more than 700 volumes for more than 150,000 pages, and many of his creations have become known around the world thanks to successful anime adaptations. Though most would point to *Astro Boy* or *Black Jack* as his best work, his "life's work" was *Phoenix*, which he began in 1967 and continued working on until his death in 1989. Perhaps the most prolific manga artist of all time, Osamu Tezuka's influence can still be felt today in a number of contemporary series.

– *Carrie Wood*

ASTRO BOY OMNIBUS VOL. 1
Dark Horse cover - 2016.
Originally published 1952-1968.
© Osamu Tezuka

ROY THOMAS

Besides being Stan Lee's first successor as Editor-in-Chief of Marvel Comics, Roy William Thomas, Jr. has made enjoyed a long career as a writer, editor and comics historian. He is possibly best known for introducing the pulp magazine hero Conan the Barbarian to American comic book audiences. With *Conan The Barbarian* and *Savage Sword of Conan*, he added to the storyline of Robert E. Howard's character and helped launch a sword and sorcery genre in comics. Thomas is also known for his championing of Golden Age superheroes to new audiences by creating *The Invaders* at Marvel and a short while later the *All-Star Squadron* and *Infinity Inc.* at DC.

Thomas also enjoyed distinctive, key runs on *The X-Men*, *The Avengers*, *Wally Wood's T.H.U.N.D.E.R. Agents* among other titles, and continues his invaluable contributions in the pages of his award-winning magazine, *Alter Ego*, which explores comics history (though generally not the history he made himself).

– *Scott Braden*

ALTER EGO #70
July 2007. © Roy Thomas

ALEX TOTH

Beginning his career at the young age of 15, and quickly rising to be one of the most iconic artists in both the world of comics and animation, Alex Toth inspired a generation of fans through his body of work, both as an artist and writer. Throughout the mid-1940s and early 1950s, Toth worked for such companies as DC, Famous Funnies, Atlas, Marvel and Visual Edition (Standard). His portfolio included work on *Green Lantern*, *Mystery in Space*, *Strange Adventures*, *Unseen*, *World's Finest*, and *Zorro*. After serving a tour of duty in the US Army, Toth began to work for Hanna-Barbera doing storyboards for *Space Ghost*, *Challenge of the Superfriends*, *Fantastic Four*, *Herculoids*, *Birdman* and *Jonny Quest*. In addition to his work in animation, Toth continued to draw comics and write columns for *Alter Ego* and *Comic Book Artist*. He passed away in 2006.

**LIMITED COLLECTORS'
EDITION C-41**
December 1975-January 1976.
© DC

TIM TRUMAN

INDUCTED IN **2016**

Whether a steely slash of Conan's blade, the muzzle flash of the Spider's side arms, or the hard driving blues of Scout's dystopic future, Tim Truman began delighting comic book audiences with his brand of action, adventure and suspense in the pages of *Starslayer* #10 in 1984. His credits include long stints as writer or artist or both on a varied number of titles and characters. After introducing Grimjack (with writer John Ostrander), illustrating *Starslayer*, and writing and illustrating the Time Beavers, Truman launched *Scout* at Eclipse Comics. It was followed by *Scout: War Shaman* and a number of spin-offs. He revived thie 1940s characters Airboy and The Heap, and developed *The Prowler* at the company as well. In addition to his creator-owned work, he's worked for other publishers as well including Dark Horse (*Conan, Star Wars, Tarzan*), DC (*The Black Lamb, Guns of the Dragon, Hawkworld, Jonah Hex, The Kents*), Topps (*Lone Ranger and Tonto*), and Valiant (*Turok: Dinosaur Hunter*), among others.

SCOUT #11
September 1986.
© Timothy Truman

MICHAEL TURNER

INDUCTED IN **2007**

Michael Turner began his career as a comic book artist in 1994 as a background artist working under Marc Silvestri at Image Comics' Top Cow Productions imprint. While there, Turner helped co-create Top Cow's *Witchblade* in 1995, which has been the company's longest running book. Following his success on *Witchblade*, he went on to create his first creator-owned property, *Fathom* in 1998.

In late 2002, Turner founded his own studio, Aspen MLT, Inc. where he brought *Fathom* and also launched *Soulfire, Cannon Hawke* and *Ekos*.

Turner was one of the most sought-after cover artists working in the industry, having done covers for both DC and Marvel Comics, as well as dozens of Independent Press books.

Tragically, he passed away in 2008 at age 37, following a long but brave battle against cancer.

WITCHBLADE #6
June 1996. © TCOW

JIM VALENTINO

INDUCTED IN **2017**

Image Comics co-founder Jim Valentino first garnered attention for his work on *normalman*, which debuted as a back-up story in Dave Sim's *Cerebus*. That was followed by the launch of a 13-issue *normalman* limited series at Sim's Aardvark-Vanaheim, but when Sim and then-wife Deni Loubert split, *normalman* ended up at Loubert's Renegade Press for #9-13. From that slightly convoluted start, he landed at Marvel, where he grabbed attention with a variety of work, which included a 27-issue run on *Guardians of the Galaxy*. That series that established him with a strong fanbase and put him in position to leave Marvel to co-found Image. There he launched his creator-owned *ShadowHawk* and followed it up with the autobiographical *A Touch of Silver*. Like his earlier work, he served as its writer and artist. After serving a stint as the company's publisher and diversifying the company's line-up, he used his Shadowline imprint at Image to launch *Bomb Queen, After the Cape* and *Sam Noir*, among other projects.

SHADOWHAWK #2
October 1992.
© Jim Valentino

MARK WAID

Starting with his stint at *Amazing Heroes*, writer Mark Waid has brought a strong, distinctive voice to both the comics he writes and the issues on which he focuses. At DC he edited a number of titles including *Gotham by Gaslight*, the first "Elseworlds" issue, before starting as a freelancer with *The Comet* for their Impact line. He firmly established himself with fans for his eight-year run on *The Flash,* succeeding where other talented writers had failed to have Wally West actually supplant Barry Allen as The Flash in the minds of many fans. His work with artist Ron Garney at Marvel on *Captain America* is widely regarded as the best of that era. Over the years his work has included *Impulse, Kingdome Come, JLA: Heaven's Ladder, Ruse, Fantastic Four, Superman: Birthright, Legion of Super-Heroes, Amazing Spider-Man, Indestructible Hulk, S.H.I.E.L.D.*, and *Daredevil*, launching the digital comics site Thrillbent, and creator-owned titles such as *Empire, Irredeemable* and *Incorruptible*. He is also co-owns The Aw Yeah Comics chain.

FLASH (2nd series) #75
April 1993. ©DC

LEN WEIN

Throughout his career, writer-editor Len Wein made significant contributions to both DC and Marvel. Wein's career began with the *Teen Titans* #18 story "Eye of the Beholder" in 1968, followed by work on romance comics, horror magazines, and TV tie-ins. Wein and artist Bernie Wrightson co-created Swamp Thing in *House of Secrets* #92 in 1971 and worked on Swamp Thing's initial run, then in the mid-'80s Wein edited *Saga of the Swamp Thing*. In the early '70s he regularly wrote for Marvel titles like *Amazing Spider-Man* and *Thor*. Wein and artists John Romita Sr. and Herb Trimpe co-created Wolverine in *Incredible Hulk* #180 (cameo appearance) in '74, followed by the X-Men revival, reformatted as *Giant Size X-Men* with Dave Cockrum. Returning to DC, he wrote *Batman*, creating Lucius Fox, wrote the *Wonder Woman* reboot, and edited the acclaimed *Watchmen*. Later in his career, Wein wrote and story edited animated shows like *X-Men, Batman,* and *Spider-Man,* wrote for Cartoon Network shows, and in 2012 he penned the *Before Watchmen: Ozymandias* miniseries.

– Amanda Sheriff

INCREDIBLE HULK #181
November 1974. © MAR

MARK WHEATLEY

Writer, artist, editor and publisher Mark Wheatley's creations include *Mars, Breathtaker, Prince Nightmare, Hammer of the Gods, Blood of the Innocent, Radical Dreamer, Frankenstein Mobster, Miles the Monster, The Mighty Motor-Sapiens, EZ Street, Lone Justice,* and *Titanic Tales,* among others. Often collaborating with fellow Insight Studios Group member Marc Hempel, studio founder Wheatley has also worked on are *Tarzan the Warrior, The Black Hood, The Adventures of Baron Munchausen, Jonny Quest,* Dr. Strange, The Flash, Argus and *The Spider*. He has won the Inkpot, Mucker, Gem, Speakeasy and Eisner awards and his projects have been nominated for the Harvey and Ignatz awards as well. His efforts have been repeatedly included in the annual Spectrum selection of fantastic art and has appeared in private gallery shows as well as the Library of Congress where several of his originals are in the LoC permanent collection. His work has also been displayed at the Norman Rockwell Museum, The Toledo Museum of Art, and The Huntington Museum of Art in Huntington, WV.

MARS TPB
August 2005. © Mark Wheatley
& Marc Hempel

MAJOR MALCOLM WHEELER-NICHOLSON

Honored in 2008 with a posthumous Eisner Award for his contributions to the comic book industry, Major Malcolm Wheeler-Nicholson might have become the forgotten titan of comic book history, except for the efforts of comics historians. The former soldier, adventurer and inventor was also a successful and prolific author and in the 1920s he made a solid living from writing novels and short stories, often for the pulp magazines. When the Great Depression forced him and his family to move back to New York from Europe, he turned his attention to a new enterprise.

Comic books had, of course, been around in one form or another, for more than 90 years, but they had almost exclusively been collections of reprinted newspaper comic strips and priced for adults. Wheeler-Nicholson not only wrote and commissioned original content, he priced them at 10¢. In 1934, he launched *New Fun Comics*. DC Comics – and with it a new form of the comics business – was born.

NEW FUN COMICS #1
February 1935. The start of
DC Comics. © DC

MIKE WIERINGO

Also known as "Ringo," artist Mike Wieringo was best known for his work on DC Comics' *The Flash*, Marvel Comics' *Fantastic Four*, and *Tellos*; the creator-owned fantasy series he developed with friend and writer Todd DeZago. In an era in which many artists rely on shock or over-the-top style, his clean, deceptively simple linework captured the heroism superheroes are supposed to embody and earned the artist a strong fan following.

Born in Venice, Italy in 1963, he joined writer Mark Waid on DC's *The Flash* with issue #80 in 1993; during their run the two co-created the character Impulse. Wieringo also illustrated *Robin* at DC, *Sensational Spider-Man* (with DeZago) at Marvel, and then created *Tellos*. He also illustrated stints on *Adventures of Superman* and (again with Waid) on *Fantastic Four*, and *Spider-Man and the Fantastic Four*, among other projects. Sadly, Wieringo passed away suddenly on August 12, 2007 at age 44.

FANTASTIC FOUR VOL. 3 #60
October 2002. © MAR

AL WILLIAMSON

Fans and historians know Al Williamson for his highly evocative art over the last fifty years, ranging from penciling and inking stories in EC's *Weird Science-Fantasy* in the '50s to inking John Romita, Jr. on *Daredevil* for Marvel in the '90s, or newspaper work including a highly respected run on the daily and Sunday *Star Wars* strip.

Al Williamson is one of only a handful of top rated comic creators who have spent their entire careers working in our industry. Too often our very best talents are lured away by promises of fame and fortune in other venues. I think that Al stands as a shining example of the lifelong craftsman who works constantly to improve his already considerable talents; by the entire scope of his career he announces to every other person in the industry that this is a field fully worth the commitment of a lifetime of creations.

He passed away in 2010.

– Mark Wheatley

WEIRD SCIENCE-FANTASY #25
September 1954.
© WMG

WALLY WOOD

INDUCTED IN 2010

Wallace A. Wood landed his first comic work with Will Eisner as a back-up artist on *The Spirit* in 1948. He also began lettering for Fox Features Syndicate, then drew stories for their love and western titles. Over the next few years he worked for Avon, Better-Standard, EC, Fawcett, Fox, Kirby Publishing Co., Youthful Magazines and Ziff-Davis.

After trying multiple genres with EC, he soon found his niche in science fiction. His work on EC's *Weird Fantasy* and *Weird Science* followed covers on Avon's *Attack On Planet Mars*, *Flying Saucers*, *Earth Man on Venus*, *Space Detective* and *Strange Worlds*. No one could draw spaceship interior instrumentation and machinery like him.

He became the first Marvel Comics artist to get a cover blurb when Stan Lee touted Wood's arrival on *Daredevil #5*. In the years that followed, he continued to produce beautiful work for DC, Charlton, Gold Key, Harvey, Tower (where he launched the T.H.U.N.D.E.R. Agents), Warren and Atlas-Seaboard, as well as a number of self-published projects.

Wood took his own life in 1981.

– Robert M. Overstreet

**INCREDIBLE
SCIENCE FICTION #33**
January-February 1956.
© WMG

BERNIE WRIGHTSON

INDUCTED IN 2017

After beginning his professional career as an illustrator for *The Baltimore Sun* in 1966, Bernie Wrightson's path was altered by a meeting with Frank Frazetta. Inspired to create his own comic book stories, his first comic work appeared in *House of Mystery #179*. By 1971, after working for both DC and Marvel, he teamed with writer Len Wein to co-create Swamp Thing. He went on to produce original work and adaptations of Poe and Lovecraft for Warren Publishing and then spent seven years on the detailed pen-and-ink illustrations for an edition of Mary Shelley's *Frankenstein*. In addition to continuing comic book work over the years, he also illustrated the one-sheet and the adaptation of the Stephen King-George Romero horror film *Creepshow*, and teamed with King for *Cycle of the Werewolf* and *The Stand*, created Captain Sternn (of *Heavy Metal* fame), and provided conceptual art for such films as *Ghostbusters*, *The Faculty*, *Galaxy Quest*, *Spider-Man*, *Land of the Dead*, and *The Mist*. He passed away March 18, 2017.

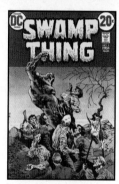

SWAMP THING #5
July-August 1973. © DC

My Top Five Favorite Guide Articles

by Robert M. Overstreet

Since our first edition, feature articles and interviews have been a vital part of *The Overstreet Comic Book Price Guide*. In our pages, contradictions have been resolved, mysteries have been unraveled, new, unsolved mysteries have been given the spotlight, creators have been honored, and previously unsung heroes have at last gotten their moment.

Our goal has always been to provide insight into the hobby through rich historical context, thoughtful guidance on collecting, and explorations of the comic industry and the people behind it.

Over the five decades of the *Guide's* history, we have had countless submissions. In the end, very few of them end up in the book each year. Over 50 years, though, that does add up to quite a few articles.

So *of course*, the staff gave me the nearly impossible task of picking my top five favorites as part of our Golden Anniversary celebration so they could be included in this book. Of course, any such undertaking is inherently arbitrary, and one knows from the outset that plenty of tremendous work by treasured friends and colleagues will be left off the list, but here are my personal top five favorite articles from the *Guide*:

In "Good Lord! Choke...Gasp...It's EC!," E.B. Boatner presents an extensive look into EC Comics. Delving into EC's "New Trend" titles, Boatner delineates their horror, science fiction, war, and humor books with insights by Bill Gaines, Al Feldstein, Harvey Kurtzman, and Jerry DeFuccio.

George Olshevsky's "The Origin of Marvel Comics" traces the roots at Timely Publications, early titles and characters that attracted readers, memorable stories, and the creators who had pivotal impacts on the comic line that would eventually become the Marvel Comics we know today.

For "L.B. Cole: The Man Behind the Mask (and Captain Aero and Catman and...)," Boatner provides an in-depth profile on the influential comic artist, editor, and publisher, with commentary by Cole himself, who recounts his work in advertising, comics, and book illustrations.

Thomas Andrae takes us to the Batcave in "Origins of the Dark Knight: A Conversation with Batman Artists Bob Kane and Jerry Robinson," in which the artists recount their introductions to comics, the creation of Batman, Robin, the Joker, and Catwoman, and the early days of Batman titles.

Harry B. Thomas and Gary M. Carter collaborate on "1941: Comic Books Go to War! Those Fabulous Comics of World War II," which transports readers back to the heart of the Golden Age, a time when superheroes fought for the war effort at home and abroad.

This selection is a small sample of the high caliber articles that Overstreet staffers, advisors, historians, supporters and others have contributed to the *Guide's* first 50 years. I hope you will enjoy them (or enjoy them again!).

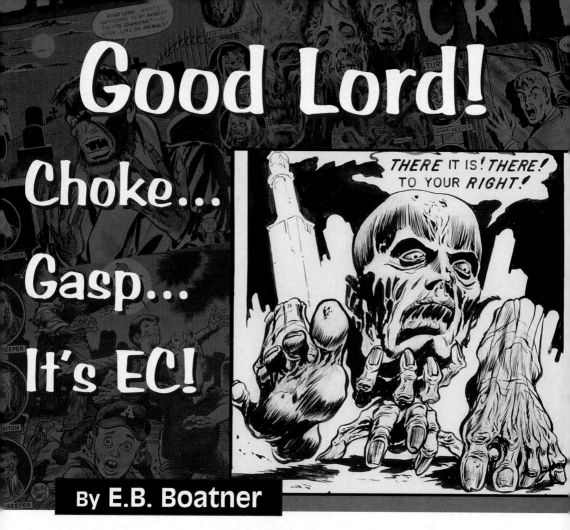

Good Lord!

Choke...

Gasp...

It's EC!

By E.B. Boatner

This article was originally published in The Overstreet Comic Book Price Guide #9 - 1979

"It was a weird tableau...the five of them! The two feet hopped along! Behind them! ... a hand dragged itself! The other hand lay, palm upward, upon the back of the moving hand! The directing hand rested in the upper hand's palm!" (*The Vault of Horror* #28).

A weird tableau for the uninitiate perhaps, but for five years between 1950 and 1955 this econoline of walking corpses was standard fare for readers of Entertaining Comics horror titles, and was typical of the startling ingenuity and inventiveness of their science fiction, suspense, war, and humor books.

In 1950, EC released seven titles in what it called a New Trend of comic books, including horror books, *The Crypt of Terror*, *The Vault of Horror*, *The Haunt of Fear*, science fiction comics, *Weird Science* and *Weird Fantasy*; crime with a twist ending, *Crime SuspenStories*; and an adventure-war book, *Two-Fisted Tales*.

Reader response to these books was immediate and enthusiastic. Here were books with a fresh approach – high quality scripts featuring plots with an O. Henry ending rather than the standard linear development, unusual and varied illustration by artists who were encouraged to develop their own idiosyncratic styles, and an editorial sense of humor that drew the reader directly into the EC ambiance.

The New Trend was the Golden Age of EC, and like all such halcyon times was preceded by a Bronze Age, and followed all too soon by a declining Silver Age. In EC terminology, these periods would be the Pre-Trend years of 1947-1950, and the New Direction and Picto-Fiction period of 1955-1956. But back to the beginning.

EC as Entertaining Comics was launched in 1947 by 25-year-old William Maxwell Gaines who took over his father's company when M.C. Gaines was killed in a motorboat accident. Before that time, as "Educational Comics," EC had consisted of a line of juvenile books: *Picture Stories From the Bible, Animal Fables, Dandy Comics, Fat and Slat, Tiny Tot Comics*, and the like.

Just as Bill Gaines was picking up the reins at EC, a young artist named Al Feldstein was growing restless with the erratic pay at Fox Studios and came to EC thinking he might get in on the ground floor of the new enterprise. Feldstein was slated to do a teenage book in the *Archie* format which never made

it to the drawing board, but he did meet Gaines which sparked a rare and happy chemistry.

They immediately dropped the "Freddy Firefly Versus Atomic Bug!" type stories (*Animal Fables* #7) to develop their line of crime, western, and romance books, including Maxwell Gaines' *War Against Crime, International Comics, Moon Girl and the Prince*, and Sol Cohen's *Gunfighter and Saddle Justice*, and their own *Crime Patrol, Modern Love*, and *Saddle Romances*. Many of the first Pre-Trend books soon underwent a series of byzantine title changes to satisfy second class postage regulations.

Gaines and Feldstein's first Pre-Trend efforts were fairly standard shoot'em ups and love books with dialogue ranging from the quaint, "ZaZa LaFleur was raised in cow country," (*Gunfighter* #10) to the obscure, "Get down off them horses yuh coyotes, before I salivate yuh! (*Gunfighter* #5). Figuring that if romance sells and oaters sell, then love on horseback should be twice as good. *Saddle Justice* was turned into *Saddle Romances*. There was even an editor-to-cowpoke advice column entitled "Chat with Chuck" similar to the "Advice from Amy" and "Advice from Adrienne" pages in *A Moon, A Girl...Romance* and *Modern Love*.

They hadn't yet hit their stride; not even the titles were all their own yet. "Like

Gunfighter," recalls Gaines, "these were mostly Sol Cohen's things. He started a book called *Gunfighter* because Gregory Peck had just come out in the movie and it was a big success. And that was about the extent of his editorial thinking." Of his own early editorship, he says, "Oh, it was fun. I never took it seriously. I was down there because my mother thought the business should be continued."

The New Trend style began to emerge through the last issues of the Pre-Trend books. Early horror and science fiction appeared in *Crime Patrol* #15, *War Against Crime* #0, and *Moon Girl* #5, while *Modern Love* #8 featured a comic industry satire titled "The Love Story to End All Love Stories." There was no attempt to test-market the proposed New Trend, says Gaines, and with the long lead time on the books, there would not have been time to assess reader response. "We put out these stories and we enjoyed them so much that we decided to change the books." The three GhouLunatics, the Old Witch, Crypt Keeper, and Vault Keeper, were spawned in the Pre-Trend stories, and they quickly set up crypt-keeping in their New Trend bailiwicks, hosting *The Haunt of Fear*, *Tales from the Crypt*, and *The Vault of Horror*, respectively.

Gaines and Feldstein wanted to be trend-setters, rather than followers, and between April and October 1950 they introduced the seven previously mentioned titles that formed the nucleus of their heralded New Trend. They came as a revelation to the jaded comic book reader. Here were unpredictable stories; stories that did not condescend, and which brought a refreshing, if macabre, sense of humor to the fledgling horror field. Their science fiction stories had substance and were not simply "Saddles in the Sky" with rockets. If the "SF was far beyond the competition," EC war stories were like nothing that had ever appeared in the heavily nationalistic books of the '40s, and the suspense books undercut everything Superman had taught about justice prevailing.

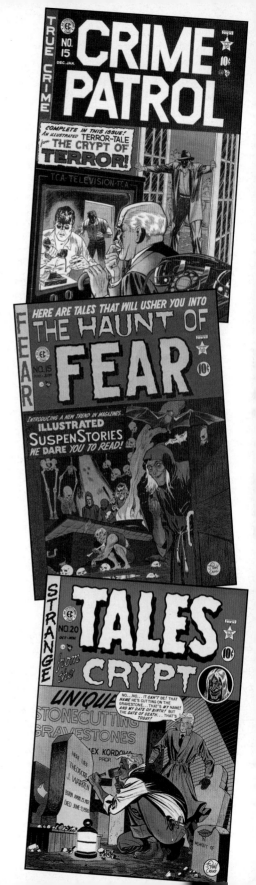

A certain synergy was generated by the Gaines-Feldstein collaboration, the transformation of their plots through the artist's rendering, and the personal interaction between the EC reader and editors via the letter pages. The small staff and Feldstein's insistence on giving the artists high visibility (Johnny Craig was featured as early as 1949 at the end of "Colorado Rose" in *Saddle Justice* #5) contributed to the personal family feeling of the books. Gaines and Feldstein made personal appearances as characters from time to time, poking fun at themselves and their creations. They are killed off at the end of "A Love Story to End All Love Stories" leaving office boy Paul Kast shouting, "I, the office boy of T. Tot Publications am the only one left! So if you like this type of story, and want to see more like it in the future issues…which I will publish…Write ME!"

The bulk of the horror, crime, suspense, and science fiction books were written and edited by Al Feldstein, who turned out four stories a week for nearly five years. Johnny Craig edited and wrote lead stories for *The Vault of Horror* and Harvey Kurtzman edited and wrote most of the *Two-Fisted Tales* (later taken over by John Severin), *Frontline Combat*, and *MAD* comics. Towards the end of the New Trend, Carl Wessler and Jack Oleck wrote for the horror books, submitting scripts which would be rewritten by Feldstein. Writers Robert Bernstein and Irving Wirstein also contributed to later books, mainly in the New Direction series.

Recalling their writing sessions, Feldstein says, "Bill and I would get together early in the morning and plot out something. First of all, we would figure out who we were writing for, because each guy had his own style. So, if we were doing an Ingles piece, we would figure out something with walking corpses, and if we were doing a Jack Kamen, we would figure on something with a love triangle, something sexy, or little kids.

"We'd try to get it pretty well plotted by lunch time, then go out and have a big lunch at Patrissy's and get bloated on Italian food, and then I'd go into my office and write. I'd lay the story out and write it at the same time so that it was written right on the boards that the artists were eventually going to draw on, the actual illustration boards. They were then given out to our letterer, who would letter what I wrote, and then the artist would draw. If I didn't write too much, they'd have some space to draw, and if I did, they had nothing and no place to draw."

The Leroy lettering was a distinctive feature of the EC books and gave a precision

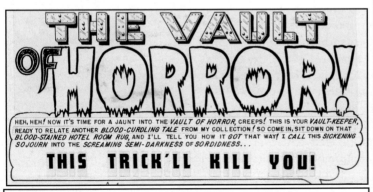
A fine example of the distinctive lettering used on the EC books.

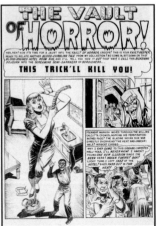

and literary quality to the already lengthy and complicated texts. EC books were written to be read, not skimmed. The lettering was done by Jim Wroten and his wife Skippy, and by Gaines' cousin Buddy Rogin. "Wroten's kind of stuff matched my personality, which is precise and exact," says Gaines. "And I could give him corrections over the phone – you can't do that with a hand-letterer." However, Harvey Kurtzman detested the rigidity of this template lettering, and after his first few stories always used Ben Oda to hand-letter his own books and his work in Feldstein's books.

After the illustration boards were returned by the artists, they were colored by Marie Severin – sister of John – who managed to color *all* of the hundreds of EC stories as well as many of the covers. Some of the artists did color their own covers.

Feldstein always left the artist free to work within the framework of his text. "I didn't believe in sketching out my conception of what the particular panel would look like," he says, "because I thought that inhibited each individual artist's style. That's like asking an artist to sign his name on my handwriting. The only thing that I asked

Al Feldstein's cover art for *Weird Science* #6.

was that they show me pencils to make sure that they had the elements for carrying the story forward.

"Every guy did his own concepts, and unless it jarred me as an editor and as author of the material, I wouldn't have any objection to it. I would just make sure that the elements that were necessary to tell the story were there."

The sources of most EC plots came from Gaines' own reading in science fiction pulps and from hundreds of "springboards" that he kept on 3" x 5" cards, one idea to a card. "I would read a story," he explains, "and I would get two or three springboards out of it. We would just take the basic premise, like making a woman out of a package of dehydrated powder in a bathtub, and fashion our own story.

"We'd gotten beyond the point of stealing the plot, we were stealing the springboard. And then one springboard would lead to another. Sometimes we would get many original thoughts from reading a story. I found reading stories was my best way to come up with original ideas. By and large, most of our ideas were original, but it all came out of reading."

An entire article could be done on the origins of EC plots, and one can ferret out numerous authors' contributions in addition to the recognized adaptations of Eando (Earl and Otto) Binder and Ray Bradbury. Roald Dahl's "The Sound Machine" for "The Sounds from Another World" (*Weird Science* #14) and Henry Hasse's "He Who Shrank" for "Lost in the Microcosm" (*Weird Science* #12) are only two.

Unfortunately for EC historians, that goldmine of 3" x 5" cards was destroyed. "We had a burglar down on Lafayette Street who would come in and steal our subscription money every so often," explains

Gaines. "Finally, because we got a safe and didn't leave money around, he got furious and burned a lot of things from my desk. One of the things he burned was my whole file of plots – hundreds and hundreds and hundreds of springboards."

Complementing the consistently high quality of the scripts was the superior art of the EC illustrators. While over 30 artists worked on the New Trend books, there is a nucleus of regulars who did most of the stories, and who can be easily recognized by their style.

Already mentioned is Johnny Craig who was drawing Pre-Trend crime, western, and romance, by 1948. All the *Crime Patrol*'s featured Craig's stunning cover art which was dominated by heavy areas of black pierced with slashes of light – spotlights, headlights, interrogation lights, and

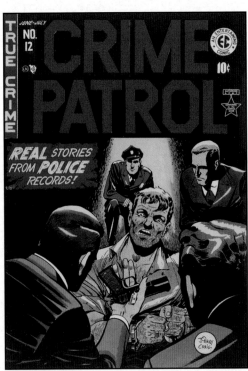

Johnny Craig's covers often showed a mastery of darkness and stark lighting. (*Crime Patrol* #12 shown)

bullet streaks. Craig delineates his characters with a fine clean line, never cluttering a panel even when there are numerous figures. ("Johnny Craig drew the only clean sewers I've ever seen," Wally Wood recalls.) Craig's killers frequently featured dapper young men, stylish ladies, or distinguished white-mustached older gentlemen who all broke out in discreet beads of sweat in moments of stress or impending death.

Most easily identifiable in the horror line is the reclusive Graham Ingles – known as Ghastly – who drew even normal people in a way that made people want to wash their hands after finishing a story. Ingles specialized in walking corpses and in people deformed in body and spirit who oozed and dripped across his pages. He did many covers for *The Haunt of Fear*, and #14 and #17 – the first one a proces-

The oozing corpses on the cover of *Haunt of Fear* #14 were a hallmark of Ghastly Graham Ingles.

sion of things with pitchforks, the second a collection of rotting heads – show the distinctive Ghastly touch.

Ingles had been an editor at Standard Comics before coming to EC. Oddly enough, he started in the love and western books where his nascent talent for the loathsome is noticeable only fleetingly in a character's skewed smile or a drunkenly tilted lamppost. "Graham was someone we pulled out of love and western," says Gaines, "and I wasn't at all sure that he could do horror. Looking back on it, it's absurd! You typecast artists just like you do actors and actresses, and I just couldn't believe that Graham was a horror artist."

Al Feldstein drew covers and stories for many of the Pre- and New Trend books in a rather heavy, deceptively simple line technique with rounded corners that gave an almost Bahaus effect. His science fiction is reminiscent of a restrained Basil Wolverton, as Wolverton drew in "The Brain Bats of Venus" (*Mister Mystery* #7 (1952)), although he was unaware of Wolverton's work at the time.

Feldstein's ghouls and corpses were tattered but not unwholesome, and his aliens had a functional appearance. A Feldstein rotting corpse wouldn't track up the kitchen floor, while the average Ingles human would have left a trail of slime. The *Weird Science* #6 cover is representative of his science fiction work, while the corpse on the cover of *Tales from the Crypt* #23 is making a tidy, albeit rotted, exit from its casket. "I'm a well-organized person," comments Feldstein, "so I guess I have well-organized aliens. I was taught in the High School of Music and Art that form follows function."

Wally Wood arrived at EC out of Eisner through Pre-Trend with Harry Harrison, where they did westerns and romances.

HORNS WERE BLOWING. COWBELLS WERE RINGING. CHIMES WERE SOUNDING OUT THE FATEFUL HOUR OF MID-NIGHT. *THIS* WAS *NEW YEARS EVE, 1953.* THIS WAS *JAM-PACKED TIMES SQUARE. THIS WAS THE SCENE OF DEATH.* HIGH OVERHEAD, IN THE WINTRY STARLESS SKY, AN ARMY BOMBER BOUND FOR MITCHEL FIELD, LONG ISLAND, SUDDENLY NOSED DOWN AND STREAKED EARTHWARD... STREAKED UNCONTROLLABLY TOWARD THE FESTIVE CROWD... *STREAKED TOWARD THE SCENE OF DEATH.* ITS ROAR WAS GREATER THAN THE CROWD ROAR. ITS WHINING SCREAMING DIVE WAS SHRILLER THAN THE HORNS. THE HORNS STOPPED BLOWING. THE BELLS STOPPED RINGING. THE CROWD FELL INTO A FROZEN TERRORIZED SILENCE. THE BOMBER'S LIGHTS EXPLODED FROM THE DARKNESS BETWEEN THE TOWERING BUILDINGS. THE SILVERY SHAPE HURTLED AT THE CROWD. AND NOW, THE SCREAMING OF THE CROWD WAS GREATER THAN THE PLANE ROAR, SHRILLER THAN ITS DIVE. AND NOW THE SCREAMING CROWD WAS *AWARE*...

AS THE GLEAMING METAL MONSTER HURTLED INTO THE SEETHING SHRIEKING MASS OF HUMANITY... TEARING INTO FLESH, CRUSHING BONE, KILLING AND MAIMING ... *THE CROWD* WAS NOW AWARE, AS *YOU* WERE ALL ALONG, THAT *THIS WAS THE SCENE OF DEATH* ...

> Wally Wood's elaborate splash page for *Weird Science* #21.

An incredibly speedy draftsman, Wood could turn out a story a week drawn with minute detail. The splash panel for "EC Confidential" (*Weird Science* #21), for example, shows an Army bomber plunging into a vast New Year's crowd in Times Square. Not only are the hundreds of figures each drawn in, but they all have faces.

Wood doted on elaborate scenes, crowded with muscular males and scantily clad females, little creatures peeping from crannies, organic statuary, and animated bric-a-brac. His multitentacled aliens had a texture midway between that of Feldstein and Ingles, giving an impression of slipperiness rather than sliminess. Both

Feldstein and Wood enjoyed drawing lush women, but Wood's had deeper cleavage and fewer clothes. The prolific Wood drew extensively for the science fiction and war books – where he excelled in space hardware and war paraphernalia – as well as for the horror, suspense, and humor.

Rebel Jack Davis added his unique densely inked artwork to the EC books in 1950. His loose redneck characters gave both a dimension of reality to the war books, and the right touch of distance and lunacy to even the grimmest horror tales. Of his brief foray into science fiction Gaines says, "Davis can do many things. On the other hand, he can't do science fiction very well. I think we gave him a cover once [three – *Incredible Science Fiction* #30-32], but Jack doesn't have it like some of the other guys did for science fiction. But he sure had it for everything else."

"Davis came up to New York from Atlanta and he was looking for work," remembers Feldstein. "Finally, he got to our place, which was a small place, so he must have tried somewhere else and didn't get anywhere. We gave him his first work, and I let him go in his own way without inhibiting him or telling him he couldn't put in the scratchy little lines or the oversized feet or anything like that. Davis has a kind of earthy style, and he's very good for war stuff.

Jack Kamen slipped easily from romance books into EC's horror, science fiction, and suspense tales, using essentially his romance characters – handsome men, voluptuous girls, and wide-eyed children. Kamen did for eyelashes what Craig did for sweat beads on nervous killers. Kamen's forte was the triangle story and the innocent – or not so innocent – child menaced by an evil adult.

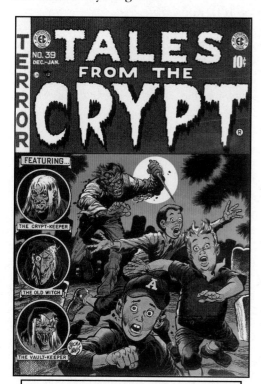

The cover of *Tales From the Crypt* #39 displays some of Jack Davis' mixture of lunacy and horror.

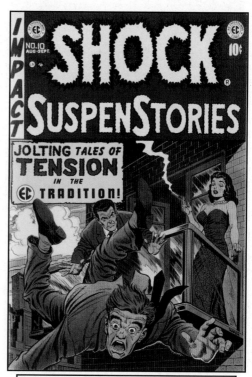

Jack Kamen's romance characters found a place on his horror covers like *Shock SuspenStories* #10.

While a Craig triangle tale usually involved a walking corpse, Kamen opted for nice wholesome family types doing each other in. The editors played up his strengths and weaknesses in "Kamen's Kalamity" (*Tales from the Crypt* #31) having mild-mannered Jack turn into a killer werewolf in an attempt to put more horror in his horror stories.

Will Elder's fine lunatic imagination came into its own with his work in *MAD*, where his ability to imitate any style of art proved an invaluable skill for parodying ads, other comic strips, movies, etc. He embellished backgrounds with his own zany

Will Elder started in horror books before making his name with *Mad* and *Panic*.

free-association graffiti, perhaps the most arcane of which was a poster in "Mickey Rodent" (*MAD* #19) reading "Attention bloodhounds – become a Donner!"

Elder worked originally as inker for John Severin's pencils. The two did many fine war stories for Kurtzman's books, and Elder made a few sallies alone into the horror and science fiction fields. The lurking satire in Elder's pen was subtly at variance with the general tenor of the science fiction books, however, and "Ahead of the Game" (*Weird Fantasy* #17), in which a demented professor wires up living heads into a computer, is too close to parody. In the same way, even though the horror books were done tongue in cheek, "Strop! You're Killing Me!" and "Last Laugh" (*Tales from the Crypt* #37 and #38), were, in Elder's hands, more a parody of an EC horror story. But he was perfectly suited for *MAD* and *Panic*.

Elder's high school chum Harvey Kurtzman, so the story goes, came to EC in 1949 looking for work in an Educational vein, unaware that Entertaining had taken over. Gaines recalls looking at Kurtzman's portfolio. "Al and I sat there and giggled and laughed all afternoon and then said, 'We're not really Educational Comics, that's a holdover from years ago. We're putting out horror and science fiction and so on. But would you like to do some of that?'

"So Harvey said yes – reluctantly, but he had to eat – and he did horror and science fiction for us. Then he came to us with the concept of an adventure book. I had no feeling at all for adventure – I didn't know what he was talking about. If you want to see a dreadful example of adventure, Al and I did one story for the first *Two-Fisted Tales*, and I don't think you'll have any trouble picking out which one it is...So I started him on *Two-Fisted Tales*. It wasn't doing well but it wasn't doing

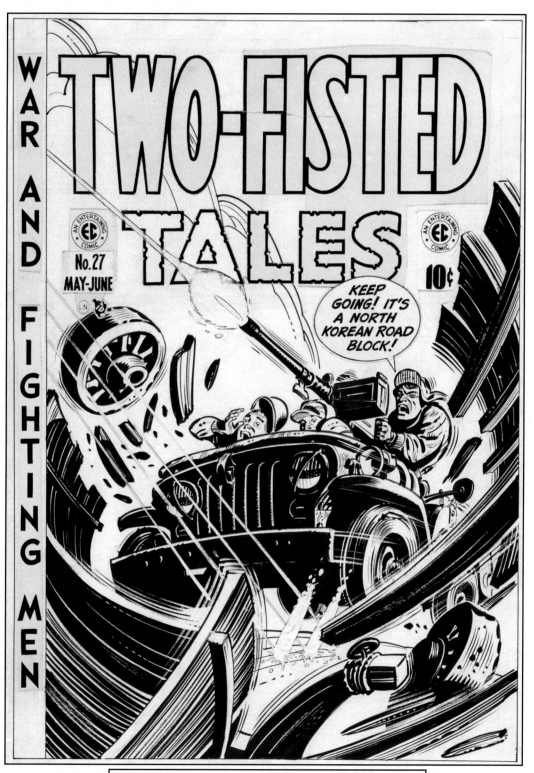

Harvey Kurtzman's original cover art for
Two-Fisted Tales #27 shows his distinctive brush lines.

badly. And then the war came, and he switched it to war and added *Frontline Combat*."

Harvey drew with thick sloopy brush lines which looked effortless but which, on the contrary, were worked and reworked by the meticulous Kurtzman. He was never comfortable with EC crime or horror – "They fell into an attitude or a system or style where it became very Freudian, very ghoulish," he says now, but he was justifiably proud of his 13 science fiction stories which included "...Gregory Had a Model T" (*Weird Science* #7) and "Mysterious Ray from Another Dimension!" (*Weird Fantasy* #16). Kurtzman drew covers and stories for his war books and covers for the *MAD* comics although he, unfortunately, did not draw any new *MAD* stories.

Al Williamson began to draw for EC in 1952 at the age of 21. Influenced by the more realistic and physical style of Alex Raymond, he beautifully illustrated prehistoric tales with amply fleshed warriors and muscular young women. He was frequently helped out on deadline by, and shared credits with, close friend Frank Frazetta, which relationship Williamson now describes as "doing a lot of stuff together, but we were not a team." Frazetta did one story alone, "Squeeze Play" (*Shock SuspenStories* #13) and a cover for *Weird Science-Fantasy* #29. This cover was originally done for *Famous Funnies* who rejected it as being too violent – it was redone for EC.

The realistic style of illustration of Al Williamson is shown in this panel from *Weird Science* #16.

Innovative Bernie Krigstein came late to EC in 1953, but his versatility of style and techniques made the reader vividly aware of his presence in the New Trend and New Direction books. Unlike Jack Kamen, Krigstein was able to adapt his style to the type of story he was illustrating, from the crude, heavily lined "Pipe Dream" (*Vault of Horror* #36), to the delicate and airy adaptation of Bradbury's "The Flying Machine" (*Weird Science-Fantasy* #23) to the stylized Hirschfield cartoon style of "From Eternity Back to Here" (*MAD* #12).

Krigstein chafed at the limitations of the six to eight-page format and often reworked the text and subdivided panels to gain more space. The most famous of these stories is "Master Race" from the New Direction's *Impact* #1, which Feldstein assigned as a six-page story, and which Krigstein expanded to eight. His cinematic technique is evident on the opening page where the repeated overlay of a figure in the final frame, for example, perfectly conveys the movement of the subway train within a single panel.

The original art from page 1 of Bernie Krigstein's Master Race story in *Impact* #1.

Other excellent artists who contributed to the new Trend, New Direction, and Pictofiction books included George Evans, Reed Crandall, Joe Orlando, Angelo Torres, Roy Krenkel, Joe Kubert, and Alexander Toth.

The fresh Gaines/Feldstein scripts and the innovative talent of these artists gave EC an impressive lineup of books with solid content and eye-catching format. EC never had the print run of Gleason and Biro's books – *Crime Does Not Pay* might sell as many as 4,000,000 copies per issue, while EC sold somewhere in the neighborhood of 1,500,000 copies monthly for the entire group, or 400,000 as a top figure for the best horror comic sale per issue – but they had a devoted following of fans who read and corresponded faithfully.

Despite distribution problems, it was an exciting time for EC's young staff. "The New Trend days were happy days from the creative point of view," agrees Gaines. "In those days I had nothing to do with the business and to speak of, so I was all involved in the editorial end, creating storylines, and creating magazines and titles. I guess there were the usual aggravations, but somehow I remember them all as very pleasant days."

It was as happy a time for Al Feldstein. "Generally, I loved doing the stuff, and it was great fun. I was a very fortunate person, and have been most of my life, in being able to earn a living at something I enjoy doing. And also, of course, it's very exciting to be able to do things that haven't been done before so that you're free within your art – from my own personal stiff-simple style, to Graham Ingels' drippy-gooky and Jack Davis' hairy-scratchy, and Jack Kamen's sweetsy-cutsie – we all had our own statements to make and we were encouraged.

"We were fortunate in having a publisher like Bill Gaines who permitted us to be that way."

Feldstein not only managed to turn out four stories a week, but he was able to keep clear editorial distinctions between the EC genres, giving the horror, science fiction, and suspense their own special flavors. Horror tales were done tongue in cheek, usually with an awful Old Testament eye for an eye retribution awaiting the villain. For example, a charlatan who offers quick weight loss to his victims and peddles them encapsulated tape worms is finally trapped in a vault and devoured by a giant worm that has battened on one of the deceased weight watchers. ("Dying to Lose Weight" *Vault of Horror* #18).

The horror reader could safely anticipate such deliciously just punishments, but as the stories grew more realistic in the crime and shock books, justice became increasingly elusive, and the reader's sense of assurance increasingly shaky. Feldstein showed that a Korean veterans' homecoming parade ("The Patriots" *Shock SuspenStories* #2) could be as lethal as the giant worm and far more likely to happen.

Feldstein played the science fiction straight, using humor on occasion as an integral part of the story, but not to lampoon the science fiction genre per se, unless the parody revolved around the EC editors, as in "EC Confidential" (*Weird Science* #21). A number of the stories were "message" plots, used to make a statement about man's inhumanity to man; "The Loathsome" (*Weird Science* #20), man's inhumanity to other creatures; "The Probers" (*Weird Science* #8), man's inhumanity to aliens; and "The Teacher From Mars" (*Weird Science-Fantasy* #24), an Eando Binder adaptation.

"The Probers" from *Weird Science* #8 with Wally Wood art.

After the first cluster of new books appeared in 1950, the New Trend was filled out with *Frontline Combat* (1951), *MAD* (1952), *Shock SuspenStories* (1952), and latecomers *Panic* (1954) and *Piracy* (1954). Title changes made *Tales from the Crypt* out of *The Crypt of Terror*, and the two science fiction books were merged, first into *Weird Science-Fantasy* and then retitled *Incredible Science Fiction*.

The five crime and horror books were EC's bread and butter, and the horror books, in particular, drew readers with Gaines and Feldstein's Planter's Punch of bad puns, outrageous jokes, and grisly grue all offered through the miasmic hospitality of the three GhouLunatics.

The reason that Gaines and Feldstein were forced to collaborate with the unwholesome three was explained in "Horror Beneath the Streets" (*Haunt of Fear* #17) where the terrified editors are pursued through the sewers of New York and forced to sign binding contracts with the Old Witch, the Crypt Keeper, and the Vault Keeper. One of the three introduced each story, trading insults with the others and inviting correspondence to their letter columns.

"Al and I had a strange rapport in those days," says Gaines, "where he could start something and I'd finish it, or vice versa, or he'd say three words and I'd say three words – we literally were writing together. And when we did the GhouLunatics, it was almost like you hear these mythological things where the ventriloquist's dummy takes over. Because we'd write a letter, and damn if one of the GhouLunatics wouldn't answer that letter, and it didn't matter whether I said, or Al said it, or we both said it – it wasn't us! It was one of those devilish creatures!"

Within this framework, the atmosphere of the horror books can be conveyed in just a few of the egregious story titles: "Ooze in the

Cellar?" (*Haunt of Fear* #11); "Horror We? How's Bayou?" (*Haunt of Fear* #17); "Ants in Her Trance!" (*Tales from the Crypt* #28); "Tain't the Meat, It's the Humanity!" (*Tales from the Crypt* #32); and "Fare Tonight, Followed by Increasing Clottyness..." (*Tales from the Crypt* #36).

Points of view varied, and stories were narrated variously by a trunk which traps a killer and squeezes him out of its keyhole like toothpaste ("Tight Grip!" *Tales from the Crypt* #38); a swamp shack forced to house a loathsome ghoul ("Swamped" *Haunt of Fear* #27); and a lonesome grave, yearning for a corpse of its own to cuddle ("The Craving Grave!" *Tales from the Crypt* #39).

EC horror opened new vistas of death from sources previously unimagined by the reader. Victims were serial-sectioned by giant machines, eaten by ghouls, devoured by rats – from inside and out, pecked by pigeons, stuffed down disposals, skewered on swords, buried alive, dismembered and used as baseball equipment, hung as living clappers in huge bells, made into sausages and soap, dissolved, southern friend, hacked up by maniacs in Santa Claus suits, and offed in unusually high percentages by their wives or husbands.

Discussing these spouse-cide tales which were also a staple of the crime and shock books, Gaines says only, "Well you have to realize that most of the EC springboards were mine, and the direction that the springboards took was the result of my neuroses. And I've probably said more than I should say at this point! For whatever reason, I got enjoyment out of those.

That's why I thought them up, much the way that Thurber did. Thurber's stuff was full of the same nuttiness. I won't say that my problems were exactly Thurber's problems but we both showed them through our work."

A popular horror feature was the "Grim Fairy Tale," the first of which was illustrated by Ingles and the remaining 13 by Kamen, the humor that Feldstein would later turn into *Panic* could be seen in "Snow White and the Seven Dwarfs" (*Haunt of Fear* #22) in which a compulsive neat Snow White drives the dwarfs to homicide and ends, 'So the seven little dwarfs stormed back into their spotless little house and proceeded to turn it into a miserable hovel again..."

"It was the biggest shock to me," Feldstein says, "when guys like Wertham and this whole catastrophe exploded on us, talking about how these comics were affecting our children and causing juvenile delinquency. I couldn't believe it. I don't believe that children are that vulnerable and that gullible that they're going to accept this as reality. Except ill children, of course, and for this country to guide its way by the standards of ill people is a frightening thing."

BELOW THE SURFACE OF THE POND, JOHN TALBOT WRITHED IN THE LOOP FORMED AROUND HIS NECK BY HIS DEAD WIFE'S ARMS AND BOUND WRISTS. AND IN THAT HORRIBLE MOMENT BEFORE THE WATER RUSHED INTO HIS TORTURED LUNGS, HER SOFT SLIMY FACE TOUCHED HIS AND HER SIGHTLESS EYES STARED AND HE COULD ALMOST HEAR HER GRINNING MOUTH WHISPER...

I'LL *NEVER LET YOU GO, JOHN...*

A spouse-cide panel from George Evans in *Haunt of Fear* #27.

It did become apparent, however, that a certain overkill marred some of the scripts. One of the most widely-quoted examples was "Foul Play!" (*Haunt of Fear* #19) illustrated by Jack Davis at his grisliest. In revenge for a teammate murdered by an opponent's poisoned spikes, the Bayville baseball team dismembers the killer and sets up a midnight memorial game.

"See the long strings of pulpy intestines that mark the base lines," intones the narrator. "See the two lungs and the liver that indicate the bases...the heart that is home plate. See Doc White bend and whisk the heart with the mangy scalp, yelling, 'Play ball...' See the batter come to the plate swinging the legs, the arms, then throwing all but one away and standing in the box waiting for the pitcher to hurl the head to him. See the catcher with the torso strapped on as a chest protector, the infielders with their hand-mitts, the stomach rosin bag, and all the other pieces of equipment that once was Central City's star pitcher, Herbie Satten..."

"One of the traps that Bill and I fell into," admits Feldstein, "was that we were beginning to formularize our material. A problem like that always happens when you're constantly pushing the stuff out. There were mistakes, no question about it. In retrospect, I'm sorry that there were some things that we did – we just got a little wild. When you're trying to outdo yourself week after week, issue after issue, sometimes you overstep the bounds and we were beginning to stretch our taste standards a bit in order to get all the stories written. That was wrong, because we got into areas that were really kind of tacky, like that baseball game thing."

"Foul Play!" from *Haunt of Fear* #19 showed a bit of EC's overkill.

"None of them ever bothered me in terms of being too horrible," he adds. The only thing that bothered me was bad taste. After all, why should a well written, well conceived horror story bother you? To me that's not bad taste; it may curdle your blood, but that's exactly what we were trying to do. That means you should be proud that you were successful."

While the GhouLunatics and their off-the-shroud humor put the reader at one remove from the mayhem in the stories, a number of EC's most vivid stories found in the *Suspense* books dealt with serious issues of racial hatred, religious intolerance, and sexual abuse; themes seldom touched in *any* media in the early '50s.

A young soldier returns from Korea ("In Gratitude…" *Shock SuspenStories* #11). He has lost an arm in a grenade explosion in which a friend died to save him. Since the friend had no family, the young soldier has brought the body back to his hometown for burial. But when he asks to visit the grave before the welcoming ceremonies, his parents confess that the friend is buried "over in Greendale."

"We couldn't go through with it, Joey!" cries his mother, and his father adds, "The whole town was on our necks, our friends…the family…I had my business to consider, son. We couldn't do it."

Standing alone that afternoon on the bunting-draped high school stage Joey faces his friends and family. "I gave my right hand defending freedom and equality and I was *proud* of it…I *was* proud, that is until today. I had a buddy in Korea. We ate together…slept together…laughed together…cried together. We fought for democracy together…he gave his life for that cause…and he saved mine in doing it. He threw himself on a live grenade… and got blown up…to save me. But when his body was sent back here, it wasn't good enough to be buried in Fairlawn Cemetery. It wasn't good enough because its skin wasn't the right color…Well that grenade that tore that skin to pieces didn't know its color…didn't care if it was white or black. What did he die for? You say you're proud of me. Well, I'm not proud of you. I'm ashamed of you…and for you!"

Not only is the message powerful, but it sustains the reader's interest through 13 panels focused on a single character delivering a monologue. Wood varies distance and point of view in his illustra-

tions, changing the focus like a movie camera, always keeping an American flag in the panel as an ironic counterpoint to Joey's bitter words.

"Hate" (*Shock SuspenStories* #5) also drawn by Wood, is a brutal story of religious prejudice in which a neighborhood gang tries to force a Jewish family to move out. Wood-illustrated stories "The Assault" (*Shock SuspenStories* #8) and "A Kind of Justice" (*Shock SuspenStories* #16) painted opposite sides of the same sexual coin, and drew reams of mail, both pro and con, from readers.

Such stories jolted the reader's complacency and his assurance that in real life justice would prevail. The horror stories and many of the lurid crime tales were too farfetched to befall the average reader, but these plots struck close to home, and were definitely unnerving. "That's a different kind of bother," says Feldstein. "That's a bother in terms of feeling badly for some innocent person, and I can understand that. We tried a lot of things that were unorthodox for their day, like having innocent people die and criminals get away with their crimes."

Horror and crime were their bread and butter, but the editors always maintained that "We at EC are proudest of our science fiction." EC science fiction *was* good. Parsecs ahead of any competition, the EC stories were lovingly scripted by Feldstein and brilliantly rendered by the science fiction artists. They have held their own against the science fiction book market over the last 25 years, and are just as readable now as the day they appeared on the stands.

For the most part following the EC formula of psychological surprise and unexpected denouement, they were on a consistently higher level than Buck Rogers' ray gun and rocket thrillers. Feldstein preferred to explore more subtle questions – how would man act in the void of outer space? What treatment would man receive at the hands – or tentacles – of aliens?

The "As ye vivisect so shall ye be vivisected" theme was repeated in stories like "The Probers" (*Weird Science* #8) where a space scientist who has been experimenting on small lab animals ends up on the other end of an alien's scalpel. Other turnaround stories, "A Gobl Is a Knog's Best Friend" (*Weird Science* #12, Wood) and "Bum Steer" (*Weird Science* #15, Orlando), offered the unpleasant possibilities of powerful aliens turning humans into pets – or pâté.

The chances for snafus and misunderstandings even among friendly or neutral races were legion. In "Chewed Out" (*Weird Science* #12, Orlando) aliens being talked down by a ham radio operator do land in the midst of a jubilant crowd – but are so tiny that ship and crew are lost in a vat of sauerkraut on a hot dog stand, and, adding injury to insult, are served up and eaten by an oblivious general.

Unfortunate earthmen managed to land on a giant gaming table, risking annihilation in a cosmic crap game ("The Die is Cast!" *Weird Fantasy* #12, Wood), touched down with a bang on a child's balloon at an alien carnival ("Snap Ending!" *Weird Science* #18) and ended ingloriously as vermin in the salad of a fastidious six-legged diner ("Revulsion!" *Weird Fantasy* #15, Orlando).

Feldstein tackled the paradox of time travel in such fine stories as "Why Papa Left Home" (*Weird Science* #11, Orlando) in which the protagonist discovers that he is his own father who deserted his mother 22 years ago, and "Sinking of the Titanic!" (*Weird Science* #6, Wood) in which attempts to return to save passengers on that fatal night causes the original collision.

March-April 1952 issue, cover by Wally Wood.

SOON THE WATERS DISAPPEAR! THE INTENSE HEAT...GROWING PROGRESSIVELY STRONGER...DRIES THE LAND! ALL MOISTURE IS GONE...

I...CAN'T...BREATH!

IT...WILL BE ...OVER... SOON...

THE EARTH IS NOW DEAD! THOSE THAT HAVE ESCAPED THE TERRIBLE ONSLAUGHT OF THE TIDAL WAVES, HAVE NOW PERISHED IN THE BLISTERING HEAT! ALL LIFE ON EARTH HAS VANISHED...SCORCHED AWAY!

THE EARTH MOVES SLOWLY INTO THE GRAVITATIONAL FIELD OF THE SUN...

IT SPEEDS TOWARD THE GIGANTIC MOLTEN MASS! ITS SURFACE BEGINS TO GLOW...RED HOT...NOW FLAMING! FASTER AND FASTER IT MOVES...

...AND THEN IT IS GONE...SWALLOWED INTO THE FLAMING GASES! A PUFF OF SMOKE...THEN SILENCE!

....AND THAT IS MY STORY, CHILDREN! THAT PLANET WAS KNOWN AS EARTH! IT IS *NOT* IN YOUR TEXT-BOOK MAPS OF OUR SOLAR SYSTEM BECAUSE IT *EXISTS NO LONGER!* BUT *I* AND *OTHER ELDERS* HERE ON *MARS,* WE REMEMBER IT WELL...GLOWING BRIGHTLY IN OUR SOUTHERN SKIES! WELL...THAT'S ALL FOR TODAY! *CLASS...DISMISSED!*

THE EDITORS OF *WEIRD SCIENCE* WANT TO KNOW WHETHER YOU LIKE THEIR MAGAZINE, AND IF SO...WHICH STORY YOU LIKE BEST! WON'T YOU WRITE AND GIVE US YOUR OPINION! IT HELPS US GIVE *YOU* WHAT *YOU WANT!*

ADDRESS YOUR LETTERS TO:-

THE EDITORS WEIRD SCIENCE ROOM 706, DEPT. 14 225 LAFAYETTE ST. N.Y. C., 12, N.Y.

8

"Destruction of the Earth" in *Weird Science* #14, art by Al Feldstein.

Feldstein himself illustrated a set of five "holocaust" or "end of the world" stories in 1950. In "Destruction of the Earth" (*Weird Science* #14), the entire world is sucked into the sun's inferno. Its absence is explained to a class of wide-eyed students by their instructor who recalls, "I and other elders here on Mars remember it well... glowing brightly in our southern skies!"

Desperately searching for a plot gimmick for *Weird Science* #11, editors Gaines and Feldstein dream up a weapon already under secret production by the U.S. Government ("Cosmic Ray Bomb Explosion" *Weird Fantasy* #14). Whisked to the Pentagon, Al and Bill are cleared by a loyalty test, but it is too late...Scientists deep in the Kremlin have already studied their copies of *Weird Science* #11. As Al and Bill stroll by the Capitol dome, the Russian bomb falls.

Basil Wolverton did an annihilation story for *Marvel Tales* #102 a year later, and a glance at "The End of the World" in this issue will show the similarity of his art and Feldstein's.

Future technologies and human-alien liaisons inspired baroque sex plots that went far beyond the triangle-adultery-murder themes of the crime and horror books. A jealous father who slips his daughter's fiancé an overdose of sex hormones ("Transformation Completed" *Weird Science* #10, Wood) is chagrined when the wedding goes on as scheduled – after she also takes a few injections. Her daughter, he conceded, "made a very handsome groom...and Lee, a lovely bride."

"Arnold, baby! I wish you'd hurry up and change...so that things can be normal," pleads the newly-bearded bride whose horrified groom has just discovered that Gastropodians change sex for the second half of their lives. ("There'll Be Some Changes Made!" *Weird Science* #14, Wood). The disgusted bride in "Right on the Button" (*Weird Science* #19, Elder) takes matters into her own hands, killing her husband on their wedding night when she discovers the loathsome alien has a navel. EC sex isn't much fun in the crime/horror present, and promises to be even more appalling in the sci-fi future when lovely women will turn out to be butterfly creatures who deposit their eggs to feed and grow in their human lovers... ("The Maidens Cried" *Weird Science* #10, Wood).

In 1952 Feldstein began a series of adaptations of Ray Bradbury's science fiction stories which evoked a heavy reader response ranging from "I thought a comic version would dim the Bradbury brilliance, but it comes across like an arc lamp" to "very interesting...but a bit over my head" (*Weird Science* #19). One surprised reader was Bradbury, who had been unaware of his part in the springboard system.

In a 1977 letter, Bradbury says "There's not much to say. EC stole from me. I caught them at it. They admitted the crime. They then proceeded to adapt 30 or more of my stories and did some fine work at it, which pleased me. Gaines has a nice sense of humor about the whole plagiarism bit. Ask him to show you a copy of my Christian letter, where I pointed out their crime, nicely, and asked for a small check which they immediately sent."

Bradbury's Christian letter of April 19, 1952 read, "Dear Sir: Just a note to remind you of an oversight. You have not as yet sent on the check for $50.00 to cover the use of secondary rights on my two stories, "The Rocket Man" and "Kaleidoscope" which appeared in your *Weird Fantasy* #13 (May-June '52), with the cover-all title of "Home to Stay." I feel that this was probably overlooked in the general confusion of office work, and look forward to your payment in the near future. My very best wishes to you."

Bradbury-EC relations remained cordial, and Bradbury was paid $25 each for adaptations of such superb pieces as "I, Rocket" (*Weird Science* #20, Williamson), "King of the Grey Spaces!" (*Weird Fantasy* #19, Severin and Elder), "The Million Year Picnic" (*Weird Fantasy* #21, Severin and Elder), "Mars Is Heaven!" (*Weird Science* #18, Wood), "There Will Come Soft Rains…" (*Weird Fantasy* #17, Wood), and "The Long Years!" (*Weird Science* #17, Wood) in addition to horror classics "The Small Assassin!" (*Shock SuspenStories* #7, Evans), "The Screaming Woman!" (*Crime SuspenStories* #15, Kamen), and "The October Game" (*Shock SuspenStories* #9, Kamen) for the other books.

Bradbury also wrote several letters to the Cosmic Correspondence pages, one of them to praise "Judgment Day!" (*Weird Fantasy* #18, Orlando – reprinted in *Incredible Science Fiction* #33) one of the most famous EC science fiction stories that Bradbury felt "should be required reading for every man, woman, and child in the United States." He wrote, "I realize you have been battling, in the sea of comics, to try to do better things. You've done a splendid thing here, and deserves the highest commendation."

The story begins as the space-suited Earthman Tarlton arrives to inspect Cybrinia, a planet of mechanical life, to see if the inhabitants are ready to receive the wonders and greatness of Earth. An orange robot steps forward to guide Tarlton around the spacious streets and gleaming plant where orange citizens are made and educated.

But what of the *blue* robots, asks Tarlton. Reluctantly, the orange guide leads him aboard a mobile-bus – where the blue citizens sit in the back – and takes him to Blue Town and the shabby plant where blue robots are constructed and educated on inferior machines. Tarlton points out that only the blue sheathing differentiates the two groups. "Would you deny that the differences between you and the blue robots are taught…in your educator?"

The orange guide replies unhappily, "You are lecturing me as though all this were my fault, Tarlton! This existed before I was made! What can I do about it? I'm only one robot." "I'm sorry, my friend!" answers Tarlton. "Yes. I know you are only one robot. That is why I am afraid that Cybrinia is not ready to join the Galactic Republic." But he leaves the orange robot with words of comfort. "For a while on Earth, it looked like there was no hope! But when mankind on Earth learned to live together, real progress first began, the universe was suddenly ours."

The great ship rockets up into the void…

AND INSIDE THE SHIP, THE MAN REMOVED HIS SPACE HELMET AND SHOOK HIS HEAD, AND THE INSTRUMENT LIGHTS MADE THE BEADS OF PERSPIRATION ON HIS DARK SKIN TWINKLE LIKE DISTANT STARS…

THE END

While thousands were moved by "Judgment Day," comics Code watchdogs in 1954 attempted to keep Gaines from reprinting it in *Incredible Science Fiction #33* "on the basis that the perspiration on the black's face in the last panel was offensive." (The slot was open because the Association had already rejected Angelo Torres' "An Eye for an Eye" – later printed in Gelman's *Horror Comics of the 1950s*.) Gaines recalls that he threatened, "'I'm going to sue you if you don't let it through,' and they said, 'All right.' They let it through and that was the end of my association with *the Association*."

While Feldstein was busy with the science fiction, crime, and horror books, Harvey Kurtzman was offering a serious look at war in *Two-Fisted Tales* and *Frontline Combat*. His books were the antithesis of the "Captain Kill Crushes the Yellow Peril" fare of the '40s. Kurtzman looked at war from Caesar's legions to the Korean conflict, examining the men who run the wars, the dog soldiers who fight them, and the hapless civilians over whose homelands and homes the wars are fought.

The first issues of *Two-Fisted Tales* were straight adventure books with standard spy tales like "Hong Kong Intrigue" (*Two-Fisted Tales* #18) which was burdened with descriptions like "evil-slanting eyes" and "obscenely fat Oriental" (and was probably the Gaines-Feldstein effort), but with the advent of the Korean War, the book went entirely to war stories, adding *Frontline Combat* in 1951.

"I think that my constant preoccupation was to put down some form of truth," Kurtzman explains. "At that time there were war stories in comic books, and they were just the worst kind of crap that you can imagine. Bad in the sense that they glamorized war. They idealized, glamorized, and made a joke of this horrible business of war."

"In any case, I was depressed by the lack of accuracy in war fiction, and I was determined to make war fiction reflect reality. That's been my underlying platform in a sense; I am constantly intrigued by areas where I sense that great lie fantasies are being built out of proportion. So, the direction that my war stories took was not satirical at all, but I was traveling a different route to arrive at the same place – a criticism of popular war attitudes in fiction and print."

Kurtzman's war is not glamorous. Qualities of bravery, cowardice, cruelty, compassion are individual – not racial or national – characteristics. And brave or cowardly, the individual's fate depends on chance; a stray bullet, a moment's hesitation, and one man's life is cut short, another's spared. Kurtzman presented the enemy as human, and his even-handed treatment of all participants gave his stories an unusual and disturbing angle, and prevented the reader from making easy judgments.

Kurtzman researched his stories meticulously, even to the point of using authentic Korean phrases in "Combat Medic!" (*Frontline Combat #4*, Davis). He and leg-man Jerry DeFuccio (who also wrote EC fillers) spent countless hours aloft in experimental aircraft, below decks in submarines, and immersed in the American History room at the Fifth Avenue Library. "Kurtzman wanted you to really absorb all the atmosphere through your pores," DeFuccio says. "He hated anything that was watered down. If you drew a weapon, it wouldn't be from another drawing or plate, it had to be from some kind of a scale model that had every bolt and rivet."

Kurtzman's accuracy paid off, both in historical ambiance and emotional impact. The reader might delude himself that the events in "Hate" or "A Kind of Justice" never happen, but he couldn't deny Kurtzman's historicity. Stonewall Jackson *was* accidentally killed by the very men who loved him, whether it happened like "Stonewall Jackson!" (*Frontline Combat #5*) or "Chancellorsville!" (*Two-Fisted Tales #35*), and the 442nd Combat Team of Japanese Americans were fighting against the Germans in 1944 (*Frontline Combat #5*).

Kurtzman experimented with several special issues, *Frontline Combat #7* and #12 on Iwo Jima and the Air Force; *Two-Fisted Tales #26* on "The Changjin Reservoir." He had hoped to cover the entire Civil War in seven books, but only three of these were completed, *Frontline Combat #9*, and *Two-Fisted Tales #31* and #35. All were exhaustively researched and executed with the legwork of Jerry DeFuccio, the aid of the American History room's Mr. Vigilante, and the advice of historian Fletcher Pratt.

Whether it was his quest for perfection or his tendency to worry, Kurtzman exercised greater control over the finished product and took longer to complete his books than did Feldstein. "He was looking for perfection in a 10¢ comic book, which is very nice, but it wasn't economically feasible," comments Gaines.

Kurtzman's tight control was not always well-received by the artist. "Sometimes my roughs inspired the artist, sometimes they made the artist angry because they boxed him in," he says. For a highly creative artist to take one of my roughs and work from it took a certain amount of discipline, because creativity does not like limitations and my roughs would limit things constantly.

The irony of Kurtzman's war plots was turned to satire and parody in *MAD*, that breath of fresh humor in the comic desert.

For the first time the comic book reader saw his everyday surroundings – including comic books – lampooned by a writer who included him in the joke. The first issue satirized the very stories that EC was publishing, and went on in later issues to tackle movies, advertising, television, the classics, supermarkets, and the McCarthy hearings which Kurtzman courageously took on in "What's My Shine!"

"The stuff I liked to do generally was provocative," he says. "I don't consider myself a good humorist, but what I did, that I think I identify with my stuff – and I can point it out in the old *MADs* – was that I did thought provoking humor."

What, for example, Kurtzman asked, would happen if comic strip violence was carried over into real life? His answer was "Bringing Back Father" (*MAD* #17) in which Elder and Krigstein did simultaneous parodies of George McManus' "Bringing Up Father." Elder, the perfect mimic, copied the original strip on one page, while on the facing page Krigstein realistically rendered the bloody homelife of characters who actually threw crockery and punches indiscriminately. The contrast is convincingly horrific, and as gruesome as the average EC tale of domesticity in the shock stories.

Davis, Elder, and Wood were the principal *MAD* artists – 22 (1955) was, in fact, an Elder tour de force: "Special Art Issue: The Bill Elder Story," taking the artist from "Childhood" to "Senility" with a Kurtzman cover and the rest drawn entirely by Elder.

MAD parodied movie and comic book favorites in such classics as Wood's "Superduperman!" (#4), "Black and Blue Hawks!" (#5), "Flesh Garden!" (#11), "Prince Violent!" (#13), and "Gopo Gossum!" (#23); Davis' "Lone Stranger!" (#3), "Mark Trade!" (#12), and "Hah! Noon!" (#9); Elder's "Dragged Net!" (#3), "Ping Pong! (#6), "Woman Wonder!" (#10), and "Starchie" (#12); and Severin's "Melvin of the Apes!" (#6).

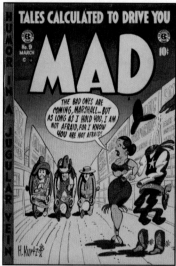

These stories alone would make *MAD* a memorable creation, but Kurtzman went further in the manipulation of his material with cover designs that mimicked the "Racing Form" or a school composition book, and experimentation with unusual visuals in the stories themselves. Jack Davis, for example, illustrated "Captain TVideo" (#15) entirely in black and white TV frames overlaid with black interference lines, while "3-Dimensions" (#12) brought the wonders of that fad to the two-dimensional page.

"When I look around me, I seem to find that there's much in this little world of ours that looks silly," comments Kurtzman. "The way people carry on. And that's where my material came from. I made fun of what the material was. Of its silliness. Of, in certain cases, its lack of truthfulness, its contradictions. Satire is the kind of thing where you really come to bear on the immediate things that are happening in the world."

MAD lasted 23 issues as a comic book before increasing censorship pressures on the whole EC line and Kurtzman-Gaines conflicts determined that it be changed to the black and white magazine format that is still going strong today. *MAD* spawned a number of imitators, the best of which was EC's own *Panic* which appeared on the stands in late 1953 and was edited by the prolific Al Feldstein along with his six other magazines.

Feldstein used other writers on *Panic*, among them Jack Mendelson together with the familiar artists Davis, Elder, Feldstein, Kamen, Orlando, Wolverton (who appeared in *MAD* #10, #11, and #17), and Wood. *Panic* had the distinction of being banned in Boston – indeed, throughout the entire Commonwealth – because of Bill Elder's lunatic rendering of "The Night Before Christmas" in #1 which featured a "Just Divorced" sign on the back of Santa's sleigh.

In the February 14, 1954 issue of the *Hartford Courant*, the first of a four-part feature by Irving M. Kravsow appeared under the banner headline "Depravity for Children – 10 Cents a Copy!" Mr. Kravsow went on to describe the offending *Panic* #1 as "having a reprint of the lovely Christmas poem "The Night Before Christmas" illustrated by gross and obscene drawings that defy descriptions." (Mr. Kravsow's descriptive faculties would have been permanently impaired had the illustrator been S. Clay Wilson rather than Will Elder.)

The spirit of McCarthy was abroad in the land, and comic books were fair game for the censorious. "It was really a frightening time," says Feldstein. "It was the time of the red herring, and parents were looking for someone who could do their job. There were also, I think, a lot of ulterior motives in terms of opening the door to censorship."

Censorship was nothing new to comics, having been on the horizon since the

Bill Elder satirizes Christmas in *Panic* #1.

mid- to late '40s, and EC was involved in all with three regulatory periods. Covers of the early EC books carry a small star labeled "Conforms to the Comics Code" under the logo "Authorized A.C.M.P." This Association of Comics Magazine Publishers was headed by one Henry Schultz, attorney and sole employee, whose job consisted of reading books and suggesting changes. When he suggested too many changes and sales went down, that was the end of A.C.M.P.

A second period of censorship, according to Gaines, was during a time of difficulty with wholesalers when his distributor, the head of Leader News, insisted that his son, another attorney named Stanley Estrow,

have the power to order changes. Craig's *Vault of Horror* #32 cover and story "Out of His Head!" must have been censored during this period, after Schultz and before the Code. An advance ad for this book ran uncensored in *Tales from the Crypt* #37 and showed a corpse with a meat cleaver wedged in its skull about to confront its killer. By the time #32 had been published the cleaver had been opaqued, leaving the corpse with an ambiguous nimbus about its head throughout the story.

IT WAS QUIET IN THE WOODS THAT SURROUNDED THE HUNTERS' CAMP-SITE. FAR AWAY IN THE NIGHT, AN OWL HOOTED. ALEX STARED DOWN AT STANLEY, CROUCHING AS IF STUNNED... THE CLEAVER SUNK DEEP IN HIS HEAD... THE HANDLE JUTTING UPWARD AWKWARDLY...

CHOKE...

The original art and cover proof show *Vault of Horror* #32 before the censors removed the meat cleaver.
Also shown is the final published cover.

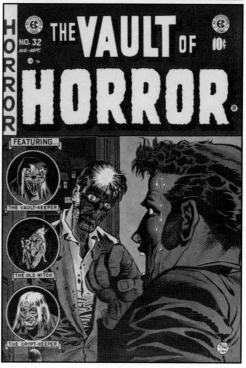

The third and final period of censorship for EC came with the introduction of the Comics Code Authority in September 1954, the year that earlier saw the publication of Dr. Fredric Wertham's *Seduction of the Innocent* and the Hearings Before the Subcommittee to Investigate Juvenile Delinquency. Gaines testified voluntarily at these hearings, and said in part, "I was the first publisher in these United States to publish horror comics. I am responsible, I started them. Some may not like them. That is a matter of personal taste. It would be just as difficult to explain the harmless thrill of a horror story to a Dr. Wertham as it would be to explain the sublimity of love to a frigid old maid. My father was proud of the comics he published, and I am proud of the comics I publish. We use the best writers, the best artists; we spare nothing to make each magazine, each story, each page, a work of art."

Later he asked, "What are we afraid of? Are we afraid of our own children? Do we forget that they are citizens too, and entitled to the essential freedom too? Or do we think our children so evil, so vicious, so simple minded, that it takes a comic magazine story of murder to set them to murder, of robbery to set them to robber?"

In the end, the Senate hearings did not produce the Code; the industry itself set up the Comics Code Authority under former New York City Magistrate Charles F. Murphy, and allowed cooperative publishers to stamp their books "Approved by the

the author of THE SHOW OF VIOLENCE and DARK LEGEND

SEDUCTION OF THE INNOCENT

Fredric Wertham, M. D.

the influence of comic books on today's youth

Comics Code Authority." Says Feldstein, "I've always maintained that the comic book industry castrated itself. The industry ran scared, and the whole thing was terrible."

The Code, which prohibited the very words "horror" and "terror," together with Gaines' existing financial and distribution problems, dealt a body blow to the New Trend books. The final issues of the horror comics in 1954 printed "IN MEMORIAM" which read in part, "As a result of hysterical, injudicious, and unfounded charges leveled at crime and horror comics, many retailers and wholesalers throughout the country have been intimidated into refusing to handle this type of magazine. We are forced to capitulate. We give up. We've had it!"

"But enough mush!" the editors continue. "This is not only an obituary notice; it is also a birth announcement!" EC rebounded from the depths of 1954 with its New Directions books for 1955: *Aces High, Extra!, Impact, M.D., Psychoanalysis,* and *Valor.* They still had *MAD, Panic, Incredible Science Fiction* (retitled from *Weird Science-Fantasy* for its final four issues) and the swashbuckling *Piracy,* which had been introduced late in 1954 and was not, strictly speaking, a New Directions book.

Feldstein edited all the new books except *Extra!* which was handled by Johnny Craig. Although the new books drew upon the same artists and added the writing skills of Carl Wessler and Jack Oleck, the New Directions died within the year. There was talent, but it was fettered by the code restrictions, and the cream of the readership, Gaines feels, had been turned away from comics by the sensationalism of the censors. The first issue of each title was published without the code seal but wholesale resistance forced Gaines to capitulate. Under the seal the books still did poorly, perhaps because of continued difficulties with wholesalers and distributors perhaps because the old spirit was gone.

Krigstein's "Master Race" in *Impact* #1 was certainly equal to the best of the New Trend, but more typical of the new scripts was "Spads Were Trump" (*Aces High* #5) also drawn by Krigstein, WWI tale in which an American ace named Muller was forced to shoot down a German ace who, improbably, is his brother. The plotting is slack, the characters one-dimensional, and there is no explanation, either psychological or logistical, for the national allegiance of either brother.

221

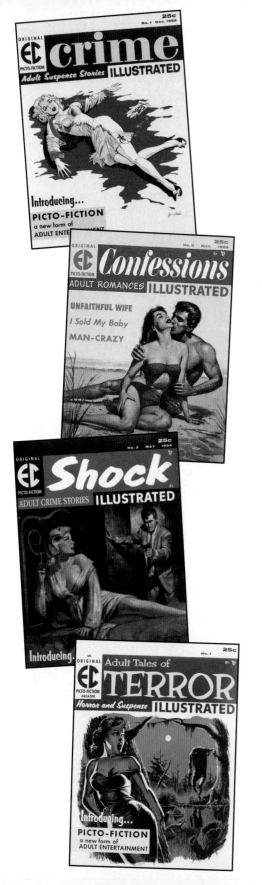

In a last ditch attempt to avoid the Code restrictions, Gaines launched the short-lived Adult Picto-Fiction books *Crime Illustrated*, *Confessions Illustrated*, *Shock Illustrated*, and *Terror Illustrated*. The four were published in *MAD*-sized magazine format, sold for a quarter, and contained black and white pictures with a block of text rather than balloon dialogue. Freed of the Code, the Picto-fiction dealt even more explicitly with themes of infidelity, sexual aberration, and abnormal psychology. Stories like "Sin Doll" (*Shock Illustrated* #3, Kamen), "I Sold My Baby (*Confessions Illustrated* #2, Kamen), and "The Lipstick Killer (*Shock Illustrated* #2, Crandall) were not bad reading, and the quality of illustration was high, but the format was static, and the content perhaps too unusual for public taste.

In any case, the financial bottom had dropped out of EC. *Confessions*, *Crime*, and *Terror* lasted only two issues, and 250,000 copies of *Shock* #3 were destroyed because there was no money to bind them. Perhaps a scant hundred were saved and handbound. There were bleak days at EC before the infant *MAD* magazine took hold and rose phoenix-like from the comic ashes. Kurtzman edited the first five magazine issues (#24-28) and then following his departure after financial disagreements with Gaines, Feldstein took over and continues as *MAD* editor today.

The question inevitably arises what might have been the fate of the New Trend books if the Code had not killed them? "The horror books never did badly," notes Gaines. "Right up to the end the horror books made money." There were plans even to the end to add a fourth horror book – *The Crypt of Terror* was to be resurrected – and ads for it had already appeared in *The Vault of Horror* #40. There were sales problems with the science fiction, but neither Gaines nor

Feldstein had any intention of abandoning them.

"That was our trick," confides Gaines. "We published everything we wanted to publish with the horror profits, which were considerable right up to the end." Adds Feldstein, "We were always going to keep the science fiction going, just for our own ego. I loved writing them, and editing them, and I loved doing the covers. We weren't going to let them go even though they weren't doing too well. The horror certainly made it up."

As for the future, Feldstein speculates that EC might have gone on to develop even better material. "I think there could have been an improvement – I think we would have perfected our art as we went along. The material was good, and we were devel-oping good writers. The whole area was wide open. In those days Bill always had a certain ambition to make money, but he also wanted to enjoy what he was doing."

Enjoyment was the word during those five years – and integrity, imagination, innovation, and talent. The EC days are gone, but time, ironically, has brought respectability. In a typical EC-style ending, in 25 years *MAD* has gone from outlaw to institution, transforming Gaines from dealer in depravity to kindly humor publisher. But scratch the surface, and EC addicts are still a crawl. Fanzine *Squa Tront* is still in print as of this writing, EC artists are in demand at cons, collectors are buying EC books at premium prices, while the beautiful Cochran reprints should assure that they will be both available and affordable for future generations. EC lives. Spa Fon!

Squa Tront was one of the earliest and most notable fanzines devoted to EC comics. Shown are issue #1 (1967) with a cover by Roger Hill and issue #9 with a painted cover by Johnny Craig.

– AFTER THE ARTICLE –

Robert Overstreet's connection with EC Comics certainly didn't end with the 1979 article. In August 1989, he and publisher Russ Cochran were invited to the Manhattan apartment of EC legend Bill Gaines to unveil and catalog the comics that Gaines' had sealed away 35-40 years ago. Seeing the light of day for the first time in decades, these prisitne copies were christened the Gaines File Copies, and when introduced to the market shortly thereafter, were enthusiastically gobbled up by the rabid EC fans.

In 2000, the 50th anniversary of EC's "New Trend" was celebrated with a pair of covers by legendary EC artists. Al Feldstein painted the familiar horror hosts while Al Williamson transported us to a fantastical sci-fi scene, lushly colored by Marie Severin.

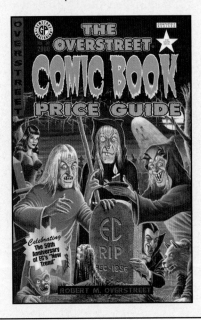

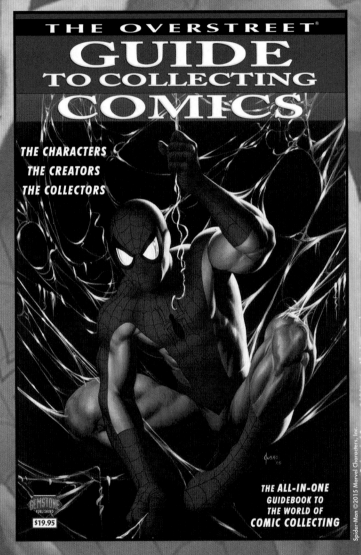

THE ORIGIN OF MARVEL COMICS

5 NEW FAMOUS
ACTION FEATURES

CAPTAIN
AMERICA
and BUCKY
HUMAN TORCH
and TORO
SUB-MARINER
THE ANGEL · BLACK MARVEL

By George Olshevsky

This article was originally published in The Overstreet Comic Book Price Guide #10 *1980*

In 1966, I began to read comic books again. For a period of about four years, I had given up comic books as simply uninteresting and juvenile. What drew me back to the fold were the Marvels. I can even pinpoint the comic book: *Tales to Astonish #78*, with the story of the Sub-Mariner versus the Puppet Master, part of a longer series in which the ultimate villain was Warlord Krang. By itself, the story was less than spectacular. But I quickly learned that it was a small chapter in the much larger story of what was beginning to be thought of as the Marvel Universe. It was this larger story that I found fascinating beyond all my expectations of what could be provided in comic books.

Two years later, I had left the ivy-covered halls of the Boston colleges for graduate work at the University of Toronto, and I took with me this novel addiction to Marvel Comics. Many times, I had entertained the heady notion of actually owning all the back issue Marvels, in order to have the complete Marvel Universe story in one library. Unfortunately, there was simply no way this goal could have been accomplished, since I was at the time quite ignorant of and isolated from the still miniscule comic fan movement.

The situation changed once I arrived in Toronto. I met George Henderson and became a regular customer at his store, Memory Lane, the first store in Canada (and, perhaps, all of North America) whose sole business was dealing in back issue comic books. "Captain George" usually sold the past year's back issues at a nickel apiece, and as the books grew older, their prices rose accordingly. *Fantastic Four* #1 was priced at $7 when I bought my first copy, while many EC comics could be had for just a dollar or two. The most expensive comic ever sold at Memory Lane (that I knew of) was a near mint copy of *Action Comics* #1, which went in a part cash, part trade deal for the then colossal sum of $500.

At Memory Lane I discovered a treasure trove of

"Captain George" Henderson, owner of Memory Lane

back issue Marvel comics, and I met several people who were in touch with the fan movement all across the continent. I learned that there were such things as comic conventions, where groups of comic collectors could gather together to buy and sell comics, meet professionals and spend many happy hours discussing the goings-on in the various "comic universes." Even more important to me in terms of my collecting interests, however, I learned that there was an extensive series of "Marvel comics before Marvel Comics," and that, even though they were a great deal scarcer than the current "modern" Marvels, they were obtainable on occasion through stores like Memory Lane and from other dealers with whom I was beginning to interact.

The job of collecting 1960s back issue Marvels was a lot easier then, than it would be today. There were only a few hundred comic books to find, and they cost an average of 10¢ to 15¢ each. So, by early 1969, I had succeeded in attaining my original goal of assembling the modern Marvel comics into one library. I also owned three of the rare "Golden Age"

Author George Olshevsky making a purchase at Memory Lane in 1970.

Marvel comics. It struck me that it would be quite a challenge to try to assemble the complete Golden Age Marvel superhero comic collection to go with the modern Marvels. Then I would have the definitively complete Marvel Universe library.

Thus, when Captain George offered a load of 40 Golden Age Marvels for sale in 1970, I bought every one. Seven years later, in July 1977, the last book I needed finally straggled in: *Blonde Phantom Comics #22*. In between buying the first and the last books, I watched the prices of Golden Age Marvels double, then double again, and then double again, while the library I built became the center of my own business and the ultimate reference source of Marvel lore, indispensable to me in my work.

The *Timely Comic Index*
by Mike Nolan

Modern Marvel Comics are very well documented as to first and last issues of runs, appearances of major characters, and artists and writers of stories. The first index to the modern Marvels appeared in 1968 (it was published in Toronto, though not by me), and fans – like myself – have been keeping track of them in minute detail ever since. In contrast, the Marvel comics of the 1940s when I first began to collect them seemed to be real antiques, relics of a truly remote era which was informationally a vast, uncharted sea. Nobody had any idea how many issues there were of any particular title, nor the contents of any particular issues. Captain George gave me a set of Jerry Bails' early fanzine, *The Panelologist*, which featured detailed data in chart form about most of the Golden Age Marvel sets. And I obtained a copy of the fabulous *Timely Comic Index* by Mike Nolan, an actual index to the stories and heroes in each individual comic. Later, after I was heavily committed to gathering the Golden Age Marvels, I learned that some of the information carried in those two sources was incorrect (an occupational hazard of comic book indexing, from which immunity is an unrealizable ideal). But by and large they were very well done and quite accurate, and they served as my road map for the years when I was putting the collection together.

Timely Publications was the name of the first company under which Marvel comics were published, starting in 1939. For this reason, the term "Timely Comics" has come to be applied to the Golden Age Marvel comics as a group – or "house" – name. Marvel experimented during the 1940s with various identifiers and trademarks to set their comics apart from all the others on the newsstands, but none lasted for any length of time. Late in 1951 the familiar Atlas globe and ribbon symbol came into use, but this was well after the superhero books of other genres. Timely comics are in fact famous for the many different names – all dummies – under which they were published, a number which exceeds 40 and may yet be augmented as research on the obscure Marvel titles continues. Any one of those dummy names could serve as a legitimate group name, but Marvel comics and Timely comics are the ones most frequently employed by collectors. I will use the two names interchangeably in this article.

Timely comics present a costly paradox to the collector. They were never very popular at the time they were published (although of course they sold well enough to make a profit), certainly not nearly as popular as Fawcett, DC, or Dell. Marvel was a second string publisher in the 1940s, with just one character (Captain America) approaching "classic" status, and only two others (Sub-Mariner and the Human Torch) at all well known. Most of the Timely titles lasted 30 issues or less, which by today's standards would be considered pretty dismal. No run exceeded a hundred issues. (Compare any of a dozen of Marvel's current titles, some of which are approaching or have passed their 200th superhero issues.) No Timely comic had sales figures in the million copy-plus range of *Superman* or *Captain Marvel*. But where many of the comic book publishers eventually left the business in the 1950s once their superhero lines folded, Marvel was able to hang on. During the 1960s, Marvel rebuilt the image of superhero comics into a more interesting and salable form than it ever had before, and they became producers of the most popular of today's comic books. Many of the original Timely superheroes have been revived – often in new guises – in modern Marvel comics, and frequent references are made to events which occurred or could have occurred during the Golden Age. As a result, the Timelys, rendered scarce by their originally moderate newsstand performance, have come into rather heavy demand as vintage examples of "what Marvel was like in the 1940s." The combination of scarcity and demand has fueled their prices as collectible issues considerably. As a group, Timely comics have become the most valuable comics of all.

The first Marvel comic was titled, appropriately enough, *Marvel Comics*. As with most such first issues, there is a story that goes with it, which I have been able to piece together with various bits of information I have accumulated and a few plausible inferences.

It all began with Funnies, Inc. an art shop founded and operated by Lloyd V. Jacquet in 1939. Jacquet had been working with comics since 1935 – he was art director and editor of *New Fun* #1, the first DC comic – and, having observed the growth of comic magazines and the art shops that kept them supplied with material, he decided to start a shop of his own. Several people were in at the beginning: Jacquet himself, with his partners John Mahon and Jim Fitzsimmons; Bill Everett,

230

who was given the job of art director; John H. Compton, who became the editor; and Frank Torpey, who was the liaison between the shop and the outside world. Working as a scripter and assistant editor was Mickey Spillane. As artists and writers, there were Al Anders, Carl Burgos, Steve Dahlman, Martin Filchock, Ben Flinton, Ray Gill, Paul Gustavson, George Kapitan, Max Neill, Michael Robard, Ed Robbins, Harry Sahle, Fred Schwab, Frank Thomas, Ben Thompson, and many others. Their studio was located at 45 West 45th Street in the heart of New York City.

The earliest project undertaken by Funnies, Inc. (They called themselves First Funnies, Inc. then) known to have reached the press was a small black and white comic book titled *Motion Picture Funnies Weekly*. It was designed to be given away as a premium by movie theaters at their Saturday matinees, something extra to keep the people coming back. Only the first issue was actually printed; cover proofs of #2-4 survive. The scheme evidently did not pan out.

The existence of *Motion Picture Funnies Weekly* was unsuspected in comic fandom until 1973, when five complete file copies (and one incomplete copy) were discovered in the estate of one of the principals of Funnies, Inc. In addition, one copy of the book apparently exists which was obtained through a movie theater in 1939 and has been saved for sentimental reasons to the present day. (The owner does not want her name known for fear of being besieged by offers from collectors, or so the story goes.) Even though it was Funnies, Inc.'s first publishing venture, *Motion Picture Funnies Weekly* would have remained an insignificant book were it not for the presence of the Sub-Mariner's origin, its earliest appearance in print. This made the discovery something of a bombshell among comic fans. It became an expensive collector's item almost immediately.

Prince Namor the Sub-Mariner, as every fan of Marvel Comics knows, is the grandson of the emperor of an Antarctic undersea empire. He is gifted with great

strength and the ability to fly using small wings on his ankles. Like all members of his underwater race of sub-mariners, he can breathe while submerged; but unlike them he can also breathe air. Because he is the son of a sub-mariner mother and a surface human father, he looks far more human than the very fishlike sub-mariners; his triangular head and pointy ears are his most obvious non-human traits. The theme running through all his stories was one of vengeance against the surface people for wrongs accidentally inflicted on the sub-mariners during a series of scientific expeditions in the 1920s. Eventually Namor was persuaded to put aside his vendetta by a policewoman named Betty Dean and – by a direct attack on his people by the Nazis – to help the United States fight the Axis. In this manner all kinds of marvelous undersea weapons were added to the arsenal of democracy. A truly original comic hero, the Sub-Mariner is by far Bill Everett's most lasting contribution to the genre.

Shortly after *Motion Picture Funnies Weekly* was printed, Frank Torpey located a publisher interested in producing a line of comic books. This was Western Fiction Publishing Co. also known as Manvis Publications and Red Circle, a pulp magazine publishing company owned and operated by Martin and Abraham Goodman. Their address was 330 West 42nd Street, New York City. They had begun in 1939 with a small line of western pulps, and by 1939 they were something of an empire, producing 14 titles with a total circulation of over half a million. They were looking for some new ventures to get involved in. The idea of publishing comics appealed to Martin Goodman, and a package was put together by Funnies Inc. on a tryout basis. Goodman created a new publishing company, Timely Publications, and brought out the first issue of *Marvel Comics*, dated October 1939. As the custom of those times dictated, it appeared on the newsstands several months in advance of the cover date, probably in late July or early August 1939.

Only four copies of *Marvel Comics* #1 are known to me with their original cover date intact. All the other copies have their dates overprinted "November 1939," both on the front cover and on the indicia on the inside front cover. This proves unquestionably that there were two separate bindings of the book, and it is a reasonable inference that it was re-dated for a separate distribution. The first release was probably a market test to selected outlets, while the second release, presumably a month later, was fully nationwide. Currently, less than 50 copies are known in collectible condition (less than 10 in Very Fine to Mint condition), and *Marvel Comics* #1 has the reputation of being the rarest newsstand comic – although this assertion would be difficult to prove.

Printed at 81 Spring Street, Newark, New Jersey, *Marvel Comics* #1 was somewhat unusual by the publishing standards of the day. The cover was printed in process colors (magenta, yellow, cyan, and black) and not primary colors (red, yellow, blue, and black), which were usually used for comic books then. This gave it a wider chromatic range, so that it resembled a pulp magazine more than a comic book. The cover, showing the Human Torch versus a criminal named Tony Sardo (his first name wasn't revealed until *Marvel Mystery Comics* #92, in 1949), was drawn by Frank R. Paul, the well known science fiction pulp illustrator. His signature is half-obliterated near the bottom of the piece. It was a 64-page comic, in size about a quarter inch narrower than the other comics of the day. Five origin stories were featured, with three of the characters appearing there for the first time ever: Carl Burgos' Human Torch (the leadoff feature), Paul Gustavson's Angel, and Al Anders' Masked Raider (Marvel's first western character). Bill Everett's Sub-Mariner origin from *Motion Picture Funnies Weekly* was reprinted there, perhaps without Goodman knowing it was a reprint, with four new pages and color added (over the black and white benday, giving it a rather murky look). Bob Byrd's jungle character Ka-Zar was resurrected from his original three-issue Red Circle pulp run (in 1936) and rendered in comic strip form by Ben Thompson. A two-page text story titled "Burning Rubber" by Ray Gill and a filler comic strip titled "Jungle Terror" by Tohm Dixon rounded out the issue. The combination of extreme scarcity, of being the first Marvel comic ever published, and of carrying all those orig-

inal stories, has made *Marvel Comics* #1 the most expensive single collector's item comic in history.

Carl Burgos' Human Torch was Timely's most popular character during their first one and a half years. He was an artificial man – an android – created by Professor Albert Horton (whose first name, too, was revealed when the Human Torch's origin was retold in *Marvel Mystery Comics* #92). Because of a defect in its construction, the entire body of the Human Torch would spontaneously burst into flame on exposure to oxygen. For this reason, Horton kept the android imprisoned in a large evacuated bell jar. Naturally, the Torch got loose. He quickly learned how to control his flame, how to project it as a weapon and how to command fire anywhere in his environment. By directing his flame backward, he was able to fly like a jet; by precisely manipulating it, he could skywrite messages and entrap criminals in intricate "flame cages." And he was a natural antagonist for the Sub-Mariner, who epitomized water the way the Human Torch epitomized fire.

Few people now remember Paul Gustavson's Angel, even though for several years he was one of Timely's better selling characters. Most likely this is because he had no elemental superpower; he was simply a well-muscled costumed crime fighter – one of the few to sport a mustache. Ka-Zar was one of a number of heroes who followed in the footsteps of Edgar Rice Burroughs' very successful Tarzan. Having lost his parents in an airplane crash in darkest Africa, David Rand was raised by a pride of lions (hence his name, Ka-Zar, which means brother of Zar, the Lion) to become a tree-swinging, muscular jungle lord. All four heroes from *Marvel Comics* #1 have returned to modern Marvel comics: the Sub-Mariner survived intact; the Human Torch was reincarnated into the teenage member of the Fantastic Four (and the actual body was used in constructing the modern Vision); the Angel's name was given to the winged X-Man; and Ka-Zar was turned into another jungle lord, Lord Kevin Plunder of the Savage Land.

So, Marvel Comics was born of the pulps. They were published by a pulp magazine publisher, the cover of the first issue was drawn by a science fiction pulp artist, and the variety of story themes in *Marvel Comics* #1 was a cross-section of the whole pulp industry. This pulpiness dominated the first years of Marvel's Golden Age until the advent of the second World War, when the comics attained a special aspect all their own.

Apparently, Martin Goodman was dissatisfied with *Marvel Comics* #1. With its second issue, he retitled it *Marvel Mystery Comics*, making *Marvel Comics* #1 the only comic book to carry exactly that title. The Bill Everett Sub-Mariner cover originally submitted for *Marvel Comics* #2 was never used (it was lent to me to be used as a motif for the cover of the Sub-Mariner volume of the *Marvel Comics Index* nearly 40 years later). A cover featuring the Angel, drawn by Claire S. Moe, a Funnies, Inc. staff artist, replaced it. Goodman evidently thought the

Angel – and the detective story in general – was more salable than Sub-Mariner, and used the Angel on many covers of *Marvel Mystery Comics* during its first year. Nevertheless, the Sub-Mariner stories in *Marvel Mystery Comics* were the only really readable stories in the title. By today's standards, most of the other artwork and stories were hopelessly crude.

Examination of John Compton's file copy of *Marvel Comics* #1, which was part of the cache of comics in which *Motion Picture Funnies Weekly* was discovered, reveals numerous marginal notes and comments concerning the printing quality of the book. Dissatisfaction with the printing was probably the reason that *Marvel Mystery Comics* #2 was printed at 8 Lord Street, Buffalo, New York rather than in Newark, New Jersey. Timely used the Buffalo printer for about a year and a half, then switched to Eastern Color Press, 169 Pratt Street, Meriden, Connecticut, who printed their books throughout the War and for many years thereafter.

There was a minor change in the story lineup from #1 to #2: the filler story "Jungle Terror" was replaced by a strip titled "American Ace," by Paul J. Lauretta, which was reprinted in color from *Motion Picture Funnies Weekly*.

The same month that Timely published *Marvel Mystery Comics* #3, Goodman brought out their second title, *Daring Mystery Comics*. Although it was clearly intended as a companion comic to *Marvel Mystery Comics*, only one real superhero was featured in the first issue: the Fiery Mask,

234

by Joe Simon. As far as I know, that was Joe Simon's first published comic book strip. Simon was never a Funnies, Inc. staff member; he had been hired by Goodman to be Timely Publications' "in house" art director and editor sometime in the autumn of 1939. A graduate of Syracuse University, Joe Simon rapidly expanded his influence in the comics field, simultaneously serving as editor and art director of Timely, Fox Publications, Centaur Publications, all of whom were also Funnies, Inc. clients. (Comic book publishing was a small world in those days, just as it is a small world today.)

The cover of *Daring Mystery Comics* #1 – dated January 1940 – featured the Fiery Mask, without his fiery mask and brandishing a mace in an attempt to rescue a helpless woman from a pair of hooded thugs driving a futuristic automobile. It was drawn by Alex Schomburg, the first of over 100 covers he would draw for Timely during the 1940s. Characteristically, it had nothing whatever to do with the story inside. Schomburg was a first rate science fiction pulp artist, and his covers are one of Timely's collectible hallmarks.

Besides the Fiery Mask, *Daring Mystery Comics* #1 carried an array of stories that were, if anything, even more pulpy than those in *Marvel Mystery Comics*. There was a war story titled "Soldier of Fortune, John Steele," by Larry Antonette (who signed it "Dean Carr"); a western titled "The Texas Kid, Robin Hood of the Range," by Ben Thompson; a magician crimefighter strip titled "Monako, Prince of Magic," by Larry Antonette, one of the many flagrant

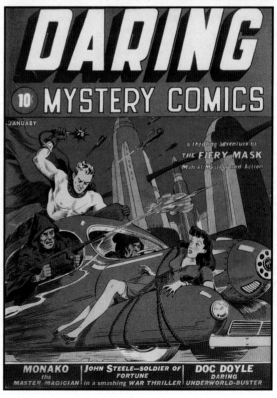

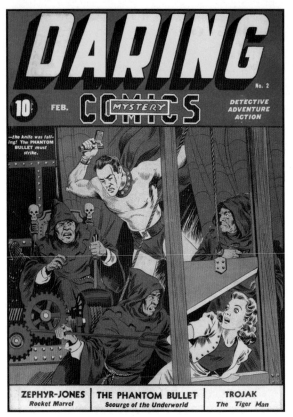

ZEPHYR-JONES | THE PHANTOM BULLET | TROJAK
Rocket Marvel | Scourge of the Underworld | The Tiger Man

(he signed himself "Dahl") "Electro, the Marvel of the Age," Marvel Comics' first, rather off-beat, version of Iron Man; and Stockbridge Winslow's "Ferret," another detective strip, drawn by Irwin Hasen. Certainly, one of the reasons *Marvel Mystery Comics* kept its readership was its reliance on continued stories: the Human Torch, Sub-Mariner, and Ka-Zar strips were all merely episodes in much longer tales. And the character was kept quite consistent from issue to issue.

Consistency of lineup was emphatically not a hallmark of *Daring Mystery Comics*. Every single character in #1 was replaced in #2 (dated February 1940, and decorated with another Schomburg cover). The book began with a science fiction strip, lifted from the very successful *Flash Gordon*, titled "Zephyr Jones and His Rocket Ship," written by Joe Cal Cagno and drawn by Fred Schwartz. This was followed by a detective hero story by Joe Simon titled "The Phantom Bullet – Scourge of the Underworld;" a jungle hero story titled "Trojak the Tiger Man," also by Joe Simon, who signed himself "Gregory Sykes" for variety; a two-page text story titled "Six-Gun Dynamite," by Russell A. Bankson (probably Ray Gill writing pseudonymously); an airplane hero strip titled "K-4 and His Sky Devils," by an artist with a very distinctive style whose name I have not yet determined; another detective hero strip titled "Mr. 'E'," written by Joe Cal Cagno and drawn by Al Carreno; and finally still another detective hero strip, "The Laughing Mask," written by Will Harr and drawn by Maurice Gutwirth.

imitations of *Mandrake*; a two-page text story (from which the title was inadvertently omitted in production) by Ray Gill and illustrated by Al Anders; a football strip titled "Flash Foster at Midwestern," by Bob Wood; a detective strip introducing the Phantom of the Underworld, titled "Case of Perrone," by Maurice Gutwirth (although the title character, the Phantom of the Underworld, was named "Doc" Denton in the story, he was billed as "Doc" Doyle on the cover); a one-page filler titled "Wartime Wonders," by Harry Francis Campbell; and a story of oceanic intrigue titled "Barney Mullen, Sea Rover," by Charles Pearson. Except for the Fiery Mask and Monako, none of those characters was ever seen again in comics.

As the months rolled on, *Marvel Mystery Comics* steadily gained in circulation. Issue 3 featured the last of American Ace, which was replaced in #4 by Steve Dahlman's

At the very end of 1939, Timely brought out its third title, *Mystic Comics*. The first issue was dated March 1940, a date which the supposedly monthly *Daring Mystery Comics* skipped. It again sported an Alex Schomburg cover (of the eight comics Timely produced in 1939, six had Schomburg covers) displaying the Blue Blaze in action against a sewer full of thugs. Inside were "Flexo the Rubber Man," an origin story written by Will Harr and drawn by Jack Binder; "The Blue Blaze," another origin story, written and drawn by Harry Douglas; the second installment of "Zephyr Jones and His Rocket Ship," again by Joe Cal Cagno and Fred Schwartz; "The 3 X's," by "Roe" (most likely Michael Robard, who later changed his name to the shorter Mike Roy), Marvel's first team of heroes in their only comic book appearance; a two-page text story titled "Tough Hombre," by Leo Stalanker (Ray Gill again?), illustrated by Harry Ramsey; "The Deep Sea Demon," by Fred Guardineer, unquestionably the best drawn strip in the book; "Dakor the Magician," drawn at least in part by Maurice Gutwirth and purchased from the Harry "A" Chesler Syndicate; and "Dynamic Man," making his debut in a story written and drawn by Daniel Peters. *Mystic Comics* was "semi consistent" – about half of the characters in #1 appeared in each of the first four issues.

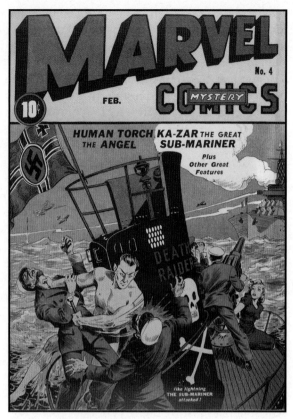

At this point, it is interesting to note that both *Daring Mystery Comics* #2 and *Marvel Mystery Comics* #4 carried advertisements on their inside front covers awarding a total of $25 in prizes to readers who sent in the best 100-word essays on their favorite characters in those respective comics. This was, of course, not an example of the publishers' generosity, but simply a ploy to survey their readers and discover which characters should be canned and which should be boosted. The results of that survey almost certainly brought about Timely's first recorded title cancellations four months later, and they were probably almost as important in determining the direction Timely would take in 1940 and 1941.

Marvel Mystery Comics, which was almost entirely composed of Funnies, Inc. strips drawn by Funnies Inc. artists, continued as Timely's flagship comic. When #7 appeared, there was a definite hint in its pages of something new and exciting: an impending battle between the Human Torch and the Sub-Mariner. Although Frank Torpey is generally credited with originating the Torch/Sub-Mariner battles, it is a natural enough confrontation that I believe it was suggested to the publishers by some reader even earlier, probably in the survey. Certainly, Timely learned that the Human Torch and the Sub-Mariner were their runaway bestselling characters, and they began to take steps to promote them heavily in their publications.

I have discussed Timely comics at some length with many persons who read comics in 1940, and all of them remember the big battle issues of *Marvel Mystery Comics* – sometimes they remember only the battle issues. There is no question that those comics were exciting to the children of that time, and it was perhaps the battle issues more than any others which elevated the protagonists into the ranks of the better known superheroes of the Golden Age.

The leadup to the battles began in *Marvel Mystery Comics* #6. The Sub-Mariner, who had done damage in New York City on his first visit there (as told in previous issues), had been persuaded by Betty Dean to return to stand trial. He was tried and astonishingly enough was sentenced to be electrocuted for the "crime" of having superpowers. Even more surprising, after being subdued and placed into the electric chair, Sub-Mariner was invigorated by the electric current, and the strength which he had lost by being kept out of water was restored. Vowing vengeance on those who would have destroyed him, he began tearing up New York in earnest, and there seemed to be no way to stop him.

In #7, the Human Torch arrived in New York to become a member of the New York Police Department. He was given the alias Jim Hamond (later changed to Hammond), and his first assignment was to stop the rampaging Sub-Mariner. Issue 8 featured the first actual meeting between the two characters. In the Sub-Mariner story, which for the first time occupied the leadoff spot in the magazine, the Human Torch was a guest star; and in the Human Torch strip the Sub-Mariner was the guest star. Both strips told essentially the same story, but from the opposite viewpoints of their title characters.

The battle in #8 was rather mild and inconclusive; but the return bout in #9 (July 1940) delivered the goods in a spectacular 22-page story written by John Compton and Hank Chapman and drawn by both Carl Burgos and Bill Everett (and more than likely some other Funnies, Inc. artists as well). The cover, another one by Alex Schomburg, was the first Timely cover to co-feature two major heroes (and one of the few to portray an actual scene from the story). Of course, neither character could ever have won such a battle decisively – it would have disappointed too many fans of the loser. So, the outcome was predestined to be a standoff. But Timely managed to drag it out one more issue by putting the final page of the story, with the battle's conclusion, into #10. Regardless of its ultimate shortcomings, it was just what the reading public wanted to see.

Marvel Mystery Comics #9 (July 1940) - The first Timely cover to co-feature their two major heroes.

By contrast, *Daring Mystery Comics* and *Mystic Comics*, with their air of being thrown together from strips rejected or shelved by other comic publishers and shops, began to falter. *Mystic Comics* lasted through #4 (July 1940) when publication was suspended. (I own a copy with the July date overprinted August on the cover, indicating that Timely returned the comic to the newsstands for a second go around.) *Daring Mystery Comics* fared slightly better, lasting until #6 (September 1940) before being suspended. Schomburg covers decorated all four issues of *Mystic Comics* and the first four issues of *Daring Mystery Comics*.

One other event of significance occurred at just this time: Jack Kirby, then in his early 20s, arrived at the Timely office looking for work. There he met Joe Simon, who was doubtless a bit exasperated with the performance of the two comics under his direct editorship (and it probably did not help that he was editorial director for several other comic companies at the

same time), and the two men sat down to discuss the future. Kirby was a fast penciller who had picked up action techniques working as an in-betweener for Fleischer Studios and had adapted his talents to the comic medium doing strips for Fiction House and various minor comic book publishers in the late 1930s.

The first thing Simon and Kirby did for Timely was start a fourth comic book title, *Red Raven Comics* #1 (August 1940). *Red Raven Comics* #1 sported a Jack Kirby cover, half of which was swiped almost line for line from a panel of the January 15, 1938 *Prince Valiant* Sunday page by Hal Foster. (When Kirby swiped, he swiped with class!) Two strips in that book were by Simon and Kirby: "Red Raven," the rather peculiar origin story of the title character, which was probably 75% Simon, and "Mercury," which introduced the gods of Olympus to Timely Comics (they were also pretty fundamental in Simon and Kirby's "Marvel Boy" strip, published a bit later in *Daring Mystery Comics* #6), which was probably 75% Kirby – it was bylined "Martin A. Bursten," a Simon and Kirby pseudonym. "Comet Pierce," a space opera strip, was entirely by Jack Kirby and the only strip in the book credited outright to him. Of the other strips, "The Human Top" was by Dick Briefer (as "Dun Barr"), "Magar the Mystic, Re-Creator of Souls," still another magician strip, was by an artist whose style resembles that of "Roe" (Michael Robard?), and "The Eternal Brain," Marvel's first version of a disembodied brain character (like Doctor Sun in modern issues of *Tomb of Dracula*), was definitely by "Roe" – his signature appears, faintly, at the bottom of the second to last panel. A two-page text story and a two-page gag strip filled out the issue.

It is unclear just what Joe Simon did and what Jack Kirby did in any of the strips credited to "Simon and Kirby." Simon almost certainly plotted each strip and scripted many of them, while Kirby penciled and inked over Simon's layouts in the early strips at least. Later, Kirby laid out and penciled while someone else inked. And there is no question that Kirby contributed heavily to the plots as well in many cases.

It was just after *Red Raven Comics* #1 was put to bed that the axe fell at Timely – probably in June 1940. Simon and Kirby just managed to squeeze their "Marvel Boy" strip into *Daring Mystery Comics* #6 (and onto its cover), when the word went out about the title cancellations. All of Timely's chips would ride on *Marvel Mystery Comics*, which was selling quite well after the Human Torch and Sub-Mariner battle issues.

The readers got to see a lot more of the Human Torch and the Sub-Mariner when Timely brought out their fifth publication, a special comic with a 19-page Human Torch story and a 12-page Sub-Mariner story as the main features. This was the first issue of *The Human Torch Comics*, and it was special in more ways than one: for the first time, the Torch was given a kid sidekick, Toro, who was discovered (the story goes) in a carnival show displaying his ability to control fire. Toro's origin story was written by John Compton and drawn mainly by Carl Burgos, and it was clearly produced in response to the spectacularly successful Robin, kid companion and foil to the Batman. Although *The Human Torch Comics* #1 appeared at the same time as *Marvel Mystery Comics* #13 (November 1940), it was not until #18, in 1941 that Toro joined the Torch in that comic book.

The Human Torch Comics #1 was dated fall 1940 and appeared September 25, two months after Joe Simon's books took their final bow. Simon and Kirby of course did not remain idle during the summer and

autumn of 1940 – far from it. Their material was incorporated into the Funnies Inc.-edited *Marvel Mystery Comics*. They did the cover of #12 (the last Angel cover to appear on that title) and initiated a new series featuring the Vision, a heroic character named Aarkis who inhabited the "smoke dimension," in #13. And they contributed a small share to *The Human Torch Comics* #1. Besides the Human Torch strip and Bill Everett's Sub-Mariner story, four filler strips appeared in that book, probably pulled from the unpublished *Daring Mystery Comics* #7. These were the final Falcon strip, drawn by George Kerr; the one-shot Microman strip, written by Paul Quinn and drawn by Harold DeLay (Marvel's first version of Ant-Man); and the one-shot Mantor the Magician strip – yes, another magician – by an artist I cannot identify. The fourth filler, the final episode of the Fiery Mask, was drawn at least in part by Simon and Kirby.

The Human Torch Comics was Timely's first quarterly comic, and there is something of an anomaly in the numbering

previous months. Earlier, in #10, Terry Vance, Schoolboy Sleuth, accompanied by his trained pet monkey Dr. Watson, written by Ray Gill and drawn by Bob Oksner, replaced Winslow and Hasen's more serious detective strip "The Ferret." "Terry Vance" was a surprisingly durable strip, running over 40 issues and last well into 1944. The hero was a teenager with a mind for unraveling mysteries instead of tending to his studies. His pet Dr. Watson could not speak but used thought balloons and gestures quite effectively, and he frequently was the key agent in the solution of the crime. Not a particularly important strip to superhero collectors, "Terry Vance" is most interesting because of its clearly derived relationship with Gus Mager's classic comic strip, *Sherlocko the Monk*.

of its earliest issues. Issue 1 is numbered Volume 1 #2 in the indicia and the next three issues continue this numbering. Issue 5 is the first issue to be numbered "correctly," so that there are two issues numbered Volume 1 #5: the "real" #4 and the "real #5. The third issue is even more inconsistent, because it has #3 on its cover and Volume 1 #4 in its indicia. The only Timely comic which could have served as Volume 1 #1 of that series is *Red Raven Comics* #1. What I presume happened was a continuation of the numbering of *Red Raven Comics* into *The Human Torch Comics* for some obscure publishing reason, perhaps to avoid paying the second class mailing permit deposit twice. It is also possible that there was an "ashcan copy" of *The Human Torch Comics*, but if so, there is no other evidence for such an issue. Finally, it could simply have been an error.

Replacing the Masked Raider with the Vision in *Marvel Mystery Comics* #13 was one of two cosmetic changes which had quietly taken place in that title during the

From July to November 1940 inclusive, Timely published only six comic books. This is less than the number of books Marvel now publishes in just one week,

though to be fair, it should be noted that Timely's comics were twice as large as today's, and carried well over three times as much story art. But bigger things were brewing at Timely. For one thing, a staff began to accumulate – something unprecedented at Timely because of the still experimental nature of the comic book publishing venture. Timely's staff became the forerunner of today's Marvel Bullpen, a "floating" assemblage of permanent and freelance writers and artists, pooling their talents to produce the comics. Joe Simon served as the first editorial director, and Jack Kirby was the art director. As people began to arrive, new publishing projects took shape.

The first staff member to be taken on was a young artist from the Harry "A" Chesler studio named Syd Shores, who walked in one day with his portfolio. He presented Kirby with a comic strip he had done as an apprentice at the studio, "The Terror" (written by Phil Sturm), and Kirby hired him. Shortly afterward, sometime in the late autumn of 1940, Timely acquired the services of a teen-age kid fresh out of high school aspiring to be a great American writer. Stanley Michael Lieber, or Stan Lee, as he signed his work, was first assigned to writing text fillers, but he rapidly advanced to scripting the comic strips themselves. In short order the Timely staff filled out with Al Avison, Al Gabriele, George Klein, Don Rico, Mike Sekowsky, and Charles Wojtkowski (who later changed his name to Charles Nicholas), all young and eager to get to work.

With this influx of new personnel, Goodman felt ready to increase the number of titles Timely was publishing. It was decided to revive *Mystic Comics* and *Daring Mystery Comics*. But instead of reviving *Red Raven Comics*, a brand new title would be brought out, Timely's sixth.

It would be dramatically relevant to the state of affairs in Europe then, foreshadowing the already widely acknowledged inevitable entry of the United States into World War II. It was destined to become Timely's best selling and most famous comic of all: *Captain America Comics*. The target month was December 1940.

The first comic to appear that December was the second issue of *The Human Torch Comics*, dated winter 1940-1941. The filler stories which ran in #1 were gone, and the book featured an honest 40 pages of the Human Torch and Toro, backed up by a 20-page Sub-Mariner story. The Sub-Mariner story was a continuation of the two-part Human Torch and Toro story, and even featured the two flaming heroes in guest appearances. Toro's storyline continued directly from #1, while the Human Torch's storyline continued from *Marvel Mystery Comics* #16. Both stories featured the Axis (including Hitler and Mussolini) as the villains. Two of the house ads in that issue featured Captain America (one for the comic, one for the Sentinels of Liberty club), and these stand as the first appearances of Captain America and Bucky in print.

Then *Marvel Mystery Comics* #17 (March 1941) opened with a giant 26-page combined Human Torch and Sub-Mariner battle, in which the two heroes teamed together to stop an Axis invasion of the United States. Continuity fans should note that this invasion was nothing more than a continuation of the one the three heroes foiled in *The Human Torch Comics* #2, the threat coming from a tunnel beneath the Pacific Ocean instead of from a flotilla on the surface. Oddly enough, the story went with the cover of #15, published two months earlier. Apparently, Timely had been harassed by the audience over not publishing stories to go with the covers, so "better late than never" stories and text filler "stories behind the covers" began to appear fairly regularly. Also featured in this issue was another contest, for the best 100-word dialogue (50 words apiece) between the Human Torch and the Sub-Mariner. The entry was, of course, to be accompanied by a feedback letter. Timely obviously valued its rapport with the readers, and certainly did their best to keep them happy.

Advertised on the inside back cover of *The Human Torch Comics* #2 as on sale December 15, 1940, was *Mystic Comics* #5, the first issue of the title after its six-month cancellation. It was obviously published as a repository for the miscellaneous inventory strips bought by Timely as its staff of artists grew. About half of the strips kicked off short-lived series, while the rest were just one-shots. The origin of the Black Marvel, drawn by George Mandel, was the cover feature. Other stories included Syd Shores and Phil Sturm's "The Terror," mentioned earlier; Paul Gustavson's one-shot "Adventures of Super Slave;" "Sub-Earth Man," another

one-shot by an artist with a very distinctive style whom I cannot identify; "The Legend of the Blackfeet," another text filler by Ray Gill; the second Black Widow story, by Harry Sahle and George Kapitan (she first appeared in *Mystic Comics* #4 before the title's suspension, Timely's first costumed female character); Fred Guardineer's one-shot "The Moon Man," and the origin of the Blazing Skull, by Bob Davis, who signed himself "Mister X."

The first issue of *Captain America Comics* (March 1941) finally arrived on the newsstands on December 20, 1940. It was only the second time that a Timely character made his debut in his own title. But where there was only one Red Raven story, *Captain America* #1 carried four stories of the superhero. His red, white, and blue costume was the ultimate in patriotic motifs designed to appeal to the readers' innate sense of pride in their country. His sidekick, Bucky, was designed to capitalize on the juvenile companion trend in vogue in the hero comics. The hard-hitting cover, drawn by Jack Kirby and inked by newcomer Syd Shores (it was Shores' very first job at Timely), showed Captain America slamming his fist "right in the Fuehrer's face." Not the first of the patriotic costumed heroes (MLJ's Shield preceded Captain America by many months and was probably the reason that Captain America's shield changed its shape from triangular to circular in the next issue), he was certainly the best conceived. There was no doubt about where he stood in response to the challenge of Nazism.

Captain America's origin is familiar to most collectors of Marvel Comics. Steve Rogers, a sickly, gaunt youth with a fierce desire to serve his country, tried to enlist in the Army, but was rejected as physically unfit. Despondent, he was offered service as a guinea pig in an experiment by the world's leading scientist, Professor

Reinstein. (Albert Einstein, incidentally, had fled Nazi Germany and arrived at Princeton a few years earlier, an event which was much in the news of the day; hence the reference.) Rogers was injected with a special serum developed by Reinstein, and in a matter of moments he was transformed into a powerful, muscular hero. Unfortunately, Reinstein was shot by a fifth column Nazi operative, and the secret of the serum died with him. Rogers became an agent of the United States government; he was given his costume and a cover at a local Army camp. Soon the figure of Captain America was striking terror into the hearts of the foes of liberty. Bucky Barnes, an orphan who was the camp mascot, became his partner after he discovered Steve Rogers changing out of his Captain America costume in his tent.

I believe the success of Captain America was motivated by much more than the mere pursuit of profit. The Goodman brothers, Joe Simon, Jack Kirby, Stan Lee,

and many others of Timely's staff were Jewish. They were very much aware of the manic antisemitism which had engulfed the German nation under Adolf Hitler. They knew of the Warsaw Ghetto, where thousands of Jewish people were systematically being starved to death each month. And certainly, they knew of the network of forced labor camps dotting central Europe – Auschwitz, Treblinka, Dachau – which in the years to follow became the scene of the Nazis' greatest horrors. As ordinary people in America, the Timely staff had little direct political influence, but through the medium of the comic book they were able to express their bitterness and frustration. The sincerity and fervor of their damnation of the Axis powers transcended the crudeness of the plot and artwork, and made their stories true comic classics.

Captain America Comics #1 was filled out with two backup stories behind the 45 pages of Captain America tales, both by

Simon and Kirby. The first reintroduced the character Mercury from *Red Raven Comics* #1, in new guise as the costumed hero Hurricane. The second introduced Tuk, Caveboy, in "Stories From the Dark Ages." This strip was the first of any published by Timely to mention Atlantis (also called "Attilan" in the story), and it was set in that long-lost antediluvian era when civilization had arisen there, but the rest of humanity still dwelled in caves. It is unquestionably the wellspring whence Marvel's current Inhumans arose.

Timely's club for Captain America fans, the Sentinels of Liberty, also premiered in *Captain America Comics* #1. By sending a dime to Timely, one could become a member, and would receive by return mail an "official badge and membership card." It is said that at its height the Sentinels of Liberty numbered over 100,000 members – quite a lot of dimes. Ads for the club, at first illustrated by Simon and Kirby, appeared in most of Timely's comics for several years. Later Al Avison's severe rendering of Captain America's face admonished the nation's children to join up. Lack of interest, perhaps fostered by the need for the metal in the badges for the war effort, finally forced the disbanding of the club in the middle 1940s.

By any standards, 1941 must be regarded as Timely's all around best year. All the writers and artists were young, full of enthusiasm and genuinely enjoyed their

craft – despite the general primitiveness of the working environment. Many were truly good draftsmen; some would later acquire fame as titans of the genre. Their ranks had not yet been decimated by the call to war, while their love for their characters and their interest in their evolution were unfettered. The field of comic literature was new, and everyone was a neophyte. There were no commercial standards to restrict technique or creativity, a situation having much in common with 1960s underground comix. The booming sales – *Captain America Comics* began to outsell *Marvel Mystery Comics* almost from the first issue – strongly reinforced the euphoric feeling that they could do no wrong.

Both *Marvel Mystery Comics* and *Captain America Comics* continued throughout 1941 as Timely's top sellers and their only monthlies. The former was primarily a Funnies, Inc. vehicle, while the latter became established as Timely's in-house comic. Twelve issues of *Marvel Mystery Comics* #18-29 (April 1941-March 1942) and 11 of *Captain America Comics* #2-12 (April 1941-March 1942, but skipping July 1941) were published during 1941.

Each cover of *Marvel Mystery Comics* in 1941 displayed either the Human Torch or the Sub-Mariner, frequently in some colossal battle with hordes of Axis invaders; all were drawn by Alex Schomburg. Carl Burgos did the honors on the year's run of Human Torch stories, of which the most memorable involved the Parrot in #24 and #26. The Parrot appeared several times in subsequent Human Torch stories – once in 1954 – and was probably the second best known Timely villain after the Red Skull. Toro joined the Torch at the beginning of the year and stayed with him in over 200 stories in the 1940s and 1950s. All the 1941 Sub-Mariner *Marvel Mystery Comics* adventures were drawn by Bill Everett, chapters of an unending novel following one another in serial order. The most unusual creatures Namor encountered were Princess Jarna of Venus and her Lavarites, a race of miniature people (Jarna herself was for some reason normal sized), in #25-26.

Marvel Mystery Comics #20 opened with a giant warning on the Human Torch story splash page, denouncing publishers thinking of swiping the flaming hero's modus operandi and noting that all of the major characters in *Marvel Mystery Comics* would forever be protected as trademarks registered with the U.S. Patent Office. This practice has continued right to the present day with Marvel Comics.

Paul Gustavson drew the Angel through #21, and in 1941 this run included a meaty three-part story in #18-20 in which the Angel fought a black-costumed female villain called the Cat's Paw. With #22, Al Gabriele and Al Avison assumed the art chores, and they stayed with the strip for some time thereafter.

The last Electro story appeared in #19, but his slot in *Marvel Mystery Comics* was not taken over until #21, when Timely quietly brought in the Patriot. The Patriot was the secret identity of newsman Jeff Mace; his first story appeared about a month earlier, in the spring 1941 issue of *The Human Torch Comics* #3, which also carried a Ray Gill text filler illustrated by Bill Everett outlining his origin. That story and the ones in *Marvel Mystery Comics* #21-23 were drawn by Art Gates. Sid Greene drew the Patriot with a fine, clean line in #24 and #25 and *The Human Torch* #4,

247

then Ray Houlihan (possibly) drew him in #26 and #27, and Al Fagaly drew him in #28 and #29.

Ka-Zar was drawn right through his final story in #27 by Ben Thompson. He was replaced by Ed Robbins' "Jimmy Jupiter" strip, which started in #28. That strip was something of a portent of things to come from Timely in the post-1941 period, being one of the first continuing "funny" strips published by that company. (Technically, "Terry Vance" was also such a strip; but it dealt with crime and adventure. "Jimmy Jupiter" was outright saccharine fantasy; it felt quite out of place in *Marvel Mystery Comics*.) Joe Simon and Jack Kirby contributed the Vision strip in #18-25. By #26 and #27 Kirby only drew the splash pages. The guts of the strips were drawn by an artist named David Walters, whose signature appeared in house ads for *Marvel Mystery Comics*. He may have inked some of the earlier Vision stories as well, and apparently also did some of Steve Dahlman's Electro strips. Following his work on the Vision, Walters dropped out of comics entirely, which leads me to suspect that the name might have been a pseudonym.

It paid to read the little text fillers in each issue; they often let the reader in on obscure incidents in the lives of the heroes. For example, #20 carried the story "High Tension," by Ray Gill, which told the origin of the Angel. Issue 23 featured "The Vision Speaks," an account of the Vision's origin by Stan Lee. "Marvel Get-Together," again by Stan Lee, described a meeting of all the heroes from *Marvel Mystery Comics* in #25, thereby proving at even that early date they all operated in the same universe. And #28 and #29 offered "The Sea of Grassy Death" and "The Ship in the Desert," two of the many early quickie text fillers by the now famous Mickey Spillane.

Captain America Comics featured either three or four stories of Captain America and Bucky in each issue, and frequently a text filler as well. Stan Lee's first published comic book work was the filler in *Captain America Comics* #3. All the comic strips were illustrated by Simon and Kirby; Syd Shores handled a good deal of the inking, and Jack Kirby inked many of the strips himself. A few others were inked by Mike Sekowsky and George Klein. At first the scripting was by Joe Simon himself; later Stan Lee took over.

Cap's stories are probably the most dramatic comic book fare published by Timely during the Golden Age; they oozed and dripped surrealistic death. Each story was concerned with the mad plot of some demented killer. Museums and hospitals became weird domains of psychotic Nazis. Webs of intrigue wove through darkened alleys and under city streets. They were a celebration of the grotesque and horrid. Obviously, the kids loved them.

As 1941 drew on, Simon and Kirby did less and less of each story. Otto Binder began to script some of the stories when the workload became too much even for Stan Lee. In the autumn of 1941, after doing the tenth issue of *Captain America Comics*, Simon and Kirby left Timely to work for DC, publishers of the top-selling Golden Age hero comics. There they wrote and drew the Newsboy Legion, the Boy Commandos, Sandman, and Manhunter. Simon and Kirby stayed together as a team until well into the 1950s, always moving from publisher to publisher, initiating series after series but for some reason never finding exactly the right combination of publisher and interest to hold them on a book for more than a few months or a year. With Simon and Kirby, the need to create greatly overpowered the desire to sustain.

In the last two 1941 issues of *Captain America Comics*, after Simon and Kirby left, the plotting, editing, and scripting were all taken over by Stan Lee, while the regular artists became Al Avison and Syd Shores.

The backup features in *Captain America Comics* were almost as interesting as the main stories. Simon and Kirby did both Tuk, Caveboy and Hurricane in #2, but the only backup feature drawn by Simon and Kirby in #3 was a two-page filler strip titled "Amazing Spy Adventures." Tuk lasted through #5 and was drawn by two or three different artists, none of whom I have been able to identify with any confidence. Hurricane lasted through #11, almost to the end of 1941, and the artist in each story from #3 up was Charles Wojtkowski. The splash page of the story in #7 includes a picture of a cigar box labeled "Baldowski Cigars" which leads me to suspect that Ken Bald, an artist who worked for Timely in the later 1940s, may have had some kind of hand in the strip as well. "Headline Hunter," a strip about a newsman, written by Stan Lee and prob-

ably drawn by Charles Wojtkowski made its debut in *Captain America Comics* #5. It ran through #13 but skipped #11, a total of eight adventures. Finally, Father Time, a costumed superhero whose weapon was a scythe, appeared in seven issues of *Captain America Comics* #6-12, in stories also written by Stan Lee – some signed "Neel Nats" – and drawn by Al Avison and Al Gabriele (#6-10), Mike Sekowsky (#11), and Jack Alderman (#12). "The Imp," a "funny" strip akin in concept to "Jimmy Jupiter," began in #12. It was written by Stan Lee and drawn by Chad Grothkopf.

Timely's thriving quarterly, *The Human Torch Comics*, was joined in March 1941 by the Sub-Mariner's own comic, another quarterly, which became Marvel's seventh title. Just as the Human Torch was backed up by the Sub-Mariner (and the Patriot in #3-4) in his own title, so the Sub-Mariner was backed up by the Angel in *The Sub-Mariner Comics*. Four issues of each title were published during 1941, all spectacles of heroic fantasy. One issue, however, stands out as perhaps the most apocalyptic comic ever produced in the Golden Age, a feast for catastrophe-lovers, the crashing climax to which Timely Comics had been building up over the previous two years. This was *The Human Torch Comics* #5, the gigantic battle between the Human Torch and the Sub-Mariner.

The impetus behind the great battle clearly came from the original battles between the two characters in *Marvel Mystery Comics*, which were excellent sales boosters. Lloyd Jacquet approached Martin Goodman with the idea of doing an enormous book-length slugfest, and Goodman thought it was a splendid idea. He ordered the 60-page story prepared over the weekend. Funnies, Inc. met the challenge with their usual aplomb. Virtually the entire studio turned up at Bill Everett's apartment to plot, script, lay out, pencil, ink, and letter the book. The place was well lubricated with beer, and the operation in shifts around the clock. Plot ideas were written and removed at whim; pages of artwork were drawn and redrawn. Chaos reigned. The final product, in which the entire planet Earth was nearly demolished, remains a monument to the spontaneity and vitality of Golden Age comic books. And on the newsstands, from all reports, it was a complete sellout.

Timely's other publications were not nearly as successful as the ones which featured their Big Three heroes. Readers who expected *Mystic Comics* #6 on the newsstands in January 1941 were disappointed. Billed in house ads as a monthly, *Mystic Comics* suffered a second suspension immediately following #5. Instead, Timely readers found the first revived issue of *Daring Mystery Comics* #7, dated April 1941. It featured a completely new lineup of characters, all of them appearing there for the first time ever. They were the Thunderer, by Carl Burgos and John Compton; the Fin, by Bill Everett; the

Blue Diamond, by Ben Thompson; the Silver Scorpion, Timely's second super-lady, by Harry Sahle (as "Jewell"); Mr. Million, by Raymond A. Burley; Captain Daring, by Joe Simon and Jack Kirby; and the Challenger, by Charles Wojtkowski (as "Nick Karlton"). A two-page text filler titled "The Valley of Time," by Ray Gill, featuring the Challenger, and a two-page gag strip, "Officer O'Krime" (signed by "Al Weine"), filled out the book. The Challenger text filler was to have been continued in the next issue, but *Daring Mystery Comics* like *Mystic Comics*, was suspended a second time after only one issue appeared, and the conclusion to the filler story never saw print.

Daring Mystery Comics #8 finally appeared very late in 1941 and was the last issue of the title. The only changes from its predecessor were the replacement of the Challenger and Mr. Million by Citizen V and "The Li'l Professor and Rudy the Robot." The startling cover was drawn by Simon and Kirby, depicting five of Timely's most obscure short-run heroes charging

out at the reader. Most interesting for inveterate indexers was a table of contents which actually identified the individual artists for each strip: Tom Benson (a pseudonym for Ben Thompson) on Citizen V; Ed Robbins and Irving Werstein on the Thunderer; Harry Sahle again on the Silver Scorpion; Bill Everett again on the Fin; Frank Borth on Captain Daring; Frank Pretsch on "The Li'l Professor and Rudy the Robot"; and Ben Thompson on the Blue Diamond.

It wasn't until the late summer of 1941 that *Mystic Comics* returned in #6, dated October 1941. All the characters in that issue had been introduced previously elsewhere (mainly in *Mystic Comics* #5) except one: the Destroyer. Dressed in a gray costume with red and blue stripes for trim, the Destroyer was the secret identity of Keen Marlow, a reporter on assignment in Nazi Germany who used this means to strike out at the foes of liberty. Two 15-page stories of the Destroyer, including his origin, were told in *Mystic Comics* #6, both written by Stan Lee and drawn by Jack Binder. Considering the late date of his initial appearance, the Destroyer proved remarkably durable. He was featured in some 42 stories altogether in *Mystic Comics* and in seven other titles, the longest-running Golden Age superhero created by Stan Lee.

Tottering on the newsstands as a result of two publication suspensions and an ever-changing cast of characters, *Mystic Comics* did not last very long after #6. Two more issues appeared in 1941, and two more after that in 1942. The Destroyer was the cover feature on all of them, drawn mainly by Al Gabriele. Accompanying the Destroyer inside were the Black Marvel (through #9), the Terror (through #10), the Blazing Skull (through #9), the Challenger (through #10), the Black Widow (in #7 only), the Witness (in #7-9 only), Davey and the Demon (in #7-10), and Gary Gaunt (in #9). Father Time made his final comic book appearance in #10, which also carried the strips "Red Skeleton" and "The World of Wonder."

Timely initiated and sustained three other titles, all quarterlies, during 1941. All of them experienced labor pains at birth. The first was *U.S.A. Comics*, which was billed as coming January 20, but which actually appeared in late April, Marvel's eighth title. Again, an entirely new cast of characters was introduced, only one of which lasted beyond the fourth issue. The Whizzer, whose superspeed was gained from an injection of mongoose blood extract, was a moderately successful Timely character who appeared in 38 stories during the Golden Age. His first story was drawn by Al Avison and Al Gabriele. With #6, well into 1942, *U.S.A. Comics* became simply a vehicle for Captain America, the Destroyer, the Whizzer and various minor military strips, while the first five issues carried a plethora of minor heroes too numerous to mention. The cover of #1 was by Jack Kirby and depicted the Defender; the covers of #2 and #3 showed Captain Terror and were also by Kirby; the cover of #4 had Major Liberty, in his beautiful colonial American outfit, drawn by Syd Shores; and the cover of #5 showed the Victory Boys, a short-run kid gang, drawn by Al Gabriele and George Klein. The first two Rockman stories (he appeared in #1-4) are particularly noteworthy because they were drawn by Basil Wolverton, practically the only time the master satirist ever drew a straight superhero strip.

Timely's ninth title was *All Winners Comics*. Originally billed as *All Aces Comics*, coming in April with all new stories of Captain America, Sub-Mariner, Human Torch and Toro, Angel, Hurricane and the Fiery Mask, the book actually appeared in late May (dated summer 1941) and featured the Human Torch and Toro, the Black Marvel, Captain America, Sub-Mariner, and the Angel. The Black Marvel and the Angel were replaced by the Destroyer and the Whizzer in #2, and this new lineup remained quite stable over the succeeding two years (the Black Avenger, formerly the Thunderer, replaced the Whizzer once, in #6). The Captain America and Bucky stories in #1 and #2 were drawn by Simon and Kirby. *All Winners Comics* showcased quite simply, all the winners of Timely's readership popularity polls. Three issues appeared during 1941.

Young Allies Comics, the first comic ever to feature a "kid gang," also appeared in the summer of 1941, probably in June. Marvel's tenth title, it ran stories of Timely's two famous sidekicks, Bucky and Toro, leading four other feisty boys – Jeff (the smart one), Tubby (the fat one),

Knuckles (the tough one, with the obligatory Brooklyn accent), and Whitewash (the token black one), all Sentinels of Liberty, naturally – on immense, multichapter quests versus the minions of the Axis. The first issue, for example, led the Young Allies around the world in a 570-page battle with the Red Skull. (Its original cover, advertised in several early house ads, was evidently scrapped; presumably the book was delayed as well.) The idea of a kid gang was conceived by Simon and Kirby, but all they contributed to the first issue were Kirby's cover (probably inked by Syd Shores) and some of the splash pages. The guts of the book were mainly by Charles Wojtkowski. Issue 2, probably drawn by Al Gabriele, was the only other issue published during 1941; the story therein continued from "The Case of the Black Talon" in *Captain America Comics* #9.

The last Timely title to be initiated in 1941, their eleventh, featured another kid gang. Lasting just one issue, *Tough Kid Squad Comics* squeaked onto the stands in December 1941, #1 (dated March 1942) with a 45-page epic origin story. There were five of them: Tom and Wally Danger, Butch, Derrick, and Eagle; and they fought the evil Dr. Klutch in their only appearance, drawn also by Charles Wojtkowski. An inventory Flying Flame story and a Human Top story filled out the book.

The years 1939-1941 were the only years during which Timely published exclusively superhero comics. With the advent of 1942, Timely brought out *Comedy Comics* (the first issue carried the number 9 because it continued from where *Daring Mystery Comics* left off), their first venture into a non-superhero comic book. To be sure, the first three issues of *Comedy Comics* carried some superhero stories interspersed among the funny animals and gag strips, but they faded

away completely once Super Rabbit made his debut in #14. Almost simultaneously, Timely started *Joker Comics*, *Krazy Komics*, and *Gay Comics*, which featured the now little known but then fairly popular Tuffy Tomcat, Ziggy Pig, Silly Seal, and a veritable zoo of others. Paul Terry, the famous cartoon animator, licensed Timely to publish *Terry-Toons Comics*, and for many years in the 1940s Gandy Goose, Sourpuss, and Mighty Mouse were in Timely's stable of funny animal characters.

But as far as Timely's heroes were concerned, the years following 1941 were not ones of great creativity or innovation, but ones of consolidation, establishment and, ultimately, decline. The popular heroes, of which there were only a handful, were expanded into a dozen different comics. Those that had failed to attract a following were quickly cancelled. Astonishingly few heroes were introduced in Timely comics after 1941, and those that were introduced lasted only a few issues. When one considers that in the years 1939-1941 no other company had produced so many heroes in so short a time, the about-face at Timely becomes truly remarkable.

I am convinced that this circumstance, the setback of the Golden Age superhero, which was shared by all the comic publishers after 1942 and not just Timely, was not entirely a function of changing public tastes. It was far more the result of dozens of young writers and artists going off to war and leaving the books to other, less capable and more conservative hands. The stories became hidebound and formulistic, and the reading public began to lose interest in them. The panache that brought forth a Captain America and the great Human Torch/Sub-Mariner battles had departed.

Thus, when the artists and writers returned to Timely to pick up their pens once more, a vastly different world confronted them. Comics were smaller. There were pro-fessional standards to be met. The ratio of mundane to superhero books was enormous; the word was jokes, women, and crime. And a New York psychologist named Wertham was raising thick, black clouds on the publishing horizon. Far too worldly wise and war weary, the artists and writers could not fit the superhero into the mold that had been erected in their absence (although they did give it a valiant try at Timely). By 1950, the last of Timely's Golden Age heroes was gone. Not counting one flash in the pan revival in 1953-1955, it would be 11 years before Timely would introduce a new dimension into the concept of superhero comics and raise the consciousness of the reading public to the point where an article like the foregoing could find an audience and a forum. The real Golden Age of the superhero, after all is said and done, is here and now.

Captain America Comics #78, the end of the 3-issue revival in the mid 1950s.

References and acknowledgements:
I am grateful to Jim Vadeboncoeur and Bob Wiener for an enormous number of insights into the publishing history of Timely/Marvel. Jerry Bails' encyclopedic works, *The Who's Who of American Comic Books* and *Collector's Guide: The First Heroic Age*, are utterly indispensable in identifying many of the less well known Golden Age artists. Jim Steranko's *History of Comics* Vol. 1, carries a highly readable account of the history of Timely Comics, although the version given therein of the genesis of the Torch/Sub-Mariner battles in *Marvel Mystery Comics* certainly applies to *The Human Torch Comics* #5 rather than the earlier, far simpler, battles. An extensive interview with Bill Everett has been published in *Alter Ego* #11, and a similar one with Syd Shores appears in *Now and Then Times* #2. As both of these prime movers of Timely have passed away, those documents remain their only extant statements on Timely's origins.

More Than Just Flower Power!

The Overstreet Guide to Collecting Concert Posters explores the connection betwe[en]
music and visual art. It features iconic musicians from several time periods and music[al]
genres. There are profiles on beloved artists with details on how they interpreted th[eir]
music for advertising as well as histories of popular venues and concert promoters.
Collectors and industry pros also share insight on collecting and the market.

Available in finer comic shops, book[?] stores, and from
www.gemstonepub.com

$15

THE OVERSTREET GUIDE TO COLLECTING CONCERT POSTERS

THE ALL-IN-ONE GUIDEBOOK FOR BOTH NEW AND EXPERIENCED COLLECTORS

BY AMANDA SHERIFF

$15.00

Overstreet® is a Registered Trademark of Gemstone Publishing. All art ©2019 their respective copyright holders. All rights reserved.

- Profiles on The Grateful Dead, The Doors, Aretha Franklin, Johnny Cash, Blondie, Prince, Jimi Hendrix, and ot[hers]
- Histories on venues and promotors Bill Graham and Chet Helms and the Family Dog
- Interviews with poster artist Mark Arminski and musician Peter Albin
- Bios on artists like Rick Griffin, Wes Wilson, and Victor Moscoso
- Understanding multiple printings, framing and storing tips, grading guides, and top sales

L.B. Cole: The Man Behind the Mask

(and Captain Aero and Catman and...)

By E.B. Boatner

This article was originally published in The Overstreet Comic Book Price Guide #11 - 1981

L.B. Cole completists have their work cut out for them: since 1936 his prolific brush has produced literally thousands of pieces of art, not only his memorable comic book cover and interior art, but advertising copy, paperbacks, magazine and digest covers, medical and wildlife book illustrations and audio-visual presentations.

Artist, editor, art director, publisher, producer, Cole is a horror artist who has assisted at autopsies; an adventure illustrator who helped teach corporate pilots to fly; a vivid animal portraitist who studied veterinary medicine. He has taught illustration at one of the world's foremost art institutes, won the prestigious Landseer award, and added a special dimension to American comic book art since 1940. Studying his diverse career is like trying to unravel the Wars of the Roses or understanding the myriad printings of *Classics Illustrated*. "It has been," he says, "a fascinating life."

Born in New York on August 28, 1918, Leonard Brandt Cole was the only child of William and Jean Cole, both of whom had artistic leanings. "My mother was a very talented illustrator," he recalls, "who used to work in a style reminiscent of Nell Brinkley. She occasionally published in the old *Journal American*." Cole's father enjoyed architectural design and "could have been a topnotch illustrator, but he was so busy doing real estate that he never did anything with it."

A voracious reader and good student, young Cole was drawn artistically and empathetically towards animals and animal portraiture. In his early teens, while living with his aunt in Lexington, Kentucky, he had the unique opportunity to work at Faraway Farm where the great Man o'War was stabled and was fortunate to use him as a model. "I was enchanted," he says, "and I drew horses almost exclusively for two or three years."

Cole happened also to own one of the original Rin Tin Tin's litter mates – Gin Tin Tin – and through him developed his life's other great interest, veterinary medicine. "Gin became ill, and when I tried to help him, I found out that you need more than good intentions, you have to have training. That's what hooked me on veterinary medicine, wanting to help creatures who need help but can't tell you about it." His parents separated when he was 14 and Cole found that animals represented a kind of extended family. "I guess I found love that was missing from my family in animals – animals are very giving. I would like to have drawn pictures

of my mother and father; instead, I drew pictures of dogs and cats and horses, and I found that I was doing pretty well."

After attending George Washington High School in New York, Cole began to work in commercial art, serving an apprenticeship at Consolidated Lithographing Co. on Grand Street and Morgan Avenue in Brooklyn. His first "published" works were cigar bands for the Consolidated Cigar Company and various liquor labels. "I designed a Three Feathers label for Calvert, Ron Rico Rum labels, and the West Point hairdressing labels. That's the only job I ever had, by the way," says Cole who since that time has always freelanced, owned, or contracted his assignments.

As early as 1939, Cole began working in the comic field, inking Don Winslow for Mac Elkan (*Four Color #2*) and for Ken Batterfield on Doc Strange, penciling and inking on the Flash and Lash Lightning for Lou Ferstadt, and some animation inking for someone he knew only as Chad. It was on that assignment that he met another young artist, Harvey Kurtzman, who later was to work briefly for him at Continental Magazines.

Cole's goings and comings at this time, and through the next decade, are complex, and it is sometimes difficult to pin down exact dates. "It's difficult for me to keep track of, too," Cole concedes. "I lived by myself from the time I was 14, so I was all over the country, did all kinds of things. Suddenly something would come up, and in any six-month period I might have been anywhere in the world."

One night, shortly after his return from one of his peregrinations, Cole and a friend took dates to the old Columbus Circle Skating Rink, now the site of the new Coliseum. Cole was attracted to his friend's date, pretty Ellen Kovack, a figure roller skating teacher. The two hit it off at once and were married in April 1942, starting a productive 38-year partnership as well as marriage. The Coles have one daughter, Jean, and today are the grandparents of Jean's only child, Scott.

Cole did a stint of advertising illustration and although he made by his account, "an awful lot of money," he wanted to go into business for himself. "I looked around for something that wouldn't take a million dollars, and thought again of comics." At 220 W. 42nd Street, Frank Z. Temerson, a former City Attorney of Birmingham, Alabama, was president of Continental Magazines (previously named EtEsGo after his three sisters, Etta, Esther, and Goldie). Cole came to Continental in 1942 as editor and art director and at once began producing the distinctive cover art that has become his trademark. His first work there was *Suspense Comics* #1 in 1943, followed by *Terrific Comics* #1. The company's five major comic titles were *Suspense Comics*, *Captain Aero Comics*, *Contact Comics*, *Catman Comics*, and *Terrific Comics*, although the company produced some 48 titles annually, including one-shots. Kurtzman did two stories for Cole at Continental, then he went his own way and made a huge success.

Aside from being a good editor, an excellent writer, and a top-flight artist, Cole

had the ability to cooperate with others. It was always with a sympathetic attitude that he reviewed the work of new writers and artists. And he will tell you today that such a viewpoint has brought to his magazines many dividends in new talent that otherwise might have been overlooked, or worse, entirely missed.

Coincidence in publishing can be very strange indeed as the following example attests to: Continental Magazines received checking copies from its printer illustrating on the covers of *Captain Aero* and *Contact* bombs being dropped. The cover of *Captain Aero* indicated a flight of P-51 Mustangs dropping a string of bombs on the homeland of Japan. The cover of *Contact* portrayed a flight of B-29s dropping bombs. The coincidence alluded to is that both of these books were received by the publisher on the day the A-Bomb was dropped on Hiroshima, and to the best of Cole's knowledge, no clear depiction of the highly classified B-29 Bomber had ever been depicted pictorially on a comic book cover. (Cole had received declassified pictorial reference through the cooperation of the Army Air Force.)

At Cole's urging, Ellen also worked at Continental lettering artwork. "I asked her to take it up. They were using Leroy lettering at that time and I didn't like it. I wanted some thick-thin variation, I needed some character. So, Ellen took an Ames guide, and within two months, I venture to say, she became one of the top three letterers in the industry. Everybody wanted her to work for them, but she was just too busy."

Between 1945 and 1948 Cole was involved in contract work with a number of publishers, producing complete packaging for books for Orbit Publications, Four Star, Palace Promotions, etc., turning out titles like *Bold, Contact, Dime, Eagle, Gold Badge, Jeep, Law-Crime (Law Against Crime), The Living Bible, Taffy, Toytown*, and many others.

"For example," he explains, "the people at So-and-So Publishing didn't have a staff so they would come to me and say, 'Len, would you produce our books with your people?' I'd say, 'Certainly,' so we would draw up a contract and produce the complete package for them. That's why some of my covers that you see were neither for Star, nor Curtis, nor Classics – they were contracted for Orbit or Sterling or Four Star or one of many others."

"All these people were smart enough not to staff themselves out of business. There was so much downtime that they would have had to pay salaries to people who were sitting around doing nothing, so it was cheaper to pay me to do the package for them." A company might come to Cole with an entire story, character, or just the vague idea for a book. "For instance, *Pilot* – I think that was for Palace Promotions. They said they wanted a book on airplanes, and we came up with a concept in two-page manuscript form. We'd also create characters and assign the artists to do them. If I didn't have enough artists of my own, I'd put an ad in the paper,

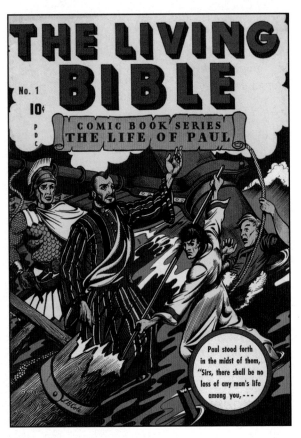

get a hundred replies the next day, and pick those I needed. The one thing I insisted on was that if I did a cover for one of these other companies, I could sign it."

In 1949-1950, Ellen was lettering for Curtis Publishing Company's Premium Group of Comics and was instrumental in Cole freelancing for them. "That's where we found *Blue Bolt*," he says. "From the time I began, I did all the covers and some of the insides of that book. By 1951 Curtis was in the throes of the blanket indictment of the comic book industry going on at that time and was getting rid of the Premium Group of Comics."

"My friend Jerry Kramer, who was a professor of Business Law at New York University and author of one of the country's foremost Tax Guides, was interested in entering the publishing field. Again, coincidence enters the scene. Jerry and I both had heard that Curtis Publishing was offering the Premium

400 titles, including the one-shots. We were running close to 200,000,000 books a year and selling virtually all of them, either in newsstand sales or on the remainder market. We never got any returns." Like the current *MAD* magazine, Star was run with a minimum of in-house staff. "Actually, there were only five people: Jerry and his secretary, myself and my secretary, and George Peltz. George was probably the best comic mind in the business, one of the craziest comic minds you will find anywhere. If I needed a book done, he would sit down and write it, illustrate it, or clean up someone else's stuff." Peltz continued on with Cole to both Gilberton and Dell.

Since Star bought everything else freelance, Cole and Kramer didn't have "the terrible running overhead of immense salaries to worry about every week," and paying in advance or upon delivery enabled them to attract a great deal of talent. Ellen, of course, continued to do lettering and proofreading. Adds Cole, "That's the way we were able to survive in the face of the giants."

The harassment of the comic book industry that caused Curtis to sell continued to plague Cole as well as other publishers, and was reflected in sales and production. "I'd say after the war things got a little hairy. Sales dropped, and money wasn't around so we cut back; a quarter of a million was where our print run balanced out, and of course we cut down on the number of our titles."

Things were "a little hairy" throughout the industry. It was the time of Kefauver Hearings before the Subcommittee to Investigate Juvenile Delinquency and the introduction of the Comics Code Authority in 1954, when comics were blamed for everything from child corruption to the Cold War. Cole denies any intentions to use sexual or suggestive

Group of Comics for sale. We both arrived at the offices of the Premium Group at precisely the same time. 'Len,' Jerry said, 'why should we bid against each other? Let's buy it together.' Curtis sold us the Premium Group, $150,000 worth of art, editorial, plates, and mats for $12,000. So, for six big ones I was in business, and that was the beginning of Star Publications."

Under the Star banner, from 1951 until Kramer's death in 1956, the prolific Cole both edited the line and did cover art for innumerable books – by the end of this period Cole had done some 1,500 comic book covers, not counting his work in non-comic lines. Cole describes Star as a considerably larger publishing venture than Continental.

"We're talking about heavy numbers at Star," he says. "We did a book every calendar day, which over the years encompassed maybe material. "In comics you have to be simplistic. It just didn't occur to us to use that kind of symbolism; we were too busy doing three to five covers a week. When the order comes through to publish one animated book, one romance book, one jungle book, one weird book, one police book a week, you'd go crazy trying to think in those terms. Obviously, you were motivated by something, but most of the time it was 'How will that stack up on the newsstand?' We tried to maintain good taste. I don't think that in any of the books that I did, or that I published, or did covers for, that I can remember anything overtly or covertly sadistic. Of course, if you're going to get in contact with a huge ape, something's gonna give – I don't call that sadism, that's just pure nature. Basically, at Star we were plotting for storyline and not for sensationalism."

"Let me put it this way. Being perfectly practical as a businessman and as a publisher, for me there was no other motive than to create a poster oriented to newsstand sales. The covers were mostly designed as posters, and when I speak of poster effect, I mean that they should be seen. If they're not seen, they're not picked up, and if they're not picked up, obviously they're not bought. I endeavored at all times to make the covers not so much attractive aesthetically, but to be as eye-catching on the stand as possible."

One of the few "theme" covers that Cole recalls was his classic *Suspense* #8, which involved a skull, a spider, and the blue-suited Mr. Nobody, Jack Grogan's character. "It occurred to me that we were so enmeshed in violence that we were almost entrapped by it – it was the first time that the newspapers had really played up the advance of crime in our society – and I illustrated that by using a spider web. So, I had the spider as the menace, Death, which was indicated by the skull, and Mr. Nobody who represented the Public. And there was a girl entrapped in the web – I couldn't just have a spider there, so I had a girl, and they tried to read a sex motif into it. I had no idea that this was a sexually devised or oriented cover; it just lent something that would sell the book."

Cole also points out that his romance and juvenile covers far outnumbered his weird and horror books. Many of these books are also excellent samples of Cole's successful exploitation of what he called the "poster effect." Packed with action and detail, presented in vibrant enameled colors, his work is so meticulously structured that it is never cluttered or confusing. A typical example is

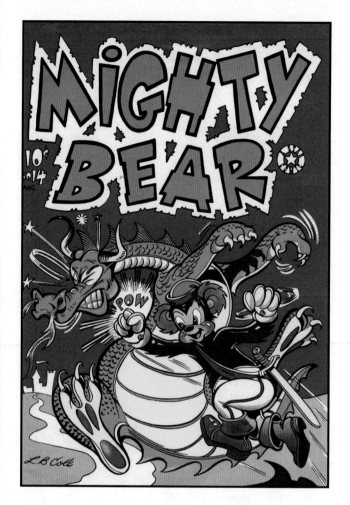

Mighty Bear #14 with its slam-bang action and brilliant primary colors. On this cover, his juxtaposition of the intensely green logo on a broad background of primary red is not only eye-catching, it is near psychedelic. The riot of action on *Frisky Animals* #53, *Fun* #11, and *Mighty Bear* #13 are set against pure white backgrounds which accentuate the carnival atmosphere of the subjects and turn the covers into little circus posters. Each unit of the drawings, down to the last bit of confetti, is planned, an integral part of the design.

"Maybe I'm just an inherent salesman, but I was always oriented toward newsstand sales, and these stylized covers drew readers. There was a riot of color out there on the stands and I figured something had to be done to catch the buyer's eye. Take a look at most of the other books: they're all done in linear technique. They were so stubborn in their design of their covers that all of the superheroes, all of the children's books, were a mass of figures kicking and punching and they all looked the same.

"A rather simple solution occurred to me one day while passing a magazine dealer who carried virtually every one of the hundreds of titles being published at that time. My thought upon viewing this riot of color confronting me was 'What would happen should a blank space seem to appear by virtue of a cover, predominately black, being placed amidst this kaleidoscope of brilliance?' Not having to receive permission from a group of editorial 'experts' I simply went ahead and produced a predominately black cover. The results were astounding…so much so that I repeated the treatment again. And again, the results were staggering. By this time word apparently got around the industry and lo and behold, mostly dark background covers appeared. It was *then* I reverted to brilliantly colored covers. Once again, I stood out on the stands. My decision for designing successful covers evolved into the use of eye-arresting blocks of vibrant, solid colors and/or a unified use of lines, all pointing toward or encompassing a single theme."

Cole's black backgrounds heightened the menace on many of his most memorable weird and horror books, *Mask* #1 and #2, *Blue Bolt Weird* #115, *Startling Terror Tales* #10 and #14, and *Captain Flight* #11. "Again, I go back to the value of black," Cole emphasizes. "What lies beyond? You don't know. The implied threat can be far more devastating than showing a guy's brains being blown out. Anticipation and culmination. The value of black is what the viewer will read into that black space. If it's a horror cover and you have a big black background, just put in some squiggly line and the reader will see it as a fang, or claw, or staring eye, and will read the most horrible aberrations into it."

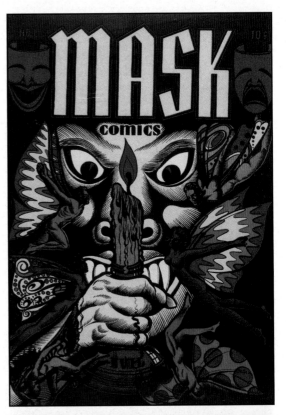

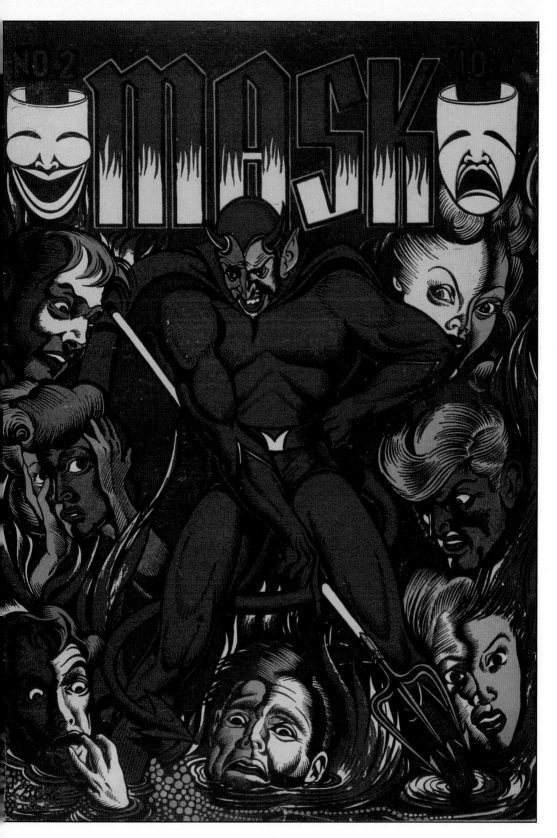

Another recurrent Cole style is seen on *Thrilling Crime Cases* #49, *Weird* #117, *Terrors of the Jungle* #18, *Confessions of Love* #14, *Love Stories (Daring Secrets of Romance)* #8, *All-Famous Police* #11, and *Startling Terror Tales* #5. These covers are the stuff of dreams - suffocating fever dreams which engulf the viewer in a closed nightmare world, leaving him prey to the demon and phantasm inhabitants. Cole contrives that we are trapped within, not viewing from without. One simply *looks* at a fiery scene in other publications, for example, but in Cole's work, the viewer himself is the center of attention, surrounded by fiendish activity one is powerless to halt. There is a restless undercurrent in these covers, many of which use flame for effect, and the swirls and eddies are intensified by the use of similar, rather than contrasting, colors. "That's the whole idea," says Cole. "You can create motion when you're using a similar color. If you have a lot of red, as on the *Love* book, you create a lot of psychedelic lines swirling into a vortex. You don't have to finish every figure; some of them just go off into nothingness."

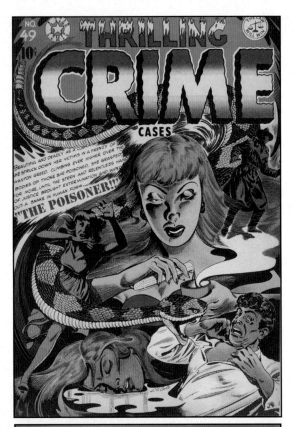

At the opposite end of the spectrum are Cole's static covers - formal, mannered pieces that push the poster concept to the extreme. *Catman* #32, for example, or *Contact* #9, both of which Cole did for Continental. Cole explains that *Contact* was one of several covers derived directly from patches of the various Air Force units, the 8th, 6th, and the Marine Corps. Commenting on the *Catman* cover, a ballet of stylized sharks and shoaling fish, he smiles, "Did you notice? Those fish are designed like a wallpaper pattern."

The fact that many of Cole's styles are readily identifiable is actually misleading. It is important to remember that he did do over 1,500 covers in all; that he covered so many different fields and in such a variety of styles that many of his covers have been overlooked to date. The *Mask* #2 or *Mighty Bear* #14 is just the tip of the Cole iceberg. In the Star line alone, Cole recalls doing covers for at least 40 titles.

Cole was indeed a swift worker, but some of his output can be contributed to the fact that he could usually draw what he pleased for Star or other companies of which he was editor or art director, and did not have to submit sketches or roughs for inspection. On occasion he had to bend to the wishes of other editors or distributors from whom he contracted work. "Charlie Biro, Bob Wood, Lev Gleason, all liked cover dialogue balloons and violent action," he recalls. "I personally didn't think that was necessary. Doesn't that go directly against one picture being worth a thousand words? It's insecurity, playing down to your audience. If you feel you have to explain every damn thing you do, then don't put a picture on the cover. Myself, I wouldn't do it with a 10-foot pen." But when required, he acquiesced. "Well, fine. They were paying the freight then, so I'd do it. And those covers worked, too. I showed everything – the glass breaking, the lamp post being broken up into a thousand pieces – but even then, if you look closely (*All-Famous Police Cases* #6) you'll see that the glass is broken in patterns; it's not just random. When the glass came out of the hole it didn't just go 'blah'

into patches of glass, it went out into a carefully orchestrated pattern."

Despite his joke about the 10-foot pen, Cole used brushes exclusively in his work. "I never used a pen in my life," he vows. "Never. I can draw a line as thin as a spider web or as thick as a pipe with a No. 3 Winsor-Newton brush. I've driven guys crazy giving them what I called 'brush drills.' They'd say, 'How did you do that?' and when I'd say, 'With a Winsor-Newton,' they'd ask, 'What kind of a pen is a Winsor-Newton?' I put my middle finger down on the board and the brush will go no further than that finger, so I can whip around into all kinds of beautiful stuff if the brush is good. In those days a No. 3 brush cost 37¢. Now they're

$9 to $10 each but they're still the same brush. I feel there's nothing a guy can do with a pen that I can't do with a brush." One of the numerous sources of non-comic Cole artwork was the Croyden paperback line also published by Star. Although the books began with copyright dates in 1945, they were not published until 1951 and were backdated to the time that the manuscripts had been acquired. These tomes had titles like *Sinner*, *Cheaters at Love*, and *Reckless Virgin*, and had the covers one might imagine – vintage Cole "good girl" art. "I would take two and put them on the same board and try to work the colors if I could, so I could just paint the backgrounds across. If that didn't work, I just did them. I'd paint them by the dozen and then say, "I'll use this one; it matches.'"

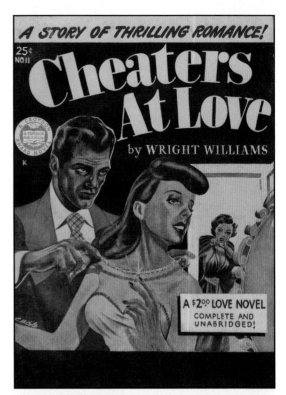

Other Star publications included crossword puzzle books, coloring books, joke books, "how to" books (*Sex, Marriage, and Love Customs Around the World; Love Omens and Charms*, which has a black background reminiscent of Cole's comic work), and the men's magazines *Man's True Action* and *Man's Daring Adventure*. The crossword magazines were highly popular; "We sold literally hundreds of thousands of these," he recalls. "We got such good reports that we took the larger format books and cut them into smaller format so that we got twice as many books and sold twice as many from the same amount of paper." Cole did innumerable covers for these magazines, some in regular full color illustrations, some in straight cartoon style, and some as a blend of the two. "Again, I would do a cover a day, sometimes doubling them up. It was no problem because I didn't have to do rough sketches or show them to anybody; I just did them. Sometimes I did two at a time, sometimes I had a big board and did four of them together,

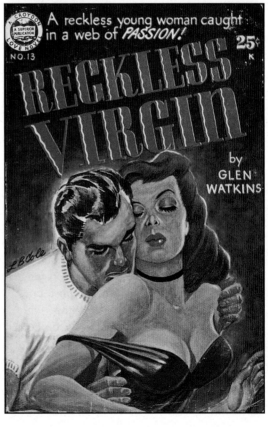

putting a red illustration to a red one – a white illustration to a white one – giving a common color trim area."

"In addition to all these pieces," Cole adds, "I have done literally 600 covers for other people and signed *their* names to them. One of the premier illustrators for the *New Yorker Magazine* had a contract with me but couldn't meet the deadline, so I did the art and copied the style." Picking up one of the Joke books Cole adds, "This is his style. See the signature there?" Cole turns the magazine on its side so that his own signature is seen clearly worked in the design down the spine edge. "I've done innumerable covers like these for other publishers."

After Kramer's death in 1956, Cole joined Dick Decker, Sales Manager at Archer St. John Publishing, to start *Alfred Hitchcock's Mystery Magazine* and *Rod and Gun* magazine, acting as art director for the first and editing and producing artwork for the second. When Decker moved to Florida and changed the format of the *Hitchcock* magazine, Cole became editor at Skye Publications with Arthur Bernhard in early 1958. Several more issues of *Rod and Gun* were published through Skye. Skye also published the adventure magazines *Power*, *Valor*, and *Epic*, men's books similar to the Star publications in which Cole's knowledge of animal anatomy stood him in good stead. The Star books regularly featured rugged men being mauled by polar bears, swamped by whales, stomped by broncos or noshed by gators, all rendered in vivid and realistic tempera. "That crocodile is quite accurate, believe me," assures Cole, pointing to the November 1957 copy of *Man's True Action*. "As a matter of fact, when my daughter Jean was 7 or 8 years old, we went out to the Bronx Zoo to get the scaling on his face accurate."

In early 1959 Cole became Art Director for Gilberton Publishing Co., succeeding Alex Blum in that position, although Cole was the only one of the two to have been listed on the masthead in that capacity. Cole was called in when the Classics Illustrated line was being refurbished. "We had to update them. They seldom did new ones; they went back and updated some of the old issues. They went by past sales records and orders from boards of education, etc. If somebody needed *Green Mansions*, they'd put a new cover on it, and either do a new inside or keep it the way it was if it was in good shape." Cole handled *Classics Illustrated*, *Classics Illustrated Jrs.*, and the new series, *The World Around Us*. When Classics began to update its line covers with four color process paintings, Cole did the cover art as

L.B. Cole's painted cover for
Classics Illustrated Green Mansions

well as the first page for *Horses #3* in *The World Around Us* series.

Cole was heir to a number of EC artists, some of whom had worked for Gilberton before his arrival, notably George Evans, Graham Ingels, Joe Orlando, and Al Williamson, all of whom were particularly visible in *The World Around Us* series. He also attracted *Collier's* illustrators Austin Briggs and John Allen Maxwell, and artists usually associated with Charlton: Sal Trapani, Ted Galindo, Dick Giordano, John Forte, and Vince and Al Fago.

As an insider privy to the company secrets, it would seem that Cole might have penetrated the veil of confusion that clings to the question of Classics Illustrated first editions and reprints. Not so. "There was *no* way of knowing," he confirms.

In 1961 Cole received an offer from Dell and moved on to run Dell Comics as editor and art director when the company was taken over from Western Printing and Litho. Dell opted for the best and had Cole take over the complete comics division. As an aside, he notes that he briefly shared an office at Dell with John Stanley just before Little Lulu's creator left Dell.

While at Dell, Cole says, "I went to more screenings than the movie critics in New York. I went to a screening almost every morning for months - *Car 54 Where Are You?*, *The Detectives*, *Bonanza*, *Beanie and Cecil*, *Barbie and Ken*…And then we had the movies - *Hatari*, every damn movie that came out we went to see…And then radio programs…" Among the plethora of canned movie, radio, and TV titles were several dozen original books, among them such diverse offerings as *Kona*, *Combat*, *Linda Lark*, *Private Nurse*, and *Brain Boy*.

Leaving Dell, Cole plunged into an even more hectic round of publishing and media activity in the graphic arts field. In 1964 he

and Ellen became involved in the audio-visual field, doing work through University Films for McGraw Hill in conjunction with Northwestern University and the University of Iowa. These programs were based on various types of cities: The Commercial City, The Resort City, and The Suburban City.

They did safety films for industry including a program titled *Safety Is No Accident* for the Joint Industry Board of the Electrical Industry in collaboration with then New York Governor, Nelson A. Rockefeller; an award-winning program for the Building Trades Employers Association with the aid of former Secretary of Labor, Peter Brennan, titled *D.O.A. (Dead or Alive)*.

Some of their medical films included a program for General Motors, titled *Alcoholism in Industry* with the cooperation of Dr. Nicholas A. Pace, Medical Director for General Motors in New York; a series of programs devoted to prenatal and postnatal care, namely *Birth Control and You* and *The Newborn Child*; and a film on preventative medicine called *So You Finally Got Your Ulcer*.

Ellen has brought her considerable organizational expertise to their AV projects. "She's a great asset," says Cole. "For example, she did not hesitate to direct a show being filmed on the upper open-construction area of the new Mt. Sinai Hospital wing in weather where the wind chill factor plummeted the temperature to 16 degrees below zero and caused the camera shutters to freeze. The cameras had to be warmed over charcoal heaters in order to function. But she got the show done.

"Another example: I can say I need a method of running a highly complex audio-visual business - that means frame by frame, all the elements in every frame including art, narration, sound effects, music, dubbing, the mixing and the timing - and she'll do it all and give me a rundown. She designed a beautiful rundown sheet that's a model for most of the Filmstrip photo houses in the country today."

In the late '70s, Cole produced AV training films for Flight Safety International (FSI) at the Marine Air Terminal at LaGuardia Airport to teach corporate pilots on flight simulators.

Although involved in AV work, Cole decided to begin republishing *Rod and Gun*, to which he had retained the rights. The name was changed to *World Rod and Gun* to avoid copyright conflicts with a Canadian publication of the same name. He reprinted some of his earlier covers and used them inside the new book as poster-quality wild-life portraits. Cole produced many stunning animal covers and inside illustrations for *World Rod and Gun* magazine. These illustrations are extremely rare and still in great demand today by astute collectors as solid growth investments.

A glance at the masthead shows an "E. Kovack" as Production Manager; throughout their marriage Ellen was proved as energetic, diverse and talented as her husband. Also listed as Art Director in most of the issues is "N. Nodel," Cole's good friend Norman Nodel who had been with him from Star days.

Cole's list of employees and co-workers over the years reads like a who's who of the comic elite, numbering among them Jay Disbrow, Joe Shuster, Don Rico, Bernard Krigstein, Ezra Jackson, Al Hollingsworth, Sam Glanzman, Tony Tallarico, and Jerry McCann.

Before he went on to run DC, the young Carmine Infantino "used to sit at my desk at Continental, watching my toy airplane propellers go around in the fan and asking me how I did this and why I did that. He certainly went on to become one of the big names. Jerry Iger? The Neanderthal Age – I've known Jerry as far back as I can remember. He is considered a building block of the comic industry. Max Elkan was a close personal friend. He was a truly brilliant illustrator who did a lot of work with Reed Crandall."

L.B. Cole's centerfold illustration for *World Rod and Gun* #1 magazine.

"Norman Nodel was another extremely talented and much under publicized illustrator who started with me at Star in 1951. He also illustrated for me at Classics and Dell and on *World Rod and Gun*. He had an opera quality voice and the God-given hands for illustrating – one of the nicest people you'll ever meet."

"There's one fellow," Cole continues, "who I think was a top illustrator in the comics and whose name is never mentioned – Bruno Premiani. He did *The Conquest of Mexico* for me at Classics Illustrated (#156), the cover and interior, and I think that would hold up for a Caldecott Award today. He was an Italian who came from Argentina. His vision was about nil without glasses, but he was a genius – I mean draftsman and an illustrator and a sensitive portrayer. He'd take a script and make a motion picture out of it. I gasped when I got back his cover original; for me it was one of the first four color illustrations that truly portrayed the essence of the interior script. Take a look at the way he delineated the story. It's very much like George Evans, who I also think is one of the top illustrators."

During his career, Cole had occasion to use works by now-famous writers such as Evan Hunter, Mickey Spillane, and Burt Hirschfeld, although they sometimes did not write under their own names.

Cole thrives on activity and diversity, energetically tackling any new project, from the 1981 *Overstreet Comic Book Price Guide* cover to graphic medical illustrations for the Queensborough Community College's *Laboratory Textbook in Anatomy and Physiology* by Professor Philip J. Costa.

Recently Cole illustrated *Practicing Vocabulary in Context* and *Practicing Reading* for Random House's reading program. He has illustrated juvenile textbooks for Simon and Schuster; and Holt, Reinhart, and Winston's Series Six on optics. His interest in wildlife has never flagged. He did the cover illustration for an Audubon Society book on robins for the Drumlin Wildlife Institute of Massachusetts; graceful watercolors of fish for Grolier's *Encyclopedia International*, and color plates for articles on "Sharks, Skates and Rays" and "Commercial Fishes of the World" for the *New Book of Knowledge*.

Then why, after nearly 25 years of non-comic art output, has Cole suddenly resurfaced in the field?

A great resurgence of interest in his work has been manifested by collectors and fans all over the country and abroad. This interest was brought to Cole's attention by Bob Overstreet who sought him out to paint the cover for this *Guide*. This began Cole's current enterprise, and fan interest in his early work has been strong enough to generate a tremendous demand for his current customized pieces, still strikingly rendered in brilliant Dr. Martin colors. The habits of work and creativity are so ingrained that Leonard Brandt Cole will always be wielding a brush or looking for new media to conquer. Looking back over the career of the polymathic Mr. Cole, his own estimate of his life – fascinating – seems grossly understated.

− AFTER THE ARTICLE −

L.B. Cole created the cover for *The Overstreet Comic Book Price Guide* #11 (1981), in which this article originally appeared, featuring pre-Code style art of a bound woman being menaced by a demonic figure. Heritage Auctions offered the original art in November 2007, and it sold for an impressive $17,925.

Cole returned to Overstreet cover duty for the 18th edition, this time featuring Superman's 50th anniversary in 1988. Two versions were created, with a white background for the hardcovers and a black background for the softcovers. Shown are the two hand colored photocopies of the black and white line art. These were photographed for the final cover art.

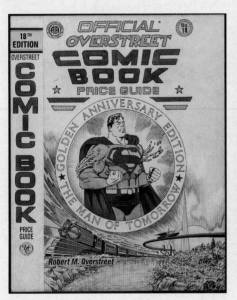 

His artwork was featured in Ernst Gerber's *Photo Journal Guide to Comic Books* in the early '90s and he contributed illustrations to the fanzine *3-D Exotic Beauties*, which ignited fresh interest in his work. Cole died on December 5, 1995. He had been honored with an Inkpot Award in 1981 and was posthumously inducted into the Will Eisner Award Hall of Fame in 1999.

COMIC AND ANIMATION ART COLLECTING REVEALED!

"Fantastic for a novice comic art or animation collector, but even better, even the most seasoned hobbyist will find some new information in many of the incredible articles. Overstreet has done it again! Another great book for our wonderful hobby!"

-- Steve Borock
President and Primary Grader
Comic Book Certification Service (CBCS)

"The perfect handbook to help understand the original comic book art market."

-- Dan Gallo
Comic Art Con

"There's no better one-volume introduction to collecting comics and animation art!"

-- Dean Mullaney
The Library of American Comics

"*The Overstreet Guide to Collecting Comic & Animation Art* is informative and incredibly exciting to read. It's full of pictures of incredible comic art, and a must-read for any comic art collector. The price is more than reasonable and the stories and art have a broad range of topics."

-- Nick Katradis
Collector

"Original narrative art is appreciated around the world. The basis of a cultural phenomenon, institutions routinely seek out and exhibit collections. It is amazing that a comprehensive guide that describes the factors and attributes that garner such attention has never been published until now."

-- Joe Mannarino
All Star Auctions

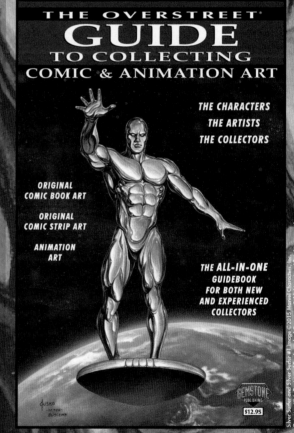

THE OVERSTREET
GUIDE
TO COLLECTING
COMIC & ANIMATION ART

THE CHARACTERS
THE ARTISTS
THE COLLECTORS

ORIGINAL
COMIC BOOK ART

ORIGINAL
COMIC STRIP ART

ANIMATION
ART

THE ALL-IN-ONE
GUIDEBOOK
FOR BOTH NEW
AND EXPERIENCED
COLLECTORS

GEMSTONE
PUBLISHING

$12.95

Insights for Beginners and Experienced Collectors Alike!
160 PAGES • FULL COLOR • SOFT COVER • $12.95
AT BETTER
COMIC SHOPS NOW!

GEMSTONE
PUBLISHING

WWW.GEMSTONEPUB.COM

COMIC SHOP LOCATOR SERVICE
comicshoplocator.com
888-COMIC-BOOK

ORIGINS OF THE DARK KNIGHT:
A CONVERSATION WITH BATMAN ARTISTS
BOB KANE AND JERRY ROBINSON

BY THOMAS ANDRAE

This article was originally published in The Overstreet Comic Book Price Guide #19 - 1989

From his first appearance in June 1938, Superman captured the hearts and minds of America's youth. His success quickly established the superhero as the reigning monarch of comic books and catapulted the medium into a multimillion dollar business – or so most histories would tell us. But the truth is more complex. While Superman was certainly the catalyst for the rapid growth of the comics industry, there was, in actuality, no immediate boom in superheroes following his debut. As Ron Goulart observes, only one costumed hero appeared in the first four months following Superman's birth – The Crimson Avenger – and he was not a superhero. He wore civilian clothes except for a cloak and mask. Appearing in May 1939, Will Eisner's Wonderman was the first to imitate Superman's costume and superpowers, but he was a pale copy and folded after one appearance and a lawsuit from Superman's publisher.

It was only after the arrival of another masked avenger that the deluge in superheroes began. Appearing in *Detective Comics* #27 (in the same month as Wonderman) "The Bat-Man," as he was called then, was unlike anything seen before in comics. With long, prominent ears that looked disturbingly like Satanic horns, and enormous batwings for a cape, he was as menacing as any of the villains he faced. More significantly, he was the first comic book superhero without superpowers. His precedent proved that superheroes need not be pallid imitations of Superman, nor even possess super-strength. Before the year was out, the Sandman, the Flame, Blue Beetle, Amazing Man, the Human Torch, and Sub-Mariner had hit the newsstands. By 1940, the Flash, Green Lantern, and Captain Marvel were added to the rolls, and scores would follow.

Batman was the creation of Bob Kane, a young cartoonist barely in his 20s. Kane began his career in 1936, drawing humorous strips like *Peter Pupp* and *Jest Laffs* for the Eisner/Iger Studio and later *Van Bragger* and *Side Streets of New York* for Circus Comics. He continued drawing humorous fillers for DC, as well as two features, *Rusty and His Pals*, inspired by

Milt Caniff's *Terry and the Pirates*, and *Clip Carson*, about a globetrotting soldier of fortune. Kane was still a novice at drawing adventure strips when he created Batman. Consequently, his art retained much of the cartoony quality of his humor strips, a style perfect for creating a surreal atmosphere of bizarre menace. "Batman's world took control of the reader," Jules Feiffer wrote. "Kane's was an authentic fantasy, a genuine vision, so that however one might nitpick the components, the end product remained an imaginative whole." Using weird angle shots, Caligari-*esque* landscapes, large moons in vacant nighttime skies, and brooding dark shadows, Kane expressively conveyed a mood of malice and derangement prefiguring the cinematic techniques of film noir detective films of the '40s and '50s.

Kane was aided by a Bronx crony, a former shoe salesman turned writer named Bill Finger. Finger had worked on *Rusty and His Pals* and *Clip Carson* and became chief scripter on the Golden Age Batman stories. Although he never received a byline while he was alive, his influence on the Batman mystique was so great that he must be considered a co-creator of the strip. Finger worked on Batman from the beginning, helping Kane to refine his first sketches of the Caped Crusader's costume and wrote the first story, "The Case of the Chemical Syndicate." Finger also named Bruce Wayne and Dick Grayson and Batman's home port of Gotham City, and created the Batcave from a photograph he had seen in *Popular Science*, as well as many of the strip's cast of bizarre villains. It was Finger who made Batman a great detective, writing what are perhaps the most finely plotted stories in the superhero genre.

A young Bob Kane at work in the 1940s.

In September 1939, Kane hired 17-year-old artist Jerry Robinson as his assistant. Robinson soon took over inking Kane's pencils, and later drew and inked his own stories as well as many of the classic Batman covers of the 1941-1946 period. Tempering Kane's style with a more illustrative look, Robinson refined the cartoony elements in the strip. Robinson is also famous for creating what is unquestionably comic book's greatest villain – the Joker. The Crown Prince of Crime was the first in a series of nemeses which would become a permanent repertory of bizarre villains comparable only to those in Chester Gould's *Dick Tracy*.

In April 1940, Kane created Robin, the Boy Wonder, adding him to the strip in order, in Robinson's words, "to humanize Batman." This dramatically altered the tone of the stories, transforming Batman from a grim, menacing loner to a paternal big brother to Robin, who had become his ward. The addition of Robin significantly lightened up the strip, the Boy Wonder's red and green costume offering a colorful counterpoint to Batman's somber blue and gray uniform. The dialogue also became cheerier, filled with the puns and badinage between Batman and Robin and the criminals that became a trademark. The first Boy Wonder in comics, Robin was such a hit that it became *de rigueur* for every new superhero to have a young sidekick.

The addition of Robin and exotic villains like the Joker made Batman so popular that he began to rival Superman's success. For years the two would vie for the title of DC's most popular superhero, with Superman usually edging out his competitor. However, recent years have seen a reversal of this trend. With the appearance of a series of soft-covered, adult-oriented graphic novels, beginning with Frank Miller's Dark Knight books, Batman has become the most popular superhero in comics. The new live-action movie, with Michael Keaton as Batman and Jack Nicholson as the Joker, could well tip the scales, giving the Caped Crusader a prominence he has not enjoyed since the Batmania of the mid-'60s. Read now the story of Batman's origins from two members of the creative team that helped make him a superstar for 50 years – Bob Kane and Jerry Robinson.

BOB KANE INTERVIEW

Overstreet: When did you become interested in cartooning?

Bob Kane (BK): I was a confirmed doodler. When I was 13, I was doodling in all my school notebooks and all over the walls and sidewalks of New York, in the Bronx. I used to copy all the comics – my dad worked for *The Daily News* in the printing department, so he brought home the Sunday papers. And I found that I could copy the comics and make them look as good as the original. My dad used to know these famous cartoonists – the creators of Moon Mullins, Popeye, and Dick Tracy – and he'd ask them how much a week they made. And they said that if you're highly successful, you could make thousands a week. Well, that really appealed to a poor kid from the Bronx. So, I set my sights on becoming a famous cartoonist.

Overstreet: How did you get involved in drawing comic books?

BK: Being at the right place at the right time is extremely propitious in life, and I was fortunate to be in on the pioneering days of the comic book industry. In 1934, the first issue of *Famous Funnies* was published – it consisted entirely of reprints of newspaper comic strips. When some of the publishers got wind that it was selling well, they decided to publish original comic art instead of reprints. One of the early comic books was called *Wow Comics*, which started in 1936. It was produced by Jerry Iger and Will Eisner. Of course, Will Eisner later became famous for creating *The Spirit* comic book. He and I went to DeWitt Clinton High School together. We were always vying to see who would be top cartoonist on our high school paper, *The Clinton News*.

After high school, I worked for Iger and Eisner doing a feature called *Peter Pupp* – it was my first good comic feature. *Peter Pupp* was drawn in a kind of Disney style. He was a puppy who had a little sidekick named Tagalong who was younger and shorter. They were kind of the basis of Batman and Robin who came along a few years later. In one story, they went to the moon in a little rocket ship, and the moon turned out to be made of green cheese. Then they stopped off at Saturn. It may be the first comic book story in which someone goes to the moon.

Overstreet: The style of Peter Pupp looks similar to that of Floyd Gottfredson's Mickey Mouse comic strip. Did it influence you?

BK: Yes. I used to copy Mickey Mouse all the time. It was one of my favorites as a kid. My dream at that time was to go to Hollywood and meet Walt Disney. But when I was 17, I got a job working for the Fleischer Studios in New York. I did fill-ins, inking, and opaque painting on Betty Boop for seven to eight months. I made $25 a week, which wasn't bad and a lot better than the $5 a week I was making with Iger and Eisner. When the studio moved to Florida, I didn't want to make the movie – I liked New York.

I started in the comic book industry again after that. I got a job at DC doing fill-in cartoons and some features like *Rusty and His Pals*, which I did in a Caniff style, and *Clip Carson*, who was a soldier of fortune and looked like me – tall, dark, and lean. I also did some strips for *Circus Comics* – one was called "Van Bragger" and was a rich man's version of the Katzenjammer Kids. He had a sister with dimples who looked like Shirley Temple. I also drew "The Sidestreets of New York," which was a take-off on the Dead End Kids. I used the name Robert Kaye on that because the editor didn't want the same name on two features in one book.

Overstreet: How did you come to create Batman?

BK: That was late in 1938 or early in January 1939. We had an enterprising editor at DC called Vincent Sullivan. One day we had a drink and I showed him some Flash Gordon drawings I had done. I was a great copyist and he said, "You know, Bob, your stuff looks just like Alex Raymond's. You could switch to the superhero stuff." I had been doing slapstick comics and fill-ins for DC. Sullivan said, "There's a character called Superman by Siegel and Shuster, and they are making $800 a week a piece." I was only making $35-50 a week at the time. I said, "My god, if I could make that kind of money!" Sullivan said, "We're looking for another superhero. Do you think you could come up with one?" This was Friday. I said, "I'll have one for you Monday."

So, over the weekend I laid out a kind of naked superhero on the page, with a muscular figure that looked like Superman or Flash Gordon. He didn't have any costume. So, I started to make sketches of a bird-man with bird wings. He looked like Hawkman with wings that were rounded out like a hawk's. Then I remembered Leonardo De Vinci's flying machine. I had made sketches of it when I was 13 and stored them in an old trunk. So, I dug them up.

I was always interested in the origins of things – how did it all begin? When I was 13, I saw this book of Da Vinci's inventions of 500 years ago – the flying machine, the parachute, the steam engine. What stuck in my mind was the flying machine. It was called an "orni" something, but it was the first airplane. It was actually a glider – a sled with bat wings attached to it with a man in the middle. He was supposed to fly by jumping off a mountain, and Leonardo actually sent men off mountains in the contraption. But in the beginning, even he made a mistake – he made wings that flapped so that, like an animated cartoon, a man would be suspended in midair, then sail down to the ground and crash. Then he noticed that seagulls would glide because their wings were stabilized. So, by stabilizing the wings of his glider, men were actually able to fly off the side of the mountain and glide to the bottom. Leonardo's sled looked like a bat-man to me. In fact, he even had a quote on the sketch – "And your bird shall have no other wings but that of a bat." So, I changed the bird-man to a "Bat-Man," with a hyphen between the Bat and Man.

My second influence was from the movie *The Mark of Zorro* with Douglas Fairbanks Sr. It gave me the idea of the dual identity. By day he was this bored Spanish count, a foppish character called Don Diego, and at night he would come out as Zorro. He rode a black horse called Tornado and would enter the cave and exit from a grandfather clock in the living room. The Batcave may have been inspired by this cave in *Zorro*. He wore this kind of handkerchief mask with slits for eyes and would carve a "Z" on the foreheads of desperadoes when he dueled with them. So, this was all engraved in my mind when I was creating Batman. In fact, at 13 I was imitating Fairbanks around my block. We had a clubhouse and called the club the Zorros; we wore black masks like Zorro.

The concept of Batman had to be different. I didn't want him to be a superhero with superpowers. I wanted a superhero, but not to imitate Superman. I needed to be original – the company wouldn't take it if it was too close to Superman. And all my influences led me to create a "Bat-Man." Batman doesn't have any superpowers. He's just an athlete. He has the athletic prowess of Douglas Fairbanks, who was my all-time favorite superhero in the movies. In films like *The Black Pirate*, in which he swung from one mast to another on his pirate ship, his daredevil acrobatics made him an "acro-Batman." I imitated all the acrobatics of Fairbanks in the early Batman books. He would do somersaults and bowl down 10 guys in a row and swing on a rope like Fairbanks.

I also saw a movie when I was a kid called *The Bat Whispers*. It was written by the mystery writer Mary Roberts Rinehart. Chester Morris, who also played Boston Blackie, was in the dual role of "The Bat" and the detective. The story was about a lot of murders in an old mansion. I remember shadowy-like figures on the wall when he was about to kill somebody. They caught up with him in the attic – he wore a costume that looked a little like my early Batman's, with gloves, a mask, and scalloped wings. He looked like a bat – very ominous. [*Note*: A prototype of the Batsignal also appears in this film.]

I was a real movie buff as a kid. Jules Feiffer says, "Bob Kane gets that fog-laden Warner Brothers look" more than any other DC artist. Movies like Bela Lugosi in the first *Dracula* film – the fog swirling up around the moors, the evil old castle – left a real indelible impression upon me. In the first year of Batman, he was a vigilante and we were more influenced by horror films and emulated a Dracula look. I loved mystery movies and serials; the Shadow on radio was also a big influence.

However, the plot thickens. I had a crony I went to DeWitt Clinton with named Bill Finger. I didn't know him in high school – he was a couple years older than I was. I met him at a party. He was a shoe salesman then and deeply into pulps like *Doc Savage* and *The Shadow*. But he had aspirations of becoming a writer. I called Bill and said, "I have a new character called the Bat-Man and I've made some crude, elementary sketches I'd like you to look at." So, he came over and I showed him the drawings. At that time, I only had a small Halloween mask, like Robin's, on Batman's face. So, he said, "Why not make him look more like a bat and put a hood on him, and take the eyeballs out and just put slits for eyes to make him look more mysterious." He wore a red union suit; the wings were black, the mask was black. I thought red and black would be a good combination. Bill said it was too bright – color it dark gray to make it look more ominous. So, I followed his suggestions. The cape looked like two stiff bat wings attached to his arms. But this was cumbersome and would get in the way of his derring-do when he was fighting or swinging on a rope. So, Bill suggested making it a cape that scalloped out like bat wings when Batman jumped through the air or swung down with a rope.

So, Bill was a contributing force right from the beginning and wrote the first story, "The Case of the Chemical Syndicate." Bill wrote most of the great stories and was influential in setting the pace of the early stories and the genre the other writers emulated. He was like "the Cecil B. DeMille of the comic strips." He would write a script by getting a photograph of a giant prop – the Statue of Liberty, a giant typewriter or sewing machine – and that would generate the idea for a story, and he would build the story around the giant prop. He was also a very good mystery writer, because of his interest in the pulps.

Bill was an unsung hero. He never realized his full potential, ever. He wrote a lot of comics for DC, created a lot of characters. But he never made much money and died broke. I never thought of giving him a byline and he never asked for one. I often tell my wife if I could go back 13 or 14 years before he died, I would like to say, "I'll put your name on it now. You deserve it." I feel a slight sense of guilt that I didn't do it. I really loved the guy. Without Bill, Batman wouldn't be as great as he is today. Now they put everybody's name on a strip – the artist, writer, inker, letterer, colorist. My editor felt that only the creator's name should be on it. I think they were afraid writers would demand more of a piece of the action, so they tried to keep them down.

Overstreet: What was DC's reaction to Batman when you first showed it to them?
BK: Vince Sullivan thought it was great; my boss, Jack Liebowitz, didn't understand it. But he thought Superman was doing well, so he said, "Let's try it." He asked me, "What is a Bat-Man?" I replied, "It's a man who wears a bat costume." He said, "It looks kind of mysterious and creepy. Do you think the public will like it?" I said, "Well, let's try it."

So, they bought the first story. It was six pages long and I got $10 per page, or $60. They gave me a five-year contract. I continued drawing *Clip Carson* and *Rusty and His Pals* for about a year. Then, when they expanded Batman, I stopped doing other comic features. Later, in 1940, my style really developed. I honed my drawing into a more professional illustrative style. Of course, what made Batman were the bizarre villains which were influenced by Dick Tracy's villains. He had marvelous villains – Prune Face, No Face, etc.

Overstreet: Tracy also had a square jaw like Batman's. Did this influence you?

BK: Yes, Dick Tracy had an influence and I always thought the square jaw connoted strength. Movie heroes like Tom Mix always had virile, square jaws.

Overstreet: Batman's jaw was almost abstract in shape, giving him an archetypal, mythical quality.
BK: Like it was carved out of stone. I also wanted my style a little cartoony – a cross between Dick Tracy and illustration. That's why the Penguin and the Joker are still kind of cartoony. I never wanted to get into full illustration – I wanted to retain the cartoon-comic quality that I admired early in my career.

Overstreet: How would you and Finger work?
BK: A lot of stories I wrote with Bill or would give him an idea and he would go home and write it. He would come over to the house and we'd kick ideas around. We would kind of co-create an idea and then he would go and write it. Bill had one problem – he was a little tardy in getting things in on deadline. He wasn't a natural writer – he had to sweat over his stuff – it didn't flow. But it came out good in the end. He was one hell of a writer.

Overstreet: Who came up with the idea of making Batman a master detective?
BK: We both came up with the fact that he would be a crimefighter. I made him a superhero vigilante when I first created him. Bill made him into a scientific detective.

Overstreet: How did you come up with the idea of making Batman a vigilante?
BK: I thought it was more exciting for him to work outside the law rather than inside it. I guess growing up as a rough kid in the Bronx, we used to be vigilantes to survive. Not that we'd steal anything, but we'd be tough. We were outsiders – outside the law. We'd break a few windows

and a cop would chase us. We'd meet at our clubhouse and cook Mickeys from potatoes our mothers would throw out the window and charbroil them over the fire.

Overstreet: How did you create Bruce Wayne?

BK: Bruce Wayne was a collaboration with Bill Finger. I suggested the dual identity from *Zorro*, and he saw *Zorro* also, so that influenced him, too. We draw ourselves or people we know into our strips. Bruce Wayne looked like me when I was young and handsome with aquiline features. Bruce Wayne was my image, Pat Ryan was Milt Caniff's when he was thinner, and Li'l Abner Al Capp's when he was younger. We emulate ourselves to a degree; the creation doesn't fall far from the creator's pen. The alliteration of the names – Bruce Wayne-Bob Kane – was probably one reason Bill came up with the name.

Overstreet: Did you encounter much censorship?

BK: In the first Batman book, he originally had a gun. He had a machine gun on his plane and used it fighting monsters.

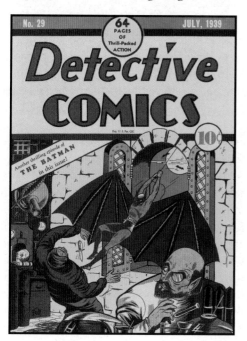

The editorial policy was to bring him over to the side of the law and get away from the vigilante he originally was and not to carry a gun. They thought this was more in keeping with the social mores of the times, and making him a murderer would taint his character. The policy was to make him an honorary member of the police force who was outside the law but still working within it. The whole moral climate changed after 1940-1941 – you couldn't kill or shoot villains. Bill Finger wrote one story in which Batman had a gun. It was his idea, not mine. It was inspired by the Shadow. We didn't think anything was wrong with it, because the Shadow used a gun. But I can't remember Batman ever killing anyone with a gun except the monsters in *Batman* #1.

Overstreet: When did you begin to use assistant artists?

BK: In 1939, the first year, I penciled, inked, and lettered the strip. In 1940, I had George Roussos come in. He did great backgrounds – I remember one of a train – he drew all the bolts in it. Then Jerry Robinson came along and did backgrounds and lettering. I always used to draw the main villains and Batman and Robin. It began to get away from me about the second year – I had Jerry Robinson do some of the secondary gangsters. I'd say the definitive Bob Kane art, art that's mostly by me, was in the first and part of the second year. I did 90% of the art in the first Batman book, Jerry did the lettering, and Roussos the backgrounds.

I feel that the ghost artist's job is to emulate the cartoonist he is imitating instead of changing the strip into his own style. That's always been a bone of contention with me. If I were to copy Dick Tracy, and in those days I did, it would look just like Dick Tracy; I wouldn't put Bob Kane into it. Dick Sprang came along and he was close to my style – very cartoony. I suppose you can't fault the ghost artists because your own style has to creep into the art no matter how closely you try to copy someone. Although when Chic Young died, his son took over *Blondie* and the style was exactly the same and did not change. After the first years, the style of Batman became more grotesque, more bizarre, and over-illustrated so that he looked like a Sloan's Liniment ad. They lost the simple, clean lines I had by throwing in another 15 or 20 lines – too many muscles, too much hay. The artists on Batman today are very fine artists, very illustrative, but any resemblance between what I drew, and their drawings is strictly coincidental. I guess they call it progress.

Overstreet: How did Robin originate?

BK: I created Robin totally by myself; neither Bill Finger nor Jerry Robinson created him. The only boy wonder prior to Robin was Junior in Dick Tracy. I was the first to create a boy wonder in a costume. The idea evolved from my wish fulfillment fantasy of visualizing myself as a 12 or 13-year-old fighting alongside some superhero like Doc Savage or the Shadow. I visualized that every kid would like to be a Robin. In their wish fulfillment dream world, they wanted to fight alongside a superhero. Instead of waiting to grow up to become a superhero, they wanted to do it now. A laughing daredevil, free – no school, no homework, living in a mansion above the Batcave, riding in the Batmobile – appealed to the imagination of every kid in the world. I got the name and costume from Robin Hood. Robin wears a tunic and shoes like Robin Hood. Batman and Robin didn't rob the rich to give to the poor, but, like Robin Hood, they had empathy for the poor and the underdog.

Oddly enough, when I brought the idea to my publisher, Jack Liebowitz, he didn't want Robin in the book. He said Batman was doing well by himself. He thought mothers would object to a kid fighting gangsters. He had a point. I said, "Why don't we try it for one issue. If you don't like it, we can take it out." But when the story appeared, it really hit. The comic book which introduced Robin [*Detective Comics* #38 (April 1940)] sold double what Batman sold as a single feature. I went to the office Monday and said, "Well, I guess we ought to take Robin out – right, Jack? You don't want a kid fighting with gangsters." "Well," he said sheepishly, "leave it in. It's okay – we'll let him go." (laughs) It was so successful that every new superhero had to have a boy wonder and a whole slew of them was created.

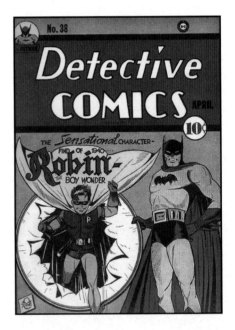

Overstreet: Which did you like best – Batman when he appeared solo or the Batman who teamed up with Robin?

BK: I preferred the first year of Batman – the more somber, mysterious character. They returned to this image about 10 years ago. Now they draw Batman without Robin. They have returned to the mysterioso roots I originally created for the character. Robin lightened up the strip by being a laughing young daredevil, and the lightness in the color of his costume was a counterpoint to Batman's somber mood and costume. Children wanted a lighter hero and a lighter mood. So, we appealed to two factions – the adults and older teenagers, and the younger children. So, there was a nice balance there. I think they are a great team. If Robin was in the strip today, if I were drawing it, I would have them pun somewhat and be light-hearted, but I would make Robin more serious. The punning got out of hand. In the early years, Robin was not the punster he later became – they made him into a buffoon.

Overstreet: How was the Joker created?
BK: Jerry Robinson will insist to his dying day that he created the Joker. But it was actually Bill Finger. The only reason I make an issue out of it is that the Joker is the best villain ever created, outside of Moriarty in *Sherlock Holmes*. Some people even like him better than Batman.

We were looking for supervillains in the first year of Batman. Bill and I were kicking around ideas about a maniacal killer who would play perennial life and death jokes on Batman that would test his mettle and ingenuity to outwit him. Then, about a week later, Bill came in with a photograph of Conrad Veidt, a fine German actor, who

had played in a movie I saw as a kid called *The Man Who Laughs*. It was based on a famous novel by Victor Hugo, about a young gypsy boy named Gwynplaine who had his mouth cut into a ghastly grin by a rival gypsy gang out for revenge. And he grew up with a ghastly smile and funereal eyes. Bill showed me the photo and said, "Why don't we create a killer with the face of a ghastly white clown?" So, I literally drew the photograph of Conrad Veidt into the Joker's face in the first Batman comic book.

Jerry Robinson was my assistant then, just an 18-year-old kid out of college. He came in with a drawing of a joker playing card, with a Joker that looked like a court jester. We used the card in a few stories as the Joker's playing card – he would drop it after he killed someone. So, somehow Jerry got in there with the card. But this was after the fact; he did not create the original concept of the Joker. Now, I don't say that Jerry is doing this intentionally, but time has eroded his memory.

I drew the Joker straighter and more illustratively than my ghost artists. They made him grotesquely clown-like, longer and thinner, and so exaggerated he looked like a buffoon. I drew him ghastly and realistically from the photo of Conrad Veidt.

Overstreet: The Catwoman was another great foe of Batman's. How did she originate?
BK: I think I came up with the Catwoman. My first girlfriend Gloria looked very feline. I always liked that type. But she was a redhead and looked like Vicki Vale and was more an inspiration for her. I had another girlfriend named Ann who had black hair and green cat eyes and was very sensual-looking. She was the inspiration for Catwoman. I made sketches of her prior to the creation of Catwoman. Then I asked her to pose as that character. In fact,

she wore a costume of the Catwoman she had made. I usually didn't use live models – I drew mainly from my imagination.

Overstreet: Were there any other sources which inspired your creation of the Catwoman?

BK: Yes, Jean Harlow had a great influence on me as a kid. I saw her in one of her first appearances in *Hell's Angels* with Ben Lyon and James Hall. At an impressionable young age, she seemed to personify feminine pulchritude at its most sensuous. Later on, when I drew the Catwoman, I kind of had her in mind, although she was blonde and Catwoman was a brunette. She was the first influence on the Catwoman; I wanted to draw somebody in her image.

We knew we needed a female nemesis to give the strip sex appeal. So, we came up with a kind of female Batman, except that she was a villainess and Batman was a hero. We figured there would be this cat and mouse, cat and bat, byplay between them – he would try to reform her, and she was working outside the law. But she was never a murderer and not all evil like the Joker. We felt she would appeal to the female readers – I figured they would relate to her as much as to Batman, or,

more likely, she would appeal to the male readers. So, she was put in the strip for the boys and girls, as a female counterpoint to Batman.

Overstreet: How did you come up with the idea of associating her with cats?

BK: It's kind of the antithesis of a bat – sort of a female version of Batman, only I made her a villain. I always felt women were feline. Men were like dogs – not that they looked like dogs, but had the personalities of dogs, faithful and friendly. Cats are cool and detached, unreliable. I feel much warmer with dogs around me – cats are hard to understand, they are erratic as women are. You feel more sure of yourself with a male friend than a woman. You always need to keep women at arm's length. We don't want anyone to take over our souls, and women generally have a habit of doing that. So, there is a love-resentment thing with women. I guess women will feel I'm being chauvinistic for speaking this way, but I do feel that I've had better relationships with male friends than women. With women, when the romance is over, somehow they're never my friend after that.

Overstreet: Who created Vicki Vale, the photographer who was romantically involved with Bruce Wayne and Batman?

BK: I created Vicki Vale. In 1948, I came to Hollywood when they were doing the second Batman serial. I went to a party after the serial was shot and met a beautiful blonde actress named Norma Jean. I talked with her and asked her to dance. "But the music isn't playing," she said. "That's okay," I replied, "That way I get a chance to hold you." We were just kidding around. She had this wispy voice. We danced together when the music played and I asked her for a date, but she said that she was married. She was only 17 or 18 years old. She had this little girl lost quality. I knew she would make it as an actress. I didn't see her again until 1958 when I came to Hollywood again, and she was on the Columbia lot. She was called Marilyn Monroe then and had become quite famous. She remembered me and I knew her for several months in Hollywood. Later, when I was in New York, she lived around the corner – she was married to Arthur Miller then. She'd wear bandanas over her head and dark glasses to camouflage herself, but she had that inimitable wiggle. We became quite friendly until she died.

After I met Marilyn, I used her image to draw Vicki Vale, girl photographer. I did some sketches of Marilyn in Santa Monica in 1948. So, when I went back to New York, I showed them the sketches and told them, "Remember to color her hair blonde," because it was Marilyn Monroe I was emulating, but the colorist inadvertently gave her red hair. Oddly enough, a full cycle later, Vicki Vale is in the new Batman movie. She is Batman's chief love interest. We kept away from romance in the early Batman stories because Batman was primarily a kid's vehicle and children think it's sissy stuff for a superhero to be involved with women.

Overstreet: Did Lois Lane also inspire you to create Vicki Vale?
BK: Yes, she had an influence. She was kind of pushy – out for a scoop like Lois Lane.

Overstreet: What was the inspiration for Two-Face?
BK: I created Two-Face. He was based on Dr. Jekyll and Mr. Hyde, who combined good and evil in one person. I saw the Frederic March movie when I was a kid. Two-Face was inspired by that – I hadn't read the book. I also came up with the idea of his flipping a coin to see whether he would be good or evil, in collaboration with Bill Finger.

Overstreet: Who created the Penguin?
BK: I did. I saw this cute little penguin on a Kool cigarette pack. To me, penguins always looked like little fat men in tuxedos. I also came up with the visual design of the character. Bill invented the Man of a Thousand Umbrellas idea and all the umbrella gimmicks he used. He was a more cartoony character – partly comedic because of his stature, but still evil and a killer.

Overstreet: What did you think of the *Batman* TV show?
BK: The camp era of the '60s, when the TV show came into prominence, has come and gone. A lot of my died in the wool fans didn't like the TV show. I thought it was a marvelous spoof and great for what it was. But it certainly wasn't the definitive Batman. I didn't have any influence over the show. I was in New York then. Hollywood is the kind of town that when you're out of sight, you're out of mind, and very often when you're in town it's out of sight, out of mind. But if you're in Hollywood, it's harder for them to deny your presence.

In 1965, they were planning to kill Batman off altogether, because sales were so terrible. I had terrible apprehensions because what else could I do – it was my life's vocation. Luckily, it was saved by the TV series and it became bigger than ever. There was a Batman hysteria in 1966. The TV show, with all its camp, caused more hysteria than any other TV show, ever. The reason it burned out so fast is that it was on twice a week with a cliffhanger on Tuesday which concluded on Thursday. If it had been on once a week, it would have lasted four or five years.

Overstreet: How did Batman become a TV show?
BK: Hugh Hefner showed the old Batman serials from 1943 and 1949 in the Playboy

287

mansion. His idea of fun was to string together 13 episodes and watch them in one long Saturday night popcorn session and, in a campy gesture, hiss the villains and applaud the heroes. Some ABC agent or executive was at the mansion that night when they showed the films, and the Bunnies and Hugh were so enthusiastic about these old serials that the agent went back to ABC and said, "You ought to see what's going on at the Playboy mansion every Saturday night. Why don't we try something like that?" And that's how the TV show started.

Overstreet: Batman is enjoying a great resurgence in popularity now, due primarily to Frank Miller's *Dark Knight* series. What do you think of it?

BK: What we have here is a transition from television to comic books – an emulation of the TV miniseries. Frank Miller is a brilliant innovator. The drawings, although sometimes grotesque – sometimes Batman looks like Quasimodo – are extremely interesting. Miller's lines are sketchy, but

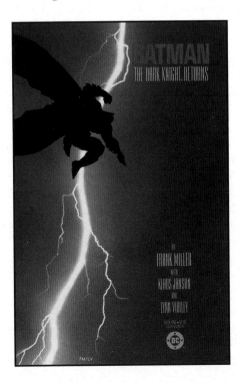

his drawings are very beautiful – very avant-garde. The color is beautiful. The story is also avant-garde – bringing Bruce Wayne out of retirement to fight crime in the Gotham City of the year 2000. I can't knock success – it's an exciting new format for comic books, trying to capture the adult as well as the children's market. It's put Batman back into the limelight.

Frankly, I don't understand Miller's storyline as well as I'd like to. There are certain political associations that I'm not sure of. Why the Nazi Swastikas on women's breasts and buttocks? I don't know what place politics has in comic books, but in the '80s maybe it has. And why does Batman fight Superman? How can Superman be disintegrated into a skeleton and come back all of a sudden full blown? Why would Miller make Robin a girl? What happened to the real Robin? And Batman looks very old – he doesn't look like Bruce Wayne as I drew him. That's what bothers me. If I drew Bruce Wayne at 55, he would look like Bruce Wayne but with gray hair and a few wrinkles. But he looks nothing like Bruce Wayne. He's balding and has a pugilistic nose – where's the straight, aquiline nose and square chin? I picture an older Bruce Wayne like John Forsythe – still a handsome man. Miller's Bruce Wayne looks like a laborer or a fighter. But, all in all, it's a brilliant book. Miller is tapping into something the public understands as the tremendous sales of the book show.

Overstreet: What is your role in the new Batman movie?

BK: I'm a creative consultant on the movie – I wrote the bible for it, to get it on the right track. We have a brilliant young director, Tim Burton, who directed *Pee-wee's Big Adventure* and *Beetlejuice*, and one of the best scripts I've ever read by a new writer named Sam Hamm, who will become a big name once the movie is out. The movie will be dramatic and definitely not a comedy. It will not be campy like the TV show. It will go back to Batman's roots – misterioso, dark, and somber. I designed a new Batplane which they will readapt, and a new Batcave. I also designed a cape which will look like a real wing and is mechanically rigged so that when Batman raises his arms, he's going to look like a real bat.

Jack Nicholson, one of the best actors in the world, will play the Joker. I've been opting for him to play the Joker for years. He will probably play it like black comedy, but not comedic. Nicholson wanted my input on the Joker, and we had lunch a few days ago. I told him that the Joker is very maniacal and psychotic, not the buffoon of Cesar Romero. He agreed that's how he should be played. "He'll be based in reality," as he said. He won't caricature it.

Bruce Wayne will be a three dimensional character – complex, brooding. Someone with a handsome, pretty face wouldn't do. He suffers, has self-doubts. He's neurotic because he feels responsible for the creation of the Joker, this wild killer, and the Joker feels he has to get revenge on Batman. So, it's a dual thing – "therein lies my own image." The Joker sees the image of Batman within him and Batman sees the Joker in himself. It's frightening when you see some of your own warped, repressed ideas in the other person. Michael Keaton with arched eyebrows looks a little like the Joker, more than a handsome guy like Pierce Brosnan or Robert Wagner would. Keaton has a mobile, expressive, tortured face. You don't want a pretty face, because he has to reflect the Joker.

I critiqued the script – it has some of my input, also. There were flaws in the film that I showed them and were corrected. For example, they made Bruce Wayne a wimp in front of the Joker, groveling on the floor. I said Bruce Wayne wouldn't grovel to anyone, because he's really Batman. So, that scene had to go. In another scene, a reporter suspects that Wayne is Batman and comes to confront him. And Bruce acquiesces and says you've caught me. Both the reporter and Bruce are in love with Vicki, so the reporter tells him to stop fooling around with his girl. But Bruce Wayne would never acquiesce – he would have a chess game with him, duel with him. So, they agreed to take that out.

Overstreet: There is some controversy about Michael Keaton, who has been basically a comic actor, playing Batman. How do you feel about this?

BK: Batman is going to be terrifying in the film. Put the costume on anyone and he'll look like Batman. The only problem is that Keaton doesn't have the strongest chin in the world – that's the problem. He looks okay with the mask full-face. The costume will look like chainmail, like the knights wore, and make him appear huskier, and they'll put lifts on his shoes so that he'll be about six feet tall. With the mechanical wings, the costume will make him look like a bat – he'll look awesome. I predict that once the movie is released, Batmania again will sweep the country like it did in 1966 with the TV show.

JERRY ROBINSON
INTERVIEW

Overstreet: When did you first become interested in cartooning?
Jerry Robinson (JR): When I was a kid, I had no interest in becoming a cartoonist. However, I had always drawn from an early age. I would lie on the floor and sketch portraits of my family as they sat and talked. One of my favorite subjects was my grandfather, whom I greatly admired. I was fascinated by his mustache and the lines on his face. I never studied art in high school because you didn't get college credits for it. But I continued to draw and was usually the cartoonist for my school newspaper. I never thought of becoming a comic artist until I met Bob Kane and began working on Batman.

Overstreet: How did the two of you meet?
JR: I met Bob the summer I graduated from high school. I was accepted at three universities – Columbia, Penn, and Syracuse, and decided to go to Syracuse to study journalism. I was interested in becoming a writer and had been an editor of my school newspaper. I sold ice cream in the summer to pay for the first year of college. They had carts on the back of bicycles – they weren't motorized. Being the latter applicant, I got the farthest franchise from the city, which meant having to pick the ice cream up and peddling five miles to the outskirts of the city to sell it. I was always thin as a rail, and at the end of the summer, after peddling all that ice cream back and forth, I could have made the 67 lb. track team. My mother didn't think I could survive the first year in college in that condition, so she persuaded me to take $25 of my hard earned savings of the summer and go away for a week in the country to fatten up.

I went to a resort in the mountains where I could play tennis, which has always been a passion of mine. The first day I was there, I went to the courts and was wearing a white house painter's jacket, with lots of pockets to put brushes and paraphernalia in. It was a fad at colleges to affect these jackets and to decorate them with slogans, fraternity insignia, and whatnot. High school kids are influenced by college fads, so a lot of us wore these jackets. I decorated mine with cartoons I had drawn for my school paper. Bob was at the courts watching the play, although I don't know what he was doing there, because I don't think he ever played. He struck up a conversation and asked me who did the cartoons on my jacket. I told him, "I did," and one thing led to another, and he introduced himself. Bob was about eight or ten years older than me, but still young enough to have rapport with someone my age. He told me he was drawing a comic book feature, which had just started, called *Batman*. To his chagrin, I had never heard of it. So, we took a walk down to the village to see if we could find a copy at the candy store. We did find an issue, but I don't think I was overly impressed with it.

I was an avid reader of the Sunday comics and had enjoyed the Cupples & Leon collections of comic strips, but this was the first comic book I'd seen.

One day Bob told me that he was going to need an assistant on Batman. When he learned that I was going to go to Syracuse, he said, "Well, that's too bad. If you were coming to New York, I could offer you a job." The pay was $25 a week. That seemed like all the money in the world to me and a lot more than the $17 a week I was making selling ice cream. It was enough I could live on. So, I immediately switched to Columbia. I didn't even go home, but went straight to New York and rented a room near Bob. There was about a month before I was to go to work for Bob, so I decided I should know something about cartooning. So, I enrolled in a school that offered cartooning courses. But they had me drawing plaster casts as an introduction – which was boring – and had no cartooning courses, so I stopped going before the month was out.

Overstreet: What were your duties when you worked for Bob?

JR: In the beginning, I just did the lettering, then I inked backgrounds and some of the secondary characters. I found it challenging, but at first, I didn't think of it seriously as a career. I was interested in becoming a writer and thought of the job as a way to pay expenses. We had to turn out a lot of work, especially after the Batman quarterly appeared. Bob began to do very loose pencils – very rough – and this was good for me, because it forced me to learn to draw. So, it was a great schooling. A couple of years later, we hired George Roussos to assist me with the inking. Within the first year I worked for Bob, I was inking complete stories.

I would work in my own apartment and then Bob, Bill, and I would get together to discuss the strip. We would talk about ideas to contribute to it and compare how well we were doing to other strips. It was very all-absorbing. We ate, breathed, and slept Batman. We felt we were doing something better than other strips – we had a better cast of characters, better plots, and a better initial concept. Superman's vulnerability, for example, made him a limited character. We felt we would always be able to inject more suspense into our stories, because Batman was human and could be harmed or killed. So, we had the best stories. Bill Finger, in my opinion, was the best writer in the business.

Around late 1941 or early 1942, I began to pencil and ink my own stories, while I continued to ink some of Bob's, as well as draw and ink my own covers. That's when I was hired directly by DC rather than by Bob. Bill Finger and I were contemplating leaving. Batman was very popular, and we had gotten a lot of offers. Other companies wanted anybody they imagined had something to do with Batman's success. Every other month, Busy Arnold wanted to take me out to dinner. He offered me several books I could write and draw by myself. But I had a sentimental attachment to Batman. I started on it and got my professional reputation from it, so I stayed. That's when DC hired me to work directly for them. They gave me a substantial raise and said I could do covers and my own stories if I continued to work for them. So, I began working at the DC office. Bill also began to work directly for DC at this time.

I rarely saw Bob after this. The cohesion of the three of us working together had split up. Bill was working on his own; other writers came in. Everyone had their own approach. I would work on my own – Bob would work on his own. The strip came to have disparate people working on it, and Bob lost control of it. It would have been much better, in terms of the quality of the strip, if Bob had kept control over it and we continued to meet so there would be a guiding nucleus. But that didn't happen.

Overstreet: What was Bob Kane like?

JR: Bob was something of a playboy at the time. He loved to go to nightclubs. This was fascinating to me as a kid from the country who, in effect, was his protégé. He would recount his adventures to me in detail. He had a great memory for comic routines. Two weeks afterwards, he could retell every joke a comic had told at the Copa Cabana or some other nightclub. And he was a very attractive looking guy – fairly tall, slim, black hair.

Overstreet: What were Bill Finger's scripts like?

JR: They were like film scripts – he wrote full scripts with not only the scene, location, mood, and dialogue, but even angle shots. He was a visual writer. He knew how the story would be visualized. If he plotted an action on shipboard where Batman was swinging down onto the deck, he would attach a photo or illustration of the deck and the construction of the ship. He would really do a lot of the research that artists normally do, but he would do it from a story standpoint as well, so everything worked and you didn't have to figure out what was going on.

It was an exciting time; we were experimenting with sequential narrative, inventing the "language of comics." Everything we tried was new – was an innovation... We were among the first to start to break up the page into different patterns for a storytelling or visual effect. We began to do vertical panels, panels of different shapes, vignettes, and other visual effects. They seem simple now, but it was new then. We stretched a panel across the top of the page so that it was the equivalent of two panels. Then, we expanded it to

maybe a third of a page until the opening shot encompassed the whole page. This was among the first splash panels. We had to fight for these innovations. The publisher's attitude was the more panels, the more they were getting for their money, and we had to battle to improve the art and storytelling.

We were all movie fans – Orson Welles, German films – and this was a major influence on us. We tried to emulate the atmosphere of German Expressionist films and consciously tried to get the surreal quality of those films into the strip. And Bill would constantly be looking for things in those films that suggested story ideas. We liked Fritz Lang's *Metropolis* and *M*, and [Von Sternberg's] *The Blue Angel*. *The Cabinet of Dr. Caligari* especially impressed us.

German lobby card for
The Cabinet of Dr. Caligari

With Orson Welles' *Citizen Kane* it was more the reverse. When we saw the film, it was a revelation, because he was doing things that we had already been doing in the comics. This was a reaffirmation that we were doing things right and were not crazy after all. We felt, gee, here not knowing anything, we were using the same techniques as Welles, and he was a genius. It was very exciting for us. We would go back and see it over and over. Once we made a bet on how many times we saw the film. I think Frederick Ray [one of the major Superman cover artists] won it. He saw the film 40 or 50 times; I was up in the 20s. We used to sit at our desks and recite whole sequences. We knew the dialogue by heart.

Overstreet: What kinds of techniques was Welles using that you also employed in Batman?

JR: The way he manipulated the camera or manipulated time. For example, he would show an event by a reaction – like the scene in which the Marion Davies character, Kane's mistress, is singing in the opera house and the camera goes up and up to the backstage scaffolding to show a stagehand's reaction to her offkey singing. The scene is told through his reaction, and you just hear her voice. Welles also used extreme low angle shots like the sequence in which Kane first takes over the newspaper, which is shot from the ground looking up at him. Welles was the first to use full sets; sets didn't have ceilings before this. We had been doing that – shooting low angle shots to get the effects up on the ceiling. Welles also used a great depth of focus in some shots. We would use techniques like that – shooting past something you wanted to make a point of, to something else. We shot through keyholes, through the floor, to give a sense of a vast room or to heighten a dramatic effect. We also began to experiment with creating illusions of time, like Welles was doing, like in the Rosebud sequence when he slowed down time to focus on the glass paperweight falling from Kane's hand as he dies.

In a way, it was fortunate that Bob and I didn't have any academic art training. Because it gave us a certain freedom in the design. It was more important how things looked than if an arm could actually twist a certain way or if the perspective was correct. The cartoony style was an advantage. We were able to give the strip a surreal look and able to draw more abstractly. Very specifically, I remember we'd look at other stuff with disdain because it was too realistic and photographic. Some of it was directly copied. We thought that was not good cartooning. We didn't want to get too photographic. I admired Foster for his great virtuosity, but Caniff was more my favorite because he was more interpretative and an impeccable storyteller. I would study his work closely. He was a great influence on Bob, too. Bob liked Foster and once in a while would adapt a pose of Tarzan or Prince Valiant. But most of the time he didn't do that – and he didn't do it deliberately.

Overstreet: How did you come to create the Joker?

JR: I was still taking writing courses at Columbia at the time. I had to do a paper for a creative writing course, some original piece of writing. With going to school at night and working for Bob during the day, I didn't have much time. So, I thought of doing a story that would do double duty – that I could write for Batman and that would serve as a piece of creative writing for the class. At that time, we needed more stories. There was going to be a new Batman quarterly and we needed some stories for that issue. I think maybe we had two of them done and needed two more. So, I told Bob I was going to work on a story, because Bill couldn't turn out that many at once.

That night I went to work on it in my little room. My first thought was to create a villain, a strong villain to oppose Batman. This was before I even tried to write any plot ideas. From my studies in literature and my own reading, I knew that all the great heroes had an antihero, and were stronger characters because they were pitted against strong antagonists. There was Moriarty in *Sherlock Holmes*, David and Goliath in the Bible, King Arthur and Mordred. And in mythology there were strong villains. At the time, there were only minor hoods in Batman, but nothing of any super-dimensions, none that I would call exotic villains. We followed the pulps and popular crime fiction of the roaring '20s, basing our villains on gangsters like Dillinger, Pretty Boy Floyd, and Al Capone. They were bank robbers, high-jackers, hold-up men – the criminal stereotypes of the era. They would be disposed of and not really be worthy of a reprise.

There was a difference of opinion in those days, by the way. It seems obvious in retrospect, but at the time it was arguable. How strong to make the villain was discussed, and it was argued both ways. There was a concern that if you made your villain too strong, it would overpower and detract from your hero so that he would not be a hero anymore. Anyway, I was not of this view. I thought the stronger the villain, the stronger the hero would be.

I knew I wanted a continuing nemesis in the vein of Moriarty or Dick Tracy – he had a marvelous cast of bizarre villains. I don't think at the time that I could have foreseen that he would be continuing to this day, but I wanted a villain that would at least last for more than one story I loved writing satire and humor, so it was natural for me to want to create a villain with a sense of humor, someone who would taunt Batman and most of the time get away with it. All the stories I had written for my high school paper had been humorous. I loved de Maupassant's and O. Henry's short stories with the twist endings, and these were the kind of stories I was writing. I thought someone with an internal contradiction would be intriguing; you don't usually think of a villain who does mean and nasty things as having a sense of humor. And, I knew that I wanted someone who was bizarre and exotic – visually striking.

For some reason or other, I drew clowns in high school or grammar school – they were one of the few things I would draw. I liked to draw pirates, cowboys, and clowns. I enjoyed drawing pirates and clowns because they had colorful costumes and an exotic, bizarre look. So, I think that also relates to my creation of the Joker. Clowns are sad – funny and sad. Contradictions like that are interesting. The pathos had an appeal for me as a kid. I loved the circus. Trenton had an annual fair – they had an old fashioned midway with clowns and strongmen, etc. It was very exciting.

When I began to toss around ideas and to deliberately make associations, somehow I thought, well, he's got a sense of humor – he's a joker. I immediately made an association with the joker playing card with that marvelous grinning face. I was

fascinated by the idea of a sinister clown. That was the contradiction I was looking for. Although I didn't know it then, the historic background of the joker on the playing card is a symbol that goes back for centuries. In all societies, they had jokers and jesters. So, it had a built-in meaning.

This is now 12 or 1 AM in the morning, and I made a frantic search throughout my room for a deck of playing cards. I felt I couldn't continue with the script until I could actually see him and get his visual appearance set. Earlier in high school, I had played contract bridge, so I found a deck and, low and behold, it was the one with the classic joker. I knew as soon as I saw it – that was it – that was how he should look. Everything crystallized then – his name was the Joker, he would give out the joker playing card as his calling card, and that would be how he looked. Then I made my first drawing of the Joker, a playing card with the Joker's face on it.

I can't tell you how excited I was. I couldn't wait to rush over to Bob's with the idea. The next morning, I told him about the story I wanted to write. The idea seemed just right for Batman. The Joker served as a marvelous counterpoint to the sinister, shadowy figure of Batman. I always saw Batman as a surreal character, and the Joker fitted this mood. Bob loved the idea immediately. Bill came over shortly afterwards and also loved it. Then came the – would you call it – the denouement? Bob said it was so great an idea that they wanted to use it for the first Batman quarterly, which was then in production. This would have been my first story, and I anticipated taking my time and developing the character. I never expected a discussion about anyone else doing it. As they persuaded me, my heart was sinking by the minute. I can still feel it today, and I was only 17 or 18 then. This would have been my first

story, and I was still going to school at the time, and it would have taken me weeks to write it. I was heartbroken, but, for the sake of the strip, I had to admit that Bill was far better equipped to write it. I never attempted to write another Batman story. I guess my experience with the Joker story turned me off.

Overstreet: Didn't Bill suggest modeling the Joker after a photo of Conrad Veidt from the film *The Man Who Laughs*?
JR: Yes. This was typical of what Bill would do. He thought visually, and my drawing of the Joker reminded him of Conrad Veidt. As I said before, he would often attach photos to his scripts. The Veidt photo reinforced the validity of the idea – so it helped flesh the concept out. That first story was a gem. Bill perfectly captured the bizarreness of the Joker using an idea many mystery writers were fond of – the closed room plot.

Overstreet: Why didn't the Joker have an origin? There was no explanation for his bizarre appearance.
JR: We did that deliberately. Later on, long after I had left the strip, they gave him an origin and explained that he looked that way because of some chemical accident. Frankly, I don't think we would have written an origin for him. I would have preferred it if his origin had always remained unknown – it takes the mystery out of the character to explain it and makes him too ordinary. It would be better if characters in the story or the readers themselves speculated about it.

Overstreet: Why the white face and green hair?
JR: The white face came from the fact that he appeared that way on the playing card. That was the idea – to give him a bizarre look and the face of a clown. The green hair was probably Bob's idea. No one else would have made a decision like that.

After we invented a new character, we usually made suggestions about how to color him. The colorist would usually have made his hair dark blue to look like black hair. The idea of the Joker being very tall was also in Bob's first sketch, I believe.

Overstreet: Wasn't the Joker originally supposed to be killed off in the second story in *Batman #1?*
JR: Yes. Bill killed the Joker off in the script he wrote, but our editor, Whitney Ellsworth, felt that he was such a great character that he had us redraw the last few panels to show that he hadn't really died. It was natural for Bill to decide to kill him off. For him to come back was a precedent. I can't think of any other villains in *Batman* that did continue before this. Batman usually disposed of them at the end.

Overstreet: You also helped create Robin, didn't you?
JR: I had a hand in it. My contribution was limited to the name, not the idea of adding a boy. I remember the day specifically. I came in, and Bob and Bill were already discussing the idea of adding a kid. Everybody loved the idea. I also liked it because it gave another dimension to the strip. I always enjoyed stories like *Treasure Island* which had a kid I could identify with. Kids relate to two things – a contemporary, a peer, or a hero figure they could look up to. This combined both – a father figure and a kid they could imagine themselves to be. It was the first boy wonder in comic books. So, we came up with a lot of firsts at this time – the first continuing villain in Batman and the idea of adding a boy wonder.

We had a big session about the name that day we were discussing adding a kid to the strip. When I came over, Bob had already started on some initial sketches of the new character. His original idea was for something along the lines of a super-costume.

And Bob and Bill had a long list of names. Our practice was to put down every conceivable idea, even if it wasn't exactly the right one, because it might suggest something. We always felt that the names were very important. For some reason, their trend of thought was more towards a supernatural name – the one I remember specifically was Mercury. They were mostly mythological names. There wasn't any one I liked among them. I thought that it should not be anything of that kind – that would be a super-character, not an ordinary kid. This would be contrary to the concept of Batman. It inferred some superpower that was in conflict with the concept of Batman being an ordinary human being. We always tried to keep Batman distinct from Superman, and I wanted to preserve that distinction. They were pretty settled on one name – something like Mercury. I kept saying, "No, no, I don't think that one is appropriate." I didn't know what to name him, but out of the depths, I came up with the name "Robin." I derived it from Robin Hood. In the beginning, I had to argue for "Robin," because their mindset was on something else.

After some discussion, it was agreed that the name Robin was best suited to the concept of the boy. Bob was at the drawing board and we were standing on both sides of him making suggestions. Once we agreed on the name, I suggested adapting the Robin Hood costume. So, Bob started drawing a costume with imitation chain-mail on the trunks and a jacket like a tunic à la Robin Hood. And he put little tails on the shoes to suggest medieval shoes and to give an illusion of speed when he was running. This also may have been a carry-over of the Mercury idea. Then Bob drew the face and two spits of hair. I think that came from an earlier character of his – it was trademark of his kids. I had designed this thing for the first letter of an opening caption – I would draw an elaborate letter like in an old manuscript in a little circle. So, I suggested adding the "R" with a circle around it as a counterpart to Batman's insignia. Actually, it is an implied circle – there is no circle around it. It is black until it hits the circle. It worked well because the red of the jacket goes through the letter. I didn't know that much about lettering. It's probably one of the few kinds of lettering I knew. I didn't go to art school where you learn all kinds of typefaces.

Overstreet: Did you create any other characters for Batman?
JR: I drew the first Tweedledee and Tweedledum story, and I think that I created them. Of course, they were based on Lewis Carroll's *Alice in Wonderland*.

Overstreet: You are also famous for drawing some of the best Batman covers of the '40s.
JR: Outside of a few specific stories, I enjoyed drawing the covers most of all. I was very interested in doing symbolic covers which weren't typical in those days. Bob did a few which were kind of symbolic, which set a precedent – like the one which introduced Robin and showed him

breaking through a circus hoop and the one of the two of them running. I was trying to do a completely symbolic cover of what the content was of the lead story, but without showing any scene from that story. Symbolic covers lent themselves to simple, strong visual images and meant I didn't have to worry about setting a natural scene and could use flat shapes like a poster. I went for the poster effect to make the book stand out visually on the newsstands. Comic books are relatively small, and you would have to examine them carefully to see all the detail if you did a full scene. We would look at them on the stands, and I would be very pleased because you could spot our covers right away.

Overstreet: Do you recall any specific covers that you did that you especially liked?
JR: I especially liked the cover with Batman and Robin wearing parachutes and landing on spotlighted targets, and the cover for a Joker story, "Slay It with Flowers," in which the Joker was a florist. I liked to do covers where the Joker would

be very large and Batman and Robin very small. The "Slay It with Flowers" cover was adapted from the splash panel and had a huge Joker coming out of a flower and spraying small figures of Batman and Robin with insecticide. Another favorite dealt with a story in which the Joker commits a crime a day and challenges Batman to stop him. It showed a huge figure of the Joker ripping out the pages of a calendar and diminutive figures of Batman and Robin being inundated by the pages. I would also color the covers I did or give color guides to the colorist.

Overstreet: What did you do after you left Batman?
JR: I wanted to do more of my own stories and characters, and felt that I needed to do something new. I worked with Mort Meskin in the '40s. He created Johnny Quick and the Vigilante for DC. Then we got other accounts and did the *Black Terror* and the *Fighting Yank* for Standard and some other titles for Simon and Kirby. In 1950, I started teaching at what is now called the School for the Visual Arts in New York. I've had a number of students become successful artists; for example, Steve Ditko was one of my students. I

also began to work for Stan Lee at Marvel in the '50s. In the mid-'50s, I collaborated on a science fiction comic strip set in the contemporary future called Jet Scott. We were syndicated in 75 papers and it lasted about two years. After that, I went into book illustration and have illustrated over 30 books on various subjects. I started doing political cartoons in 1961 for my syndicated newspaper panel, "Still Life." It's still going, and is now titled "Life with Robinson." I have also started my own newspaper syndicate, the Cartoonist's and Writer's Syndicate, which represents cartoonists from 40 countries. Most recently, I have collaborated on a musical called *Astra*, which combines science fiction and political satire, and am exploring the possibility of adapting it for films.

- AFTER THE ARTICLE -

In 1989, Bob Kane published his autobiography *Batman and Me* and then released the updated edition *Batman and Me, The Saga Continues* in 1996. After the '89 *Batman* film, he was a project consultant on the three sequels released in the '90s. He was interviewed by Stan Lee for the documentary *The Comic Book Greats* in '92 and was inducted into the Jack Kirby Hall of Fame in '94 and the Will Eisner Comic Book Hall of Fame in '96. Kane died on November 3, 1998 at the age of 83. He was posthumously added to the Overstreet Hall of Fame in 2013 and given a star on the Hollywood Walk of Fame in 2015.

Jerry Robinson went on to curate, produce, and consult on numerous art exhibits around the world. He created the comic series Astra in 1999, and his art was featured in the documentaries *Adventures into Digital Comics* in 2006 and *Secret Origin: The Story of DC Comics* in '10. He was inducted into Comic Book Hall of Fame in '04 and the Overstreet Hall of Fame in '10. Robinson died at age 89 on December 7, 2011. He had been interviewed for the documentary *Superheroes: A Never-Ending Battle*, which eventually aired in 2013.

Whether you've known him as The Dark Knight,
The World's Greatest Detective or simply as Bruce Wayne,
there's no denying the impact that Batman has had on pop culture.

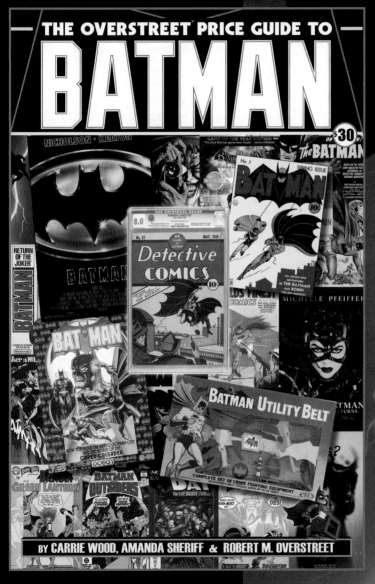

Softcover
$30

ON
SALE
NOW

The Overstreet Price Guide to Batman celebrates the character's 80th anniversary
by taking a look at the characters and creators that have influenced his history,
and will include in-depth pricing on comics, video games, movie posters, toys,
and many other Bat-related collectibles.

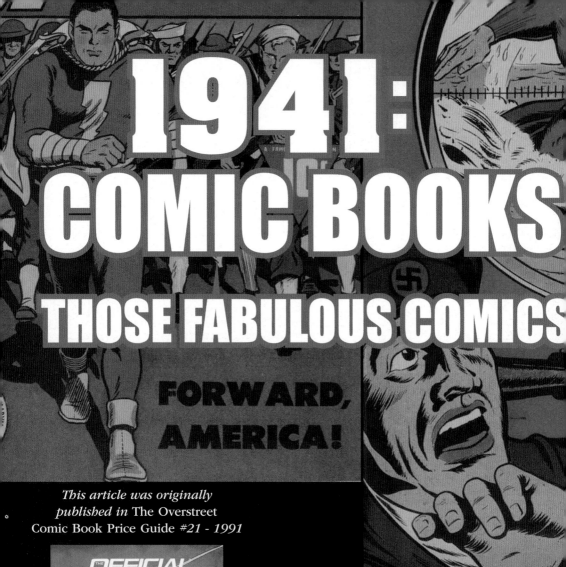

1941: COMIC BOOKS

THOSE FABULOUS COMICS

FORWARD, AMERICA!

This article was originally published in The Overstreet Comic Book Price Guide #21 - 1991

By Harry B. Thomas and Gary M. Carter

Dateline 1939...*The Wizard of Oz* and *Gone with the Wind*...Jack Benny and Fred Allen...Batman and the Human Torch...The New York World's Fair and The World of Tomorrow...and regrettably, for the millions of wounded and dead, the war in Europe and Adolf Hitler. The well worn quote was never more applicable; "it was the best of times, it was the worst of times." It was a time in our history when the drums of war began to echo across America... and as the national anti-axis sentiment began to gel, the comic book industry jumped on the bandwagon. For several truly historic years, World War II and the

A FAWCETT PUBLICATION

GO TO WAR!
OF WORLD WAR II

YOU STARTED IT!
NOW- WE'LL
FINISH IT!

Golden Age of comics walked hand in hand, as it were, down the path of history.

Nationalism was at an all-time high, and with it came a veritable litany of media, fueling the fires of patriotism from Maine to California. One Hollywood film after another played out the horrors of the Nazi war machine in Europe. Movie stars with ties to Great Britain began to volunteer for military service. Newspaper editorials warned that the occupation of Manchuria was only the precursor of further Japanese Imperialism in the Pacific theater. Newsreel footage graphically depicted the agony of thousands of innocent Chinese refugees. *Life* and other magazines published pictorial evidence of Germany's savage and ruthless blitzkrieg. Radio programs satirized the leaders of the Axis powers in a steady stream of skits and monologues while others used villains with obvious German and Asian accents. Sunday comic strips had a field day with a seemingly endless parade of military protagonists.

Pulp magazines chronicled spies plotting to undermine the American military establishment and steal the latest secret weapon (right out from under the collective noses of the defense industry). Highway billboards and storefront recruiting posters pleaded, cajoled, ordered, and inspired young men and women to rush to the aid of their country.

But what of America's new entry into the mass media community? As 1939 marched on and the full extent of Hitler's evil became known to the public, the 7-year-old comic book industry quickly established itself as one of the most stalwart defenders of truth, justice, and the American way.

In late 1939 and early 1940, the comic book industry began using more and more war theme covers. This early cover art was basically generic in nature, in that there were no indications that soldiers or weaponry belonged to any specific country. No swastikas, iron crosses, or rising suns overtly labeled the enemy, but the readers knew… they knew!

Classic examples of these war covers can be found on DC's *Action Comics* #10, #11, #15, #17, #19, and #21. These covers all feature non-identifiable soldiers and/or weapons. And all these issues are from 1939 and early 1940! America may not have been officially at war, but (as illustrated by the covers of *Action* #10, #17, #19, and #21) its famous son from the planet Krypton was getting things started on his own! One of the most poignant covers from this pre-World War II era is the cover of *Action Comics* #31 (December 1940). In what appears to be a European country overrun by the Germans, Superman flies in at the last moment to protect the victim of a firing squad from a hail of deadly bullets. Like the rest of the first 84 *Action* covers, there is no speech balloon to explain. The interpretation of the cover is dependent on the non-verbal emblems of helmets, fixed bayonets, and the European-esque buildings in the background. Also important to the interpretation of the cover of *Action* #31 is Superman's clenched fist and facial expression. It's clear that ole Sup' is about to clobber these guys… and what kind of guys does he usually clobber? Bad guys, that's who! If we can depend on anything, it's that Superman knows who the bad guys are. This is very important because this cover was published more than one year before Pearl Harbor! To lend further credence to Superman's ability to identify the enemy far ahead of the government, note the covers of *Action Comics* #35 and #39 (obvious German helmet), #40 (German cross on tank), #43 (German paratrooper with swastika arm band, first swastika used on an *Action Comics* cover), and #44 (German helmets and swastika), all on the stands before Pearl Harbor.

Action Comics #17.
Generic Superman war cover by Joe Shuster.

Action Comics #31.
Another generic Superman war cover.

Marvel Mystery Comics #4.
Sub-Mariner battles Germans.

Pep Comics #1 introduces The Shield,
America's first patriotic hero.

When it came to identifying the bad guys early, Superman was in good company. In February 1940, (nearly two years before Pearl Harbor) Timely published the cover of *Marvel Mystery Comics #4*. This amazing cover depicted one of Timely's most popular heroes, the Sub-Mariner, punching it out with a submarine crew somewhere on the Atlantic. The Death Raider submarine is clearly emblazoned with a German swastika and flies the black and red German battle flag with a large swastika as its central design element! The covers of *Marvel Mystery Comics* continued to dish out punishment for the Third Reich on 13 more covers that hit the stands before Pearl Harbor.

By 1940, the youth of America were scouring the newsstands, not only for Superman, Batman, Sub-Mariner, and the Human Torch…but for any new hero who might be making a first appearance. There didn't seem to be enough of these new costumed heroes to appease the comic book buying public! To fill this demand, hundreds of new comic book titles would appear on the stands before the close of 1940.

As the war in Europe edged ever closer to America, established costumed heroes began to do their part against the Axis. Another group of comic book heroes was created expressly for this task. These champions of liberty are often defined as patriotic heroes. The Shield, first of these red, white, and blue heroes, was created by MLJ Publishing (now Archie) and appeared in *Pep Comics #1* (January 1940). The front of his costume was made to resemble a shield (which, in actuality, it was) adorned with bars and stars borrowed from Old Glory. Couple this with leggings, boots, and a mask and America's first patriotic hero was born!

The Shield was billed as the G-Man *extraordinary* and as such, most of his early adventures were centered around homegrown criminals. He was later cast in stories of intrigue and espionage. The Shield would remain MLJ's premier character through the early years and *Pep Comics*, their flagship publication. The only other MLJ character to get much attention was the Hangman, whose adventures would also be associated with the war.

Covers are, and always have been, one of the most important aspects of comic books. Editors and retailers still argue that the cover sells the comic. Many enthusiasts collect old comics based entirely on their covers. The war years produced an incredible number of wonderful covers, that can be loosely classified into two categories, the war cover and the patriotic cover. The war cover usually depicts the heroes in pitched battle against the enemy. The "patriotic cover" was much more symbolic in nature and often employed the use of flags, eagles, swastikas, the rising sun, etc.

MLJ Comics mostly featured war covers; however, special notice should be given to the cover to *Pep* #20, one of the top patriotic covers published during the war. *Pep* #20 featured a giant swastika that takes up two thirds of the cover, with flames and hands coming up through it. In the background, rushing to help free the oppressed people trapped by the giant swastika, are the Shield, Dusty (his boy companion), and the Hangman. This cover ranks as one of the finest covers using the swastika as its central theme.

In March 1941, Timely's Captain America, the greatest of all the patriotic comic book heroes, stormed onto America's newsstand. To help launch the new title, the cover featured an appearance by der Fuhrer himself!

No hero of the patriotic genre would create such excitement in comic books. The creative team of Joe Simon and Jack Kirby, considered by most as the best creative masters of the Golden Age of comics, would share the credit for the creation of America's hero. With the introduction of Captain America, all patriotic heroes, before and after, would pale by comparison.

Cap, as Captain America is fondly referred to by collectors, had a true all-American origin. After failing his army physical, a weak and skinny American youth Steve Rogers volunteers to be the test subject of a top secret experiment. An army research scientist injects Steve with a serum that instantly transforms him into a muscular, athletic, and superior human specimen – the perfect warrior! Somewhat predictably, the scientist is assassinated by Nazi spies, the secret formula is lost forever, and Steve Rogers assumes the guise of Captain America!

Many have argued that Cap's costume ranks as one of the top, if not the top, costumes of the Golden Age. It was artistically original and visually stunning! The blue hood, the wings on either side of the large 'A' emblazoned on the forehead, the blue chainmail jersey with a white star on the chest, the vertical red and white stripes around the waist, the blue tights and red seven-league boots, the red gloves, and of course, the symbolic circular red, white, and blue shield, make Simon and Kirby's creation America personified!

Although there were none, the character would have been a perfect medium for patriotic covers. Instead, most issues sported an incredible action cover with a tantalizing caption calculated to entice a young reader to plunk down a dime! Consider these exam-

Captain America Comics #1.
One of the top costumes of the Golden Age.

Captain America Comics #2.
Hitler appears on cover.

Captain America Comics #3.
The Red Skull's first cover appearance.

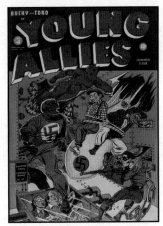

Young Allies Comics #4.
The Red Skull appears on the cover.

ples of intriguing cover captions and note how well they illustrate Cap's penchant for the melodramatic. "Was Bucky to be the next victim of the horror hospital," "Was the senator to be the next victim of the ringmaster's wheel of death?," "Would Bucky's be another terrible death in the chamber of horrors, or would Captain America be there in time?," "Can the mighty Captain America be in time to save Bucky from the horror of the feuding mountaineers?," "Are Captain America and Bucky doomed to become pygmies for all time?" In every case, these compelling questions could be answered by simply buying the comic book or, better yet, sneaking a peek at the end of the story before the newsstand owner spotted you. In either situation, no fan could resist.

Whether by Simon and Kirby, Al Avison, Sid Shores, Alex Schomburg, or their successors, each cover stands as a monument to the American ideal of helping the underdog and taking the bad guys to task with no quarter asked...and no quarter given.

Captain America spawned one of the most memorable villains of WWII...the Red Skull! An awesome sight to behold, the horrible blood red skull sat atop a figure attired in a one piece coverall outfit with a giant swastika on the chest. As villains go, the Red Skull was really not that different from other Timely antagonists of the period. He was just another crazed German agent, totally devoted to Hitler, world conquest, and the superiority of the German race. Even though his appearance made the Red Skull a pretty scary proposition, little was done to develop him into the potentially world class villain he might have become. Though he was written into numerous war era stories, the editors seemed to communicate a similar lack of confidence in the Red Skull, allotting him but a single cover appearance during the war years (issue 3). He would also make a cover appearance on *Young Allies* #4 which featured Cap's sidekick Bucky along with the Human Torch's sidekick Toro. Even though his potential may not have been fully realized, the Red Skull remains one of the most recognizable World War II villains ever created. This fact can be supported by the many Golden Age collectors who prize Red Skull issues above all others.

Captain America was Timely's most acclaimed character, but Timely had others that were almost as popular with the comic book buying public. Two of these other heroes appeared in the monthly anthology that served as the flagship of Timely Publications...*Marvel Mystery*!

With the publication of *Marvel Comics* #1 in November 1939 (it would not be *Marvel Mystery Comics* until the second issue), the

Human Torch and the Sub-Mariner began their long careers at Timely. The Torch and Sub-Mariner would alternate cover duties (along with five appearances by the Angel) during the first two years. The Human Torch was featured on nearly all the remaining covers.

As noted earlier, the Sub-Mariner was already at war with the Germans by the fourth issue, but that should have come as no great surprise. Sub-Mariner was at war with everybody! As a matter of fact, Subby even fought against a fellow hero, the Human Torch, both in *Marvel Mystery* and the Torch's own magazine. It's important to note that (at least conceptually) the Sub-Mariner was most likely the first comic book antihero.

By mid-1940, the story content of *Marvel Mystery* had taken on the same characteristics found in all the Timely publications during the war years. They dealt entirely with their costumed heroes battling the German minions or the crafty Japanese.

The covers for the entire run of *Marvel Mystery* are so similar (especially after Alex Schomburg took over the artistic chores) that young readers had no difficulty spotting the distinctive look of their favorite title, even at some distance from the display rack. Schomburg covers, even though similar, are distinctive and fantastic beauties to behold.

Schomburg could literally cram a cover full of heroes, Germans, Japanese, ships, bombs, planes, artillery, explosions, and of course, an obligatory torture machine or two, to round out the scene. Something thrilling was happening in every inch of a Schomburg cover! Most comic book collectors and historians alike credit him as the best war genre cover artist of the Golden Age and certainly one of the most prolific. Not only did he draw practically every cover for every title at Timely during the '40s, he was also producing a massive amount of covers for Nedor/Standard! It has been suggested on more than one occasion that no collection of Golden Age books would be complete without one of Schomburg's graphic gems.

While nearly all of Timely's covers were war covers, they did produce a smattering of patriotic and symbolic pieces. The cover of *All Winners* #4 ranks among the very best of the entire war! The first issue of *All Winners* was dated summer 1941 and was likely published as Timely's answer to DC's very popular *All Star Comics*. Like *All Star*'s format, Timely placed their most popular characters (Captain America, Human Torch, Sub-Mariner, the Whizzer, the Destroyer, etc.) into one regularly published magazine. The important fundamental difference between the two titles was that DC's heroes banded together as a team (starting with the now famous third issue) for a book-length

Marvel Mystery Comics #48. One of the many classic Schomburg war covers.

All Winners Comics #5. America's heroes stop the Nazi invasion fleet.

All Winners Comics #8.
American heroes attack German troops.

All Winners Comics #9.
German U-boat war cover.

---

adventure. *All Winners* was an anthology book, segregating its heroes in separate, individual adventures (like *All Stars* #1 and #2). Just imagine a Justice Society of Timely superstars...wow...that would have really scorched the newsstand!

The covers of the first eight issues of *All Winners* are truly outstanding and make this title a particular favorite with collectors. The first three covers are more or less war themes but are rendered with a touch of symbolism. And then came #4. All the heroes appearing in that issue are seen rising like giants of freedom over a world aflame and overrun by mad Germans. No better cover produced during the war years can be found at Timely! Other particularly nice patriotic covers were #6 – a flag cover which also featured Hitler, Mussolini, and Hirohito – and #8 featuring the heroes in a jeep mowing down terrorized German troops.

This leads us to an important question. If Timely characters and titles were so popular, why did the company nearly die out so quickly after the war? This can at least be partly answered by reviewing just a few factors. First, *All Winners* and the other Timely action titles were all war-oriented. If there is no war, then it is easy to see how quickly the interest of the "fickle public" will be focused elsewhere. Even the very existence of the

characters becomes hard to justify. This sudden lack of social relevance at wars-end would lead directly to the failure of many of their titles.

Secondly, Timely used what at best could be described as skimpy plot development and, with the notable exception of the Sub-Mariner, character development was virtually non-existent. While other major comic book publishers such as DC and Fawcett were building enduring characters, intricate plots, and essential supporting casts, Timely seemed to manufacture a nearly continuous stream of the standard anti-German/Japanese stories. One notable comic book researcher described Timely as the absolute master of the all-action, no brains story.

When the war ended, Timely was left with no continuity to build on...there were no recurring villains (to speak of) such as the Joker, Penguin, Luthor, or Sivana...nothing to keep people coming back for more. After the war, Timely's heroes were basically left in a vacuum.

Timely's six-year reign as the number one publisher of war theme comics would cost them dearly in popularity when the war ended, but those astonishingly beautiful issues from 1940 to 1945 will always be considered classics by historians and collectors alike!

Over at DC, possibly the number one comics publisher of the time, things were being handled very differently. DC was building for the future. They balanced war stories and covers with a mixture of other themes, including crime, horror, murder, comedy, and even holidays. DC also established good secondary characters to populate their comics. This continuing line of character actors would develop a following that would continue long after the war.

For instance, such characters as Doiby Dickles and his taxi Goitrude, the 3 Dimwits, Lois Lane, Jimmy Olsen, Perry White, Lex Luthor, the Joker, the Penguin, Two-Face, Shiera, Alfred, Etta Candy and the Holiday Girls, Steve Trevor, and many more, were introduced in various titles. These characters came to play an essential role in the legends of the main characters. Consider the fact that most comic fans can readily name the strips each of the above second bananas appeared in! In contrast, Timely had their heroes so involved with Hitler, Hirohito, Mussolini, and their assorted henchmen, that when the war ended, there was no cast of secondary characters or villains to build on.

DC had its own red, white, and blue clad character – Wonder Woman. She had a boyfriend (Steve Trevor) who was a military officer and her costume was DC's own embodiment of the American flag motif. Even though the number of war theme covers on *Wonder Woman* and *Sensation Comics* can be counted on both hands, it must be noted that there were many war-oriented stories involving Wonder Woman and Steve Trevor.

On reflection, it is really a mystery that Wonder Woman in her all-American costume was not used on the covers of her books in a more patriotic effect. In spite of all her exploits, moral fiber, and nationalistic spirit, her "gender-constricted" readers persistently clung to the idea that Wonder Woman was afflicted with an overwhelming and incurable genetic handicap. She was a woman!

While the lack of exploitation of Wonder Woman as a patriotic symbol is a bit of a puzzle, there is little mystery as to why Superman was chosen to carry the flag (both figuratively and literally). In 1941, Superman was DC's most popular character and considered by many to be the most popular character in comic books.

Superman war stories had to be tough to write. Even the youngest of readers were asking the obvious question – why doesn't Superman just fly over to Berlin and knock the stuffin's out of the whole darned German army? Even the most ergonomically deficient first graders figured out that Superman, all by himself, could easily win the war in no time at all.

Wonder Woman #1. One of the few Wonder Woman patriotic covers.

Superman #18.
Superman bombs the Japanazis.

Superman #24.
Classic flag cover.

Superman #34.
American Red Cross cover.

To overcome this thematic catch-22 DC kept the Superman stories self-contained and on an adventure by adventure basis, not worrying much about philosophy and continuity. When they did feature a war story, it would be treated as any other tale and kept within the context of that individual story. The writers never gave the reader paradoxes to ponder or plots that required excessive thought. And why should they? After all, the explosive sales of *Superman* and *Action Comics* communicated to the publishers that the strip had all the literary excellence that it required.

It would be on the covers, though, that Superman would really let his colors show. Nothing was held back! *Action Comics* and *Superman Comics* from 1941 through 1944 featured more of the war and patriotic/symbolic genre covers than any other of DC's major publications. Two of the covers of *Superman Comics* during this period are true classics of the patriotic/symbolic genre. On the cover of *Superman* #14, he is seen standing, full-bodied, in front of a red, white, and blue shield. His arm is raised and on it is perched an eagle. The background is solid black, giving the whole cover a fantastic, almost surreal, three-dimensional effect.

The second exceptional cover is similar to #14 in that it also employs the same black background. *Superman* #24 boasts the famous American flag cover and is a classic of American symbolism. Longtime followers of *The Overstreet Comic Book Price Guide* may remember way back to the 1972 (#2) issue where many a collector was first mesmerized by the cover of *Superman* #24. Both covers are truly breathtaking and once they find their way into someone's collection rarely find themselves back in the hobby marketplace.

The last Superman war cover appeared on *Action Comics* #86. It depicts Superman inundating a high-ranking Japanese officer with a huge pile of war bonds. Superman's disclaimer is simply stated in his speech balloon – "And it isn't Superman who's doing this – it's the American people!"

Though *Action Comics* was doing its patriotic duty, some of the other publications at DC had amazingly few (if any) covers that were directly war related. Notable exceptions to this general lack of patriotic fervor were the covers of their single character books *Superman*, *Batman*, and *Green Lantern*, which were more likely to feature war theme covers.

Green Lantern, for instance, had some outstanding war related covers (and stories). Issue 3 featured the world covered with flames and swastikas while a threatening Green Lantern stands gigantic above it all. *Green Lantern* #4 shows the Green Lantern in his civilian identity (along with Doiby Dickles) marching across the cover in military uniforms. This cover is a dead ringer for a recruitment poster. With his power ring, Green Lantern battles a German tank on the cover of #5.

Batman, DC's second most popular character, may not have had many war theme covers as the lead feature of *Detective Comics*, but he made up for it in his own title. *Batman* #12 (August/September 1942) began the series of war covers on that title with Batman and Robin riding in an army jeep. Batman's first words on any cover were "War savings bonds and stamps – keep'em rolling!" *Batman* #13 had a classic cover by Jerry Robinson, showing Batman and Robin descending from a solid black night sky with billowing white parachutes. High grade copies of this cover are enough to give you collecting shivers! Another well loved Batman cover was done for #15 and shows Batman firing a water-cooled machine gun complete with tripod. Robin is expertly feeding belts of cartridges into the side of the weapon with the look of someone who is having a great time. Issue 17 depicts the dynamic duo astride the back of a giant eagle while giving the victory sign. Robin speaks up for the first time on a cover with the words "Keep the American eagle flying! Buy war bonds and stamps!"

Other more "cartoony" examples of Batman and Robin at war can be found on the cover of #18 (featuring caricatures of Hitler, Hirohito, and Mussolini) and #30, the first issue where both Gotham City crusaders actually speak on the cover. Set on what appears to be a Pacific island, Batman hands over a new M1 rifle to an American soldier and states "Here's a new gun from the folks back home, soldier!" Then the Boy Wonder chimes "Yep! The folks that're backing the 7th war loan!" Marines all over the world cringed at Batman's faux pas. They had just spent agonizing weeks in boot camp learning never to call a rifle a gun!

Very few Batman stories would take the hero to the actual warfront. Instead, he would confront homegrown menaces, expose espionage agents, promote patriotism, and support the sale of war bonds and stamps. Keeping its heroes off the frontlines would be the common policy in most of DC's titles.

By 1941 Simon and Kirby had left Timely (a whole article in itself) and were busy at DC. It was here that their artistic talents matured to a high level of excellence rarely matched in the world of comic books, even to this day!

Simon and Kirby had experimented with kid groups at Timely, but it was at DC that Jack and Joe would really perfect this unusual

Green Lantern #3.
One of the most collected war covers.

Batman #18.
Hitler, Hirohito, Mussolini cover.

Star Spangled Comics #7, first appearance
of The Guardian and the Newsboy Legion.

Boy Commandos #2.
Simon and Kirby at their best.

genre. Two of the most popular strips at DC during the years 1941 through 1945 would be kid groups originated by these two comic book geniuses.

In the summer of 1941, #7 of *Star Spangled Comics* hit the stands. Taking over the cover spot (previously occupied by a distinctly patriotic hero, the Star Spangled Kid and his sidekick Stripesy) was S&K's newest smash feature, the Guardian and the Newsboy Legion! The first story disclosed that the Newsboy Legion was made up of four New York slum kids with very different personalities. The Guardian was the costumed alter ego of a New York cop who took the kids under his protective wing. The Newsboy Legion proved to be one of the most popular features ever produced by DC and was not only strong enough to survive the departure of Simon and Kirby, but even survived past the end of the war.

The artwork by Simon and Kirby is among the best ever done in the superhero genre and the covers they created for this series are absolutely stunning! It is amazing that this superb title remains so low in value when compared to other DC publications of the same time period. Like Batman, there were numerous stories of the Guardian and his pals foiling the un-American antics of villain after villain.

The other (and apparently more popular) "kid" group created by the Simon and Kirby team was another assemblage of preteens, this time with an international flavor. The Boy Commandos had their origin and first appearance in *Detective Comics* #64 and their only cover appearance in *Detective Comics* #65.

This "two-fisted" group's protective adult was army Capt. Rip Carter whose only costume was his military uniform. One major difference between this group of heroes and most of the other strips at DC during this period was that their adventures would take place at the front rather than in the U.S.A. The Boy Commandos proved so popular that in the winter of 1942 they were given their own magazine and the Simon and Kirby covers on the first few issues are again shining examples of the team's classic talents. Simon and Kirby's wonderful cover to *Boy Commandos* #2 is an enduring classic. It features the boys giving the bum's rush to no less than Hitler himself! Rip and the four boys would continue to battle with the Axis on the first 13 of their 36 covers.

In one of their most flavorful and famous stories (published in *Detective Comics* #106 (December 1945)) the Boy Commandos "Meet the Commandos from Nippon!" They are Bugi (World's Greatest Acrobat), Fugi (World's Greatest Jiujitsu Expert), Mugi

(World's Greatest Sniper), and, last but not least, Yugi (World's Greatest Knife Thrower). In typical Boy Commandos fashion, Alfy, Andre, Jan, and Brooklyn swiftly dispatch (as in kill) the rival Commandos one by one. In the last panel of the story, the four dead Nipponese commandos, standing on clouds, argue with each other about the failure of their mission while a sign in the foreground reads "Broken-down land of honorable ancestors overcrowded!" This attempted insult of something very sacred to the Japanese may have backfired. Perplexed readers across the country now had graphic proof that, contrary to popular opinion, the Japanese went to Heaven too!

While the idea of kid groups might seem silly to the more cynical readers of today, the concept was incredibly successful. The Newsboys Legion and the Boy Commandos were among the most popular wartime features at DC.

DC did not relegate Simon and Kirby to drawing and writing only kid groups. They were also responsible for the (new) Sandman and Manhunter strips in *Adventure Comics* during this same time period. Their work on these two strips, however, did not seem to reveal the same enthusiasm as the kid heroes. Some notable *Adventure Comics* covers with war themes (some by S&K, some

S&K lookalikes) are #78, #79, #82, #86, #88, #91, #95, and #96.

With the exception of the Boy Commandos, DC utilized war stories and covers on a more or less intermittent basis. Their costumed heroes seemed to take on their war duties as a somewhat lower priority than the standard fare offered by ordinary adventures. *All Star* #4 (the first bimonthly issue (March/April 1941) introduced an important change in this editorial policy.

On the last page of *All Star* #3, below a drawing of the eight heroes shown on the cover, the editors announce two things. First, that *All Star* will be published every two months instead of every three months. And secondly, that "In the next issue of *All Star Comics* – you will follow the adventures of all your favorite characters, pictured on this page, in one big episode in which they work hand in hand with the chief of the FBI in Washington, and we know you will get even a greater kick out of the next issue than you got out of this one!"

Issue 4 begins at that Washington meeting where the FBI director (J. Edgar Hoover, no less) proceeds to enlist the members of the Justice Society of America (JSA) to fight national internal espionage which is threatening to undermine freedom and democracy

Adventure Comics #79.
Manhunter stalks a German U-boat.

All Star Comics #4. The Justice Society goes to Washington.

All Star Comics #11.
Hawkman battles a Japanese soldier.

All Star Comics #12.
"V" for victory cover.

in America. This incredible issue has one of the most beautiful patriotic covers of the entire 57-issue run. Beginning with #4, *All Star* would be DC's most war-oriented costumed hero title.

All Star's war theme cover "hall of fame" continued with #7 (members raising money to help feed war orphans in Europe), #9 (symbolic eagle and shield), #11 (which featured Hawkman in a man to man duel with a Japanese soldier). Issue 11 also stated that the JSA was being disbanded so the various team members could join the armed services in their civilian identities and "properly serve their country in time of need." All the current JSA membership (Hawkman, Dr. Fate, Sandman, the Atom, Dr. Mid-Night, Starman, and Johnny Thunder) proceeded to join the armed forces. Only the Spectre, as a bonafide ghost, was unable to pass the physical. In spite of this minor setback, he declared he would continue the fight on the home front while the other members went off to Europe.

After arriving at the front, it didn't take long for the heroes to don their costumes and help the troops. It soon became obvious to the military hierarchy that the JSA had secretly enlisted. This news resulted in the disruption of normal military procedures and the commanding officer persuaded the JSA to form an elite and exclusive fighting group called the Justice Battalion to remain in effect until war's end.

The distinctive and beautiful cover of *All Star* #12 depicts the JSA team members in a full cover "V" for victory. Wonder Woman, now a full-fledged member, forms the base of the "V." *All Star* #14 made a rare wartime statement with the cover blurb "Food for staring patriots." This subdued and historically significant horn of plenty cover is still relevant, considering the present state of world hunger. *All Star* #16 featured a symbolic cover with the JSA members surrounded by Americans of all walks of life and a banner along the cover bottom reading, "The Justice Society for a united America!" Issue 22 is the famous American flag cover, with renderings of Washington and Lincoln in the background in case the flag alone did not stir you to patriotic feelings. Issue 24 ranks as one of the most unusual covers and stories of the series. Rarely, if ever, would DC make such a blatantly propagandistic, distorted, and racist statement as in the story "This is Our Enemy." In contrast, #27 suggests love, care and understanding, and explores the tragedy of disabled veterans returning home from war.

Only one other company would so effectively exploit the notion of America at war. That company started with a single world... "Shazam!"

From the standpoint of pure physical attractiveness, the Fawcett comic books published in the early '40s were a real class act. This was because Fawcett covers were printed on higher quality, heavier paper stock than any other company's. Many collectors have noted that the spines of DC and Timely comics from the '40s tend to flake easily when opened. The spines of Fawcett books seem to resist this defect to a much higher degree. Also, due to the better paper stock, the colors of Fawcett covers seem a bit brighter and seldom have serious browning so common in the majority of other contemporaneous comics. Fawcett could also claim the most popular costumed hero of the 1940s – Captain Marvel!

Considered by many comic book researchers and collectors to be the best superhero origin story ever published, Captain Marvel and *Whiz Comics* seemed destined for success right from the beginning.

Billy Batson, a young boy who looked to be somewhere between 11 and 13 years of age, was given the power to become the adult Captain Marvel by saying the magic word, Shazam! Actually, Billy did not become Captain Marvel. He and the "Big Red Cheese" merely exchanged places when the magic word was spoken. Readers were never given an explanation of where Captain Marvel came from (or who he was), or where Billy would disappear to. No one seemed to mind because the popularity of C.C. Beck's wonderful hero spread like lightning all across the country.

Captain Marvel's adventures only got better and better as each story was published. His tales were always just slightly "off center" – never quite planting the reader in reality. In fact, this surreal quality seemed to actually advance the popularity of Captain Marvel stories.

Captain Marvel was portrayed as shy, not overly smart, impetuous, laughable (his #1 nemesis, Dr. Sivana, invented the humorously derogatory term "the big red cheese"), dedicated, heroic…in other words, one of the few really interesting personalities in a world populated by bland, two-dimensional heroes.

C.C. Beck was the genius behind the good Captain throughout most of his long career, including a great deal of input into the stories. C.C. Beck was an innovative master of comic book illustration and one of the few to seriously challenge the team of Simon and Kirby!

Beck's style was deceptively cartoonish but upon closer inspection reveals a stylistic intricacy and has yet to be equaled. He was one of the few illustrators to make a comic book hero actually appear to have weight and substance. Captain Marvel was rounded, making the costume appear full. This contrasted

All Star Comics #24.
"This is our enemy" issue.

Whiz Comics #2 (#1). First Capt. Marvel, the most popular hero of the 1940s.

Captain Marvel Adventures #12.
Captain Marvel joins the Army.

Captain Marvel Adventures #14.
Captain Marvel swats the Japanese army.

greatly with the more common illustrative method of sharp angles and costumes which looked as though they were part of the hero.

Billy Batson and Captain Marvel were both dedicated to goodness and fair play, so when Hitler and his cohorts started the nasty business of world conquest, they both stepped forward to do their patriotic duty.

In *Captain Marvel Adventures* #12, Billy Batson's attempted enlistment in the Army failed because he was underage. Billy walked out of the recruiting office, spoke the magic word "Shazam," reentered and signed up as Captain Marvel.

The Army was ecstatic to get so perfect a specimen! They appeared to have never heard of Captain Marvel (again, that hint of being slightly beyond the accepted bounds of reality) and treated him as just another recruit. (…Almost sounds like Elvis.)

At the story's end, old Shazam, who had granted Billy Batson the power to become Captain Marvel, appeared as an army officer (he had joined due to his belief that America would need him to defeat the evil of Hitler), and told Captain Marvel he could best serve the world by remaining free and independent of the Army. Sadly, Captain Marvel agreed and his stint in the U.S. Army came to an abrupt end.

Later in #12, Captain Marvel, now a civilian, would have one of his many confrontations with Hitler himself. The two foes would meet many times during the course of the war, supplying Captain Marvel with many opportunities to totally embarrass the German leader. In all of Hitler's many appearances in Fawcett comics, he was always depicted as a jumping, screaming, mad clown, with a severe case of spoiled brat syndrome.

Whiz Comics, of which Captain Marvel was the cover and lead feature, and *Captain Marvel Adventures* would both feature loads of patriotic/war covers. Fawcett excelled in cover art and almost any cover on any of their titles during the early '40s could have been used for poster art!

The main villains in *Captain Marvel Adventures*, Dr. Sivana (a mad scientist) and Mr. Mind (a worm from outer space bent on world conquest) gave outstanding performances over the years and were examples of genuine unique literary creations.

At different times, and independent of one another, the two villains joined forces with Hitler (as well as with Hirohito and Stalin) in their drive for world conquest, but with a twist – Sivana and Mr. Mind both planned to betray the Axis powers at the earliest opportunity and to take over the world themselves. However, both Sivana and Mr. Mind soon withdrew their aid from Hitler and his gang, determining that they (the Nazis) were too stupid to be of much use to them. How embarrassing – even the villains at Fawcett had no use for the Axis!

Some outstanding examples of Captain Marvel World War II covers can be found on *Captain Marvel Adventures* #12 (Captain Marvel leading an Army troop through barbed wire and shell bursts), #14 (swats the Japanese), #15 (paste the Axis), #16 (Marvel and Uncle Sam side by side, rolling up their sleeves to take on the enemy), #17 (fantastic and rarely done painted cover of Captain Marvel in an aerial dog fight with enemy planes), #21 (swastika cover), #26 (flag cover), #27 (Captain Marvel joins the Navy), #28 (Uncle Sam pins medal on Captain Marvel), and #37 (buy war stamps).

Whiz Comics also had many, many war-related covers, two of the very best being #31 which featured Captain Marvel posing beside a poster of General MacArthur and the visually stunning #44 with Captain Marvel leading our troops onto an enemy beachhead while carrying an American flag!

While Captain Marvel was the mainstay at Fawcett, his protégé, Captain Marvel Jr., was also very popular and was possibly the most successful boy hero of the '40s. Captain Marvel Jr. was driven with a vengeance against the Hun, and with good reason. Hitler and the war were directly responsible for the creation of Captain Marvel Jr., and his origin trilogy of stories in *Master Comics* #21, *Whiz Comics* #25, and *Master Comics* #22 form one of the best character introductions in the history of comic books! Not only did the trilogy introduce the very successful Captain Marvel Jr. – it also introduced another of the major WWII comic book villains, Captain Nazi!

Captain Nazi was a unique stroke of genius for Fawcett in that unlike the more commonly done villains that were parodies of German, Japanese, and Italian foes, Captain Nazi was the personification of German aggrandizement and Aryan perfection. He was tall, muscular, movie star handsome, blond, and totally dedicated to Hitler's warped ideals and goals.

Captain Nazi made his first appearance in *Master* #21, with a cover featuring Captain Marvel and Bulletman standing on either side of a grinning, arrogant, green-clad Captain Nazi. Readers knew this issue contained something very special – and they were right!

As the story began, Hitler introduced (to a gathering of his generals and allies) his latest and greatest secret weapon, Captain Nazi. Hitler proudly announced that this new German superman would defeat any super-

Captain Marvel Adventures #16.
Patriotic Uncle Sam cover.

Master Comics #21. Captain Nazi's first
app. & part 1 of Capt. Marvel Jr. origin

Whiz Comics #25.
Part 2 of Capt. Marvel Jr.'s origin.

Master Comics #33.
One of the best swastika covers.

hero that America might send against him.

Captain Nazi possessed superpowers except for the ability to fly (and he would acquire that power a little later in his career). Where he attained those powers was never revealed.

Captain Nazi's first stop in America was in *Master Comics* #21 where he began making a shambles of Bulletman's territory. However, Billy Batson just happened to be visiting the area, and one Shazam later, Captain Marvel himself joined Bulletman. The team proved too much for the super German agent and, as Captain Nazi fled, he threw out a challenge to Captain Marvel – "I'm headed for *Whiz Comics*. If you (C.M.) are brave enough, I'll be waiting."

Nazi arrived at *Whiz* just in time for the 25th issue (December 1941). Captain Marvel immediately proceeded to give him a good thrashing, the last blow of which sent the evil German far out and into a giant lake. An old man and his grandson in a fishing boat watched Captain Nazi hit the water, rushed to his aid, and dragged the villain into their small boat. As a reward for this kind act, Captain Nazi beat the old man to death with a boat oar and swatted the young boy into the lake. Captain Marvel spied the drowning lad and rushed him to a hospital, where he was informed that the boy, Freddy Freeman (a name symbolic for the times), had been mor-

tally injured. Blaming himself, Captain Marvel took Freddy to his mentor, Old Shazam, and asked him to save the boy. Old Shazam not only saved Freddy, but gave him superpowers similar to those of Captain Marvel.

The artist of Captain Marvel Jr. was Mac Raboy. Raboy was more of an illustrator rather than a strip artist, taking his inspiration from the likes of Alex Raymond whose comic strip, Flash Gordon, he would one day draw. Each panel of a Raboy comic strip was lovingly rendered in a posed format, making it stand out individually much like an illustration in a novel. Raboy's art is nothing short of breathtaking and is often reminiscent of near-photographic accuracy. Raboy's skill as a cover illustrator was rarely equaled.

The highly symbolic and colorful covers of *Master Comics* from the war years are the epitome of comic book patriotic/war covers. The most outstanding of these covers appeared on the following issues: #27 (V for Victory), #28 (Liberty Bell), #29 (Hitler and Hirohito), #30 (stunning flag cover), #32 (American eagle), #33 (the very best cover ever done using the swastika as a symbol), #34 (Captain Nazi), #36 (absolutely breathtaking Statue of Liberty cover), #40 (another fabulous flag cover), and #41 (tribute to the armed forces). Raboy covers on Captain Marvel Jr. are also worthy of note, including #4 (Jr. standing in front of a fiery shell burst), #11 (war theme), #13 (Hitler's football game), and #25 (with yet another outstanding flag cover).

Though Captain Marvel and Captain Marvel Jr. were by far the two most popular war years heroes at Fawcett, the company had many more excellent characters such as Minute Man (their answer to the red, white, and blue clad patriotic hero), Bulletman, Mr. Scarlet, Captain Midnight, Mary Marvel (check out her tribute to the wartime effort of American women on the cover to *Wow Comics* #11 and the equally beautiful flag cover on #15 of the same title), and one of the most popular war-related heroes of them all – Spy Smasher.

Fawcett was so filled with support for the war that they even furnished their buyers with a specially illustrated mailing envelope (featuring all their characters) with which the reader could supply comics to the troops overseas. Fawcett expended a great deal of patriotic effort yet established a line of strong titles and characters that would be successful long after the war.

Other companies that enjoyed various degrees of success during the war years were Holyoke, Prize, Harvey (the Green Hornet), Hillman (Airboy), Centaur, Ace, and Nedor/Better (the Black Terror, Fighting Yank). Fiction House, with their two publications *Wings* and *Fight*,

proved that cheesecake could sell war comics. Actually, they proved that cheesecake could sell any title! Dell Comics, publisher of primarily comic strip reprint titles (such as *Popular, Super, Crackajack Funnies, Walt Disney Comics and Stories*) had its fair share of war theme covers.

During the early part of the war years, Dell even introduced two of the earliest war comics, both featuring original stories. *War Comics* had a four-issue run starting with #1 in May 1940 and *War Heroes*, which appeared in 1942 and lasted 11 issues. Neither title was that successful, supporting evidence for the theory that war theme comics needed the pizazz of a costumed hero to be really successful. Dell did have some outstanding patriotic covers on their books, the best of which, surprisingly, appeared on their two funny animal titles, *Walt Disney's Comics & Stories* and *Looney Tunes*.

Quality Comics – and they were quality – introduced two extremely popular strips to comic book fans in the early '40s – Blackhawk in *Military Comics* and Plastic Man in *Police Comics*. When introduced in *Military* #1 in August of 1941, before America's official entry into the war, Blackhawk was a Polish freedom fighter. As a result of Hitler's atrocities to his country and family, he formed a band of international air-fighters from various countries who were

Captain Marvel Jr. #4.
Classic Raboy cover art.

Wow Comics #15.
Patriotic flag cover.

Military Comics #21.
Crandall art in these issues is unbeatable.

Daredevil Battles Hitler.
One of the best Hitler covers.

also victims of Nazi aggression. At a later date, Blackhawk's origin would be revised, giving him an American nationality. The exact number of team members that made up the early Blackhawks was not clear in the first few issues of *Military*, but soon stabilized at seven. The earliest adventures were drawn by Charles Cuidera, with inspiration and guidance from the great Will Eisner.

With #12, Reed Crandall took over and delivered some of the very best work done during the war. Crandall was a fantastic talent and his work on #12 through #22 of *Military Comics* are unbeatable! His attention to detail is amazing and his ability to illustrate women was unequaled during the war years.

The Lev Gleason Company published relatively few titles, but those they did publish were among the very best of the era. Their two most popular titles from the war years were *Daredevil* and *Boy Comics*. Daredevil's first issue was titled *Daredevil Battles Hitler* starring, once again, the mad man of Germany. After that first issue, *Daredevil Comics* was more like DC and Fawcett titles in that the character would do a mix of stories – some involving the war and some with other themes.

Daredevil, as well as Crimebuster (the lead feature in *Boy Comics*), tended to be a little more realistic and adult-oriented than their contemporaries. Even though the stories could, at times, prove to be extremely gruesome, they are still among the most original ever published.

Couple these beautifully crafted stories with the artistic virtuosity of Charles Biro, and the result was great reading! Biro was a premier Golden Age artist and very prolific, not only doing the work at Lev Gleason, but also doing covers and lead features at MLJ Comics.

As inspired as Biro's work may have been on the Daredevil stories, it paled when compared to his efforts on the Crimebuster strip in *Boy Comics*! *Boy Comics* started with #3 (the first two issues of the book had been called *Captain Battle*) dated April 1942. It not only introduced Crimebuster and his pet monkey Winks, but also the most sinister and cruel World War II villain of all, Iron Jaw!

In #3, teenager Chuck Chandler's mother and father are destroyed by Hitler's ace agent, Iron Jaw. Iron Jaw was a fearful sight to behold. Crew cut hair, snub nose, and a lower jaw replaced with a massive cast iron piece with two sets of serrated teeth. These deadly dentures were used primarily to tear out the throats of his enemies.

Hitler himself would be considered the only war villain more evil than Iron Jaw, and that would be questionable as #5 of *Boy Comics* would prove. Issue 6 was the best single issue of that title, featuring one of the most outstanding stories to come out of the war era. The book featured the first appearance of Iron Jaw on the cover, then proceeded to tell of his origin inside. But the full extent of Iron Jaw's evil nature was revealed with the introduction of his son in this same issue.

Iron Jaw had his son brought to America to serve alongside him as an agent of Hitler. He did not anticipate that his son would soon forsake his and Hitler's ideals and convert to democracy. Rather than see his offspring embrace the causes of freedom, he proceeded to kill his own son! Strong content for World War II comic books!

Even though Chuck Chandler was the title character of those early Crimebuster tales, Iron Jaw was the real star of the show. Never, even in *Dick Tracy*, was there ever a villain more vile and contemptible! Fans and historians of the comic book's Golden Age suggest that he is second in villainy only to Batman's foe, the Joker. All the Crimebuster stories in *Boy Comics* #3-15 were of above average fare. Issue 15 is worthy of special note because it contains the death (he came back) of Iron Jaw. Some of the truly graphic covers that should be noted in this same period are #5 (great war cover), #7 (flag and Hitler), #9 (classic Statue of Liberty/Iron Jaw piece), #10

(equally classic swastika/Iron Jaw cover), #12 (Japanese torturing American soldier), and #17 (a beautiful flag cover).

It would take a book rather than an article, to completely chronicle all the notable comic books published during World War II. Although this effort just begins to scratch the surface of this fascinating topic, it does permit a number of interesting conclusions to be drawn. First, nearly every comic book company of the time produced war covers and stories. Second, no other thematic idea was so readily embraced and so universally exploited by the comic book industry. Third, the nationalistic and patriotic effect of war theme comics, although inferred by many, will be a great challenge to future historians to conclusively prove. And fourth, although war comics were produced in conjunction with other wars, they never attained the extreme popularity of those published during World War II.

When comic books went to war half a century ago, they did so in a grand and glorious manner. How much patriotic fervor they developed among their young readers may never be accurately measured. What can be qualified, however, is the intense interest of collectors who will always strive to obtain these fascinating, gorgeous, and are artifacts of the past – the comic books that went to war!

Boy Comics #6.
Origin & 1st app. of Iron Jaw.

Boy Comics #11.
Classic Iron Jaw cover.

Available in Hardcover
for the First Time!

ON SALE APRIL 2021 • Cover by Billy Tucci

Newly Revised & Expanded • Full Color • $34.95 HC • $24.95 SC

WWW.GEMSTONEPUB.COM

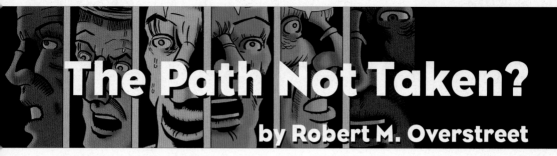

The Path Not Taken?

by Robert M. Overstreet

We've often said that if not for EC Comics, The Overstreet Comic Book Price Guide wouldn't exist. It's not that it wasn't needed or that someone wouldn't have done it, just that it wouldn't have been Bob Overstreet. Even at a young age, he was very serious about collecting and studying the ECs. What many don't know, though, is that Bob is a very talented artist as well as a price guide guru.

While we're very glad that Bob followed his price guide muse and not his artistic one, the story on the following 11 pages are enough to make us ask "What if...?" (much like our friends at Marvel Comics). We're pleased to present "March 25th" restored and for the first time in color, but first, here's the story behind the story.

———————————————

I think it was 1964 when **L.C. Chesney** and I were in touch with **Bill Spicer**, who was publishing a new fanzine, *Fantasy Illustrated*. Chesney did the cover to #1 and #3. We had our first comic book story, "A Study in Horror," ready for *Fantasy Illustrated #3*.

We drew this story in the EC tradition as true EC fans at the time. "A Study in Horror" was illustrated by Chesney and me, and we drew ourselves as the main characters in the story. Both of us posed for each panel and took pictures of ourselves to work from.

Spicer was so impressed with "Study" that he asked me if I would consider doing another story by myself. I said that I would, and he began sending me scripts hoping to find one that I liked. The one I settled on was "March 25th." It was written by a fan, Ken Finnerty, who I had the pleasure of meeting at a Houston Con a few years later.

Chesney was really good at lettering and he did all the lettering on "Study." He even had a photo of me inking one of the pages of that story, which we published in *The Overstreet Comic Book Price Guide #30*.

Bill Spicer created all the panel layouts for "March 25th" on illustration board and sent me all 11 pages of the story lettered and ready for me to fill in the art. He also sent me a rough breakdown with suggestions of what he thought the art should show. I still have these rough layouts that he penciled.

I spent several weeks creating the panel art by first drawing the art in blue pencil and then inking the final version. It was the only comic story that I did completely on my own and I was very happy with the way it turned out.

In addition to the original credits, which you'll find on the story, I would like to thank **Dawn Guzzo** of Atomic Studios for cleaning up the images of the original art so beautifully, **Mort Todd** for his wonderful colors, and **Gary Guzzo** for managing the restoration and color process. As happy as I was to see the original in print, seeing it in such beautiful color was an incredible bonus.

A Story Revisted

by Bill Spicer

OH GOD! *THIS THING WAS ACTUALLY HAPPENING!*

"March 25th" is a good example of the time when I fancied myself being a minor league Harvey Kurtzman or Bernard Krigstein, influenced as I was by their page layouts or breakdowns at EC in the 1950s. I did almost all the lettering for stories in early *Fantasy Illustrated* issues, plus the layouts as well which probably, for better or worse, made me something of a control freak. In that department "March 25th" was no exception. If anything, it went overboard with prep work compared to every other story up to and including those in this #3 issue, highlighted by back and forth discussions going on just about each week between Bob and myself.

Ken Finnerty's original manuscript ran very long, needing at least 24 pages to be used "as is," so it had to be pared down to a more manageable length for Bob to illustrate while keeping key dialog and plot continuity intact as much as possible. The final version ended up being a largely experimental effort with more panels than an average 11-page story would have, thanks to some special effect sequences scattered throughout and various panel repetitions. It took quite a bit of time, but Bob eventually received pre-lettered and laid out pages from me so he could get started on doing the actual artwork. Up to that point, most things for me were still more or less theoretical.

As a nightmarish psychological horror story, Bob did a great job of getting across just the right amount of foreboding atmosphere and moody paranoia, certain parts of all that benefitting from an assortment of what we liked to call camera angles. Looking back on it now, I would have to say some of those experimental effects I orchestrated did better than others. The one that stands out to me today as best of all is the page 7 lineup of 12 jurors, Bob going the extra mile by giving each one a distinctively individual appearance.

MEMBERS OF THE JURY--HAVE YOU REACHED A VERDICT?

WE HAVE, YOUR HONOR.

MARCH 25TH

Written by Ken Finnerty

Drawn by Bob Overstreet

Lettering and page layouts by Bill Spicer

MARTIN CROWSON, REGISTERED PHYSICIAN AT THE NEW YORK CENTRAL HOSPITAL, BENT OVER THE BODY, REALIZING HOW PECULIAR IT SEEMED THAT THE BODY HAD NOT BEEN SEVERELY BROKEN BY THE IMPACT OF THE FALL...

OHHH--

SOME OF THE PEOPLE STARTED TO BACK AWAY, BUT MOST STAYED ON TO SEE WHAT WOULD HAPPEN NEXT. THEY SAW HIM KNEELING OVER THE BODY, AND WAITED TO TALK WITH THIS INCREDIBLE MAN WHO HAD LIVED AFTER FALLING FROM A HEIGHT THAT SEEMED WOULD BRING CERTAIN DEATH...

I'M--ALL RIGHT-- LET ME UP-- LET ME UP--

I GUESS I'M PRETTY LUCKY TO BE WALKING AWAY FROM HERE, HUH?! WHEN I FELL FROM THAT WINDOW I SAID TO MYSELF, JOHN, I SAID, THIS IS IT-- IT'LL ALL BE OVER IN A FEW SECONDS...

HOW DID YOU SURVIVE? HOW COULD A PERSON POSSIBLY GET UP AND WALK AFTER FALLING THAT FAR? WHY, YOUR BODY ISN'T EVEN DAMAGED!

THAT'S A QUESTION I CAN'T ANSWER, FRIEND--

CHALK IT UP TO CLEAN LIVING!

NOW IF YOU'LL EXCUSE ME, I'LL BE ON MY WAY BACK TO THE OFFICE--

WAIT-- I'D LIKE TO CHECK YOUR PULSE TO SEE IF YOUR HEART HAS REGAINED ITS FULL COORDINATION-

NO, I'M ALL RIGHT-- YOU DON'T-*!*

THE NEXT THING JOHN MYERS KNEW HE WAS SITTING IN FRONT OF AN X-RAY MACHINE. HE OPENED HIS EYES AND LOOKED UP AT THE FORM OF DR. CROWSON, WHO WAS JUST ENTERING THE ROOM...

WHAT-- WHAT AM I DOING HERE? I'M ALL RIGHT-- I JUST BLANKED OUT...

WHY ARE THESE COPS HERE?

CALM YOURSELF. WHEN YOU BLACKED OUT I COULDN'T FIND A HEARTBEAT SO WE BROUGHT YOU TO THE HOSPITAL HERE TO CHECK YOU OUT. TO FIND YOUR HEART.

FIND MY HEART?

YES. AND YOU DO HAVE A HEART, SIR, BUT...

BUT WHAT?

WELL, ACCORDING TO OUR TESTS--

YOUR HEART IS NOT FUNCTIONING.

THIS IS CRAZY! I'VE GOT TO HAVE A HEART THAT WORKS-- I'M ALIVE AREN'T I?

AND WHAT ARE THESE COPS STANDING AROUND FOR?

I DON'T WANT TO KEEP YOU HERE, MR. MYERS, BUT I'M AFRAID YOU'LL HAVE TO GO ALONG WITH THE POLICE IF YOU FEEL UP TO IT--

WHY DO I HAVE TO GO WITH THEM? AM I UNDER ARREST, OR SOMETHING? ON WHAT CHARGE--

ILLEGAL BREATHING?

MR. MYERS, YOU WILL HAVE TO BE BOOKED AND HELD ON TRIAL, EVENTUALLY. IF DOCTOR CROWSON SAYS YOU'RE OKAY TO GO, WE'LL HAVE TO TAKE YOU DOWN TO THE STATION NOW.

WHAT IS THIS-- A JOKE?!

YOU'RE ALL *NUTS!* HEARTBEAT OR NOT, YOU CRAZY FOOLS, I'M LEAVING--

WOMP!!

WHEN JOHN MYERS WOKE, HE WAS IN A JAIL-CELL.

HE REALIZED WHAT THIS PLACE WAS AS SOON AS HIS SENSES WERE REGAINED. HE STOOD UP QUICKLY AND BEGAN TO SCREAM OUT LOUD INTO THE EMPTY, DARK CORRIDOR...

HEY!

LET ME OUT OF HERE!

I DON'T BELONG HERE--

I HAVEN'T DONE ANYTHING WRONG!

HOW COULD I HAVE COMMITTED A CRIME?

WELL? WHAT HAVE I DONE?

TELL ME, SOMEONE!

CLIK!

WELL, THAT'S HARD FOR A FELLOW TO ANSWER--

BUT SOME GUY IN THE NEWSPAPER BROUGHT UP THE POINT THAT A PERSON WHO DOESN'T HAVE HIS HEART OPERATING, AND STILL WALKS AROUND, SHOULDN'T BE CONSIDERED A--

--A HUMAN BEING.

WHAT IS THAT SUPPOSED TO MEAN? THAT I'M LOCKED UP HERE BECAUSE I'M NOT AN ALIEN FROM OUTER SPACE, BUT I'M NOT A MEMBER OF THE HUMAN RACE EITHER? IS THAT IT?

NOT QUITE.

YOU SEE, I'M AFRAID YOU'LL HAVE TO GO TO COURT TO PROVE YOUR INNOCENCE. CERTAIN PEOPLE HAVE BROUGHT TO THE ATTENTION OF THE COURTS THAT A PERSON WITHOUT A BEATING HEART SHOULDN'T BE PERMITTED TO *LIVE*.

THAT'S RIDICULOUS! WHAT WOULD THEY DO IF I WERE FOUND-- "GUILTY"? SEND ME TO THE ELECTRIC CHAIR?

I DON'T KNOW *WHAT* THEY'D DO EXACTLY, BUT IF YOU'RE PROVEN GUILTY-- I IMAGINE THAT YOU WOULD HAVE TO BE DISPOSED OF.

IN NEW YORK CITY? IN THIS COUNTRY? YOU'RE OUT OF YOUR MIND! YOU MUST BE NUTS TO THINK THAT I COULD POSSIBLY BE PUT TO DEATH FOR-- FOR NOTHING!

I DON'T THINK YOU UNDERSTAND YOUR SITUATION, SIR...

I DON'T THINK YOU UNDERSTAND AT ALL...

MEMBERS OF THE JURY--HAVE YOU REACHED A VERDICT?

WE HAVE, YOUR HONOR.

AND WHAT IS YOUR VERDICT?

WE FIND THE DEFENDENT, JOHN MYERS, GUILTY AS CHARGED.

YOU, JOHN MYERS, HAVE BEEN FOUND GUILTY...

BY THE AUTHORITY VESTED IN ME BY THE STATE OF NEW YORK...

I HEREBY SENTENCE YOU TO BE BROUGHT TO MEMORIAL CEMETERY ON MARCH 25th-

AND BURIED ALIVE.

IT WAS A WEEK LATER. MARCH 25th. NOW JOHN MYERS WAS CALM, NOT TENSE AND EXCITED. HE EVEN MANAGED A SMILE WHEN THE POLICE CAME TO HIS CELL AND TOLD HIM THAT IT WAS TIME TO GO...

THEY CLIMBED INTO THE BACK SEAT OF A SQUAD CAR AND PROCEEDED TO THE CEMETERY. WHEN THEY ARRIVED, PEOPLE WERE THERE, WAITING--HUNDREDS OF THEM-- TO WATCH THE CEREMONY...

THERE HE STOOD, NOT MAKING A SOUND OR A MOVE. AFTER A MOMENT OF SILENCE, FOUR MEN CAME FORWARD. THEY HAD BEEN PAID TO PERFORM THE OPERATION...

TWO OF THEM GRABBED MYERS BY THE ARMS AND BROUGHT HIM OVER TO THE LARGE WOODEN BOX AND ONE OF THE OTHER MEN OPENED THE LID...

IT WAS A BEAUTIFUL COFFIN, MYERS NOTED. HAND-CARVED SCROLLWORK ON THE SIDES AN TOP-- IT EVEN HAD HIS NAME INSCRIBED IN A REGAL SCRIPT. SUCH A WONDERFUL PIECE OF ART, HE THOUGHT, TO BE PUT OUT OF SIGHT UNDER THE GROUND...

MYERS TOOK A STEP FORWARD. THE CROWD WATCHED. THE OTHER MEN TOOK HIS FEET AND THEY CARRIED HIS BODY TO THE WOODEN BOX AND PLACED IT INSIDE...

MYERS DID NOT SEEM TO CARE WHAT WAS GOING TO HAPPEN, OR PERHAPS HE HAD TALKED HIMSELF INTO THE FACT THAT DYING WAS NOT SO BAD AFTER ALL. HE SLOWLY CLOSED HIS EYES, AS A SIGNAL THAT HE WAS READY FOR THE ORDEAL...

NOW THE FOUR MEN LIFTED THE COFFIN FROM THE GROUND AND CARRIED IT TO THE DEEP HOLE WHICH HAD BEEN MADE WEEKS AGO -- EVEN BEFORE THE TRIAL...

THEY CAREFULLY LOWERED THE CASKET INTO THE PIT UNTIL IT RESTED SECURELY AT THE BOTTOM... AND AS THEY LET GO OF THE ROPES, A MUFFLED CRY WAS HEARD...

THE FOUR MEN PICKED UP THEIR SHOVELS AND BEGAN TO COVER THE HOLE WITH EARTH...

THE CRIES OF MERCY NOW SEEMED TO BE FAR AWAY AND AFTER A WHILE, THEY VANISHED ALTOGETHER.

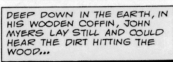

DEEP DOWN IN THE EARTH, IN HIS WOODEN COFFIN, JOHN MYERS LAY STILL AND COULD HEAR THE DIRT HITTING THE WOOD...

THUD! THUD!

HOW DARK IT WAS -- AS IF HE WERE NOW A BLIND PERSON WITH NO PLACE TO TURN. NOW IT WAS TOO LATE -- NOTHING COULD SAVE HIM NOW, HE THOUGHT...

HE WOULD JUST HAVE TO CLOSE HIS EYES AND GO TO SLEEP AND PERHAPS THIS THING WOULD NOT BE AS BAD...

HOW HAD THIS HAPPENED TO HIM? WHAT KIND OF INSANITY WAS THIS, TO BURY ALIVE AN INNOCENT MAN LIKE HIMSELF? HE GASPED FOR AIR, AND BEGAN TO PRESS AT THE SIDES OF THE CASKET, FRANTICALLY, AS HE CAME TO FULL REALIZATION...

OH GOD! THIS THING WAS ACTUALLY HAPPENING!

NO-- PLEASE--

JOHN MYERS SAT UP SUDDENLY FROM HIS PERSPIRATION-SOAKED COT. NOW HE WAS AWAKE-- FULLY AWAKE-- FREE FROM THIS HORRIBLE NIGHTMARE. THE SAME NIGHTMARE THAT HAD BEEN RECURRING TIME AND TIME AGAIN BEFORE...

THE DREAM-- THE DAMN DREAM AGAIN--

HE SLOWLY ROSE FROM THE COT, STEADIED HIMSELF, AND WALKED SHAKILY OVER TO THE DOOR. FOR WHAT SEEMED LIKE THE THOUSANDTH TIME, HE TRIED TO OPEN IT. AND FOR WHAT ALSO SEEMED LIKE THE THOUSANDTH TIME, IT WAS UNYIELDING...

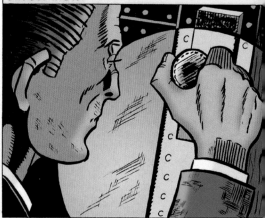

THE MONEY. ALL FIVE HUNDRED THOUSAND DOLLARS OF IT WAS STILL HERE, OF COURSE. WHO COULD STEAL IT FROM HIM NOW-- IT WAS PERFECTLY SAFE FROM THE POLICE, JOHN THOUGHT, AS HE HIMSELF WAS...

PERFECTLY SAFE...

SO PERFECTLY SAFE.

TOO BAD...

HE MUST HAVE DIED ONLY A DAY OR TWO AGO....

THE POLICE SERGEANT TOOK A GRIM LOOK AT THE BODY OF JOHN MYERS LYING ON THE COT BY THE SOLID STEEL DOOR OF THE FALLOUT SHELTER.

YEP. THIS IS MYERS, ALRIGHT--

... HAD ALL THE MONEY DOWN HERE WITH HIM, TOO--

HE GAVE US A REAL CHASE, HE DID...

FINALLY GOT A LINE ON HIM, THOUGH...

HE SHOULDN'T HAVE KILLED THE OWNER OF THIS CABIN. THAT'S WHERE HE MADE A BIG MISTAKE-- NOT THAT IT WOULD HAVE MADE ANY DIFFERENCE, I SUPPOSE, WE WOULD HAVE CAUGHT UP WITH HIM EVENTUALLY--

TRACED THE OWNER THROUGH RELATIVES WHEN WE RECEIVED A REPORT OF HIS DISAPPEARANCE...TURNS OUT IT LED US RIGHT TO MYERS...

POOR MYERS-- HE STAYED DOWN THERE FOR OVER THREE MONTHS, UNTIL THE FOOD RATIONS AND WATER WERE USED UP. THAT JAMMED DOOR LOCK-- IT'S LIKE BEING BURIED ALIVE...

ENOUGH TO GIVE A FELLA NIGHTMARES!

Overstreet

AFTERWORD
by J.C. Vaughn

As we started planning for *The Overstreet Comic Book Price Guide's* 50th anniversary a couple years ago, it hit me that I'd been on board for half of the *Guide's* existence. I have to admit I like being able to say that.

I've been aware of the *Guide* almost as long as I've been collecting comics, since I first saw *CBPG* #6 with the great Will Eisner cover in Eide's Entertainment's old location on Federal Street, where PNC Park now stands in Pittsburgh. Not long after that, I saw Joe Kubert's *CBPG* #5 cover, still a favorite of many all these years later, and realized that this came out every year!

CBPG #8 was the first one I got to pour through time and again after Rob Miller purchased it and thereby upped both of our collecting games. We spent hours looking at the ads and the listings, learning all sorts of stuff we didn't know before.

As the years passed, it was always great seeing who Bob Overstreet got to do the cover. Little did I know that one day finding artists for the cover would become one of my responsibilities (and a bit of an obsession).

In fact, they're a great metaphor for life. I have a pretty solid track record at picking great cover artists and the right subject matter for them at the right times. And yet, I can't draw the covers myself or execute their designs. In fact, almost no one could do this alone. Bob Overstreet would be the first to tell you that a legion of collectors, dealers, and historians made the *Guide* what it is (Just check his thank-you page every issue).

For me, my thanks include Bob, Steve Geppi (for putting me in charge of the daily operations and years of encouragement), Carol Overstreet for hiring me (I've decided to forgive her), Mark Huesman (for 23 years of incredible work), Amanda Sheriff (for her perspective and dedication), Gary M. Carter (for causing all of this by repeatedly giving me freelance work), and John K. Snyder, Jr. (for more than he'll ever know).

This journey wouldn't have been what it has been without Mark Haynes, Scott Braden, Joe Rybandt, Jeff Dillon, Benn Ray, Todd Hoffer, Joe McGuckin, Mike Wilbur, Jamie Blagg, Courtney Benhoff, Lindsey Wallace, Missy Bowersox, Josh Geppi, Sammi Cohen, Alex & Heather Winter, Michael Solof, John Clark, Russ Cochran, and so many others that we'd need another section of this book if I kept listing them.

To all of those named and unnamed, to our Overstreet Advisors, our advertisers, and our readers, while it will always seem insufficient, I can only say *Thank-You.*

Here's to the next 50!

J.C. Vaughn
Vice-President of Publishing